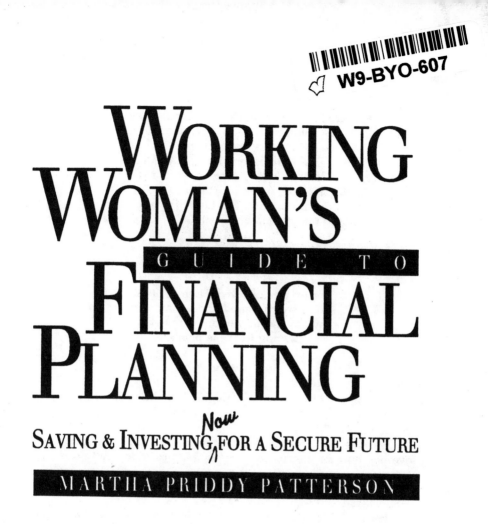

WORKING WOMAN'S

G U I D E   T O

FINANCIAL PLANNING

SAVING & INVESTING *Now* FOR A SECURE FUTURE

MARTHA PRIDDY PATTERSON

PRENTICE HALL
Englewood Cliffs, New Jersey 07632

Prentice-Hall International (UK) Limited, *London*
Prentice-Hall of Australia Pty. Limited, *Sydney*
Prentice-Hall Canada, Inc., *Toronto*
Prentice-Hall Hispanoamericana, S.A., *Mexico*
Prentice-Hall of India Private Limited, *New Delhi*
Prentice-Hall of Japan, Inc., *Tokyo*
Simon & Schuster Asia Pte. Ltd., *Singapore*
Editora Prentice-Hall do Brasil, Ltda., *Rio de Janeiro*

© 1993 *by*
Prentice-Hall, Inc.

10 9 8 7 6 5 4 3 2 1

Library of Congress Cataloging-in-Publication Data

Patterson, Martha Priddy.
   The working woman's guide to retirement planning: saving &
investing now for a secure future / by Martha Priddy Patterson.
      p.   cm.
   Includes index.
   ISBN 0-13-952813-X
   1. Women—Finance, Personal. 2. Retirement income—United States.
3. Women—Pensions—United States. I. Title.
HG179.P294   1993
332.024′042—dc20   92-42610
                                                                    CIP

ISBN 0-13-952813-X

PRENTICE HALL
Career & Personal Development
Englewood Cliffs, NJ 07632

Simon & Schuster, A Paramount Communications Company

Printed in the United States of America

DEDICATION

To Bonnie Priddy Spaugh, who gave me the best assets any woman can have, a sense of humor and a dedication to self-sufficiency. And to Laurence I. Barrett, who gave me a triumph of hope over experience.

ACKNOWLEDGMENTS

Thanks are in order to a number of people. First, thanks go to my colleagues at KPMG Peat Marwick who provided valuable advice, Vince Amoroso, Peter Elinsky, Roy Oliver, and Deborah Walker and colleagues who gave me important comments and reviews, Dominick DiCosimo, Tracie Henderson, and Rick Taylor. Anna Rappaport, an actuary who specializes in work force demographics, first interested me in the subject of women's retirement planning. Aquil Ahmed, a former colleague, supplied the actuarial calculations that provide the bedrock of the book. Susan Korn and Drew Douglas at the Bureau of National Affairs first gave me a forum to discuss the issue. Ruth Mills, the editor at Simon & Schuster, was the quintessential literary adviser; whenever she offered a suggestion, I invariably thought, "I wish I had done that in the first place." John Turner and Daniel Beller at the U.S. Department of Labor provided valuable data and insight. And saving the best for last, Laurence I. Barrett, whose writing and reporting skills impressed me long before I knew him, helped me put complex ideas in simple sentences. As usual, if there are mistakes, they are of my own making.

ABOUT THE AUTHOR

Martha Priddy Patterson is director of employee benefits policy and analysis for KPMG Peat Marwick. She is a lawyer who has worked in the employee benefits area for many years, advising clients ranging in size from *Fortune* 500 companies to individuals. She first became interested in the special retirement savings problems of women by working as one of the primary authors of a major study on pension plan portability and the effects of job changes on women's retirement benefits for the American Association of Retired Persons. She authored "Retirement Income Versus Family Responsibility: 10 Ways to Protect Working Women's Pension Benefits," for the Bureau of National Affairs Special Report Series on Work and Family. She is also the author of *An Employer's Guide to Retirement Plans*, published by the Human Incentive and Resource Education Institute. She is the creator and author of many of KPMG Peat Marwick's "THE BASICS," a series of primers on various types of employee benefit plans.

Ms. Patterson is a member of the bars of the District of Columbia, Texas, Virginia, and the Supreme Court of the United States. She is a frequent speaker on employee benefits issues before clients and women's groups.

CONTENTS

INTRODUCTION

Why should women suffer "pension envy"? Why should there be a book devoted solely to working women's financial planning for retirement? And why should this lawyer be writing it? The first question is easy—too many women end their final years in poverty; *only 9% of women over 40 receive or expect to receive a retirement benefit,* and if they receive a retirement benefit at all, *it is usually less than one-third of that received by their male colleagues.* These facts reflect different, and usually more complex, problems women encounter in establishing secure benefits for their retirement years. The second question is easy, too. Every day I saw a need for a guide to help women understand and plan for their retirement, and there was nothing available to help them do that. As a female employed by companies of varied types, I've dealt with those differences as an individual. As an attorney who came to specialize in employee benefits law, I've studied the subject from professional perspectives as well.

One of the first things you learn is that small variations in the work pattern—those typical of women's careers—can have very large impact on retirement income. For instance, a woman who takes 7 years away from the job during a career spanning 40 years may get *half* the retirement benefits received by someone who stayed in the work force for the full 40 years.

This dramatic loss, totally out of proportion to the time spent off the payroll, is not the worst-case scenario. Many women work for years for various employers who provide retirement benefits, but these women don't stay long enough with one enterprise to earn an irrevocable right to the benefits. They retire after a lifetime of work with no employer-provided retirement plan at all. Many more women than men work for firms which do not provide any retirement benefits. These facts aren't going to change soon—if ever. And future changes in retirement-benefit policy aren't much help if you are 45 or 50 now and have already spent many years in the work force.

Women can achieve economic security in retirement only if they start planning for it while they are in the work force. Your first day on the job isn't too early to start. You must understand how retirement plans—your employer's and your own retirement savings—work legally and financially.

I've been a lawyer for 18 years, 11 of them spent concentrating on employee benefits law. From my employers, I have vested in only one retirement plan—which will pay me $4,000 a year 22 years from now! Still, this is the most generous plan any of my employers provided. Half of my employers did not provide retirement benefits at all. Shortly after I began to specialize in benefits law, it became clear to me that if I was going to have a financially secure retirement, I would have to be the primary contributor to it—not my employer, and certainly not the Social Security system.

Research and personal observation of other women convinced me my experience was typical. The need for this book screamed at me after I had watched a female colleague deliver an hour-long lecture on litigation strategy without notes to an audience that hung on her every word. Later, as we were talking, she mentioned her employer had a 401(k) plan to which she contributed. But, she inquired, was her contribution with pretax dollars or after-tax dollars? The big advantage of 401(k) plans that every employer stresses is the fact the savings are made with pretax dollars and all the earnings on those savings avoid tax until the money is withdrawn. In terms of retirement planning, this lawyer's question was like asking whether the tennis ball should go over the net.

Clearly, smart, hardworking women are not paying attention to their financial retirement future. Others don't know where to begin because the law and retirement benefit plans seem so complex. The following chapters eliminate some of the confusion and provide a planning map. Remember, for retirement planning, the future is now.

Martha Priddy Patterson

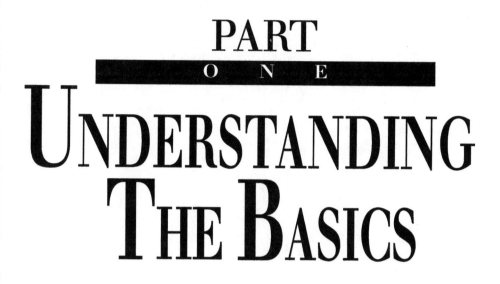

PART
ONE
UNDERSTANDING THE BASICS

WHY RETIREMENT PLANNING IS DIFFERENT FOR WOMEN

Alice, now age 60, has been in the nursing profession all her life, and she would like to retire within the next few years, certainly by the time she is 65. Over the years she was out of the profession only 3 years, 1 year for the birth of each of her two children and 1 year to care for her dying mother and settle the estate. But when Alice does retire, she can expect her retirement benefits from her more than 30 years of work to be at least 10% less than a male nurse who followed her same career pattern. She earns that much less than her male colleague, and her retirement benefits will be based primarily on earnings. (If Alice were an assembly-line worker, the difference between her earnings and that of a male coworker would have been even more pronounced—about 26%.) Additionally, her retirement benefits will be less than half of what they would have been had she not taken just those 3 years out of the work force and had stayed with one employer over the years. She can also expect to live at least 5 years longer than her male coworker.

Why are retirement savings and financial planning different for women than for men? After all, money is money whether you are male or female. Or so you thought. But Alice's wage and career pattern experience shows us why saving for retirement income and security is different—and more difficult—for women.

Of course, in many other ways retirement saving is not different for the two sexes. Starting early and keeping up a steady pattern of investment is equally important for women and men. Court cases and federal laws of the 1970s and 1980s have equalized most retirement plans for the sexes. There is little, if any, inherent gender preference in employer retirement plans or individual retirement savings plans. Yet it will be years before past inequities are corrected and women begin to receive parity in benefits. For example, the General Accounting Office recently reported in over half of the small-employer defined benefit plans, men earned more than $1.10 in benefits for every $1.00 women earned, even when the calculations were corrected for the fact women earned less wages and had fewer years of service. But most larger plans allocated benefits equitably.[1]

For example, by law plans can no longer reduce annual pension payments to individual women because women in general tend to live longer than men.

But as Alice has shown us, retirement savings planning is substantially different for women—in part because of several easily documented statistical facts and in part because of several social pressures that are less easily documented but are fully familiar to most women.

This book acknowledges those facts and pressures and urges you to cope with them in two ways. First, begin your retirement savings from the day you walk on the job. Second, plan to depend more heavily on your own savings for retirement security rather than relying on employer-provided plans and Social Security retirement benefits as your male colleagues are better able to do.

Chapter 4 compares the retirement benefits earned by four women with fairly typical career patterns (including Alice) with the retirement benefits they would have earned from their employer had they followed a single-job career more similar to men's career patterns. Throughout the book we will use these examples of Alice, our 60-year-old nurse; Susan, a midlevel manager age 50; Bonnie, a lawyer of 40;

and Jennifer, a secretary of 30. The differences in their retirement benefits when compared with their career benefits are startling!

TEN REASONS WOMEN MUST SAVE AND PLAN MORE FOR RETIREMENT

Here are the plain, documented facts:

1. Women live longer than men.
2. Women earn less money than men.
3. Women change jobs more frequently than men.
4. Women leave and rejoin the work force more frequently than men.
5. Women tend to work in jobs less likely to have employer-provided retirement benefits.
6. Women in the work force before the enactment of the Equal Pay Act, the Civil Rights Act of 1964, and ERISA in 1974 were adversely affected by laws restricting jobs, overtime, and hours.
7. Women who do receive retirement benefits receive significantly lower benefits than men.

Social pressures make women's retirement planning more difficult, too. People can argue about social pressures, but most women believe the social factors affecting retirement security are equally as valid as the documented statistics:

8. Women are most likely to leave the job market to provide care when family matters require care giving.
9. Women are most often the "trailing spouse" who gives up a job and benefits when a family must move because a spouse has been relocated.
10. Women don't have a role model for retirement planning.

Some of these social facts may be changing. According to the Department of Labor, women's work patterns are getting more like men's. And males have been known to stay home with the children while their wives continue working. But, on balance, things aren't changing that rapidly. Frankly, telling a 50-year-old woman the women's wage gap is closing (even if it were true, which it isn't) does not give her the money lost from this wage gap over the previous 30 years of her working life. Nor does it give back the years when she was "protected" from working overtime or in hazardous—and high-paying—jobs. Her retirement benefits earned to date and the personal savings for retirement she was or wasn't able to make reflect that wage gap. And so will her Social Security benefits when she reaches age 65.

Leaving aside social pressures, just look at the facts.

Women Live Longer than Men

In 1988 a 40-year-old woman could expect to live another 41 years; a 40-year-old man could expect only another 35 years. A 20-year-old woman can expect to live another 60 years; her male colleague only another 54 years.[2]

The longer you live, the more money you need. Clearly, a woman will need to build up a bigger retirement nest egg to see her through financially secure retirement. Moreover, many married women also see their own retirement savings greatly eroded to pay for the medical expenses of their husbands.

Women Earn Less Money than Men

You are constantly being told the wage gap is closing, and any gaps that do exist result from a woman's shorter time in the work force, lower level of education, and so on, and so on, ad nauseum. But according to the U.S. Bureau of the Census, the facts disprove these claims.

In 1955 women annually earned 63.9% of male's wages. In 1989 women who worked year-round full time earned 68% of wages earned by men.[3]

If you look at weekly earnings comparisons and include only those wage earners over 25, the gap between men and women remains. For example, in 1988 a woman earned 68.6% of a man's wages, using those criteria.[4]

Another way to look at it is to compare earnings in specific professions. Table 1.1 compares women's and men's weekly earnings for three occupations: department heads, assembly-line workers, and nurses, according to the Department of Labor January 1990 data.

	Women	Men	Percentage of Male Wages Women Earn Weekly
TABLE 1.1			
Comparison of Weekly Earnings of Women and Men, 1989			
Department heads	$458	$698	66%
Assemblers	236	366	64
Nurses	564	629	90

Source: U.S. Department of Labor, Bureau of Labor Statistics, *Employment and Earnings* (Washington, D.C.: U.S. Government Printing Office, January 1990).

Most people seeing these figures for the first time sympathetically tell me I have made a typographical error! Unfortunately, the error is not in the type, but in the wages. We haven't come a long way, baby. We are at best only 90% of the way there and that's after having been at 63.9% in 1955.

You might expect the wage difference for department heads based on the excuse—sorry, explanation—of more seniority, and so on. But the wage difference for nurses is harder to accept. If the explanation for women's lower wages is based on seniority, one has to assume a traditionally female occupation where presumably the people with the most seniority are women would have minuscule wage differences between the sexes. Clearly, that is not an accurate assumption. So the expectation the wage gap will disappear as women become more senior in their fields is at best questionable.

And it doesn't get better with increased education or age. In 1988, all males with 4 years of college earned a mean income of $40,415, while females earned $25,674 (63% of male wages); males with 5 or more years of higher education earned $50,262, white females earned $31,189 (62% of male wages). When divided into age brackets, the gap remained consistent. The highest mean earning bracket for women with 4 years of college was $27,220 for women age 35–44. The lowest mean earning bracket for males with some college was $26,486, for men age 25–34 with 1 to 3 years of college. These figures include only full-time, year-round workers over age 25.[5]

This wage gap is a double whammy on retirement planning. First, there is the obvious fact that if you make less money, you have less discretionary income and a more difficult time saving for anything, but especially something so seemingly far away as retirement. A less obvious, but perhaps more important, effect is the fact almost every employer-provided retirement benefit, as well as Social Security, is based primarily on your salary while you were working. Therefore, *a low salary while you are working guarantees a low retirement benefit later.*

Women Change Jobs More Frequently than Men

Women over 25 stay with an employer only 4.8 years as compared to 6.6 years for men of that age.[6] Frequent job changes have several impacts on retirement planning. First, most employers require that you work for them for a minimum amount of time (by law this period can't be longer than a year in most cases) before you are eligible to begin earning any retirement benefits. So each time you change jobs you have a period during which you earn no retirement benefits other than Social Security, even if you go directly from one employer to the next.

Second, most retirement plans require that you work for the employer for a minimum amount of time before you have a irrevocable right to the retirement benefits you are earning. Achieving this irre-vocable status for the benefit is called *vesting.* By law, an employer can require that an employee serve 5 years before she "vests" in all the earned benefits or serve at least 3 years before vesting begins to occur gradually. Prior to 1989, the vesting requirement was 10 years. Obviously, with an average service period of only 4.8 years, a woman might work continuously throughout her life, but for different employers *and never receive a retirement benefit, because she never vested.*

Table 1.2 shows the relationship between time with a "primary employer" and pension coverage.

Women Are Out of the Work Force More Often than Men

For whatever reason—care giving to children or elderly parents, seeking work as a trailing spouse, or loss of jobs—women are out of the work force more than men. A 25-year-old man will spend 70% of his remaining life working, while a 25-year-old *woman is estimated to spend only 44% of her remaining life on a payroll.*

TABLE 1.2 Years with Employer Compared with Pension Coverage for Women and Men Full-Time Workers		
	Years of Service with Employer	
Years with Employer	All Women	All Men
Less than 1 year	19%	17%
1 to 4 years	37	33
5 to 9 years	18	17
10 to 14 years	10	11
15 to 19 years	6	7
20 years or more	5	11
	100%	100%

Percentage of Employees with Pension Coverage in Each Years-of-Service Bracket		
Years with Employer	Women with Pension Coverage	Men with Pension Coverage
All years	43%	50%
Less than 1 year	13	18
1 to 4 years	37	39
5 to 9 years	63	62
10 to 14 years	70	73
15 to 19 years	72	77
20 years or more	75	82

Source: Testimony by Dr. Sophie Korczyk before the U.S. House of Representatives' Select Committee on Aging Subcommittee on Retirement Income and Employment, March 26, 1992, entitled "Pension Coverage and Portability Issues Facing Employed Women," the author's calculations based on data from the Employee Benefit Research Institute tabulations of the May 1988 *Current Population Survey.*

Obviously, when you are not on the payroll, you are not earning a salary to use for savings. But the losses don't stop with just your salary. You are also missing seniority leading to promotions and pay increases. From a retirement savings perspective, you also are not earning credits for retirement benefits from either an employer or from the Social Security system when you are not on the payroll.

Chapter 8 discusses some of the ways you can shelter retirement savings through Individual Retirement Accounts and self-employed retirement plans when you are off the payroll.

Women Are More Likely to Work in Jobs that Don't Provide Retirement Benefits

Among workers and retirees over 40 years old, 23% of men expect to receive or are receiving an employer-provided retirement benefit, as compared with 16% of women.[7] Certain industries can be classified as more heavily served by one gender than the other. On this basis, agriculture, durable goods manufacturing, wholesale trade, transportation and public utilities, construction, and mining are "predominately male worker" industries, whereas professional services, finance, insurance, and real estate are "predominately female worker" industries. Some industries are "gender neutral" in the makeup of their work force. Men fare equally well in pension coverage in both male and female industries. Women have the highest pension coverage in male industries: about 56% of women in such industries are covered by a pension. By contrast, *women in predominantly female industries have only a 49% pension coverage rate.*[8]

Women are also heavily concentrated in occupations that have lower pension coverage. For example, women dominate the "technical, sales and administrative support" job classifications, where only 38% of employees are offered retirement benefits plans. Men are most heavily concentrated in the managerial classification, with a 58% rate of pension coverage; mining, with a 61% coverage rate; and transportation, with a 60% coverage rate.[9]

Comparing men and women in 1983, age 25–46 working full time, and at their current job for at least one year, 73% of men are likely to be offered a retirement benefit plan as compared to 66% of women.[10] Things are improving in one sense. In 1990 figures show 57% of men and 53% of women working for employers who offer retirement plans. But when you look at that same group, you find only 39% of women actually earning the rights to future benefits as compared with 47% of men earning rights to benefits.[11]

The gap between *coverage,* which defines whether an employer has a retirement plan, and *participation,* which defines whether an employee is actually earning retirement benefits, may be attributed to several factors that the data do not reveal. That is, women may not be eligible to participate in the plan and earn benefits because they have not worked for the employer long enough or do not work enough hours to meet the threshold requirements to participate. Or, if the plans require the employee to contribute to the plan in order to participate in the plan, women may be choosing not to contribute to the plan and thereby denying themselves the value of the employer's contribution.

Women Have Lost Wages Through Legally Sanctioned Pay Discrimination

A woman who is 55 today entered the job market in the late 1950s. At that time it was entirely legal to pay a woman less for the same job than the man sitting next to her received. And employers did. In fact, some union contracts required it!

Many states "protected" women through laws limiting the number of total hours women could work each week and the hours of day they could work. Certain hazardous jobs or classifications were barred to women completely—by law. These jobs frequently were high-paying jobs when compared with the relative small amount of education or training required. Certain professions required a woman to quit her job or at least take a leave of absence if she became pregnant.

Women did not have the legal right to equal wages until the enactment of the Equal Pay Act of 1963, and reforms were not immediate. Women in their 30s reading this book may be shocked by these facts. Although it is good to remember the strides women have made, realism requires acknowledging facts. Many retired women today live in poverty, and many women close to retirement today are not financially prepared for it. In part, their poverty and their lack of financial preparation stem from the legally sanctioned discrimination in wages and job opportunities they faced prior to the equal pay and civil rights laws.

Women Who Do Receive Retirement Benefits Receive Significantly Lower Benefits than Men

The most recent data on pensions trends come from a December 1989 *Current Population Survey,* compiled and analyzed by the Department of Labor in *Trends in Pensions 1992.* In comparing current pension benefits payments by gender, the authors say:

> The median retirement age of 62 is the same for men and women. Similarities end there. Comparing medians, men have 50 percent more service, 67 percent higher earnings, 200 percent higher benefits, and 53 percent higher replacement rates [of final earnings as compared with retirement income].[12]

These figures speak eloquently. The fact women have 50% less service than men, coupled with the fact they have only 67% of men's earnings means that *a woman's retirement benefits will be one-fourth the size of her male colleague's.* The relationship between work and entitlement to retirement benefits is *not* one to one. It is critical to remember the benefit calculation relationships magnify lower wages and less time in the workplace at retirement. A dollar less in salary is not just a dollar less now. It may mean three dollars less in retirement benefits as well.

The numbers in Table 1.3 reflect only the women who are actually receiving retirement benefits. The averages are not pulled down by the many women who do not receive retirement benefits at all. Some of the reasons for this gap will be illustrated when we look at the experiences of Alice, Susan, Bonnie, and Jennifer, our hypothetical career women, in Chapter 4.

These latest data demonstrate that women are not catching up on the retirement benefit track. Penis envy may be an outmoded psychological thesis. But the numbers released by the U.S. government prove there is every reason for pension envy among women.

WHY WOMEN SHOULD NOT RELY ON THEIR SPOUSES' RETIREMENT INCOME

One accurate criticism of this book is that the planning discussions do not take into account the fact many women plan retirement as an economic unit with their spouses. None of the examples, advice, or worksheets here include any mention of the spouse's potential retirement income. Spouses are not included in the planning because the data show that for the majority of us there will be no spouse at all. Even if we begin retirement with a spouse, we are likely to spend most of our retirement alone. As a nation we no longer consist primarily of married households. Husbands are wonderful, but they tend to disappear. Loyal, dedicated ones die, or they get sick and look to their wives for support, emotionally and financially; others of the breed decide they want to be fully married to their jobs or to another person.

TABLE 1.3 Comparison of Annual Pension Benefits Payments for Men Versus Women				
	1978		**1989**	
	Men	Women	Men	Women
All Industries				
Mean	$4,450	$2,290	$9,460	$4,330
Median	3,480	1,630	7,020	2,570
Manufacturing				
Mean	4,730	2,880	8,190	4,600
Median	3,860	2,320	6,070	1,870
Nonmanufacturing				
Mean	3,970	1,780	10,550	4,200
Median	2,640	1,260	7,500	2,680

Source: Daniel J. Beller and David D. McCarthy, "Private Pension Benefits," in John A. Turner and Daniel J. Beller, eds., *Trends in Pensions 1992* (Washington, D.C.: U.S. Department of Labor, Pension and Welfare Benefits Administration, U.S. Government Printing Office, 1992), Table 10.18.

But even if you are confident of old Harry's fidelity and health, read these recent words from Congressman William J. Hughes, chair of the retirement subcommittee of the Aging Committee:

> Almost three-quarters of the elderly persons living below poverty are women. Half of elderly women living alone have incomes less

than $9,500 per year. Something is seriously wrong with our retirement policies when the General Accounting Office reports that *around 80% of the widows now living in poverty were not poor before the death of their husbands.* (emphasis in the original).[13]

This entire book tends to be based on the worst case scenarios—which include the possibility that you may not retire with a financially secure spouse. If you can, congratulations. You can spend your extra retirement income vacationing in the south of France or Georgia, buying the racy sports car you always wanted, or endowing your favorite charity. This is not to say you should not consult with your husband and coordinate your investment strategies and retirement planning. You definitely should. Certainly as you near retirement, you should agree on life-style and location. *But you should also plan financially as though you will be your own independent economic unit.* The statistics say you will be independent at least for some of your life. Besides, there has never been a single documented case of a woman's feeling herself to be less of a person because she was financially secure in her own right.

CONCLUSION: WOMEN MUST PLAN FOR THEIR RETIREMENT IN DIFFERENT WAYS FROM MEN

For all these reasons, women must use different planning techniques in establishing financial security for retirement. You are never too young to start saving for retirement. Your own savings will be much more important for you than for your male colleagues because, as shown, the statistics tell you several undeniable facts: your benefits will be less than a comparable male worker your same age, and you will live longer than he will. Fortunately, women are accustomed to working harder for financial security, so this is not a surprise. What may be surprising is the large difference a few years out of the work force at the wrong time can make on employer-provided retirement benefits and what a positive difference early and steady savings, even on a small basis, can make for financial security at retirement. The next chapters will begin to detail these differences.

NOTES FOR CHAPTER 1

1. U.S. General Accounting Office, "Private Pensions: 1986 Law Will Improve Benefit Equity in Many Small Employers' Plans," GAO/HRD-91-58, March 1991, pp. 18–19.

2. U.S. Bureau of the Census, Statistical Abstract of the United States: 1991, 111th ed. (Washington, D.C.: U.S. Government Printing Office, 1991), Table 107.

3. Ibid., Table 736.

4. U.S. Bureau of the Census, Statistical Abstract of the United States: 1990, 110th ed. (Washington, D.C.: U.S. Government Printing Office, 1990), Table 671.

5. U.S. Bureau of the Census, 1991 Statistical Abstract, Table 740.

6. Bureau of National Affairs, "Retirement Income Versus Family Responsibility: 10 Ways to Protect Working Women's Pension Benefits," The BNA Special Report Series on Work & Family, No. 29 (Washington, D.C.: The Bureau of National Affairs, 1990), p. 6, citing October 22, 1987, data from the Bureau of Labor Statistics.

7. Daniel J. Beller and David D. McCarthy, "Private Pension Benefits," in John A. Turner and Daniel J. Beller, eds., *Trends in Pensions 1992* (Washington, D.C.: U.S. Department of Labor, Pension and Welfare Benefits Administration, U.S. Government Printing Office, 1992), Table 10.3, pp. 236–237.

8. Testimony by Dr. Sophie Korczyk before the U.S. House of Representatives' Select Committee on Aging Subcommittee on Retirement Income and Employment, March 26, 1992, entitled "Pension Coverage and Portability Issues Facing Employed Women;" at pp. 3–4. The author's calculations based on data from the Employee Benefit Research Institute tabulations of the May 1988 *Current Population Survey.*

9. U.S. Bureau of the Census, *1990 Statistical Abstract*, Tables 671 and 678.

10. Emily Andrews, *The Changing Profile of Pensions in America* (Washington, D.C.: Employee Benefits Research Institute, 1985), p. 65.

11. Employee Benefit Research Institute, "New Findings from the March 1991 CPS on Pension Coverage and Participation," *EBRI Employee Benefit Notes*, March 1992, Table 2.

12. Beller and McCarthy, "Private Pension Benefits," in *Trends in Pensions 1992*, pp. 226–227.

13. Opening Remarks of the Honorable William J. Hughes, chairman, Subcommittee on Retirement Income and Employment, Select Committee on Aging, U.S. House of Representatives, Hearings held on March 26, 1992.

BASICS OF RETIREMENT SAVINGS AND PLANNING

You need a three-legged stool for retirement planning—your own savings, Social Security, and employer-provided retirement programs such as a pension or a 401(k) plan. You must realize immediately that only one of these legs is under your direct control—your savings. This chapter briefly discusses the roles of each "leg" and explains a financial concept critical to retirement planning, the *time value of money*. We will work through some sample calculations to illustrate how to consider time value of money in your own planning.

SOCIAL SECURITY—DON'T DEPEND ON IT AS THE SOLE SOURCE OF YOUR RETIREMENT INCOME

Social Security will probably always be available during your life-time—unless you are reading this book in 2050. But levels of Social

Security for today's workers who will be the twenty-first century's retirees are questionable at best. Under the current system, Social Security will replace about 42% of your pay if you earn average wages. If your earnings are lower than average, Social Security will replace a greater percentage of your income, perhaps as much as 88%. If you have higher earnings, you can expect a smaller percentage, closer to 24% to 27% of the portion of your salary that was subject to Social Security taxes.

TABLE 2.1 Social Security Contributors and Beneficiaries, 1945–2030			
Year	Covered Workers (Millions)	Recipients (Millions)	Workers per Recipient
1945	46.9	1.1	42.6
1950	48.3	2.9	16.6
1960	72.5	13.7	5.3
1970	93.1	22.6	4.1
1980	112.2	30.4	3.7
1985	120.1	32.8	3.7
1990*	132.8	35.4	3.8
2000*	144.6	39.0	3.7
2030*	152.0	68.2	2.2

*Projections. Under other alternatives projected by the Board of Trustees using different assumptions, the numbers are different with the "workers per recipient" ranging from a high of 2.5 to a low of 1.9 in 2030.

Source: Report of the Board of Trustees of the Federal Old-Age and Survivors Insurance Trust Funds (Washington, D.C.: U.S. Government Printing Office, 1990).

These levels of income replacement are more generous than the original replacement ratios enacted in the 1935 Social Security law. Social Security was never intended or designed to be the sole source of retirement income. It alone will not give you a secure retirement. Yet too many retirees have refused to recognize this fact, until it was too late. Don't be one of them. Common sense tells us that a system that used over 42 working payers of Social Security taxes to support 1 Social Security recipient in 1945 cannot continue to grant as generous a benefit when only 2 to 3 workers are supporting and paying taxes for each recipient receiving benefits. People have a limit to the amount of tax they are willing to pay! Table 2.1, which compares Social Security taxpayers to Social Security recipients, tells the whole story.

The Social Security "surplus" that was supposed to be generated by the increased payroll taxes of the 1980s is a myth. The federal government has spent the money and left a series of IOUs in the form of Treasury bonds, bills, and notes to pay the "age wave" of baby boomers who will retire early in the twenty-first century. The projections show big Social Security deficits rather than a surplus at that time.

The political prospects for maintaining the 1990s Social Security benefits levels when the age wave begins to retire in 2010 are uncertain. Intergenerational equity is also an issue. We can only maintain the 1990s Social Security levels by increasing Social Security taxes on young workers or by reducing federal spending for other purposes, such as health care and education. Actually, we will need to increase taxes *and* reduce spending, if we intend to maintain 1990s Social Security levels for all the retirees of the twenty-first century.

Currently, more than 30% of the federal budget goes to provide Social Security, Medicare, and other pensions for the oldest portion of our population. Federal spending for all other health care and all education and training, including that amount devoted to children's health care and education, is 6–7% of the budget. If we do not develop our children into an educated, healthy work force for the twenty-first century, there will be too few productive workers to continue contributing to the Social Security system to finance Social Security payments to retirees.

The real issue on budgeting for the 1990s is whether we really want to continue to "eat our young" by spending an increasingly large portion of the federal budget on the oldest segment of our population while we neglect to spend money on the health and education of our children. If we reject cannibalizing our children and choose instead to invest more in their future, the next generation of Social Security recipients will almost certainly receive lower benefits.

Gwendolyn King, former commissioner of Social Security, disagrees vehemently with the idea that Social Security is in any jeopardy or that spending for Social Security reduces the funds available for the young. She criticizes "nervous politicians, sleazy misleading advertisers or even the budding, would-be best-selling authors" who say there are problems with Social Security.[1] She argues correctly that Social Security, through its survivors' benefits, is one of the biggest suppliers of aid to children. She cites the 1991 annual report of the Social Security Board of Trustees stating Social Security will be able to pay benefits with no increase in taxes for the next 50 years. But that was under the Board's most optimistic scenario. Traditionally, the Board of Trustees develops several alternative scenarios based on different assumptions about interest rates, employment, and demographics. Under what the Board considers its "best estimate," Social Security begins to run a deficit after 26 years. That does not include the deficit from the Medicare trust fund, which, by their estimates, causes the combined programs to go into deficit in 2009.[2] Certainly, we all hope Ms. King is correct, and we hope the more optimistic assumptions of the Board of Trustees come true. But rosy scenarios from the federal government have faded before.

There will probably always be some Social Security system for those who have paid into it. This book assumes so, and Chapter 9 discusses Social Security's current operation and coverage in detail. But, almost as certainly, future Social Security payments will be proportionately smaller than the benefits received by today's retirees. You must factor that possibility into your own retirement planning, and, most important, into your own retirement savings. Dorcas Hardy, former commissioner of the Social Security Administration, takes a far less optimistic view of Social Security's prospects than her successor; among her recommendations for reforming the Social Security system, she recommends increasing individual private savings, as the "safest, surest, most logical solution for all future retirement income. . . ."[3]

EMPLOYER-PROVIDED RETIREMENT INCOME—BEWARE OF DECREASING BENEFITS

Employer-provided benefits are an important source of retirement income. In 1989 approximately 41% of retirees over age 55 were receiving or had received a retirement benefit, with the median annual benefit being about $4,400. For those who retired in 1988 and 1989, that figure jumped to about $5,800.[4] About 52 million workers (i.e., about 39% of the working population) are currently working for employers with retirement benefit plans, although not all those workers are eligible for the retirement plan, due to hours worked, length of service, and so on.[5] Unlike Social Security, most of those benefits are in trust funds that cannot be touched by the employer. Under this arrangement, the money is guaranteed to be available when the workers retire.

But there are employer retirement plans that are underfunded. Defined benefit plans, the so-called "pension plan," are usually backed up by the government-run Pension Benefit Guaranty Corporation (PBGC). But with numerous liquidations in the 1989–1991 recession, PBGC is being strained. Further, PBGC has limits on the amount of benefits it will pay. Thus, very rich benefits to those with the most seniority or highest wages during their working years may not be fully guaranteed.

Another risk is that pressures on employer-provided retirement benefits will grow as companies face increasing international competition where benefits are provided by the foreign governments, rather than employers, or where benefits are nonexistent. Many of the largest companies, which have tended to have the most generous retirement benefits, now face heavy debt generated during the takeover craze of the 1980s. All employers have suffered from the early 1990s recession. *In fact, retirement benefit plan coverage percentages are declining.* According to a study in the mid-1980s by Emily Andrews, a researcher with the Employee Benefits Research Institute, the rate of coverage for all workers fell from 56% in 1979 to 52% in 1983.[6]

The manufacturing industries are already showing a decline in the benefits provided. From 1978 to 1989 real retirement benefits per retiree declined 12%, and wage replacement ratios—the amount of retirement benefit received from the employer divided by the recipient's former salary—declined by 23%. Women in those industries saw an even sharper decline—a 58% reduction in real benefits and a 42% reduction in replacement ratios! Fortunately, nonmanufacturing industries showed an increase in per retiree benefits over the same time, with benefits increasing by 27% in real terms and 35% in replacement ratios.[7]

Continuation of generous employer-provided retirement plans is also threatened by the cost of employer-provided health care. In past decades retirement plans were the most expensive benefit provided by the employer. In the 1990s, health care programs are more expensive than retirement plans. Employers have only so many dollars to spend on labor costs, including both salary and benefits. The more dollars employers spend for employees' health care, the fewer dollars remain for retirement plans—or salaries.

Finally, employer retirement plans are of little use when you are off the payroll, as women may be from time to time.

PERSONAL SAVINGS—THE ONLY RETIREMENT BENEFITS YOU CAN CONTROL

Individual savings are the critical leg of the retirement security stool; for women, it should be the major one. This is the one part of the triad you can control. Personal savings are especially critical for women because women lose employer benefits as a result of lower wages and time out of the work force.

There are several "tax-favored" retirement savings opportunities available to individuals. These include Individual Retirement Accounts, Keoghs, universal life insurance, and deferred annuities, all of which will be discussed in detail in Chapter 8.

You must recognize *now* that Social Security and employer-provided retirement benefits are only parts of your retirement security. The important point is to *begin saving as soon as you start working*—in any sort of safe account. If you begin saving in your early 30s, when you have about 35 years before you retire, an annual investment of $1,845, which is slightly less than the $2,000 you can put in an IRA each year, will give you *a half-million-dollar nest egg at retirement*. If you wait until you are 45 to start, you will need to save $8,730 annually to have that same half million dollars. And if you wait until you are 50, you will have to save a whopping $15,737 a year![8] Have you ever heard anyone say, "Gee, I'm sorry I started saving money so early"?

Making Money Work as Hard as You Do— Understanding the Time Value of Money

To recognize the importance of your own savings and to begin your own retirement saving program, it is vital to recognize the concept of the "time value of money." If you save $100 today, rather than spend it, and even if you invest it very modestly at 7%, it will be worth:

$140 in 5 years
$197 in 10 years
$387 in 20 years
$543 in 25 years
$761 in 30 years

Would you rather have another new dress today or $387 20 years from now? Granted, $387 is not going to make or break your retirement. But let's say you decide to pass up spending just $100 each year from the time you are 35 until you retire. You invest that $100 each year at 8%. When you retire, you will have accumulated more than $11,300, which could make a very nice difference in your retirement.

Appendix A contains tables that are more empowering than 20 self-help treatises. These tables will help you determine the time value of money by providing you with various factors to use as multipliers in given situations. In all this Chapter's discussions we are using constant dollars that will not take inflation into account. Inflation is a critical element in retirement planning, and in Chapter 11, we discuss it in detail. For our purposes now, just remember that inflation effects can be calculated just like interest rates. If you want to know what a sum would be in today's dollars, treat the interest rate as an inflation rate in any of the examples that follow. *The tables do not reflect the effect of taxes on your savings, so keep in mind that tax will be due on the amounts you are saving.* Chapter 5 compares the impact of taxable, tax-deferred, and tax-exempt investments on your retirement saving. Let's see how the tables work for you.

Calculating the Future Value of Money

Appendix A.1 shows how a given sum grows at different interest rates over different time periods. Simply multiply the factor under the applicable interest rate and next to the applicable period of years by the amount of money you are saving or investing (or spending for that matter) to determine what the sum would be worth after the period of years.

For example, suppose you are thinking about spending a windfall of $2,500 on a painting you've always wanted, but you're also thinking about investing the sum in a 9% tax-free municipal bond for 10 years. Look down the 9% column to the 10-year figure and you find a factor of 2.367. Multiply $2,500 by 2.367 and you find your investment would be worth $5,917.50 in 10 years. Regardless of whether you decide to spend or invest, you can at least weigh more accurately whether you would rather have the painting now or almost $6,000 10 years from now.

Calculating the Contribution Needed Today to Reach a Future Goal

Use Appendix A.2 to see how much money and the rate of interest it must earn to accumulate a given sum over a period a time. For example, let's say you want a $500,000 nest egg at retirement. At age 35 you have 30 years until you retire, and you believe you can invest the money at 9%. How much do you need to invest today to reach your $500,000 goal? Look at the present value table. The factor under 9% over 30 years is 0.075. Multiply $500,000 times 0.075, and you will find that $37,500 invested today will provide you with $500,000 at retirement.

Calculating the Future Value of Known Annual Retirement Savings

Few of us can set aside a lump sum like $37,500 all at once for retirement. We need to make annual or monthly payments. Appendix A.3 shows you the future value of given annual payments over various periods of years at different interest rates. For example, suppose you intend to save $2,000 per year in an Individual Retirement Account from age 35 until you retire at 65. You want to invest it in a mutual fund that you think can earn 10% per year. Looking down the 10% column and across the 30-year row, you find a factor of 164.494. Multiply this by $2,000. You find you will have $328,988 at age 65 if you contribute each year and the fund earns the expected 10%.

Calculating the Immediate Value of Future Promised Amounts

Appendix A.4 tells you how much you will need today to reach a given sum at various interest rates and periods of time. For example, suppose your employer has offered to buy out the remaining 4 years of your employment contract beginning with payments of $30,000 a year for the next 4 years. You fear the company won't last that long, and you want a lump sum now. Assuming you could invest the money at 7% after taxes, how much should you demand from your employer now to give you the equivalent of $30,000 per year for 4 years? Look at the 7% column; find the 4-year row and multiply the factor, 3.387, by $30,000. You find that a payment of $101,610 now would be the equivalent of $30,000 each year for the next four years. Your boss thinks she's saving over $18,000 because she doesn't understand the time value of money, and you get the lump sum.

Other Uses for Time Value of Money Tables

The tables can also show you how important higher rates of return are over long periods of time. This will help you balance the advantages of higher rates of return with the risks of investment that usually come with those higher rates. For example, compare the difference in the multiplier factor over 20 years between 7%, which you might get in a certificate of deposit, and 12%, which you might get from a mutual fund. At 7% the factor is 3.87, while at 12%, it is 9.646. The sum of $1,000 invested for 20 years at 7% will give you $3,870, but at 12%, it would provide $9,646.

The tables will also show you the eroding effect of inflation. For example, using the future value of a dollar table, you will find, if inflation runs at 4% each year for 10 years, you will need $1,480 then to purchase $1,000 worth of goods in today's dollars.

Using the "Rule of 72" to Calculate Compound Interest

Another handy rule to remember is the "Rule of 72." Unlike the useful tables, you can keep this rule in your head to remind yourself of the wonders of compound interest. Divide the interest rate on any investment you are considering into 72, and the result will tell you how many years will pass before your money doubles. For example, suppose you are considering investing $2,000 in an 8% certificate of deposit. Divide 8 into 72 and you find your $2,000 will double to $4,000 in 9 years. If you could find a 9% certificate of deposit, your money could double in 8 years.

Conclusion: Build Your Personal Savings to Be a Major Portion of Your Retirement Income

Employer-provided retirement benefits and Social Security are obvious sources of retirement income. Chapters 7 and 9 discuss these sources in detail. But begin to think of your own individual savings as a necessary and critical element in your retirement planning. *Start saving now for retirement—whether you are 25 or 65!* Even if it must be a small amount, begin now. As you spend or save cash, think of it in terms of the time value of money. Get in the habit of using the tables in Appendix A to calculate future and present values of money when you are weighing a spending or saving option. You will be surprised at how different you may feel about spending and saving money when you know how much the sum in question could be worth after a few years at different investment rates. Chapter 8 spells out the various tax-favored retirement savings vehicles available for your individual savings, and Chapter 11 can help you determine how much you will need for retirement. Chapter 12 discusses savings and investment programs in more detail.

NOTES FOR CHAPTER 2

1. Excerpts from an address by Gwendolyn S. King, commissioner of Social Security, before the National Press Club, Washington, D.C., March 3, 1992.

2. *1991 Annual Report of the Board of Trustees of the Federal Old-Age and Survivors Insurance and Disability Insurance Trust Funds* (Washington, D.C.: U.S. Government Printing Office, 1991), pp. 1–2 and Table F5, p. 149.

3. Dorcas R. Hardy and C. Colburn Hardy, *Social Insecurity: the Crisis in America's Social Security and How to Plan Now for Your Own Financial Survival* (New York: Villard Books, 1991), p. 65.

4. Daniel J. Beller and David D. McCarthy, "Private Pension Benefits," in John A. Turner and Daniel J. Beller, eds., *Trends in Pensions 1992* (Wash-

ington, D.C.: U.S. Department of Labor, Pension and Welfare Benefits Administration, U.S. Government Printing Office, 1992), p. 217.

5. U.S. Bureau of the Census, *Statistical Abstract of the United States: 1991*, 111th edition (Washington, D.C.: U.S. Government Printing Office, 1991), Table 685.

6. Emily Andrews, *The Changing Profile of Pensions in America* (Washington, D.C.: Employee Benefits Research Institute, 1985), p. 13.

7. Daniel J. Beller and David D. McCarthy, "Private Pension Benefits," *Trends in Pensions 1992.*

8. Charles Schwab & Co., "Guide to Retirement Planning," March 1990, Table III, p. 15.

CHAPTER THREE

RETIREMENT BENEFITS BUZZWORDS

Retirement planning and benefits can be lathered with seemingly impossible jargon and buzzwords. Understanding some basic concepts and terms commonly used in discussing retirement plans is an important step for planning your retirement savings strategy. If you don't know the terms, you can't talk as easily or listen as carefully with the human resources people where you work or with financial planners or sellers of retirement saving products. You cannot really begin your planning until you understand the retirement benefits your current or potential employer is offering and how those benefits will grow for you over the years. Familiarity with the "buzzwords" will make the retirement planning process less complicated.

This chapter presents some of the basic terminology. The concepts are discussed in the order of importance to you. We start with you—otherwise known as the *plan participant*—and describe how you earn benefits, legal protections for retirement plans, who controls the plans, how your benefits are paid, and how various plans differ. Chapters 7 and 8 discuss the various employer-provided and individual plans in detail, including the advantages and disadvantages of each. The glossary at the end of the book also provides a handy reference to retirement and benefit plan terms.

THE BASIC TERMINOLOGY

Eligible Participant—Getting into the Retirement Benefits Game

You are the "participant" in an employer benefit plan. If your employer has a retirement plan, in most cases you become eligible to be a participant after you have worked for the company *full time* for 1 year or when you turn 21 years or, whichever comes later. Companies may permit you to become a participant sooner. An employer may also delay making you a participant for as long as 2 years, but, if so, you must then immediately own the right to any plan benefits you earn when you do become a participant.

"Full-time" employment is defined as 1,000 working hours per year. An employer may also permit you to be a participant if you work part time. But, if you work more than 1,000 hours a year, the employer *must* allow you to participate in any plan, even though both you and the employer consider you to be working "part time."

Plan Sponsor—the Keeper of the Keys

The plan sponsor of a retirement program is usually your employer. However, in some cases, usually involving "multiemployer plans," the plan sponsor may be a union or a combination of unions, with the trustees of the plan consisting of representatives from both the union and the employers contributing to the plan. (Multiemployer plans are discussed in more detail at the end of this chapter.)

Summary Plan Description

The Summary Plan Description, usually called the SPD, outlines the basic provisions of your employer's plan. This will be the document you receive from your employer when you are eligible to be a participant in the plan. An SPD is supposed to be written in plain English, understandable by the ordinary employee. But it is also supposed to describe and disclose all the provisions of the plan accurately and completely.

These two goals are almost mutually exclusive. As a consequence, employers fear the "plain English" summary plan description will leave something out or misstate an important point, such as the distinction between accrual and vesting. Omissions or misstatements could lead to lawsuits and unhappy retirees. So the employer errs on the side of protecting itself, and the "plain English" SPD can become as complicated as the original plan document. Some employers even give up entirely and simply state the plan document is the SPD. In general, the SPD will set out the provisions of your plan in relatively clear language.

Your employer plan SPD is the most useful document in understanding your employer-provided retirement benefit. The SPD may not be as simple as you would like, nevertheless, you should get a copy and read it. It will tell you:

❖ How you earn benefits.

❖ When you will have a nonforfeitable right to those benefits.

❖ How your benefits will be calculated.

❖ Whether you have to contribute money to receive an employer contribution.

It will also tell you all the other facts you need to begin to use your employer's plan as part of your retirement planning.

Benefit Accrual and Vesting—First You Earn It, then You Own It

With employer-provided benefits you usually begin to *accrue* (i.e., earn) benefits as soon as you become a participant. But it will probably be several years before you are *vested* in those benefits.

Benefits "accrue" as you earn them over the course of working. Generally, after a year with an employer, you have become a participant and you begin to earn benefits in the retirement plan. That means you are being credited with such benefits. For certain purposes, you may even be credited with the time you worked before you became a plan participant.

Although you may have accrued substantial benefits with an employer, your accruals will be subject to forfeiture if you do not continue working for the same employer for a fixed period of time. You will not own the benefits until you "vest" in them. *Vesting* means you have not only earned the benefits, but you are entitled to keep them if you leave the company or become disabled. If you die before you retire, your surviving beneficiaries can receive your benefits. This is frequently referred to as having a *nonforfeitable right* to the benefits you have accrued.

By law, there are basically two maximum vesting periods your employer may choose—cliff vesting or graduated vesting. Under *cliff vesting plans*, you vest in 100% of your benefits earned to date and all future benefits after you have worked 5 years with the employer. If the plan sponsor uses *graduated vesting* (also called *graded vesting*), you may have a nonforfeitable right in a portion of your benefits each year over a period of 7 years, beginning with 20% after 3 years of service and increasing by 20% each succeeding year. The details of vesting are discussed in Chapter 6 on ERISA.

Years of Service—How We Keep Score

Your right to participate in the plan is keyed to completing a *year of service*. Future rights to benefits, such as counting for vesting and for determining the *credited service* used to calculate most defined benefit plan payments, will be based in part on years of service. Under retirement plan laws, a year of service is defined as any 12-month period, defined by the retirement plan. The 12 months could be a calendar year, a tax year or what is referred to as the *plan year*. A plan year can be any 12-month period stated in the retirement plan document.

There are three ways to count years of service. One way is the *general* or *standard hours' method*, which simply counts actual hours worked. As a rule, however, many employers do not count actual hours worked. Instead, they keep track of work on a weekly or daily basis. In calculating "service" for retirement plan purposes, these employers may use another way to count years of service: an *equivalency system* based on weeks, payroll periods, days, or shifts. These periods are assigned an hourly equivalent, higher than the hours likely to actually be worked during the period. For example, a day is equivalent to 10 hours. Under the equivalency method, 870 hours worked will be the equivalent of 1,000 hours. If either of these methods is used, most plans require you to have worked 1,000 hours during the year to be credited with a year of service.

The third way to count years of service is simply counting the period of time since the date you started working for the employer. This *elapsed time method* does not count hours. Under this method, 12 months after you started working for your employer, you will have a year of service, regardless of how many hours you worked during that time.

You cannot earn more than 1 year of service during a 12-month calendar period, regardless of the number of hours you work.

Breaks in service are periods in any year when you work fewer than 500 hours. A break in service can occur when you quit or are laid off, or if you are assigned to a part-time job when you had been working full time. You may take up to approximately 6 months for the birth of a child without that leave being counted as a break in service.

If you have a break in service and return to your employer, your first years of service prior to the time you left will count for vesting and benefit calculation unless the break was longer than 5 years or the number of years you had worked before you left, whichever is greater. For example, suppose you work for Acme full time from 1985 to 1989, when you leave for another job. In 1992, Acme asks you to return and you agree. Your earlier 4 years of service will count for vesting and benefits calculations because it is greater than your 3-year break in service.

Portability of Retirement Benefits

The concept of *portability* for retirement benefits can mean several things, but basically it means the right to keep vested retirement benefits when you leave the employer where you earned these benefits. *Portability of benefits* simply means you have vested in the benefits, and when you retire, even though you may have left the plan sponsor years before, the plan sponsor will provide you with the benefit. By law most retirement plans must permit this type of portability. *Portability of assets* means you can actually take the money with you when you leave. As noted earlier with *portability of service*, prior years of working for other employers are counted in determining benefits at retirement. But portability of service is rare. Chapter 4 discusses the effects of portability in specific careers.

ERISA—the Cop on the Beat and Your Legal Protection

ERISA is the acronym for the 1974 federal law, the Employee Retirement Income Security Act. ERISA controls all retirement benefits provided by most employers, as well as most other benefits such as health and life insurance. Chapter 6 discusses this law in detail. ERISA does not cover plans provided by state and local governments, the federal government, or churches. ERISA is enforced by the Department of Labor (DOL) and the Internal Revenue Service (IRS).

Qualified Plan

You may hear employer retirement or welfare plans referred to as qualified plans. Qualified retirement plans receive preferential tax treatment under the Internal Revenue Code and under most state income tax provisions as well. To be "qualified," the plan must meet stringent IRS statutes and rules, many of which are identical to the ERISA statute. Usually, an ERISA retirement plan is also a qualified plan, and vice versa. However, many of the qualified plan tax rules do apply to plans exempted from ERISA. For example, government and church plans are subject to tax limits on the size of benefits, to nondiscrimination rules, and to distribution rules.

Unfortunately, the DOL and the IRS each write their own rules interpreting the statutes that Congress has passed. The DOL and the IRS don't always agree on how the statutes should be interpreted. So, for example, what may be a "highly compensated" employee for IRS rules may not be for DOL purposes. These inconsistencies are lots of fun for the two agencies, but not much fun for plan participants or plan sponsors.

Fortunately, it is usually the employer, rather than you, who is charged with the duty to resolve the rules. You need remember only that what you have been told about a plan and its IRS rules may be augmented when you add on the layer of DOL rules. If certain explanations of the plan sound slightly inconsistent, it may be because the plan is trying to satisfy two sets of rules. Or it may be because the speaker doesn't understand all the rules.

Defined Benefit or Defined Contribution Plan—
Tell Me Later, Tell Me Now

Retirement programs are usually classified as either defined benefit plans or defined contribution plans. A *defined benefit plan* literally specifies the payment you will receive at retirement. For example, the plan ordinarily will state that when you retire, you will receive an annual benefit of 1% of your annual compensation times the number of years you worked. The benefits will be paid monthly for the rest of your life. Under this plan, a 30-year employee earning an average of $40,000 annually would be entitled to $12,000 annually at retirement.

You have probably guessed that in a *defined contribution plan* it is the "contribution" made by your employer—or occasionally you— which is specified in the plan document. For example, a plan document may provide that each year your employer will contribute 2% of your compensation or the employer will match 50% of any amount you contribute (up to legally set maximums). For example, if you earned $40,000 this year, your employer's 2% contribution would be $800 for this year.

These words will frequently be used to delineate the type of plan your employer has and will affect how you do your own planning. Typically, a defined benefit plan is referred to as a *pension. 401(k) plans* or *profit-sharing plans* are common types of defined contribution plans.

A typical question from employees is, "Which plan is better?" The obvious answer is: *the plan that pays the most money.* In fact there is no definitive answer to the general question. It depends on several factors: the amount of money involved in each plan, your age when you ask the question, and how long you will stay with the employer.

In general, the defined contribution plan is better for younger employees who have been with the employer a shorter time, and the defined benefit plan is better for older workers with long service with the employee. In Chapter 4, we will see the actual difference in retirement benefits generated by the two types of plans, in various career patterns. Look at the scenarios in Appendix B, Tables B.1–B.4, to compare the buildup of benefits for a one-job career under a defined benefit and a defined contribution plan. Chapter 7 also has more detail on the comparisons.

Pensions

Pensions are defined benefit retirement plans that ordinarily pay you on a monthly basis when you retire until you die. If you choose, the payment can also continue after you die for the life of your surviving spouse or other beneficiary.

401(k) Plans—You Fund Your Own Retirement

401(k) plans are named after the section of the Internal Revenue Code that created the plan. These are employer-provided plans which allow you to save your own wages without paying federal (and in most cases state) income tax on the savings or the earnings on the savings until you retire or take the money out of the plan. (You will have to pay Social Security taxes on the money you contribute.) Frequently, employers will also contribute to your account by matching your contributions. This may be on a dollar-for-dollar basis or on a percentage of what you contribute.

401(k) plans are sometimes also referred to as CODAs (*Cash or Deferred Arrangements*) by the IRS or benefits specialists. *If your employer has a 401(k) plan, this is the first place to begin saving. It is the best retirement savings vehicle you can possibly have because of the pretax benefit and possible employer contributions.*

Other Types of Employer-Provided Retirement Plans

Other types of employer-provided defined contribution retirement plans include the following:

- ❖ *Profit-sharing plans*—these allow an employer the *option* of contributing to your retirement plan each year.
- ❖ *Money purchase pension plans*—here, the annual contribution is not optional; instead, the employer must contribute a percentage of pay for each plan participant each year.
- ❖ *Stock bonus plans*—these are simply plans in which the employer's contribution is made in the form of company stock.

- ❖ *ESOPs* (employee stock ownership plans)—these consist of a hybrid stock bonus plan that must consist primarily of employer stock with the highest voting rights and powers.
- ❖ *Thrift plans*—these essentially permit you to save money with after-tax dollars (unlike the 401(k) plans, which take pretax dollars). The employer may match your contribution.
- ❖ *Target benefit plans*—here, the employer establishes a "target" for the benefit you should have at retirement and the employer contributes an amount each year designed to reach the target based on the assumptions used for the earnings on the money in the plan.

Chapter 7, on employer-provided retirement plans, discusses each of these plans in detail.

Pension Plan Integration—Accounting for Social Security

Retirement plans that take into account payments from Social Security—or other types of retirement plans—in some form when setting the benefits under the plan are called *integrated plans*. Employers are permitted to "integrate" pension plans to receive credit for the employer-paid portion of Social Security payroll taxes. Integrated plans usually permit the employer to contribute a lower amount to the plan for the wages that are subject to the Social Security taxes (currently wages up to about $57,600) and to contribute a higher amount for those wages in excess of the Social Security taxable wage base. There are strict limits on the amount of integration permitted.

A typical integrated defined benefit pension plan might base benefits as follows:

1% of pay up to the Social Security wage base times years of service

+

1.25% of pay in excess of the Social Security wage base times years of service

A typical defined contribution plan might have a formula such as:

3% of pay up to the Social Security wage base

+

6% of pay in over the Social Security wage base

Simplified Employee Pensions (SEPs)

Simplified employee pensions (SEPs) permit an employer essentially to set up an individual retirement account for each employee. Annual contributions can be up to 25% of compensation or $30,000, whichever is less. You are immediately vested in the contribution. We will look at the rules in detail in Chapter 7.

Keogh Plans

Keogh plans, named for their congressional sponsor, Congressman Eugene Keogh, are also referred to as H.R. 10 plans, for the bill which enacted them into law. Keogh plans are retirement plans for the self-employed. Even if you are employed and have a retirement plan through your employer, you may also have a Keogh plan if you earn income as a freelance worker or independent contractor. For example, suppose you work for a printing company and have a retirement plan there, but you also have a graphics design business at home. You may open a Keogh account and put up to 25% or $30,000 of your net earnings from the graphics arts business into the account on a pretax basis. When you retire, you will pay tax as you withdraw money from the plan. We look at Keogh plans in detail in Chapter 8, on your individual savings for retirement.

Annuity or Lump-Sum Payments—How Do You Get Your Money?

Retirement benefits, life insurance policies, and certain other financial investment vehicles are paid out to the recipient in one of two ways—as an "annuity" or in a lump sum. The *lump-sum option* is obvious: you get all the money or assets of the investment at once.

In contrast, an *annuity* provides payments periodically over the course of a stated period of years or over your lifetime, and in some cases the life of your beneficiary. A true annuity keeps paying as long as you are alive. This is generally the form of payment for employer-provided pensions. Annuities may also be paid over a stated number of years such as 15 or 20.

Joint and Survivor Annuity—You Can't Take It with You

By law the ordinary form of payment to married employees in most employer-provided retirement plans is a joint and survivor annuity, unless you and your spouse agree otherwise. Under this type of payment, you receive the benefit from the retirement plan in monthly payments for as long as you live. When you die, your spouse continues receiving payments. The payment you receive when you first retire is less than the payment you would have received if there were no survivor benefits. The benefit received by your surviving spouse is usually reduced again after you die. These annuity forms are discussed in more detail in Chapter 14, on marriage and benefits.

Preretirement Survivor Annuity—A Cushion for Survivors

Also by law, most employer-provided plans must provide payments to a spouse if the employee held any vested benefits at death before retirement. These payments must begin no later than the employee's earliest retirement date had she survived. Chapter 7 provides more information on preretirement annuities.

Plan Trust—the Protected Piggy Bank

The funds for the employer's promised retirement benefits are held in the *plan trust*. As with any trust, there are guardians of the funds, called trustees. Under ERISA, the trust and its funds must be used "exclusively" for the benefit of the plan participants and their beneficiaries and to defray the reasonable expenses of the plan. The employer has no right to the funds in the trust, and neither the employer nor its creditors may reach the money unless the plan is terminated and all benefits paid. Likewise, your creditors may not reach your share of the trust fund.

Pension Benefit Guaranty Corporation

ERISA created the *Pension Benefit Guaranty Corporation* (PBGC) to guarantee defined benefit retirement plans, that is, the true pension. PBGC is funded by "insurance premiums" paid each year by employers sponsoring pension plans. If a plan is terminated by a company without sufficient funds to cover all the benefits, the PBGC will pay a portion of those unfunded benefits. Chapter 6 on ERISA discusses the role of PBGC in detail.

Fiduciaries

A *fiduciary*, by law, is any person who is charged with the duty to act at her discretion for another in the other's best interests, without consideration of the fiduciary's own interests. For example, guardians of minor children are fiduciaries to the child. Trustees are fiduciaries to the trust. Corporate boards of directors are fiduciaries to the corporation.

A *retirement plan fiduciary* is any person or entity with discretion or authority over the plan or its assets. Such a fiduciary must act for the exclusive benefit of the participants of the plan and with the care and diligence a prudent person in the same or similar circumstances with the same business goals would use. The employer is a fiduciary to the plan if the employer exercises discretionary control over the administration of the plan. The *named fiduciaries*, usually chosen by the employer to act as the plan's trustees, are, of course, fiduciaries. Anyone deciding how the general plan assets are invested or choosing investment options for plan participants is a fiduciary. The plan *administrator* who decides how the plan will be interpreted is a fiduciary. Mere record keepers for plans, who are also some times casually referred to as "administrators," are not fiduciaries because they have no discretionary authority. If a plan participant is not dealt with legally, the plan fiduciary is the legally responsible party and is liable for suit.

Actuaries

Actuaries tell employers how much money to put in defined benefit pension plans to ensure that there is enough money to pay you when you retire. In short, it is a noble (if unexciting) profession.

Actuaries are mathematicians who make financial projections based on assumptions regarding interest rates, risks, the life expectancies within a group of individuals, and so on. *Pension actuaries* make projections based on life expectancies (usually referred to as mortality rates), employee turnover, expected retirement ages, and rates of return on investments made by the pension plan. These calculations tell the plan sponsor how much money should be placed in the pension plan trust to have adequate funds to pay benefits as the plan beneficiaries retire.

Enrolled actuaries certify to the IRS, the Pension Benefit Guaranty Corporation and the Department of Labor that pension plans are funded in compliance with law. *Actuarial assumptions* are the estimates and projections an actuary uses to reach the funding calculations. By law, such assumptions used in qualified plan calculations must be "reasonable" in the aggregate.

Nondiscrimination Rules—Retirement Plans Are Not Just for Executives

Nondiscrimination rules in qualified retirement plans are not concerned with race, sex, or religion. They refer to discrimination in plan benefits between "highly compensated employees" and those benefits given to "nonhighly compensated employees." These rules basically forbid executives and owners from receiving disproportionately higher benefits than other employees. For example, a defined contribution plan giving everyone 5% of compensation is not considered discriminatory, even though it's clear that executives will receive more in absolute dollars than the rank and file. It would not be permissible to give everyone earning less than $30,000 a contribution of 3% and all those above $30,000 a 10% contribution. Nondiscrimination rules are also designed to ensure that most employees are, in fact, covered by the benefit plan, if the employer establishes a plan. For example, tax-qualified retirement plans cannot be set up to cover just the executives. Companies may create special executive plans that do not receive preferential tax treatment.

Although the concept of nondiscrimination sounds simple enough, the nondiscrimination rules are among the most complex area of retirement law. The testing required by these rules can be expensive, time consuming, and confusing to employers. Employers are bound by these rules, so why should you care if they are complex and cumbersome? Because the complexity and expense of these rules discourage employers from setting up plans in the first place. For existing plans, excessive red tape means that money that could be spent on benefits is spent administering the plan. We need the nondiscrimination rules, but we don't need them to be so complicated.

Highly Compensated Employees

A *highly compensated employee* is an intricately defined IRS term (the regulations account for 15 pages of fine print). Basically, highly compensated employees are roughly those employees earning over $64,000 in 1993, acting as officers and earning over $57,000, or owning more than 5% of the company. As you've already guessed, *nonhighly paid employees* are the rest of us. The dollar limitations are adjusted for inflation each year.

Multiemployer Plans

Multiemployer plans are any sort of benefit plan sponsored by unions and arising from the collective bargaining process. Unlike *single-employer plans*, which are sponsored by only one employer, multiemployer plans depend on the contributions of several employers who have employees belonging to the union conducting the collective bargaining. As a participant in a multiemployer plan, you have "portability of service," meaning your years of service with all employers in the plan are counted. You are not penalized by moving from one employer in the plan to another employer in the plan. As you move to a new employer in the plan, you are considered to take the service with you; hence, you have a type of pension "portability."

The rules for multiemployer plans differ from those for single-employer plans, especially in the areas of funding and employer contributions. The most important difference from an employee's point of view is the difference in vesting rules. Multiemployer plans may still require 10 years of service before the employee is 100% vested. In this book, we refer primarily to single-employer plans. But where multiemployer plans are different, the differences are usually noted in the book.

CONCLUSION: USE YOUR KNOWLEDGE OF BENEFITS BUZZWORDS TO REVIEW YOUR RETIREMENT BENEFITS OPTIONS

A grasp of the basic terms will give you the confidence to question your employer, accountant, or investment adviser and to begin the process of retirement planning. Now that you have mastered these terms, take a look—hopefully not for the first time—at your employer's

SPD for your retirement plan. It should be easier to read now that you know the difference between "accruing" and "vesting" and a "joint and survivor annuity" as compared to a "single annuity." As you discuss retirement savings, you can focus on the substance of the plan or investment vehicle and its underlying value without being distracted by wondering about the terminology.

In the next chapter, we meet four women as they put these terms to practical application. We see by concrete example the differences in the various plans and how time off the payroll radically changes retirement benefit growth.

CHAPTER FOUR

ALICE, SUSAN, BONNIE, AND JENNIFER: FOUR CASE STUDIES THAT SHOW HOW RETIREMENT BENEFITS CAN GROW-OR DISAPPEAR

How do women's career patterns really affect their retirement income? Specifics show us better than theory. Four examples—Alice, Susan, Bonnie, and Jennifer, each with career patterns common to many women—illustrate exactly how women can be robbed of huge amounts of employer-provided retirement income because of time out of the work force and job changes. These case studies show how even a few years out of the workplace, combined with changing employers, can result in the loss of *more than half* the employer-provided benefits one would receive after a career with a single employer. These dramatic losses result primarily from:

❖ Failure to vest in benefits
❖ The effects of inflation on benefits earned early in one's career
❖ Cashing out and spending benefits before retirement

These factors inflict more damage on the purchasing power of employer-provided benefits than do losses from the actual time out of the work force. The chapter concludes by discussing how portability of retirement benefits affected our sample population and how it may affect you.

Appendix B provides the benefit calculations for each woman. The salary of each woman is based on Department of Labor data for their job classification, adjusted for inflation to 1992 real dollars. Note that unless otherwise stated, the dollar figures we will discuss throughout the chapter from these scenarios are constant 1992 dollars. So, for example, when we say Bonnie will have an annual employer-provided benefit of $35,000 when she retires some 25 years from now, the actual dollar figure will be higher. She will have the equivalent buying power at that time of $35,000.[1] Each appendix calculates benefits for Alice, Susan, Bonnie, and Jennifer and compares their career benefit accumulations with a person who held one job over the same career span, earning the same salary with the same types of employer-provided retirement plan. Retirement payments are shown both as lump sums and as annuity payments until death.

These payments are also shown with alternatives that assume the benefits earned from jobs held prior to retirement either were cashed out and transferred into an individual retirement account (IRA) for reinvestment or were left with the employer until retirement age and then taken out. Because we use the same earnings assumptions for the money, you immediately ask, "What's the difference?" If the transfer option is chosen in a defined benefit plan, the employer may reduce the benefit payout slightly based on a "mortality" factor. Remember that in a defined benefit plan, the employer (or the actuary, actually) bets that some of the potential beneficiaries will die before retiring and receiving a benefit. When you withdraw your vested share before retirement age, the law permits this reduction because you are avoiding the possibility of dying and forfeiting the benefit before you can draw funds at retirement age.

ALICE: A NURSE AT 60

Alice, now 60, began her nursing career at age 21. She is just now beginning to think seriously about retirement. In financial terms, however, she is not sure that she can swing it. Her own savings are small, and she would be relying primarily on any employer pensions due her and on Social Security.

Alice's Career Path

Alice has worked full time for six different employers over her 39-year career, and she now earns $36,750. She served 8 years at her first job with a large hospital, and then took 1 year off for her first child. She went back to work in the emergency room at a smaller hospital, working full time for 4 years and then took another year off for her second child. After that she worked for 7 years in a hospital nearer her home so she could be close to the children. She was offered a supervisory position at a different hospital and accepted that job, which she held for 8 years. She then took a year off to care for her mother, who was terminally ill, and to help settle her mother's estate. She then joined a clinic specializing in children's care for 6 years. Two years ago she moved to her current job as supervisor of a neighborhood clinic. She plans to stay in this job until she retires.

What Alice Has in Pensions

If Alice retires at 65, *she will receive an annual pension of less than $4,650. Compare that with a pension of $12,700 she would have received* if she had stayed with one employer over her career or had received credit for all her years of service! What happened to Alice? Her pension is only about one-third of what it would be had she stayed with one employer and still taken 3 years off over her 39-year career.

What Happened to Alice's Retirement Benefits?

Basically, Alice's dramatically lower pension results from lack of vesting. Over the years as she left her various jobs, she left behind valuable retirement benefits because she had not stayed with her employer long enough to vest in the benefits and to have the right to take them with her or receive payments when she did eventually retire. During much of her career, the law allowed employers to require 10 years or more of service before an employee vested in retirement benefits—and Alice never stayed with any of her employers for 10 years or more.

The lump-sum value of the benefits Alice left behind in each job tells the tale:

	Value at Date of Termination in 1992 $	Approximate Value at Age 65 in 1992 $
First job	$1,229	$15,500
Second job	977	9,200
Third job	3,261	17,200
Fourth job	7,512	22,200

Alice usually worked at her jobs for several years. If the 5-year vesting required by today's law had been in effect during her career, *she would have been entitled to all these lump sums* except the $977 from her second position, where she worked for only 4 years. Five-year vesting did protect her in her fifth job. She earned the right to an annual pension of $1,670, worth a lump-sum value of $10,700 when she left the job, and the estimated aggregate pension of $4,650 includes that annual $1,670 from the fifth job.

Could Alice Have Protected Herself?

Could Alice have protected herself in some way against these losses? Possibly, but only with her own diligence and demands. For example, in three of her jobs, she left after more than 7 years. In the first job, if she had delayed child bearing for 2 years, or taken the year off after the baby was age 2, she would have vested. But babies don't observe timetables, and most prospective parents don't plan families around pension vesting.

When Alice changed employers to move up in rank, she could have attempted to negotiate a bonus from the new employer as compensation for lost benefits. Such a special payment would lack the automatic tax-deferred status of regular pension credits. However, she could have then invested the extra money in a tax-deferred instrument such as an annuity or a tax-free municipal bond fund. Earnings would then accrue on a tax-favored basis.

The most certain way to have protected herself would have been through her own personal savings. Diverting just 5% of her income to a tax-free investment would have given her $2,660 when she left her first job. By retirement at age 65, this amount would have grown to approximately $14,700, assuming a 5% rate of return and no further contributions. She could have done the same in each of her jobs and had her own retirement account of approximately $112,000 at age 65, by saving 5% of her earnings and investing them at 7½% in a tax-deferred account.

What Should Alice Do Now?

At age 60 there is little Alice can do realistically to change her bleak retirement future dramatically. Working full time a few more years, perhaps even past age 65, is a necessity. Part-time work after retirement may be another option. Nursing is a physically demanding job, and Alice may want to find something else for her part-time work. What follows will provide Alice with some detailed advice, but it won't be as helpful as it would have been when she was 30 or 40 or even 50.

Investigate Exact Amount of Social Security Benefits. First, because all of her employers offered defined benefit pension plans integrated with Social Security, Alice should contact Social Security and be sure that the agency has an accurate wage history for her. It will also tell her what her expected benefit would be if she retired at 62.

Second, she should look at her current employer's summary plan description (SPD) and determine at what age she can retire and what the reductions for early retirement before age 65 might be. If she retires now, she would receive an annual income from this job's pension of only $1,077, which with her income from the prior job's pension would give her an annual income of only $2,747, clearly not enough to live on, especially considering that she will not be eligible for Social Security until age 62. If she stays another 5 years, her annual pension for this job will be $2,960, more than twice its current value.

The dramatic increase in the worth of Alice's pension illustrates the value and the buildup of defined benefit pension plans for older workers during their final years of service. Nevertheless, Alice will by no means have a financially secure retirement from her pension alone. At age 65, the two pensions will represent just 12% of her previous income. With the addition of Social Security, her retirement income will be just 42% of her final earnings. Even with optimistic estimates that retirees need only 70% of prior income (these projections are not realistic, as we will discuss in Chapter 11), Alice will need additional revenue. Certainly, she does not have the income to retire now, even if her plan would allow retirement at 60. Without savings of her own, Alice will be strapped, and her financial condition will only get worse over time because her pension income is not going to grow with inflation. Her Social Security payments will increase with inflation—at least under current law.

Consider a Lump-Sum Payment Form.   To protect against inflation, Alice could consider taking one or both of her pensions in a lump sum at retirement and reinvesting the amounts. The lump-sum value of her pension when she is 65 will be $14,100 from her former job and $25,062 from her current job (compared with a lump-sum value of $107,400 for a one-job career with the same defined benefit pension plan). These sums could be rolled directly into an IRA without paying taxes on the money until it was taken out. Investments could be purchased which might give her a greater annual return than she would receive under the pension. But such a move would require very sound financial advice. Chapter 8 discusses in detail using the lump-sum payment form to protect against inflation.

Redouble Savings Efforts.   Third, Alice should begin—or hopefully redouble—her efforts at saving now. She should look for investments that will protect against inflation. If she has her own home, she might consider trading down to a smaller, less expensive residence. If Alice chooses this option, she has time over the next 5 years to observe the housing market and sell at her convenience. Money remaining after the purchase of a smaller place should be invested for retirement income. Alternatively, she might consider renting part or all of her home if that could be made profitable.

Look for Forgotten Benefits.   Fourth, Alice should contact all her former employers and inquire about any potential retirement benefits. This is a very big long shot, but benefits plans do change, sometimes retroactively and for the better. Memories can become confused or perhaps Alice overlooked a benefit. After all, when she left these employers, pinning down her future retirement benefits was not a high-priority item, even though, with hindsight, it should have been. Clearly, if the employer does not know where she is today, it cannot deliver the good news that she has a retirement benefit waiting. Her investment is a little time and a postage stamp or a phone call. Even a few hundred dollars each year can pay the phone bill for a year.

Work After "Retirement". Finally, Alice should think about a part-time job after retirement. After age 65, Alice can earn up to $10,560 annually (in 1993 dollars) without having her Social Security benefits reduced. At age 70 she may earn as much as she wishes without any Social Security reduction. Any pension benefits she receives are not included in this limit. At any age she may have to pay tax on as much as half of her Social Security benefits if she has income of more than $25,000 per year, which does include pension payments. (Couples pay tax on part of their Social Security benefits if they have income of more than $32,000).

If Alice feels nursing will be too rigorous after age 65, she should begin thinking now about other possible job opportunities. Are there less onerous jobs at the clinic? Are there paying jobs at the museum where she volunteers? Five years before retirement is not too early to begin thinking about possibilities, even if it is too soon to begin sending out résumés. Of course her best retirement financial move would be to work more years for her current employer. Because she will likely be receiving a larger salary each year and because the pension plan is based on the last 5 years of work and on the number of years worked, she will be increasing two important variables in her ultimate pension benefit formula. Additionally, if she postpones receiving Social Security benefits past age 65, when she does retire Alice will receive an increased Social Security benefit for the rest of her life.

SUSAN: A MIDDLE MANAGER AT 50

Susan began working when she was 20 and she has never stopped. Over her 30-year career she has had five jobs, and she plans to stay with her management job at a small auto parts manufacturer until she retires. Susan likes her job and she doesn't plan to retire until she is 65. But when she does retire, she would like to travel, like her brother who retired last year after 30 years with the same company Susan works for. She currently earns $25,200.

Susan's Career Path

Susan worked as a secretary at her first job for 4 years. Her employer did not have a retirement plan, and at age 20 she never gave retirement a thought. She then moved to another firm which promised some marketing training and worked there for 5 years. Her employer had a defined benefit retirement plan, but she did not vest in it. Susan then took a job with a large appliance manufacturing company in marketing and moved into management. The company had a defined benefit plan. Susan stayed with the company 10 years and vested in her benefit. She moved to a new position with a start-up company, but was part of a "down sizing" after 5 years because the company was not growing. At that point she went to work with her current employer, which has a defined contribution plan.

What Susan Has in Retirement Benefits

When Susan retires at 65, she can expect an annual income from all her employers' retirement plans of about $4,700. Of this, $570 will be from her defined benefit plan earned with the appliance manufacturer, where she spent 10 years, and $4,130 will come from her current employer's plan. These amounts will represent about 16% of her final earnings. Compare this with the $8,300 she would have received annually from a single-job career under a defined benefit plan or the $10,600 annually she would have received under a defined contribution plan in a single-job career. Under these plans she could have received 29% or 37%, respectively, of her final earnings.

When Susan retires at age 65, she will have worked full time continually for 45 years. She will have about half of the retirement benefits a one-job career would have given her under plans similar to those of her employers.

What Happened to Susan's Retirement Benefits?

Susan's first job had no retirement benefits, but at age 20 she never gave that fact a thought. Although that may be reasonable for a 20-year-old, let's look at what Susan missed in her early 20s by comparing her with a friend, Linda. Linda earned the same salary as Susan, but Linda worked in a company with a defined contribution plan devoting 5% of salary each year to her account. Contributions vested immediately, so Linda was entitled to a lump-sum benefit worth $4,000 in today's dollars after working 4 years. Or she could have opted for an annual benefit of $1,200 when she retired at 65, even if she never worked another day in her life! Not so shabby for earnings from age 20 to 24. Linda's situation is a simple illustration of how seemingly meaningless amounts of money saved early in life really mount up.

When Susan left her second job after 5 years, she had earned a lump-sum value in the pension plan of $450, which she left behind because the benefit was not vested. That sum would have paid her $150 annually at 65 if she had vested in it. Granted, not enough to live on, but enough to buy a new coat every year or pay a month's utility bills.

Fortunately, Susan stayed for 10 years at her third job, which had a defined benefit plan integrated with Social Security. Because she stayed 10 years and because ERISA was enacted during those years, and because ERISA required as a minimum 10-year cliff vesting or graduated vesting over 15 years, she had the right to retirement benefits when she left. Susan had earned a benefit with a lump-sum value today of $2,900, which will pay her at retirement $570 annually. If Susan could have taken that amount on termination and rolled it into an IRA when she retired, it would be worth about $7,300, assuming a 7% rate of return, or about $12,000, assuming 9%.

Her next job also offered a defined benefit plan, but she did not vest in the benefit she accrued. Susan was there only for 5 years, and the law did not require 5-year vesting at that time. In that case she left on the table a lump sum of about $1,600 in today's dollars, which would have paid annually $387 when she retired. If she could have taken the lump-sum amount and rolled it into an IRA at 9%, she would have about $7,600 at retirement, growing to about $9,800 if she left it untouched until she was 68.

Compare that $7,600 amount to the lump-sum value of Susan's current benefit under her employer's defined contribution plan of $9,200. Again we see small amounts casually left behind at an earlier employer grow to be significant at retirement.

Susan's annual income from her appliance manufacturing pension is suffering from what is known as "preretirement/retirement inflation." The $570 annual amount is based on the salary she was earning when she left more than a decade ago. The benefit will not be increased to reflect inflation since then or any other increases in wages Susan has had. Because the last decade has not been one of high inflation, this erosion is not terribly dramatic, but it is there. If the years before Susan's retirement are high inflation years, she may see a very dramatic erosion.

Susan actually was lucky. She could have lost even more benefits because each time she changed jobs her new employer was entitled to keep her out of the plan for 1 year. Although that first year counts for vesting purposes, it does not have to count for benefit calculation purposes. Under some plans your first year will not be included in calculating "credited service," a concept used especially in defined benefit plans formulas. If your employer has a defined contribution plan, chances are you will not receive a contribution for that first year. If you have 6 jobs, you may automatically lose six years of benefits simply because of these waiting periods.

How Could Susan Have Protected Herself?

Susan could have been less cavalier about benefits in her first two jobs. For example, after she had been in the work force for 8 years, she had no retirement benefits. By contrast, her friend Linda by that time had a defined contribution benefit with a lump-sum value of $8,500, which would pay her $2,700 a year at retirement even if Linda earned no further benefits. Compare this to the annual $4,700 Susan will have after working 45 years!

Moral of the story: the early years count. The earlier you start, the easier it is to accumulate a significant retirement pool of capital. If Susan had "paid herself" 5% of her income, just for those early years, and invested it in tax-free investments or in an annuity, she would have an extra $2,700 a year at retirement. If she had done this throughout her career, she could retire with an annual income of $10,600 from her own personal retirement plan earnings in addition to the employer pensions she has.

When she was part of the layoff at her fourth job, she might have tried to negotiate taking the $1,600 lump-sum value of her benefits. True, this is only a possibility. But $1,600 is a small sum to a company and even a company in economic difficulties feels guilty about letting good employees go. As we saw, that $1,600 would have grown over the 22 years to about $7,600, a very tidy sum for Susan. It never hurts to ask.

What Should Susan Do Now?

Susan is much more fortunate than Alice. Susan has begun to look at retirement income needs 10 years before Alice has. A lot of savings can accrue in the 15 years between now and Susan's retirement. Unlike her brother, who retired from the same company with a benefit that gave him 37% of his prior earnings, Susan will have only 16% in employer-provided retirement benefits if she follows her plans to remain with her current firm until retirement. Social Security will provide another 40% or so, giving her 56% of income at retirement. She doesn't think that's enough, and she is probably correct, as we will see in Chapter 11, How Much Do You Need for Retirement?

First, Susan can practice her own savings program for the next 15 years. Second, because her employer has a defined contribution plan, the company is also likely to have a 401(k) program to which she can contribute. That money is taken out of her pay on a pretax basis. No tax is due on the money or the earnings until she begins to withdraw it at retirement.

Third, she can also fully fund an IRA each year. Under current law, her contribution is only partially deductible because she earns more than $25,000. But she earns only slightly more than that, so $1,960 of the $2,000 will be deductible. And the earnings are tax deferred until she begins to use the money. She won't pay tax again on the amount she could not deduct originally. A $2,000 annual contribution to an IRA over the next 15 years will provide her with an account of $46,550 if it earns 6% annually and $54,300 if it earns 8%. She might consider mutual funds with high income, where returns of 14% are not unusual, in which case she would have an IRA worth $87,000 at retirement.

BONNIE: A LAWYER OF 40

Bonnie did not enter the work force until she was 24 and out of law school. Since then she has had five jobs and taken off a year to be with her baby. She hopes to remain with her current employer, a *Fortune* 500 company engaged in food processing, until she retires. But, given the corporate world of mergers, acquisitions, down sizing, right sizing, and management upheavals, she realizes that this may be difficult. She hopes to retire at 62. As assistant general counsel, Bonnie earns $85,000.

Bonnie's Career Path

In her first year after law school Bonnie clerked for a judge and then worked for a local public interest group for 2 years. From there, she moved to a law firm where she worked for 4 years. At that point she took 1 year off to spend with her family and decided to go to work in a corporate law office for a retail operation, hoping for mere 50-hour weeks rather than the 60-hour weeks at the law firm. After 5 years—and only 50-hour weeks—with the corporation, Bonnie was offered the assistant general counselship with the food processing corporation's law office. She gave her employer a chance to meet the offer, and when it didn't, Bonnie took the offer with the new corporation. Bonnie has worked for 16 years and she plans to work another 22 years.

Bonnie's Present Retirement Benefits

In her first three jobs Bonnie received no retirement benefits. The clerkship and the public interest group had no retirement plans. The law firm had a defined contribution plan, but Bonnie did not vest in the plan because she was there for only 4 years and the law permitted the plan to vest benefits after 10 years.

In her first corporate job, Bonnie participated in a defined benefit plan integrated with Social Security. Before she left that job, the law was changed to require 5-year vesting or 7-year graduated vesting. The corporation adopted 5-year vesting. With 5 years of service, Bonnie just qualified for a benefit under the plan before she moved to her current job. From that 5 years with the retail operation, she will be entitled to an annual pension of about $1,680 or a lump sum of about $13,000 at age 62. Without the change in the law in the late 1980s, she would not have been eligible to receive this amount.

At her job now, Bonnie also has a defined benefit plan integrated with Social Security. If she follows her plan and remains with her employer, at age 62 Bonnie will be entitled to a total annual pension from both corporate employers of $34,700, or 33% of her final earnings. A one-job career under the same plan would provide $41,300 annually, or 40% of final earnings.

What Bonnie's Experience Shows

Bonnie's experience illustrates the advantage of having a defined benefit plan later in life. If Bonnie had held just one job throughout her career, but had only a defined contribution plan, she would receive only $27,500 annually, representing just 27% of her final earnings. The actual experiences of Bonnie and Susan, who had a defined contribution plan late in her career, show why it is impossible to say categorically that defined benefit plans are better than defined contribution plans or vice versa. It depends, at least in part, on the time in your career when you participate in the plan. All things being equal, the experiences of Bonnie and Susan show that you are better off with a defined contribution plan early in life while the benefits have years to grow and a defined benefit plan later in your career when the employer must fund your benefit rapidly over the shorter time before you retire.

Still, 34% of income is not sufficient to face retirement at age 62, given that Bonnie can expect to live another 20 years during which inflation will reduce the buying power of that percentage. With Social Security, Bonnie will have approximately 58% of earnings at retirement, still not enough to provide a secure retirement under most circumstances.

Bonnie's situation also illustrates the value of pension plans integrated with Social Security for highly compensated employees. We will discuss this in detail in Chapter 8, but briefly, it works like this. Bonnie has always earned more than the Social Security wage base, which is the amount of wages subject to Social Security taxes and used to ultimately calculate Social Security benefits. That part of her salary above the Social Security wage base (and hence not subject to Social Security taxes or benefits) will receive a proportionately higher retirement benefit under the integrated plan to compensate for the fact Bonnie will not receive Social Security benefits for that higher wage. By contrast, Susan has always had all her earnings subject to the Social Security wage base. As a result, Susan receives a lower employer-provided retirement benefit for all her wages under the integrated plan, because she will receive Social Security benefits based on all her wages. If Susan had worked in one job all her career with an integrated defined benefit plan, she would receive only 29% of final earnings from her employer-provided retirement benefit, as compared to the 40% a one-job employee would receive at Bonnie's earning level under the same plan. But Susan will receive Social Security benefits equal to about 40% of her preretirement wages, while Bonnie will receive a Social Security benefit at normal retirement age of only about 24% of her preretirement earnings.

Theoretically, Social Security will balance out the difference in benefits under an integrated plan. But it may not, especially for women who do not work the maximum number of years for full Social Security payments.

What Should Bonnie Do Now?

Bonnie's retirement planning outlook is much brighter than Alice's and Susan's for a number of reasons. First, and most obvious, she earns much more money. Her employer-provided retirement income will be based on those higher earnings, so retirement income will be higher. But she also has other advantages. She was helped by changes in the law that allowed her to vest in her benefits in a shorter period of time. Those changes came after Alice and Susan were well into their careers and the changes were not retroactive. Bonnie could set up IRAs earlier in her career; they weren't available to the others until later in their careers. Finally, Bonnie is starting earlier to begin retirement financial planning.

Things look fairly good for Bonnie. Indeed, some retirement or financial planners might tell her she is close to having all the retirement income she will need with 58% of preretirement income due to come from employer-provided pensions and Social Security. They would be wrong! Those planners are assuming Bonnie's employer never changes the current retirement plan. *Many employers terminate defined benefit plans and replace them with defined contribution plans.* The planners are assuming Bonnie will continue to want to stay with her current employer for another 22 years, and they are assuming Social Security will still pay the same wage replacements for highly paid workers 22 years from now. These assumptions are risky at best.

Bonnie is not entirely set for retirement, but she has time to build her own personal savings, the most important part of any retirement financial planning. Bonnie already realizes that, much as she might like to stay with her company for the next 22 years, it may not be possible. What if her husband were transferred to a higher-paid job than hers in another city and she really wanted to follow? Or what if her company is merged with another and suddenly she is "redundant"? What if she were offered a really powerful government job or a judgeship? All these are plausible possibilities. Some are even pleasant options. Bonnie wants to be prepared to meet each of them and still have a financially sound retirement.

Her own retirement savings will be the key to creating the security she needs to avoid being chained to her current employer if opportunity or disaster knock at her door.

JENNIFER: A SECRETARY OF 30

Jennifer entered the job market after graduation from college at age 21. She has held three jobs, taken 1 year off, and has been in her present job for 4 years. She currently earns $21,000.

Jennifer's Career Path

Jennifer's career path is still to be mapped and traveled. So far she has had a difficult start. With a bachelor's degree in psychology, the entry-level jobs she found allowing her to use her training paid less than secretarial work. Lacking the money to go on for a master's and doctorate, Jennifer took a job as a secretary. The job was hellish and boring. It did offer a defined benefit plan, but of course after only 1 year on the job, she did not vest in any benefits. After 1 year she took an interesting-sounding job as secretary to the president of a small exporting company. Jennifer found the work varied and low pressure, and she liked the fact the company had a defined contribution plan. She could easily see benefits being added and growing each year in her account. She worked there for 3 years. By that time she had saved enough on her own to take a year off to go back to school. She did not vest in the benefits in her defined contribution plan because she had been there for only 3 years and the plan had 5-year cliff vesting.

The money she saved didn't last as long as she had hoped and she returned to full-time work after only a year off. Jennifer has been with her present employer for 4 years, and she really doesn't think she will go back to school for an advanced degree in psychology. She is wondering what her retirement benefits would look like if she just stayed in her present job for the next 35 years—an unheard of proposition in today's work atmosphere, but an idea nevertheless.

What Jennifer's Retirement Benefits Might Be

If Jennifer stayed in her present job, which has a defined benefit plan integrated with Social Security, she would receive an annual benefit of $8,000 in today's dollars upon retirement at age 65. Her full Social Security benefits would not be available to her at that time because, for people born in 1962, the normal Social Security retirement age is 67. She could receive a reduced amount at 65. Or she could wait until 67 and receive her full benefit, which should replace approximately 42% of her final earnings, assuming no change in Social Security earnings replacement ratios over the next 37 years.

Her $8,000 annual pension represents approximately 28% of her final earnings. This is the same amount she would earn if she had held one job her entire career because her plan, like many retirement programs, grants benefits for a maximum period of only 30 years of service. Jennifer will have been in her job for 38 years when she is 65, so under this defined benefit plan, 8 years of her work will not be valued for benefits purposes other than to take account of her higher earnings in the last years of her career. By comparison, a defined contribution plan contributing 5% of earnings over every year of her working life would provide Jennifer with $10,400 annually or about 36% of her final earnings.

Jennifer was right to appreciate the defined contribution plan at her second job. When she left that job, her nonvested benefit had a lump-sum value of slightly over $3,000. If she had vested in that sum and rolled it into an IRA earning 8% for the next 35 years, it would have been worth over $33,100, and about $63,000, if she had earned 10%. If she had vested in even this small amount and left the money in the plan, at age 65 she would be entitled to $915 annually. True, this sum represents only 3% of Jennifer's final earnings at retirement. But the amount itself could pay the car insurance for a year or support a modest vacation each year.

What Should Jennifer Do Now for Retirement Planning?

Jennifer is really the only one of our examples who is beginning to look at retirement planning at an early enough age. She can make choices now which will drastically affect her retirement. Even very small amounts of money saved now can accumulate to give Jennifer a significant retirement income. Jennifer realizes that she can expect to have less than a third of her final earnings made up by an employer-provided benefit, under the best of circumstances. That assumes she stays with her current employer another 35 years.

Jennifer needs to begin her own savings program now. Because she earns less than $25,000, an IRA contribution will be tax deductible to her even though she has an employer-provided plan. If she places $2,000 a year in an IRA, she will save $300 a year in federal taxes alone. After 30 years she will have accumulated $189,000 if her IRA investments return 7% and $226,600 if she earns 8%. Her own savings will give her a lump-sum three times bigger than the lump sum value of her pension. Starting now on her own retirement savings will not only give Jennifer a more financially secure retirement; it will also provide the freedom to change jobs if better opportunities come along without jeopardizing her retirement future.

LESSONS LEARNED: APPLYING THE CASE STUDY SCENARIOS TO YOUR RETIREMENT PLANNING

Believe it or not, in many ways, the examples of Alice, Susan, Bonnie, and Jennifer are "best case" scenarios. As you apply the lessons of their cases, remember several facts. *Only 18% of women over age 40 expect to receive or are receiving any employer-provided retirement benefits.*[2] Most of the jobs discussed actually *had* retirement plans. Many working women today do not have any employer-provided retirement benefits. These benefits plans in our scenarios are relatively generous. Our benefits estimates were based on the fact each of our friends held full-time jobs for most or all of their working lives. Many women today work part time for several years while their children are growing, and even if the employers provide retirement benefits, workers with fewer than 1,000 hours annually usually do not earn benefits. Alice, Susan, Bonnie, and Jennifer remained—or are planning to remain—with one employer late in their career, and those employers' plans account for most of the retirement benefits. If they had been unable to stay with their late-career employers for a substantial number of years due to layoffs or the need to care for ailing parents or husbands, their benefits would be much reduced.

Don't Spend Your Retirement Benefits Before Retirement

Another reason why our group provides a best case scenario is their wisdom in never cashing out and spending any retirement benefits due them when they leave a job. Alice, Susan, Bonnie, and Jennifer are unusual in saving it all. However, recent data suggest women may be ahead of their male colleagues in understanding the importance of saving rather than spending lump-sum distributions. The research indicates slightly more women than men save at least a part of their distributions and among those receiving $10,000 to $15,000, 88% of women save some portion of it while only 70% of men save a portion.[3]

Although more people are coming to realize the importance of saving these distributions, experts estimate as much as 34% of the recipients spend their entire retirement cashouts as they leave various jobs over their careers.[4] If Alice had cashed out her one previously vested benefit before she moved to her current job, her retirement income would be only $3,000 per year as opposed to her projected benefit of $4,600 per year. *She would have reduced her retirement income by 36%.* If Susan had cashed out her retirement benefits from an early employer, she would have lost about 12% of her final retirement income or almost $600 a year. Alice and Susan dramatically show why *you should never, never, never spend retirement benefits you receive when you leave a job prior to your actual retirement.*

The growth of defined contribution plans that also permit employees to invest their own pretax money may be encouraging employees to cash out and spend their money as they move from employer to employer. Frequently, these retirement plans are erroneously explained as "savings" plans, leading young employees leaving their jobs to feel it is perfectly acceptable to spend the money. After all, they "saved" it, so now it's time to spend it. Nothing could be farther from the truth. It is true, you have savings. But those savings are what you must live on for the rest of your life after you stop working. If you spend the savings on a new car each time you leave an employer, chances are you will never retire. You won't have the money!

The imposition of an early withdrawal penalty in the form of a 10% federal tax in the Tax Reform Act of 1986 should help to discourage early consumption of retirement benefits. In 1987, the first year in which the penalty tax was in effect, only 18% of the money was used entirely for consumption, but in 1988 the proportion of preretirement lump-sum consumption was up to 26%. At least according to this sample, the penalty tax doesn't seem to be having much effect.[5] The recent requirement that employers withhold 20% of any lump-sum distribution which is not transferred directly to an IRA or another employer's plan may also discourage preretirement spending.

Data suggest preretirement spending is highest among the young, and as people age they tend to save preretirement distributions.[6] Although this suggests people nearing retirement are at least beginning to look out for their long-term security, it also means younger workers are cheating themselves out of years of investment growth. Remember Susan's experience as compared with her friend Linda on the importance of early benefits earnings and their savings in developing retirement capital.

HOW PENSION PORTABILITY ENHANCES RETIREMENT BENEFITS

Many people argue that retirement security could be guaranteed and the reliance and political demands on Social Security reduced if "pension portability" were enhanced. Pension portability is a recurring issue of debate for retirement consultants and social planners.

Because the entire U.S. population is changing jobs more frequently, whether on their own or with the "assistance" of their employers in down sizing, the issue of loss of pension benefits due to job shifts is increasingly important. Even with 5-year vesting and no spending of cashed out retirement funds, *when workers change jobs, they stand to lose an average of 15% of their retirement benefits,* according to compensation experts using assumptions based on job and pension patterns in the mid-1980s. Of all workers, an estimated 41% would have no loss because they kept one job for 35 years or more. But among the remaining 59% of workers, the loss was 23%, or about $5,000 of annual pensions per worker.[7] Some economists argue enhanced pension portability is vital to avoid "job lock" and produce the type of flexible work force and economy required if the United States is to compete in the world market.[8]

Portability of pension benefits is a difficult, yet vague, concept. It is discussed here, immediately after you have seen the effects of portability in actual situations, rather than in the earlier chapters on "theory," because you can more easily see the impact and importance of portability in the experiences of Alice, Susan, Bonnie, and Jennifer.

Portability of Service—Receiving Benefits for All the Years You've Worked

What exactly is *pension portability*? The Social Security system is the best illustration of a fully portable pension plan. You receive credit for every year you have worked, no matter how many employers you have. You never lose the benefit, no matter how short a period you may stay with the employer, and the plan is always the same with each employer. Social Security gives you portability of service and it provides the best protection for retirement benefits. You receive credit for all the years you have worked, and your benefits are based on your full career earnings, including those important last years, which are usually the highest earnings and those least eroded by inflation. So, for example, in Alice's case under a system with portability of service, she would receive credit for 30 years of service over a 33-year career (remember her 3 years off at various times), and depending on her plan's formula, those years would be multiplied by career average earnings or final 5 years' earnings.

If Alice had been in a union, her benefits might have been calculated by using years of service among many different employers who belonged to the plan. Many union plans, also called multiemployer plans because a number of employers contribute to them, provide for this kind of pension benefit calculation based on portability of service, at least counting service with those employers who are part of the multiemployer plan. But in the case of these plans, employee benefits calculations and employer contribution calculations are easier. There is only one plan, so all the benefits are calculated under one formula. The employer knows the provisions of the plan and knows his contribution for the year. The multiemployer plan itself is responsible for the record keeping and the administration of the plan through the board of trustees, usually made up of both employers and union officials.

As long as the employee works for an employer contributing to the union plan, she will enjoy portability of service at least among those employers. But if she goes to work for an employer outside the union plan, she will not receive credit under the union plan for service with the new employer. So in these cases the multiemployer plans provided only limited portability of service.

Employers generally oppose the portability of service concept because it is expensive and complex. The final employer fears she will have to come up with all the funding to pay for benefits. If the earlier employer is required to contribute, she has had no control over the employee's earnings in the later years, and the earlier employer fears she will be contributing to a much more generous benefit than had been contemplated. Record keeping for hundreds of employers and tens of thousands of employees would be expensive and difficult. As a practical matter, employers' pension plans probably differ too greatly to be able to calculate benefits for a given employee under portability of service, at least under our current retirement plan scheme.

From time to time over the last three decades, suggestions have been made for a clearing house at the federal level to serve as holder of pension funds to permit portability of service. These proposals are dismissed as too expensive and too complicated for the government to run effectively. Others have criticized the idea of having the federal government responsible for the investment of the huge sums of money that would be generated by such a program. Certainly, based on the federal government's trusteeship of the Social Security system where the federal government has essentially embezzled the funds and left IOUs, you might not be comfortable with the idea that the same trustee now has discretion over your employer-provided pension funds, as well.

Portability of Assets—Rolling Over Benefits from One Employer to the Next

Portability of assets permits the benefit you have earned to go with you when you leave an employer, either to be rolled over into an IRA or into another employer's plan, if the new employer's plan will allow it to accept the contribution. Many retirement plans today permit portability of assets. Again, the problem with portability of assets is too many people fail to save the money for retirement. Congress is considering additional limits on the use of preretirement distributions, such as requiring the distributing employer to place the money only in an IRA of the employee's choice or in the new employer's plan.

A second and more difficult problem is investing the money wisely to receive an acceptable rate of return. Most retirement plans do give an employee a very modest rate of return if the money is left in the plan, so you don't need to take high risks with your benefit or be an investment genius to earn more money for your benefit outside the fund than you would have had if you left it in the fund. Of course, if you have a plan that is paying you an above-average rate of return, simply leaving the money there is a wise decision.

Portability of Benefits—Cashing In at Retirement

Portability of benefits simply means the employer will give you your benefit at retirement. All ERISA plans now provide for this type of portability by requiring that you vest after a legally defined maximum number of years. But as Alice and Susan have demonstrated, early benefits are heavily eroded by inflation. It is true the benefit exists, but by the time you receive it, its purchasing power may have been severely diminished.

Congressional actions to require widely increased portability of benefits do not seem likely. Congress has taken a few steps to make portability of benefits a bit easier, such as simplifying the rules regarding the benefit distributions that can be accepted by employer plans, and Congress has considered prohibiting cashouts unless they go directly to the employee's retirement account. But a mandated universal system for service portability does not seem in the cards.

Still, as our examples show, preretirement consumption of employer-provided benefits is a big cause of the loss of retirement benefits. Under current law, only the participants of the pension savings plan themselves can prevent this benefit loss. It's simple—all they have to do is roll the money into an IRA or leave it in the former employer's plan. Congress is much more likely to enact more laws to prevent recipients from spending the money before retirement than to pass laws requiring other forms of pension portability.

CONCLUSION: RECOGNIZE THE IMPACT OF CHANGING EMPLOYERS ON YOUR RETIREMENT BENEFITS

The experiences of Alice, Susan, Bonnie, and Jennifer show you why taking a year away from work is not *just* losing you a year's pay. Depending on your employer plan's vesting provisions and whether you return to that employer, the year off may lose you significant retirement benefits. Their experiences also show us how a new job, even with an increase in pay, can cost retirement benefits. Equally important, their experiences reveal how dramatically "cashing out" retirement benefits early in your career can affect your retirement finances.

The one-career job is now a rarity for both women and men, so you and your spouse will face many of the same issues in changing jobs or taking time off. The important thing is to recognize the impact of a job shift on retirement income as well as on current career plans. Whenever possible, *time your job changes to maximize your retirement benefits,* and either take your vested benefits with you and put them in an IRA or keep track of them, including keeping your former employer informed of your current whereabouts. You can't run your career based on retirement considerations alone, but you must at least realize the effect of job moves on your ultimate retirement income.

NOTES FOR CHAPTER 4

1. The scenarios involved here have the following assumptions unless otherwise stated. The retirement plan provisions are:

   Defined benefit plan formula—1.25% of final 5-year average earnings times years of service to a maximum of 30 years

   Integrated defined benefit plan—1% of final 5-year average earnings for wages subject to FICA tax and 1.65% for wages above that base

   Defined contribution formula—5% of earnings each year

   The economic assumptions are:

Rate of inflation	5.0%
Salary increase rate	6.0
Defined contribution plan interest rate	7.5
Rollover interest rate	7.5

   The annual and lump-sum figures are usually rounded to the nearest hundred dollars. *Note that all figures are in constant 1992 dollars, so the nominal dollars at retirement will be much larger.* Comparisons remain the same in percentage terms.

2. Daniel J. Beller and David D. McCarthy, "Private Pension Benefits," in John A. Turner and Daniel J. Beller, eds., *Trends in Pensions 1992* (Washington, D.C.: U.S. Department of Labor, Pension and Welfare Benefits Administration, U.S. Government Printing Office, 1992), Table 10.3, p. 237.

3. Testimony of Dr. Sophie M. Korczyk, "Pension Coverage and Portability Issues Facing Employed Women," Table 13, Hearings before the House of Representatives' Subcommittee on Retirement Income and Employment, Select Committee on Aging, March 26, 1992. Dr. Korczyk relies on Employee Benefits Research Institute tabulations of May 1988 *Current Population Survey* data.

4. Employee Benefits Research Institute, *EBRI Issue Brief No. 98, Preservation of Pension Benefits* (Washington, D.C.: EBRI, January 1990).

5. Ibid., Table 5, based on May 1988 *Current Population Survey* data.

6. Ibid., Tables 4 and 5.

7. Ibid., p. 14, quoting Hay/Huggins Company, Inc., Mathematica Policy Research, "The Effect of Job Mobility on Pension Benefits" (paper prepared for U.S. Department of Labor, Pension and Welfare Benefits Administration, 1988). The General Accounting Office, reporting on work of the Congressional Research Service, found the same types of erosion of benefits we see in the scenarios involving Alice, Susan, Bonnie, and Jennifer. See *Private Pensions: Portability and Preservation of Vested Pension Benefits*, GAO/HRD-89-15BR, February 1989.

8. Pat Choate and J. K. Linger, *The High-Flex Society: Shaping America's Economic Future* (New York: Alfred A. Knopf, 1986), pp. 247–250.

CHAPTER FIVE

HOW TAXES AFFECT RETIREMENT PLANNING- AND RETIREMENT INCOME

Most of the retirement planning devices we've mentioned have one thing in common: they provide for deferral of taxes on savings and on the earnings of those savings until the money is withdrawn from savings during retirement. Table 5.1 illustrates why. The premium derived from tax-deferred savings, as compared with after-tax savings, is dramatic: *you'll have $92,117 more after 30 years if you save in a tax-deferred savings plan.*

Pretax dollars are those on which you have not paid taxes, such as your gross salary quoted you by your boss. After-tax dollars refer to money that has been taxed, such as your take-home pay.

Of course, funds sheltered during your working years will be taxed eventually as you withdraw them from the tax-deferred retirement plan. But until that point, you have had the advantage of using money that otherwise would have gone immediately to pay taxes instead to earn additional interest or other income. The Congressional

Budget Office calculates that $1,000 saved under a tax-favored plan using tax-deferred dollars, such as a 401(k) or a tax-deductible IRA, provides a 37% greater rate of return after 15 years at 8% if you are in the 28% tax bracket and an 18% greater rate of return if you are in the 15% tax bracket. This comparison assumes that you stay in the same tax bracket when you retire. If your bracket is lower, the advantage is even greater.

Even if your original contributions to a plan consist of after-tax dollars—as in an employer's thrift plan or a nondeductible IRA— you still realize significant benefits. The earnings on those contributions are tax-deferred. That deferral improves the compounding factor over many years. In such cases the 28% taxpayer has an 11% greater return and the 15% taxpayer has a 6% greater return in a tax-deferred plan than in a savings plan which is taxed annually. These higher rates are calculated after all tax has been paid on the amounts. The figures also assume the tax bracket is not lower at retirement. If the tax bracket is reduced from 28% while working to 15% at retirement, the difference between taxable and tax-deferred savings could be as great as 62%.[1]

TABLE 5.1 Tax-Deferred Versus Taxed Savings*		
Year	Tax Deferred	After-Tax Savings
1	$ 2,000	$ 1,440
10	31,875	22,950
20	114,550	82,476
30	328,988	236,871
*Assumes a 10% rate of return and a 28% tax rate.		

These savings calculations don't include the amounts you save on state taxes, which could be proportionately similar. Most, but not all, states also give favorable tax deferral treatment to all federally tax qualified plans.

HOW FEDERAL TAX POLICY AFFECTS
RETIREMENT SAVINGS

One of the motivating factors for the growth of retirement plans in the 1940s was the ability to fund such plans with tax-deductible dollars and hence save corporate earnings from the very high tax rate of those days. Today, it is estimated the tax deferral permitted to individuals for retirement plans combined with the tax deductions granted employers for the various retirement plans cost the federal government over $60 billion a year in revenues which would otherwise go into IRS coffers! This is the single largest tax break, or *tax expenditure*, as the IRS calls it, in the Internal Revenue Code, and it is bigger by $6 billion than the home mortgage deduction and used by more people, some of whom may not even be aware of the fact they benefit from this tax break.

Looking at it another way, on a federal deficit of more than $300 billion per year, eliminating the tax-favored treatment of private retirement plans would reduce the deficit by about 20% per year. Fortunately, Congress has not looked at it that way. But it is not surprising that congressional and IRS tax writers are constantly tinkering at the margins to shave a few million off the retirement plan tax breaks. This tinkering means not only a loss of the tax advantages, but also constant changes in an already devilishly complex law.

Given these facts, along with the seemingly intractable federal deficit, more changes in the tax treatment of retirement savings can be expected. You should also expect some of the tax advantages to be reduced. Such changes are likely to apply only prospectively, however. Congress has usually been sensitive to not changing the rules for money already saved for retirement. And this sensitivity to the protection of money already saved argues only more vigorously for the wisdom of saving as much as possible now while significant tax advantages are still on the books.

CHOOSING TAX-DEFERRED VERSUS
TAX-EXEMPT SAVINGS VEHICLES

Most retirement savings plans defer the payment of taxes until payment begins at retirement. That does not mean you never pay tax on the money, but simply that you will not pay tax on it until you begin to take the money out of the plan. This should not be until you retire around the age of 65. Even then, you may take employer money in a lump sum and transfer it into an IRA. In that case you can defer tax on the money further, but you cannot defer paying taxes on the tax-deferred retirement money after age 70½. At that point, the IRS will treat all such monies as though they were being distributed to you over your remaining life expectancy or the life expectancy of you and the named beneficiary of the retirement accounts you may have.

If you do not begin taking money out of these accounts and paying taxes on the distributions, you will be hit with a 50% excise tax on the amount you should have taken. This will not be a problem for most of us, since we will have begun using our retirement savings well before age 70½. Our concern will be making the sum last through our life expectancy, not sheltering it from taxes!

Municipal Bonds. Of course, a substantial part of your retirement savings could be in currently tax-exempt investments, such as municipal bonds or municipal bond mutual funds. No other sources of tax-exempt income are easily available. But even this source of income may be subject to the federal alternative minimum income tax and may be subject to state income taxes as well. These investments also have a relatively low rate of return, which makes them unsuitable for long-term retirement savings. Also tax-exempt investments should not be part of your IRA because their income will become taxable once it is withdrawn from the IRA.

401(k)s and IRAs. In general, the major portion of your contributions to retirement savings should first rely on tax-deferred savings vehicles such as any 401(k)s available to you and IRAs for two reasons. First, these retirement savings accounts enable you to earn more money than tax-exempt investments without paying taxes while the money is growing in the retirement plans. Second, buying other investments such as stocks and stock mutual funds for your 401(k) or IRA also permits you to diversify your investments beyond just tax-exempt bonds. Diversity of investments is an important rule for any investment strategy. Once you have fully funded all the tax-deferred retirement savings plans available to you, you can move on to tax-exempt and taxable savings vehicles in addition to these tax-favored accounts.

Fortunately, no one who is earning income or is married to a person earning income is totally denied access to a tax-deferred retirement savings plan. If your employer does not have a retirement plan, you can set up a tax deductible IRA on your own. That money and its earnings will not be taxed until you begin to withdraw it at retirement or if you become disabled. If you are self-employed, you may set up a Keogh or a "simplified employee pension" plan which permits you to save tax-deductible amounts, again deferring tax on that amount and its earnings until retirement.

Annuities. Annuities and universal life insurance policies are another tax-deferred method of saving. Annuities, usually underwritten by insurance companies or banks, are basically pensions you purchase yourself with after-tax dollars. Generally, a fairly large initial investment of at least $2,000 or more is required. Depending on the annuity, you may make additional investments over a period of years. The earnings on the money invested is not taxed until you begin to receive payments from the annuity. Universal life insurance works much the same way; however, it usually does not require a high initial investment, but it does require subsequent payments. Chapter 8 discusses these investments in detail.

BEWARE OF EARLY WITHDRAWAL TAX PENALTIES

Of course, the IRS does not give you these tax breaks without some strings. We have already been introduced to some of the rules surrounding tax-favored retirement plans. Another "string" (or noose, if you prefer) is the early withdrawal penalty tax imposed on withdrawals from tax-favored plans, including IRAs, Keoghs, annuities, and 401(k) programs. If you withdraw money from these plans before age 59½, you pay an additional 10% penalty tax.

There are a few exceptions. If you die or become disabled, no penalty tax applies. If you begin receiving the money in a "life stream" over the number of remaining years you are expected to live, there will be no penalty. You may also escape the penalty tax if the withdrawals are as a result of early retirement after age 55 or if used to pay deductible medical bills (without the restriction on that such bills exceed 7.5% of your income). These last two exceptions do not apply to IRAs.

These penalties are designed to enforce the purpose for the tax breaks in the first place—money in these accounts is to be saved for retirement. The accounts are *not* to be used as a tax-favored way to save for your luxury car or a trip along the Grand Canal—at least not until you are past age 59½.

Should You Pay the Tax Now to Avoid Higher Tax Later?

Today's tax rates are lower than they have been in decades. Already, the rates have crept up a point or so from the low after the Tax Reform Act of 1986. Some tax advisers argue it is wiser to pay current tax on earnings and investments now and avoid what are certain to be higher rates in the future at retirement. This argument cannot be dismissed totally. However, the advantage of tax deferral over a number of years, such as you have in retirement savings plans that exist for decades, is still likely to outstrip the possible loss from higher taxes for most individuals unless the federal income tax rates become very high. Certainly, given the federal deficit, tax rates will likely increase eventually. But when and how much are unknown. Even if tax rates are increased, more tax brackets will be created, and as a retiree you are likely to be in the lower brackets of the increase.

CONCLUSION: SAVE EVEN IF YOUR SAVINGS PLAN ISN'T TAX FAVORED

Unless you are already vested in a very generous retirement plan or you can begin saving the maximum Keogh amount each year early in your career, you probably will not be able to provide a secure retirement simply by using tax-favored retirement plans. Remembering the Duchess of Windsor's dictate, "You can never be too rich or too thin," certainly you should save beyond the amounts permitted to you under the employer, Keogh, and IRA tax-favored plans. You will want to make other investments. Just be sure you use the tax-deferred retirement programs to their fullest before you start other retirement savings programs.

You have seen how valuable tax-preferred investments can be to savings growth. But never let retirement or any other type of savings or investment plans be totally driven by tax considerations. A bad tax-exempt investment or a bad tax-deferred investment is still a bad investment. True, not making money is the ultimate tax dodge, but it's a painful way to avoid the IRS.

Finally, even if tax rates are increased in the future, remember the amounts represented by your after-tax savings won't be taxed again when you spend them at retirement.

NOTE FOR CHAPTER 5

1. Congressional Budget Office, *Tax Policy for Pensions and Other Retirement Saving* (Washington, D.C.: U.S. Government Printing Office), April 1987, Table 1, p. 4.

ERISA-THE EMPLOYMENT RETIREMENT INCOME SECURITY ACT

ERISA is the federal law enacted in 1974 that regulates and protects employees' rights to employer-provided pension and health and welfare plans. This chapter sketches the protections ERISA can—and cannot—provide for your employer's retirement plans.

Neither ERISA nor any other federal statute requires employers to provide such benefit programs. But once employers do undertake to provide benefits, ERISA outlines the rules the employers must follow. Indeed, when ERISA was enacted, many pundits predicted the end of employee benefits because the employers would terminate the plans. The reasoning: no employer would want to be subject to such complex, expensive rules. Fortunately, the pundits were wrong. Since the enactment of ERISA, the number of plans has grown from just over 311,000 to over 729,000.[1]

PRE-ERISA LAW

The federal government had some rules on tax-favored employee benefits and retirement plans prior to ERISA. Because most retirement plans receive favorable tax treatment, the IRS first set the rules for retirement plans. During World War II, the quantity and type of benefits, including retirement plans, increased dramatically, largely because under wage and price laws, pay increases were limited, but benefits were not restricted by the emergency regulations. Employers, desperate for workers, lured them with benefits rather than with higher wages.

As early as 1942, Congress began to place some limits on tax-favored retirement plans. If the employer offered such a program, it had to comply with the following rules.

- ❖ The plan had to be in writing and be permanent, and the employees had to be told about it.

- ❖ The plan had to cover a broad cross section of employees, not just owners and executives.

- ❖ The plan could not provide disproportionate benefits for executives or owners.

ERISA's BEGINNINGS

Congress remained concerned with pensions, from time to time imposing additional disclosure requirements. But in 1963 the Studebaker car company closed, leaving many of its vested employees with less than their earned pensions. Pressure to regulate the pension and retirement plan area more carefully increased. Extensive hearings and debate occurred almost immediately. But the first comprehensive pension protection bill was not introduced until 1967, and it became law only after 7 years of legislative wrangling.

As with many proposed laws, the opponents viewed it as the "end of civilization as we know it"—or at least the end of the private pension plan system. The supporters envisioned it as less protection than they wanted, but more than they had. And lawyers and actuaries saw it as guaranteed income for themselves. Only the lawyers and actuaries were completely correct.

THE BASICS—SECURE FUNDS
AND A GUARANTEED RIGHT TO THEM

ERISA provided two basic and far-reaching protections for employees. First, it required retirement plans to be funded adequately through a trust which could not be reached by either the employer or its creditors. Second, it required that a plan have a stated vesting schedule, not to exceed 15 years, after which an employee received a nonforfeitable right to some benefits, whether she was fired, she quit, the plan terminated, or the company went bankrupt.

THE ENFORCERS—IRS, THE DEPARTMENT
OF LABOR, AND YOU

ERISA is enforced by both the Internal Revenue Service and the Department of Labor. Generally, the IRS enforces the issues involving funding, participant rights, benefits levels, and "discrimination" in benefits between executives and the rank and file. The DOL enforces the disclosure and fiduciary issues.

ERISA employs two enforcement mechanisms. First, to receive a tax deduction for benefit plan contributions and other breaks, the employer must comply with the tax code provisions of ERISA. Failure to comply can "disqualify the plan," resulting in all contributions being taxable and in employees being taxed for the value of their benefits vested in the plan, but not yet received. Second, failure to follow ERISA rules subjects the employer and/or the plan to fines, some as high as $1,000 per day.

You as an employee or a plan participant also have the right to enforce ERISA rules by going directly to federal court. Unlike many employment laws such as the civil rights laws, you do not need to go first to a federal or state agency to seek enforcement through the agency procedures. You must first complete any appeals procedures outlined in the plan before you go to court. Once in court, you will not be able to seek a jury trial in most cases, and your only relief will be the benefits to which you were originally entitled. Even reimbursement for your attorneys' fees and court costs will be at the discretion of the judge.

ERISA uses a number of methods to achieve the goals of retirement plan security for employees ranging from disclosure and reporting to employees to heavy penalties. The rest of this chapter describes how ERISA provides retirement benefits security.

WHO AND WHAT IS COVERED?

ERISA applies to virtually every employer and union plan, except the federal government, state and local governments, and churches. ERISA applies to retirement plans and to *welfare plans*. Welfare plans cover medical and hospitalization benefits, benefits for sickness, disability, and vacations, training programs, and so on. Welfare plans are generally covered only by the reporting and disclosure portions of the law; they are not covered by the vesting and participation requirements. The Department of Labor takes the position ERISA does not cover off-site dependent care programs, and most sick leave programs are not considered to be covered by ERISA. Unfunded retirement plans for executives are also only covered by ERISA disclosure and reporting requirements.

ERISA covers *multiemployer plans*, developed under a collective bargaining process with a union. In multiemployer plans, the union negotiates with several employers to create and maintain a plan covering a particular trade such as carpenters or the needle trades. As a member of the union you remain in the same plan even though you work for a number of different employers so long as the employers contribute to the plan. The ERISA rules for multiemployer plans are somewhat different, the most notable difference being that they can require 10 years of service before you vest in the plan. Congress has frequently considered requiring multiemployer plans to adopt the same vesting schedule as single-employer plans, and at some point, this change is likely to occur. Multiemployer plans are also subject to different rules regarding employer withdrawal from the plan and plan terminations.

Note, this book does not attempt to address the operation of the federal, state, and local government or church retirement plans. Because many institutions such as hospitals and schools are run by churches, plans in these institutions may not be covered by ERISA. Except where specifically noted, the book assumes the retirement plans are covered by ERISA. While specific rules for government and church plans are different, many of the basic concepts are the same as for other plans. Additionally, many non-ERISA plans closely track ERISA rules.

DISCLOSURE OF PLAN PROVISIONS AND FUNDING

ERISA requires a number of reports and disclosures. These include a summary plan description (SPD), the formal plan document and any amendments, and the summary annual report and benefits statement.

The Summary Plan Description—A Plain English Guide

Each benefit plan must have a "summary plan description," mentioned in Chapter 3 as one of the benefits buzzwords. The SPD must spell out the provisions of any employer plan in understandable words of "plain English." If a significant number of employees do not understand English, the SPD must be in Spanish or any other language a significant percentage of the employees can read or understand. The retirement plan SPD tells you:

- ❖ Whether the plan is a defined contribution plan or a defined benefit plan
- ❖ When you are eligible to be a participant
- ❖ How you accrue benefits
- ❖ When you vest in those benefits
- ❖ When they will be paid to you
- ❖ How benefits will be paid to you, that is, lump sum or annuity
- ❖ Who the plan administrator is
- ❖ Where and how to get more information about the plan
- ❖ Whether you must contribute to the plan
- ❖ Limits on the amount of money you can put in the plan
- ❖ Your rights under ERISA to get information about the plan
- ❖ Your rights to appeal any denial of benefits
- ❖ Your right to contact the Department of Labor for help if you believe the plan is not being properly applied to you
- ❖ Your right to go directly to court if you don't get the information you are entitled to or if your appeal under the plan is denied

❖ Your duty to keep the plan administrator informed of your where-abouts

Because the plan sponsor has so much information to cover in the SPD and because the plan sponsor bears a heavy legal responsibility to be sure the SPD is both accurate and thorough, the sponsor tends to err on the side of length and complexity. SPDs are rarely "summary," and they frequently lapse into pension jargon. Don't be put off. After Chapter 3 you know the buzzwords—or at least most of them.

Don't worry if you have to read the SPD or certain sentences in it three or four times. Frequently, the "experts" do too. Retirement plan concepts can be complex, especially when you are just beginning to learn them. Read the SPD carefully, as soon as possible. If you don't understand it, make an appointment with your company's human resources person and ask questions. Keep asking until you get clear answers. This is your future you're asking about. If the human resources person doesn't know, ask him or her to find out.

The "Plan Document"

You have the right to see the actual plan document and any amendments, in addition to the SPD. After you have read and understood the SPD, you may want to get a copy of the plan document and go over it. But in most cases, the document will be too filled with jargon to be understandable. However, you will definitely want a copy of the plan document if you are nearing retirement and have doubts about the proper calculation of your benefit, even if you have to hire an expert to help you interpret it. The plan document is the legally controlling document. A rare court has held the SPD will control, but this is usually in cases where there has been a blatant attempt by the plan sponsor to hide or obscure information. If there is anything contradictory between the SPD and the plan document, rely on the plan document.

Summary Annual Report and Benefits Statement

You have a right to a summary annual report, which should show the assets and the liabilities of the plan. Additionally, once a year you can ask for a summary of your benefits, which will tell you how much of a benefit you have accrued to date and whether you are vested in those benefits. Realizing that employees have a right to ask for their benefits statement annually, many employers provide all employees with this information once a year at the same time, without waiting for employees to request the information.

Other Information to Which You Are Entitled

If the plan is changed in a significant way, the employer must notify you.

Once a year the plan must file a report with IRS that is jointly shared with DOL too. This Form 5500 annual report contains detailed actuarial and financial analysis, including an audit of the funds, as well as information on the number of participants. The Form 5500 is not likely to provide you with any additional relevant information under ordinary circumstances.

As a plan participant, you have the right to all relevant documents about the plan. This obviously includes the items just listed, such as the SPD, the plan document, and a summary annual report, but it also includes the Form 5500s and other documents under which the plan is established and operated. ERISA imposes a fine of up to $100 per day for each day the employer refuses to provide the documents after a 30-day waiting period. The employer may charge a reasonable fee for such documents.

ERISA's Standards for Participating in a Company Retirement Plan

Under ERISA you must be able to participate in a plan after the later of:

❖ Your 21st birthday or

❖ One year on the job in which you worked at least 1,000 hours

An employer may keep you out of the plan for 2 years of full-time work, but in such cases, when you do become a participant in the plan, you must be immediately vested in any benefits you earn.

If you join your employer when you are near retirement, you cannot be kept out of a plan just because you are older. Prior to 1988, employees could lawfully be kept out of a defined benefit pension plan if the employee joined the company within 5 years of the normal retirement date under the plan. That is age 65 in most plans. Some employers took the position that once an employee reached retirement age, no further retirement contributions of any kind would be made. Congress has now required that retirement contributions continue for employees working past age 65. It is still permissible for a plan sponsor to limit the years of service it will count for an employee. For example, a plan may provide that after the employee has 30 years of credited service, no further service will be recognized for benefits calculations or no further contributions will be made to the employee's defined contribution plan.

VESTING STANDARDS

You "vest" in retirement benefits when you have a nonforfeitable right to benefits accrued under the plan. You are always vested in any money you contribute to an employer's retirement plan. ERISA requires that plans vest benefits earned by employees under one of two schedules. These are maximum time periods. Your plan may permit vesting with fewer years of service. But it cannot exceed these periods.

A plan may have a vesting schedule which gives you the right to 100% of your benefits after 5 years of service with the employer. This 5-year/100% vesting schedule is often called *cliff vesting*. Or a plan may have a gradual vesting according to this schedule:

Years of Service	Percentage of Benefit Vested
1–2	0%
3	20%
4	40%
5	60%
6	80%
7	100%

This schedule is frequently called *graduated vesting*.

Vesting also occurs automatically when you reach the plan's designated "normal retirement age" if that retirement age is 65 or younger, regardless of the number of years of service you have. If the plan's normal retirement age is over 65 and if you joined the plan within 5 years of the plan's retirement age, you will be vested after 5 years of participation. For example, if the plan's retirement date is

67 and you joined the plan when you were 62, you will be fully vested when you turn 67 even if the plan has graduated vesting for everyone else. Vesting also occurs if the plan is terminated.

If yours is a union-sponsored multiemployer plan, the vesting schedule by law can require ten years of service for cliff vesting.

Vesting is based on years of service, not years of participation in the plan. To calculate vesting, in most cases you begin counting from the date you started working for the employer. But an employer need not count years you worked before age 18 or years you worked before the plan was put into place.

Once you are 100% vested, you own all benefits as soon as they are earned. You don't have to wait for a period of years after earning each benefit before it is vested.

Prior to 1989, vesting could be 100% after 10 years or graduated over 15 years. "Class year" vesting was also permitted. Under class year vesting you vested in a benefit 5 years after you earned the benefit regardless of how long you had worked for the employer.

Because the 5-year or 3- to 7-year vesting schedules only began to apply for plan years beginning in 1989, many women now in the work force who have worked steadily, but changed jobs every 5 or 6 years, may never have vested in a pension. Remember the situations with Bonnie, Alice, Susan, and Jennifer. Each of them lost benefits because they changed jobs before the vesting period for the employer plans was completed.

FIDUCIARY DUTY OF THOSE MANAGING THE PLAN

Each ERISA plan must have a named fiduciary charged with the responsibility and discretion of operating and managing the plan. Any other person who exercises discretionary authority or control over the plan or its assets is considered a fiduciary. ERISA fiduciaries must act "solely in the interest of the participants and beneficiaries" of the plan. All fiduciary actions are to be only for the "exclusive purpose" of providing benefits and paying the "reasonable expenses" of administering the plan.

The fiduciary is also bound by the "prudent man rule" (okay, okay, "prudent person"). The prudent person rule requires the fiduciary to operate the plan, including its investments, "with the care, skill, prudence, and diligence," which would be used by one acting in similar circumstances with the same goals.

The importance of this from your point of view is that the administrators, the investment managers, advisers, and others must make decisions based on your best interests, not that of the employer. While representatives from the company will usually be the trustees and administrators of the plan, in their dealings with the plan, their considerations should be for the employees, not the employer. Needless to say, this requirement demands a strong lack of self-preservation on the part of the employee/fiduciaries. It also raises some difficult issues in the case of certain plans such as ESOPs and 401(k) plans, which can and do invest heavily in employer stock.

Fiduciaries and other "parties in interest" such as the plan sponsor, corporate executives, company owners, and major stockholders cannot do business with the plan. These "prohibited transactions" or "party-in-interest transactions" cover almost any business dealings other than providing office space and support staff for the plan administration. For example, suppose a bank acts as a record keeper for a number of plans operated by others. The bank also keeps records for its own plan and charges the plan the same fee it charges other customers. The Department of Labor has viewed that as a "prohibited transaction" because the plan sponsor makes a profit on servicing the plan. Plan sponsors can apply to DOL for an exemption to the prohibited transaction rule in specific cases. If DOL determines the transaction would benefit the plan, DOL will grant an exemption.

WHO MANAGES THE TRUST FOR PLAN ASSETS?

All plan assets must be held in an irrevocable trust managed by trustees or the named fiduciary. The employer has no control over the funds or the trust. Most important, the creditors of the employer cannot reach the funds in the trust. The trust must be audited once a year, which in most cases provides all the incentive a good faith plan sponsor requires to keep the plan funded up to legally required standards. Once the assets are in the trust, the employees can be relatively confident the funds will be there to pay benefits at retirement.

In a defined contribution plan, the employer knows exactly how much money must be placed in the plan trust each year because the contribution amount is literally "defined under the plan." As a result, defined contribution plan trusts are rarely short on funds to pay accrued benefits to the individual accounts under the plan.

In a defined benefit plan, the employer must engage a pension actuary to calculate the amount of money to be contributed to the plan each year. IRS also strictly regulates the amount of money which can be deducted for contributing to the plan. An employer is subject to fines if it places too little money in the plan *and* if it places too much money in the plan. By law, the plan is discouraged from immediately funding the plan for the amounts which it will eventually need. As a result, even if the plan is funded up to legal requirements, there may not be enough assets to pay all benefits, if the plan terminates. The amount of money an employer must contribute depends in part on the amount of income earned by the plan's investments. When stock market share prices are high and investments have done well, the plan may become *overfunded* without any action by the employer. If investments do poorly, the plan may become *underfunded*, even though the employer has made contributions at the expected rate each year. Employee turnover and retirement decisions may also affect plan funding status.

Underfunding does not become an issue unless the plan is terminated, either by the employer or by the Pension Benefit Guaranty Corporation, which insures the benefits. In the section on plan terminations in the following pages, we discuss the underfunding problem and its cures.

How to Challenge a Denial of ERISA Benefits

ERISA gives you the right to challenge a denial of benefits in several ways. For purposes of this discussion, "denial" of benefits also includes the granting of benefits at a level you believe to be incorrect. First, the plan itself must contain an appeals procedure. ERISA does not detail this procedure, so the employer has a great deal of discretion in constructing the system. But at a minimum, the plan's appeals procedure must be spelled out in the summary plan description. You must be told in writing that your benefits are being denied and that you have the right to appeal to the plan administrator or other named person or body within a specified reasonable period.

The denial of benefits must give the reasons for the denial in understandable language and offer a complete and fair review of the denial. You must be given at least 60 days in which to appeal the denial.

If you follow the plan's appeals procedure, but are not satisfied with the result, you can proceed to the Department of Labor for help or go directly to federal court. The DOL's Pension and Welfare Benefits Administration can provide limited guidance on benefits questions. You should at least start by contacting that office at:

> Division of Technical Assistance and Inquiries
> Room N-5658
> Pension and Welfare Benefits Administration
> Department of Labor
> 200 Constitution Avenue, N.W.
> Washington, D.C. 20210-0999
> (202) 523-8784

If you call, you will first get a long series of recorded messages, but eventually a live person will talk with you. Depending on the details of your problem, this office may be able to give you or your employer guidance to resolve the problem. The national office may refer you to a DOL office closer to you.

DOL does not have a formal internal complaints procedure to resolve differences between plan participants and employers. This can be both a blessing and curse. Unlike civil rights laws, which do have elaborate administrative procedures to follow before you can get into court, under ERISA you need not wait for action by DOL or get permission from DOL to protect your rights. No agency official has legal authority to resolve the case by urging the employer to "do the right thing" or, conversely, explaining to you why you don't have a case. The down side is you must get a lawyer to represent you almost immediately.

Unfortunately, ERISA lawyers for individuals are not easy to find. While there are thousands of them, they work mostly for employers. They may not be willing to represent an individual. A lawyer who does not specialize in ERISA, even though she may be brilliant, will have great difficulty in efficiently and expertly advising you, because this area of law is so complex. At a minimum you may wind up paying for the lawyer's time to master ERISA's intricacies—an expensive and time-consuming project. Should you need counsel, shop carefully and don't be reluctant to ask whether a lawyer has dealt with ERISA cases on the employee's side previously. Referrals may also be available through the Pension Rights Center, 918 Sixteenth St., N.W., Suite 704, Washington, D.C. 20006.

Also remember—and remind your employer, if necessary—that ERISA protects you from any retaliation for exercising your rights under the Act.

HOW ERISA HANDLES CHANGES TO THE RETIREMENT BENEFITS PLAN

Employers may change their plans under ERISA, but such changes must be prospective only if they affect benefits. Any benefit which you have accrued and in which you vested cannot be reduced retroactively. For example, you have a plan which pays 1% of compensation for each year of service, you have worked for your company for 15 years, and the company changes the plan to 0.5% of pay for each year of service. Assuming no other changes in the plan, when you retire 10 years from now, your benefit must be calculated as follows:

15 years at 1% of compensation (under the old plan)

+

10 years at 0.5% of compensation (under the new plan)

=

20% of compensation as your retirement benefit.

Even though the plan at your retirement date provides for 0.5% of compensation for each year of service, you remain entitled to the provisions of the earlier plan for the years when you accrued benefits under those provisions.

WHAT ERISA REQUIRES IF YOUR EMPLOYER TERMINATES THE PLAN

Under ERISA, employers are free to terminate plans completely, but employees must retain all the benefits earned to date of termination. If you are not vested and the employer terminates the retirement plan, you become immediately vested in any benefits you have accrued to the date of termination.

Let's look at an example. You have been with Midnight Banking for 30 years and you will soon retire. Your colleague, Sallie, has been there 4 years, and Judith is just completing her first year. The Midnight plan requires 1 year of service before participation and 5 years' service with 100% vesting. Midnight decides to terminate the pension plan. You are entitled to your full 30 years of service-accrued benefits. Although Sallie has accrued 4 years of service and benefits, she is not yet vested under the rules of the plan; however, because the plan is terminated, Sallie is vested in her 3 years of accrued benefits (she could not participate in her first year). Judith will not receive any benefits, because she has not yet become a participant or accrued any benefits in the plan.

At the termination of the plan, the plan sponsor may distribute the lump-sum present value of the benefit earned to date or may purchase an annuity to pay the benefit when the employee reaches the retirement age specified under the old terminated plan.

If the plan is terminated, all participants immediately vest in the benefits earned to date. While benefits accrued over such a short period are not likely to be large, they are at least a reward for work completed.

In the event there are plan assets remaining after all accrued benefits are paid out, those assets may be returned to the employer provided that for at least the previous 5 years the plan contained language expressly permitting such reversions. The employer will pay a 50% "reversion" tax and regular income tax on such assets. Some employers, recognizing the penalties, have distributed the "excess" assets to the plan participants. Employers may avoid the 50% reversion tax and pay a lower tax on some of the excess assets if the assets are transferred to a successor plan covering most of the same employees and meeting other designated criteria. Some lawmakers have suggested that all assets from terminated pension plans should be given to plan participants and that the employer should have no reversion rights. Others fear this draconian treatment of excess assets will encourage employers to underfund plans or to avoid setting up plans at all.

All this debate skirts the real issue, which is the employees' reliance on the "promise" there will be a retirement payment when the employee reaches retirement age. When you join a firm with a defined benefit or a defined contribution plan, you expect a certain amount of money from that plan when you retire. You make your personal retirement savings plans, and sometimes even your career plans, based on this promise. Let's say you joined Acme at age 35, planning to stay there until you retire at age 60. In part your decision was based on the fact Acme had a pension plan and you realize that in 25 years you will have accrued a substantial monthly retirement check. If the plan is terminated after you have been with Acme for 15 years, the amount you will receive from your accrued benefits is far less than what you expected. You will miss the contributions for the next 10 years, which under a defined benefit plan would have been the years of greatest accumulations for you. In effect, Acme has given you a substantial pay cut, and you will need to scramble to revise your personal savings plan. True, Acme never promised you it would never change the plan, but you never expected to receive a substantial pay reduction after years of loyal service, either.

PENSION BENEFIT GUARANTY CORPORATION—INSURANCE FOR DEFINED BENEFIT PLANS

Even though ERISA protects plan assets with a trust, problems can arise in defined benefit plans, if the plan has not been fully funded. And, as we have seen, a perfectly lawful plan may not contain sufficient assets at termination to pay all benefits. Defined benefit plans are based on numerous variable factors, and ERISA permits funding at various levels. Additionally, for many years the IRS had the authority to grant defined benefit plans "funding waivers" for a year. As a result, some defined benefit plans are not adequately funded even though they have fully complied with ERISA and tax-law funding rules. If an employer goes bankrupt or terminates the plan, there may not be adequate funds to pay all the promised benefits.

ERISA created the Pension Benefit Guaranty Corporation to deal with the problem. The PBGC is a government corporation, financed by "premiums" paid by plan sponsors. Each sponsor of a defined benefit plan pays a premium of approximately $20 per plan participant (the dollar amount is frequently adjusted). Underfunded plans pay an additional premium amount based on the amount of the underfunding.

PBGC oversees the terminations of defined benefit plans. A termination may be "voluntary," meaning the employer has decided to terminate the plan. In such cases if the plan does not have enough assets to meet all benefit liabilities under the plan, the employer must promise to contribute enough money to meet the obligations. This is referred to as a *standard termination*. If the employer wishes to terminate the plan but cannot fulfill the plan's liabilities, it must prove that continuing the plan will cause the business to collapse. These *distress terminations* are unusual and are rarely granted except in cases of bankruptcies. The PBGC itself may involuntarily terminate a plan if it finds the plan's liabilities are unlikely to be fulfilled either by plan assets or by the employer.

If a plan sponsor defaults on the plan and the plan is terminated, the PBGC will pay basic benefits up to a certain level for plan participants. Retirees currently receiving benefits will be paid up to a maximum amount based on the average wage earnings in the United States, currently about $2,000 per month. For participants who are still working, PBGC will guarantee benefits these workers had accrued at the time the plan terminated. They will not provide the benefit the worker would have earned had she continued working until retirement. Additionally, the PBGC will not fully pay benefits based on increases from new plan provisions granted within the last 5 years or benefit increases granted while the plan was not in compliance with the law. For example, if your plan had provided for 1% of final average pay for each year of service, but was increased to 2% last year and was then terminated, PBGC would pay your benefits based on the old 1% rate and would pay only 20% of the increased benefit.

Different rules apply for multiemployer plans. Because several employers are involved in such plans, PBGC will become responsible for the plan only if it becomes insolvent. Employers who cease participating in the plan remain liable to contribute to the plan for a number of years; thus the financial health of the plan is not tied to the fate of one employer. If PBGC does pay benefits for the plan, the payment limits are much lower than are those for single-employer plans. The maximum benefit multiemployer benefit guaranteed is only $600 per month for a 30-year participant! And PBGC will not pay for any benefit increases granted in the last 5 years.

Even after the PBGC takes responsibility to pay plan benefits, the plan sponsors remain liable to PBGC for the amounts owed the plan. However, in cases of bankruptcy, the courts usually rule PBGC is an unsecured creditor and, as such, unlikely to collect the debt in most cases. PBGC is actively working to improve its status as a priority creditor in bankruptcy cases, but to date it has been unsuccessful with either the Congress or the courts.

WHAT TO DO IF YOUR EMPLOYER TERMINATES THE PLAN

Unfortunately, if your employer decides to terminate your benefit plan, you have few options. You will receive a notice of the termination. If the plan is a defined benefit plan guaranteed by PBGC, you must receive a benefits statement showing your accrued benefit and the facts used to calculate the benefit such as your age, date of hire, earnings, and so on. Be sure to double-check these facts and inform the plan administrator immediately if you disagree with any of the data. If your plan is a defined contribution plan, you may only receive a notice the plan is being terminated and later a check for your accrued benefit. If you don't get a benefit statement, ask for one immediately. Be sure those records match your records of your benefits.

You may be given the choice of receiving your benefit in a lump sum or as an annuity held by an insurance company. Even if the plan has been previously guaranteed by PBGC, that agency will not guarantee the validity of the annuity. In recent years annuities issued by insurance companies such as the Executive Life and Mutual Benefit insurance companies have reduced payments because of the financial difficulties of these issuing companies. But hundreds of thousands of other annuities have been safe and paid regularly. Ask the plan administrator who will be paying the annuities and try to research that company.

Or take the money as a lump sum. You can then transfer it into an IRA and invest the money any way you wish. If the terminating plan is a defined contribution plan invested in stocks or mutual funds, find out whether there is the possibility of receiving your account in assets rather than a check. This may not be a good time to sell the assets in your defined contribution plan, and if you can receive the assets, you may be able to hold them until the price increases.

Do not fail to put any assets you receive from the plan into an IRA. Arrange to have these assets transferred directly to the IRA or another employer's plan, if you have access to another employer plan. If you don't have the amount transferred directly to the IRA or other plan, the employer must withhold 20% of the amount for federal taxes. You can still transfer the entire value of the benefit amount you should have received before the withholding, if you put the money into an IRA and file for a refund of the withheld amount. But you may not have the extra money to make up for the 20% withheld when you fund the IRA. If you don't get the money into an IRA within 60 days after you receive the check, you will pay income tax on the entire amount, and you will pay the 10% preretirement withdrawal penalty, even though you didn't "withdraw" the money. Unless you use the IRA, the only way you will escape the 10% penalty is if you are 59½ at the time you receive the money or are 55 or over and fit under the early retirement provisions of the terminating plan.

Strategy Plan for ERISA: Know Your Rights Under ERISA

- ❖ Get up-to-date copies of all employers' summary plan descriptions. Do this for both current and former employers.
- ❖ Begin a file folder for all materials on employer plans.
- ❖ Read each SPD and note dates relevant to you on the front cover such as date of hire, date of vesting, and date of your leaving the employer, if it is a previous employer.
- ❖ Arrange a meeting with your employer's benefits specialist to discuss areas of the SPD or other forms where you have questions.
- ❖ Do a rough calculation of your benefits under your employer's plans. We will use those calculations in later chapters to determine your savings needed for retirement.

NOTE FOR CHAPTER 6

1. Daniel J. Beller and David D. McCarthy, "Private Pension Benefits," in John A. Turner and Daniel J. Beller, eds., *Trends in Pensions 1992* (Washington, D.C.: U.S. Department of Labor, Pension and Welfare Benefits Administration, U.S. Government Printing Office, 1992), Table A1, p. 590.

PART
T W O
SOURCES OF RETIREMENT SAVINGS

EMPLOYER-PROVIDED RETIREMENT PLANS

Alice, Susan, Bonnie, and Jennifer are among a minority of employees because each of them now works for an employer that provides a retirement plan. Although more than 729,000 such plans cover some 51 million active employees, that translated into coverage for only about 43% of the work force in 1990.[1]

Even so, employer retirement plans contain nearly $3 trillion in assets to pay benefits, a significant sum in comparison with a gross national product of approximately $5 trillion. Pension assets not only represent an important source of retirement security for Americans, but a powerful source of investment capital for national savings and growth.

As we have already seen, these plans are heavily regulated by the federal government. This regulation helps protect the rights of employees, but it also means the laws affecting retirement plans are extremely complex. This chapter will examine—and simplify—some of that complexity by explaining the basic outlines of some common employer retirement plans and listing the advantages and disadvantages of each.

TAX BREAKS AND CHANGING LAWS

These employer-provided retirement plans enjoy tax breaks worth approximately $56 billion in fiscal year 1993, the largest single area of tax preferences in the federal budget.[2] The complexity of employer-provided benefit plans is increased by frequent changes in retirement plan laws. These alterations stem from the fact that during the last decade of unprecedented deficits, Congress has constantly needed new sources of revenue. In its search to raise revenues, Congress has repeatedly shaved away at the tax breaks given both retirement and health employee benefits. With over $100 billion of employee benefits at stake, Congress changes the benefits rules for the same reason Willie Sutton said he robbed banks: it's where the money is.

The material in this chapter is based on the law as it exists today. Changes are possible at any time, and you should be certain that you—and your employer—are operating under the most recent effective law. Usually, when Congress changes the law in this area, the effective dates are delayed 1 to 3 years to give employers time to amend their plans and inform employees about required changes. But some employers do not keep up with changes as rapidly as they should. In their defense, unless one has access to the very expensive special service publications that report employee benefits law changes, it is difficult to find the current law in this area. You should look for dates on any summary plan descriptions you have. If your company's SPD is more than 5 years old, it is likely out of date. Either the SPD has not been changed to reflect plan changes or—worse—the plan has not been changed to comply with the latest law. If you are concerned about a specific provision, ask the human resources department to confirm the provision does, in fact, represent the latest version of the plan and the law. If you are still concerned, contact the Department of Labor's Pension and Welfare Plan Administration and pose the question to them.

HOW NEW LIVING PATTERNS CAN CONFLICT WITH OLD RETIREMENT PLANS

For many people the retirement benefits provided by their employers will be the largest segment of their retirement income. But as we saw from Alice's experiences, *significant retirement benefits will be available only if you worked for one employer for several years or if you contributed heavily to the retirement plan with your own money.* For example, on average, recent data show an employee with a defined benefit plan and 10 years of service with her employer could expect her benefits to replace 10–12% of wages; with 20 years of service, she could expect 20–23%; and with 30 years of service, 29–35%.[3] Because women frequently change jobs or take time off the payroll, it is more difficult for them to receive the full benefit of employer retirement plans that require long, uninterrupted service.

Originally, retirement plans were designed to reward many years of continuous service. Many still operate that way. This goal may have been appropriate when employers sought to keep employees for decades and when one-earner families were common. Today, employers frequently *want* employees to move on after a few years. Two-earner families often need one of the earners—still usually the woman—to take time off the payroll to care for families or to relocate. As our examples have illustrated, these changes in the way we live make some retirement plans less effective for women than the employer may have intended.

Some employers are addressing their changed goals for retirement plans, recognizing that since they no longer want workers who are dedicated to the company solely by the promise of a large pension, the companies should change their retirement plans. Other employers simply want to spend less money for benefits. Both these desires are fueling a move to defined contribution plans and away from defined benefit plans. The number of private employer defined benefit plans has shrunk from more than 175,000 in 1983 to about 146,000 in 1988, whereas defined contribution plans have steadily grown from about 207,000 in 1975 to more than 580,000 in 1988.[4] Defined benefit plans still cover more people than defined contribution plans, but that difference is rapidly eroding as well.[5] As we have seen, since defined contribution plans emphasize the need to begin saving early in your career, it becomes all the more important to begin retirement saving from your first day on the job!

INVESTIGATE EMPLOYER PLANS EARLY—NOT AT RETIREMENT

To achieve the maximum benefit from employer plans, you must understand how your employer's plans operate. By law, the employer must help inform you. The SPD for each plan must be given to you when you become eligible for the plan. Most employers give you these SPDs as soon as you join the company. Most employees ignore them. Be the exception—read the SPD! Other plan documents must be given to you, if you request them. Employers are eager for you to know about and understand your retirement benefits. Employers spend literally millions on these plans, and they are happy to publicize them. Getting information usually won't be a problem.

But you have to read and understand the materials the employer gives you. And to plan effectively for maximizing these benefits at retirement, you have to read and understand the provisions and act on them early in your career, not two weeks before you plan to quit or retire. The language may at first seem confusing. Frequently, it is. This chapter explains the basic legal framework of some common types of employer retirement plans. Your employer's plans will probably have additional rules. In general, an employer's plan may be more generous than the law requires, but plans may not be more restrictive than outlined here.

UNDERSTANDING THE BASIC DIFFERENCES BETWEEN DEFINED BENEFIT PLANS AND DEFINED CONTRIBUTION PLANS

You know employer-provided retirement plans come in two basic varieties: *defined benefit plans* and *defined contribution plans.* The first *defines* the benefit you will receive when you retire. For example, the benefit defined might be 1% of pay times years worked. Under a defined benefit plan, if you live longer than average, you beat the system, because you will be guaranteed a payment as long as you live.

In contrast, a defined contribution plan specifies the amount the employer will deposit in a trust fund each year you work in that firm. Such contributions are usually based on a percentage of your salary. For example, such plans might promise to contribute 5% of your pay each year. At retirement you have a lump sum of money which you can spend or invest any way you want. If you invest well, you may be able to make the money last for your lifetime and leave some behind for your heirs. But if your investments don't prosper or you live a very long time you may run out of money.

Generally, defined benefit plans are thought to favor older workers who have been with the employer for a long time, or who plan to work for the employer for a long time. This is because the money needed to supply defined benefits for a young employee with only a few years of service is very small. Only when a worker is near retirement and has served many years with the employer does the money needed for the benefit reach a significant sum.

By contrast, defined contribution plans are usually considered to be more favorable for young workers with few years on the job. There are several reasons for this. First, the size of the employer contribution is usually not dependent on the number of years worked or the employee's age. Second, a contribution put into an account for a young employee has more years to earn investment income before that employee retires. For example, assume Alice, age 60, and Jennifer, age 30, both earn $24,000 per year and receive a contribution of 1% of pay this year. That $240 will earn interest for 5 years before Alice retires, giving her a mere $307 when she retires. But Jennifer's $240 will earn interest for 35 years before she retires and give her $1,324 at retirement. (This example assumes a modest 5% rate of interest; the differences would be even more dramatic if higher interest rates are used. See the "Future Value of a Dollar" table in Table A.1 and work your own examples.)

Defined contribution plans are usually more "portable" than defined benefit plans. Defined contribution plans' values can be easily calculated when an employee leaves. The sum can be transferred to another employer's plan, in some cases, or to an IRA. Once invested, the amount can grow. By contrast, many defined benefit pension plans do not permit "cashouts" when an employee leaves. Because the pension payment is fixed as of the date the employee leaves the plan and is based on the employee's salary at the time of termination, the benefit does not grow and can be eroded by inflation. For example, in Alice's case, she vested in a defined benefit plan in a previous job, but the annual amount for that benefit is frozen for 8 years before she retires. Preretirement inflation erodes the value of that amount each year. Even if the pension plan does permit "cashouts," the value of the benefit will be reduced by a "mortality" factor, which takes into account the possibility the employee might have died before collecting the pension. These reductions are not made in defined contribution plans.

LIMITS ON THE AMOUNT YOUR EMPLOYER CAN PROVIDE

While it is rarely a problem for most women, there are limits on the amount an employer can contribute annually for you under a defined contribution plan and limits on the amount of benefit you can ultimately receive under a defined benefit plan. There is also a combined annual limit on the amount of benefits you can accrue under one employer's plans, if the employer has a defined contribution plan and a defined benefit plan or more than one of either plan. These limits are sometimes referred to as the *415 limits* for the section of the Internal Revenue Code setting them out.

Contributions under all the employer's defined contribution plans for an employee in 1 year may not exceed the *lesser* of:

❖ $30,000 (which will be adjusted for inflation in the future) or

❖ 25% of the employee's compensation

Once you retire, benefits annually under all defined benefit plans from one employer cannot exceed the *lesser* of:

❖ 100% of the employee's average highest 3 years of compensation or

❖ $90,000 adjusted annually for inflation (the 1993 dollar amount is $115,641)

The benefit limit will be further reduced if you retire prior to Social Security retirement age or prior to having completed 10 years of service or participation in the plan.

DEFINED BENEFIT PLANS—ALSO KNOWN AS "PENSIONS"

Defined benefit plans are usually what you think of when you hear the word "pension," so we will refer to defined benefit plans as *pensions* throughout this chapter. Pensions are the most complicated retirement benefit plan, both for you as an employee to understand and for the employer to fund and administer. As with all employer-provided retirement plans, pension plans are regulated by the Internal Revenue Service and the Department of Labor, which are responsible for all ERISA-covered employee benefits. But pension plans are also regulated by another quasi-government agency, the Pension Benefit Guaranty Corporation, the agency which partially insures the pension plan's assets to be sure there are adequate funds to pay your promised benefits when you retire.

Common Formulas for Pension Calculation

Most pension plans base their formula for ultimate retirement benefit payments on a percentage of your "compensation" times your "years of service" with the company. The formula used for the unit defined benefit plan in the Chapter 4 career examples' comparisons was 1.25% of the final 5 years of pay per year of service with the company up to a maximum of 30 years. Under this formula, if you earn $25,000 per year after 20 years with the company, your payment per year would be:

$$1.25\% \times \$25,000 = \$312.50$$
$$\$312.50 \times 20 \text{ years} = \$6,250 \text{ per year}$$

Such payments are usually made on a monthly basis, so you would receive $520.83 per month for life.

Other common formulas are a percentage of salary, for example, 50% of compensation, or a flat dollar amount per year of service, such as $2 times years of service per month. Flat dollar amounts are frequently seen in union-sponsored pension plans.

Different Definitions of "Compensation" Can Affect Your Benefits

These formulas seem simple enough, but in actual operation, several complex factors come into play. *Compensation* can be defined in many ways. For example, it could be:

- ❖ The average of compensation over your career (so-called "career-average plans")
- ❖ The average of your compensation over the last 5 years you worked
- ❖ The average of the highest 5 years of compensation you received (or over some other period of years)

There are other variations of these definitions, and they can have a big impact on your actual benefit. For example, a "career-average" definition of compensation will produce a much lower benefit than a definition of compensation based on your highest 5 years of compensation. A definition based on the highest year of compensation, obviously, provides the largest benefit, but this is not a common definition.

For example, assume you worked for Acme for 20 years, you currently make $25,000 annually, and you will receive a retirement benefit of 1% of compensation times years of service. If the plan uses final year's compensation, your annnual benefit will be $5,000. If the plan uses the average of the highest 5 years, the annual benefit would be $4,600 (assuming raises of $1,000 year each of the last 5 years). If the plan is a career-average plan, your earliest years of compensation will be averaged in to determine the benefit. Assuming you started at $10,000 and received steady increases each year, your annual benefit would be far less than the benefit calculated under other models.

Your benefit will also be affected by the earnings included within the plan's definition of "compensation." For example, depending on the plan, compensation may or may not include overtime, bonuses, commissions, or amounts from your paycheck which are deducted before taxes to pay for your health insurance or other benefits such as 401(k) plan contributions.

If you have been working overtime or used bonuses to meet daily living expenses and your retirement plan does not take those earnings into account in calculating your pension benefits, you may have a more difficult time living on your pension than you anticipated. The plan's definition of compensation is a good example of information you should have and consider early in your career while you can still adjust your personal retirement savings plan accordingly. For example, as a salesperson you may receive a very modest base salary, but you earn commissions that increase your income significantly. To plan the amount of money you need to save for retirement, you need to know now whether your pension will be based on your $10,000 salary or on your salary plus your annual $40,000 of commissions.

Defining "Years of Service" to Determine Pension Benefits

Years of employment or so-called *years of service* are also subject to various meanings. A single pension plan may even use different definitions of "years of service" for different purposes. For example, plans frequently require an employee to work for a year before she is eligible to participate in the plan. In such cases the first year of service may not be counted for benefit calculation purposes, but will be counted for vesting purposes.

Years of service for vesting purposes may not be the same as years of service for benefits calculation purposes. Recall that the concept of vesting determines when you have an irrevocable right to the benefits you have earned. By law you must have such a right to all benefits earned to date after 5 years, the so-called "cliff vesting," or earn a right to benefits at 20% per year after completing your second year of service until you become 100% vested in all benefits after your seventh year of service. Plans can provide for faster vesting.

Prior to 1989, plans could delay vesting for up to 10 years for cliff vesting and permit graduated vesting over 15 years. Plans could also permit vesting under a *Rule of 45* whereby vesting occurred gradually under a schedule based on your combined age and years of service. For this reason many women who have been in the work force for years and changed jobs only a few times may still have never vested in a retirement plan. For example, Alice worked for an average of 7 years for her first four employers, but she never vested in any benefits with those employers. Each of her early employers required 10-year vesting. Only the recent change in the law enabled her to vest with her last two employers. *Her earlier years of work get no credit with the current employer in benefit calculations under that employer's plan.*

Frequently, the years of service used to calculate the benefits are referred to as *credited years of service*. As with vesting, by law only the years in which you worked at least 1,000 hours are required to be counted. For example, when Jennifer works part time and later moves to a full-time position with the same employer, her part-time years will not count as years of service if she did not work more than 1,000 hours during those part-time years. Of course, an employer can design a plan that credits part-time work for retirement benefits, if the employer wishes.

The Difference Between Accruing Benefits and Vesting in Benefits

By law an employer may not prevent an employee age 21 or older from participating in the employer's retirement plan for more than one year after the employee begins full-time employment, or 2 years, if the plan provides immediate 100% vesting of benefits. If the employer's plan only allows employees to *enter the plan* at certain times during the year, a waiting period before the plan "entry date" may be tacked on. Most plans permit employees to "enter" the plan at least twice a year. An employee *must* be permitted to enter the plan either (1) at the beginning of the plan year after she satisfies the one- or two-year rule or (2) six months after satisfying the one- or two-year rule, whichever date is earlier.

For example, in February Jennifer goes to work at Acme, which has a pension plan and a 401(k) plan. Both plans require employees to work for 1 year before they can participate. The plans also provide that employees may enter the plan only on January 1 and July 1. Jennifer is eligible for the plan the following February, but she will not be able actually to contribute to the 401(k) plan or have her service counted for the pension plan until the next plan entry date, which is July 1. Jennifer really loses 17 months of benefits because of the participation rules.

Once she begins to *participate* in the plan, she begins to *accrue benefits.* If the employer's pension plan gives 1% of pay per year of participation, on the July following the July she entered the plan, she will have "accrued" or earned the right to a future benefit of 1% of pay for the one year of participation. But if she leaves after that year, she will receive no benefit, because she did not vest in the benefit she accrued. Until she vests, the accrued benefit is simply a contingent promise of the employer to provide the benefit. Once the initial vesting period has elapsed, Jennifer will own all benefits as she accrues them. She does not have to wait after accruing the benefit actually to vest in the benefit.

Receiving Benefits—Life Stream Versus Lump-Sum Payments

Pensions are designed to be paid in regular installments over the course of your lifetime after you retire. This is called the *annuity form of payment* as opposed to *lump-sum payments.* The concept is to provide you with an income for as long as you live. These payments are not adjusted for inflation in private plans, except in very rare cases. Only about 3% of those receiving a private employer pension receive an automatic, plan-required benefit increase.[6] Pensions provided by federal, state, and local governments frequently do provide for some inflation adjustment, usually referred to as a *cost-of-living adjustment,* or *COLA*. If you live for several years after you retire and/or inflation increases rapidly, the buying power of your monthly annuity payment is likely to erode significantly.

Some pension plans do permit retirees to receive the current value of their pension plan in a lump sum. This sum will be calculated based on the retiree's age at retirement and current interest rates. The lump-sum amount equals the total amount which the retiree would have received had she fulfilled her life expectancy according to established mortality tables, discounted for the amount the lump sum will earn over the period until her expected death. Alternatively, the lump sum may reflect the interest it would earn as well as a mortality factor. The mortality factor represents a reduction based on the probability the retiree might have died earlier than her established mortality, but is now guaranteed to have the money regardless of the time of her death.

The law requires plans to use a single table for all employees, whether they are men or women. Most plans use a unisex mortality table or a mortality table based on male life expectancy. These tables anticipate fewer years of life than a female mortality table, because women live longer than men. Because of this difference, a healthy retiring woman will almost always receive a lump sum *lower in value* than the amount she might ultimately receive by taking payments over her lifetime.

There are exceptions. If the retiree is in poor health, she may not reach her life expectancy. In that case the lump sum may provide the larger sum of money. If the retiree believes she can invest the lump and generate a greater return than the pension plan, she should also take a lump sum. This ability to generate a greater return on the lump sum may not be as difficult as it seems in times of very high inflation. For example, in the double-digit inflation of the 1970s, the buying power of pension payments begun in 1970 eroded to less than half by 1979. Because interest rates were equally high during much of that period, a retiree might have been able to protect her income much more effectively by taking the lump-sum payment and investing it rather than taking a life stream. But such market timing is extremely difficult. Moreover, in times of high inflation, the assumed earnings rate used to estimate your lump-sum payment will be high. The higher the interest rate assumption used to calculate your lump sum, the lower the amount of money you will receive in your lump sum. The mathematics are fairly simple: the higher assumed rate of earnings on the amount of money used to pay your benefit, the less money you need.

Choosing Payment Forms If You Are Married

Under the changes to ERISA made by the federal Retirement Equity Act, if you have a spouse, the pension payment form will automatically be paid as a joint and survivor annuity, unless you *and your spouse* request a different form of payment. To make up for the possibility the payments will have to be paid over two lifetimes—yours and your spouse's—the monthly payment you receive will be reduced at the beginning of your retirement. Once you die, the payment to the survivor may also be reduced, depending on the provisions of the plan. Joint and survivor annuities are almost always a bad method of pension payment for a woman's own retirement plan, because her husband is not likely to outlive her, and the reduction in her benefits during her lifetime will have been for naught. If you die before you retire, your spouse may receive a payment at the time when you would have reached retirement age. This payment form is a *qualified preretirement survivor annuity.* Chapter 14 discusses these payment forms in detail.

How Your Company Pension Ties in with Social Security

In a retirement plan—whether it is a defined benefit or a defined contribution plan—employers may take into account their contributions toward Social Security taxes on your salary by "integrating" the plan with Social Security. In more up-to-date legal language, the plan is said to recognize "permitted disparity" between wages earned that fall below the Social Security taxable wage base and wages earned above the Social Security taxable wage base. These adjustments for Social Security payments are more common in defined benefit pension plans than in defined contribution plans.

Prior to the Tax Reform Act of 1986, such Social Security integration could dramatically reduce benefits. For low-income workers, Social Security integration sometimes totally wiped out the pension benefit. For example, a pension plan might provide for 1.5% of compensation times years of service minus an amount equal to one-half of Social Security. For a woman who had an average compensation of $15,000 and worked for 15 years the formula would be:

$15,000 × 1.5% × 15 years = $3,375
Social Security benefit = $7,650
½ Social Security benefit = $3,825

The ½ Social Security benefit, $3,825, exceeds the benefit calculated under the pension, thus *no pension payment was due.*

Workers who thought they would have a pension found at retirement, in fact, the pension was nonexistent. Social Security replaced enough of their wages to satisfy the pension plan formula with no further payments from the pension plan. These reductions were permitted by law, so the employees and retirees had no right to claim fraud. The employee simply never read the fine print and calculated the complex formula for the benefits with Social Security. But retirees felt defrauded, regardless of the legality of such reductions.

After a series of tearful congressional hearings in which retirees described their disappointment and financial difficulties caused by the Social Security integration rules, Congress made changes. Although plans can still recognize Social Security benefits in calculating benefits under the plan, the retirement plan benefit cannot be reduced to less than half what it would have been if there had been no recognition of Social Security.

There are other extremely complex rules surrounding the use of "permitted disparity" based on Social Security. The bottom line is that pension plans must always give some credit for wages earned at or below the Social Security wage base. This base, frequently called "covered compensation," is averaged over years to account for the increasing level of wages subject to Social Security taxes. For example, a permissible pension plan using Social Security integration or "permitted disparity" could have a formula such as:

1% of pay up to the covered compensation limit
+
1½% of pay in excess of the covered compensation limit
×
years of service

An example illustrates the concept. Assume Patti's pay as defined by the plan is $60,000, covered compensation at her year of retirement is $25,000, and she had worked 30 years when she retired. Her annual benefit would be:

$$1\% \text{ of } \$25,000$$
$$+$$
$$1\frac{1}{2}\% \text{ of } \$35,000 \text{ [}\$60,000 - \$25,000\text{]}$$
$$\times 30 \text{ years } =$$
$$\$250 + \$525 \times 30 = \$23,250 \text{ per year}$$

By contrast, if the plan did not take into account Social Security, by providing a lower benefit for wages at or below the Social Security wage base, she would receive $1\frac{1}{2}\%$ of all pay, and her annual benefit would be $27,000 per year. Of course, the employer could also argue that, without taking into account his payments to Social Security, he could only afford to fund a plan which paid 1% of pay times years of service. In that case Patti's benefit would be only $18,000 per year.

Pension plans which take Social Security into account in calculating benefit payments will spell this out in the summary plan description. If you have a pension plan with your employer, *be sure you read this section of the SPD carefully and remember to take into consideration the effects of this Social Security adjustment.*

Additionally, while the laws have changed to limit the reductions that can be made for Social Security, the changes were not effective until 1989. For benefits earned before 1989, the old rules can apply and greater reductions can be made. A more typical illustration of Patti's case would show the calculation using the old rules for Patti's first years of service and the new Social Security integration rules only for those benefits earned since 1989. The SPD should explain any reductions made under the old rules. These rules are complicated, and even pension experts frequently must read the plan provisions or SPDs several times to get the precise meaning. Don't be intimidated—if you don't understand this section of the SPD the first time you read it, read it a few more times. If you still have problems, ask your employer to explain it with an example based on your benefits earned to date.

Advantages of Defined Benefit Plans

Guaranteed Payments. Defined benefit pension plans guarantee a specific benefit payment as long as you live. You don't have to worry about how to invest the money or how to divide the money to ensure it lasts a lifetime. Indeed, as discussed earlier, if you are willing to receive a lower monthly payment, you can even be sure it lasts to cover the life of your husband or, in some plans, another beneficiary such as a dependent child.

No Investment Decision Required. Unlike defined contribution plans, where the employee is frequently encouraged to contribute her own money, which in turn requires decisions on how much should be contributed and how it should be invested, with a defined benefit plan, the employee usually has no investment decisions. The plan trustees decide how to invest the money, and the actuaries, guided by law and regulation, tell the employer how much money to contribute. The benefits are guaranteed by the Pension Benefit Guaranty Corporation. Even if there are insufficient funds in the plan trust, plan beneficiaries will receive all or most of their benefits. Some very large benefits may be reduced, if PBGC has to pay, but minimum benefits will always be available.

No Investment Risk for the Employee. The employer bears all the investment risk of the plan's trust fund. If the investments made by the trust don't earn as much money as projected, the employer has to supply more money to the trust to be sure the trust is fully funded to pay the promised benefits. By contrast, in a defined contribution plan, such as a profit-sharing plan or 401(k) plan, if the assets in the employee's account don't earn acceptable returns, the employee simply has a smaller account than she expected. The employer is not required to contribute any additional money.

Disadvantages of Defined Benefit Plans

Low Benefits for Young Employees. By design, defined benefit pension plans provide the greatest advantage to older workers who stay with one employer for several years. Pension plans' benefits are heavily back loaded. This means the benefits build up very slowly for a younger employee with little service.

This is how it works. The benefits are based in part on numbers of years of service. Obviously, the fewer years of service, the smaller the benefit. But the plan investment for the employee is also based on the amount of money needed today to provide benefits for the employee when she reaches retirement age, usually 65.

Assume Linda has worked at Acme for 15 years, since she was 20, and assume the pension plan formula is 1% of compensation times years of service. The benefit she has accrued after 15 years of service at age 35 in today's dollars is the amount of money invested today at a reasonable rate of interest (spelled out in the pension plan document) which will provide her with 15% of her pay when she reaches age 65. When Linda is 35, even though she has 15 years of service, this amount of money is relatively small because she is entitled only to an amount that would pay her 15% of her salary 30 years from now. The amount of money needed to fund that obligation is small, because it has 30 years to grow with investments. In contrast, assume Barbara is an employee with 15 years of service and making the same amount of pay as Linda, but Barbara is 60 today. Barbara's accrued benefit is much larger than Linda's because the amount of money needed to provide Barbara's 15% of pay benefit at age 65 has only 5 years to grow.

This growth period between the time the money is contributed and the retirement date of the employee is also the reason why defined contribution plans favor younger workers. The money contributed to the defined contribution plan has more time to earn income before the employee retires. Pension plans reward long service and encourage loyalty to the employer. Both of these goals are admirable. But, while this goal of encouraging loyalty and long service from employees is a worthy one, the goal may not fit the reality of the 1980s or the 1990s. Women's career patterns do not fit the pattern of long continuous service with one employer. Hence, women tend not to receive the maximum benefit from defined benefit plans.

Demographic trends show that in general both men and women are staying in jobs for shorter periods of time and having more employers. Many public policy analysts argue that the United States needs workers who are more flexible and willing to learn new jobs and relocate more often. Defined benefit plans discourage this flexibility. Moreover, particularly in the 1980s, many jobs were eliminated and workers forced to change employers, leaving behind benefits in pension plans which had not vested or which were very small.

Possible Plan Terminations.   Another disadvantage of pension plans occurs when a plan that is being counted on by the employee in her retirement planning is terminated long before the employee is ready to retire. If the employer does terminate the plan, the employee is entitled to all benefits she has accrued to date. But as we have seen, the "accrued benefit" for a young—or even middle-aged—employee may be quite small in relation to what she had expected if she had worked until actual retirement age.

No Adjustment for Inflation.   Finally, pension plans are rarely indexed for inflation once the benefits are accrued or the payments begin. A few years of high inflation can substantially reduce the buying power of the monthly pension payment. Because women live longer than men, they face more years of inflation eroding the payment. If inflation is particularly high when an employee retires and has the choice to take annuity payments or a lump sum, she may attempt to avoid inflation's ravages by taking the lump sum and investing it. But if inflation jumps after she has retired, there is no way to change the benefit payments.

DEFINED CONTRIBUTION PLANS

Many bigger companies provide both defined contribution plans and defined benefit plans and may even provide more than one defined contribution plan, such as both a profit-sharing plan and a 401(k) plan.

Defined contribution plans come in many varieties and each variety has a number of options and alternatives. There are some elements common to all defined contribution plans. First and most obvious, the employer makes a contribution for each employee or permits the employee to contribute for herself. The amount and timing of that contribution and the method for calculating it for each employee are spelled out in the plan document. Unlike defined benefit plans, the employer does not make a general contribution based on actuarial calculations of the work force as a whole. Defined contribution plans frequently permit the employees to contribute to the plan on their own account. Defined benefit plans rarely permit employee contributions. For record-keeping purposes, each employee has her own "individual account," unlike a defined benefit plan. The amount in your individual account will depend, not only on the employer's contributions, but on any contributions you are permitted to make, as well as on the earnings of the contributions and the expenses of the plan, if the employer requires the plan to pay expenses. Some employers pay for the expenses of the plan, thus increasing the growth of your benefits.

Choosing How Your Contribution Is Invested

Many defined contribution plans give you some options for how the money in your account is invested. With these options, you become responsible, to a degree, for the growth of your retirement account. Remember, unlike defined benefit plans, the Pension Benefit Guaranty Corporation does not guarantee any of the funds in defined contribution plans.

Where investment options are available, the plans usually offer two to four different investment choices. The employee is given the option to invest portions of her defined contribution individual account in these different choices. The investment choices range from *guaranteed income contracts* (GICs), which provide a fixed rate of return for a given period, to bond or stock funds. These funds may be mutual funds which are also available on the open market, or they may be funds set up and managed by the trustees of the plan. These are usually a mixture of growth funds, income funds, or fixed rate funds. One of the investment choices is frequently the employer's stock, if the stock is publicly traded. As with most investments, the higher the rates of return, the greater the likely risk of loss or decline in the value of the funds. Funds which are safer are likely to have a lower rate of return.

The major exceptions to this rule that the lower the rate of return, the lower the risk to your investment—in my personal opinion—are the so-called "guaranteed income contracts." *Your investment in these contracts is in no way guaranteed by anyone other than the company sponsoring the contract!* The only thing that is "guaranteed" is the rate of interest, and that "guarantee" is usually only for one year. The assets in the "contract" are dedicated to repaying the investment in the contract, but those assets may or may not hold their value. Many of these contracts are offered by insurance companies or by banks. Neither of those industries is considered to have especially rosy financial prospects for the next few years, although there are individual exceptions.

Yet these contracts usually offer a substantially lower rate of return than other funds offered in many defined contribution plan investment elections and thousands of employees invest in GICs, believing their money is as safe as a certificate of deposit. Nothing could be farther from the truth. In investing in GICs, you may be getting the worst of both worlds—a low rate of return and potentially high risk. No total losses have occurred with GICs—yet. But the risk seems too high in proportion to the earnings on the investment. After all, if you invest in a mutual fund with your defined contribution assets, the value will go up and down, it is true, but to lose your total investment, every company the fund has invested in has to go bankrupt. With an individual GIC investment, only one company, the GIC sponsor, has to go bankrupt for you potentially to lose all your retirement plan investment! Some plan sponsors have reduced this risk to some extent by offering GIC funds which consist of several GICs offered by different companies. When GICs have failed, employers have sometimes stepped in to cover the losses to employees. These steps reduce the risk, it is true, but they don't increase the rate of return on GICs.

Employees, even sophisticated employees, make a retirement planning mistake by investing their accounts in the lowest-paying funds because these funds tend to be the most conservative and safe investments among the options. As a result, their account's growth is dramatically reduced over the years. For example, if you invested $4,000 per year for 25 years in your 401(k) plan in the conservative GIC account paying 4%, at the end of that time you would have $166,584, but if you invested it in a mutual fund that returned 6% you would have $219,460. A fund paying you 9% would provide a lump sum of $338,800. Clearly, your life-style in retirement will depend to some extent on the risks you're willing to assume during your working years with your retirement savings.

Extremely conservative investments with low rates of return are an especially poor investment for young employees. Young employees have a great deal of time to accrue investment earnings. Even if a young employee's investment has a low return or drops in value for a year or two, the younger employee has plenty of time to wait before she needs the money. As an employee nears retirement, it may make sense to move to more conservative investments to preserve asset value, but for younger employees, overly conservative investments cheat them of growth in their money.

Receiving Benefits: Payout in Lump Sum

Defined contribution plans usually pay the retirement benefit to you in a lump sum when you retire or leave the employer. You are responsible for investing and spending the lump sum to give you an income for the rest of your life. Some defined contribution plans allow for conversion to an annuity form of payment—in regular payments over the course of years—but these annuities may not guarantee payment for a lifetime.

Advantages of Defined Contribution Plans

❖ The contributions for younger, less senior employees (a common status for women because they change jobs frequently) are proportionately larger than they would be under a defined benefit plan.

❖ Defined contribution plans frequently permit you to add your own money to the plan, thus providing you with a tax-deferred place to hold your retirement savings.

❖ You may have a choice of specific investments.

❖ Defined contribution plans are more "portable" because such plans are more likely to permit a lump-sum distribution to you when you leave the employer. You can then invest the lump sum in ways designed to protect it against the ravages of inflation.

Disadvantages of Defined Contribution Plans

❖ You bear the risk of investment of the plan's assets. If the investments in the plan don't do well, you will simply have less money than you had planned on for retirement. The employer will not provide more money to the plan just because the investments perform poorly.

❖ The funds are not guaranteed by the Pension Benefit Guaranty Corporation.

❖ The employer may be placing too much of the burden of retirement saving on you by providing a very small employer contribution or no contribution at all.

TYPES OF DEFINED CONTRIBUTION PLANS

Let's look at some different types of commonly offered defined contribution plans and the unique advantages and disadvantages of each:

❖ Profit-sharing plans
❖ Money purchase pension plan
❖ Thrift plans
❖ 401(k) plans
❖ Stock bonus plans
❖ Employee stock ownership plans (ESOPs)
❖ Simplified employee pensions (SEPs)

Profit-Sharing Plans

Profit-sharing plans are really misnamed in some respects. The employer does not need to have profits to make contributions to the profit-sharing plan. Nor is the employer required to contribute to the profit-sharing plan because the company has profits in a given year.

Profit-sharing plans, when used as retirement programs, simply permit, but do not require, an employer to make a contribution to your retirement account. A profit-sharing scheme gives the employer the discretion to fund the defined contribution retirement plan from year to year.

Not all profit-sharing plans are used as retirement plans. There are three basic types of profit-sharing plans:

1. *Current or cash profit-sharing plan.* The employer gives a profit share in cash to the employee. This money is immediately taxable to the employee. Current or cash plans are not used as retirement plans, although the smart retirement planner will use this usually unexpected sum to fund an IRA or to set aside other forms of savings for retirement.

2. *Combination profit-sharing plan.* The employer declares the profit share, but the employee decides whether to take the money in cash, pay taxes on the money and use it as she wishes, or "defer" the profit share money into the retirement savings plan set up by the employer. If she elects to put the money in the profit-sharing retirement plan, she pays no tax on the money—or on its earnings—until she withdraws the money at retirement.

3. *Deferred profit-sharing plan type.* The employer permits the profit-sharing contribution to be used only for deferrals into the retire-

ment plan. The profit share is set aside in each employee's account. That account is available when she retires or leaves the employer. The employee pays no tax on this contribution until she retires or otherwise takes the money out of the account. Earnings on this money accumulate in the employee's account and are not taxed until she receives the money.

Usually the contribution the employee receives is based on compensation. For example, a profit-sharing formula may be based on the ratio of an employee's salary as compared to the total payroll. That percentage of the profit-sharing contribution will be contributed to the employee's account. For example, if Alice earns $30,000 and the employer's total payroll is $1 million, Alice will receive 3% of the profit-sharing contribution. If the employer's total profit-sharing contribution is $100,000, Alice will receive $3,000 in her profit-sharing account for that year.

Some profit-sharing plans base contributions on a simple percentage of compensation, for example, 5% of compensation. Profit-sharing contributions can also be based on a formula which combines compensation, age, and/or years of service. For example:

❖ Employees age 21 with 1 to 5 years of service might receive 2% of pay.

❖ Employees age 30 or older with 5 to 10 years of service receive 4% of pay.

❖ Employees over age 40 with 10 to 15 years of service receive 6%.

❖ Employees age 45 and older with over 15 years receive 10% of pay.

Such plans are referred to as "age- and service-weighted profit-sharing plans." Such plans are becoming popular, especially in smaller companies, because they enable an older, higher-paid worker to receive more benefits than she would under an ordinary profit-sharing plan, while allowing the plan to satisfy the IRS nondiscrimination rules, too.

Profit-sharing contributions may be made in cash or the employer's stock. If the employer's stock is used, the plan may also be referred to as a stock bonus plan or employee stock ownership plan, also called an ESOP (pronounced "e-sop," like Aesop's fables—

you'll see why later). ESOPs and stock bonus plans are discussed in detail later in this chapter.

In addition to the per employee limits on yearly contributions we discussed at the beginning of the chapter, employers sponsoring profit-sharing plans may not deduct contributions in excess of 15% of the total compensation for all participants in the plan.

Advantages of Profit-Sharing Plans

❖ As do most defined contribution plans, profit-sharing may give younger or less senior employees proportionately larger benefits than they would receive under a defined benefit plan.

❖ The account balance in a profit-sharing plan is easy to understand and easy to calculate.

❖ Profit-sharing plans, like most defined contribution plans, are more likely than defined benefit plans to permit lump-sum cashouts if the employee terminates prior to retirement age, thus providing greater portability of benefits.

Disadvantages of Profit-Sharing Plans

❖ The employer has the discretion each year to fund—or not to fund—the plan, and she may not want to fund every year.

Money Purchase Pension Plan

Money purchase pension plans require the employer to contribute an amount each year based on a percentage of your salary. There is no discretion to eliminate a contribution in any year. These plans are commonly integrated with Social Security. If the plan is integrated, the contribution percentage for salary below the Social Security wage base will be lower than the contribution for salary above the wage base. A money purchase pension plan might be integrated with a formula such as:

3% of compensation up to the Social Security taxable wage base

+

5% of compensation in excess of the Social Security taxable wage base

These yearly contributions, plus earnings, provide your "pension" at retirement. Unlike other defined contribution plans, the payout for these plans is frequently in an annuity form.

Advantages and Disadvantages. Money purchase plans share most of the advantages and disadvantages common to defined contribution plans; however, with money purchase plans, the employer's contribution is not discretionary. Contributions must be made each year, unless the plan is terminated. This lack of discretion is an advantage for the employee and a disadvantage for the employer.

Thrift Plans

Thrift plans basically require the employee to fund at least part of her own retirement. A thrift plan may consist of only the employee's contributions and the earnings on those contributions. Or, if the employer does make contributions to the thrift plan, the employee generally must contribute to the plan to receive those employer contributions toward retirement savings. Frequently, the employer contributions are in the form of a matching contribution.

As with profit-sharing plans, each employee has a separate account to track her contributions and the contributions of the employer, if any, and the earnings and losses on those contributions. Thrift plans, too, may permit the employee to choose among a number of different investment funds. An employee may contribute to the thrift plan with money on which she has already paid taxes. If you contribute on an after-tax basis, you will not receive a tax break on your contributions during your working years, although the earnings will accumulate on a tax-deferred basis. But when you retire, you will pay no tax on your contributions as they are withdrawn, because you have already paid tax on that amount. You will pay tax on the employer's contribution and the earnings on all contributions, because that money has not been taxed before. The tax rules for determining what portion of the benefit payments will be treated as your contribution and what portion represents employer contributions and earnings are extremely complex.

Thrift plans may also be designed to allow employees to contribute with their salary before the money has been taxed. If you contribute on this pretax basis, the thrift plan is called a 401(k) plan after the section of the Internal Revenue Code which permits such pretax contributions. These 401(k) plans have become common and have almost completely replaced after-tax thrift plans. Because 401(k) plans are covered by such complex rules, they deserve separate discussion.

401(k) Plans—Cash or Deferred Arrangements

401(k) plans are thrift plans in which you contribute dollars before federal taxes are paid or withheld on that amount; that is, contributions are on a pretax basis. Such plans are also known as cash or deferred arrangements—or CODAs—because you may take the money as part of your ordinary salary in cash or you can "defer" that part of your salary into the 401(k) retirement plan. Another name for 401(k) plans is *salary reduction plans*, because you "reduce" your take-home salary by the amount you contribute to the 401(k).

The money you contribute to your 401(k) plan will not be subject to withholding for federal income tax, and in most states, there will also be no withholding for state taxes. The money will be subject to Social Security and unemployment taxes. The benefit of this pretax savings is apparent when you realize even at the lowest tax bracket, for every $1.00 earned, you have only $0.85 left for savings through ordinary savings plans. The first $0.15 of each dollar earned must be paid in federal taxes. In a 401(k) plan, you only need to earn a dollar to save a dollar. As with other defined contribution plans, you do not pay taxes on any employer contributions to the 401(k) or on any earnings on your account until you retire or take the money out of the plan for other reasons.

Popular with employees and employers, 401(k) plans have grown phenomenally over the last decade even though they are governed by extremely complex tax rules. The number of 401(k) plans increased from 1,703 in 1983 to more than 45,000 in 1987, and the growth continues.[7] Employers like 401(k) plans because they can be inexpensive. The employee is essentially funding her own retirement plan. Additionally, the 401(k) forces the employee to think about the need for retirement savings and requires her to take some responsibility for her retirement security. Unlike a pension plan, where the employee has no idea how much the employer is contributing for her each year, if the employer contributes to the 401(k) on her behalf, the employee knows exactly how much was contributed. Human nature as it is, most people appreciate a definite and known contribution to a 401(k) plan more than the vague buildup of pension rights which are difficult to see in terms of actual dollars until actual retirement.

Employees like 401(k) plans because they are usually paid as a lump sum on termination, the plan is easy to understand, and a 401(k) provides both significant immediate tax breaks for current salary and long-term tax shelter for the earnings on the salary that is saved in the 401(k). And, when you move to a new employer, the 401(k) account can easily go with you. You can transfer the 401(k) money to the new employer's plan, if the new employer accepts transfers, or you can "roll over" the money into an IRA.

Because your account will primarily consist of your own money and earnings on that money, which is always fully vested, the issue of vesting is less important than with a defined benefit plan. Vesting rules affect only the amounts, if any, the employer contributes. Additionally, because the benefit consists of your individual account, which is easily and obviously calculated, there is no confusion about the value of the benefit you receive, as there frequently is with pension plans which are based on a number of factors including years of service, age of the employee, number of years to retirement, and so on.

Basic IRS Rules. You may not contribute more than 25% of your compensation (including employer contributions, if any) to a 401(k) in any one year. You may not contribute more than $7,000 per year to the 401(k). This $7,000 limit is indexed annually for inflation, and was up to $8,994 for 1993. This $7,000 limit does not include any amount the employer may contribute.

For example, assume Kathy, who earns $85,000 annually, elects in December 1991 to make as her 1992 contribution 10% of her salary on a pretax basis. Her $8,500 contribution meets both the percentage limit and the 1992 dollar limit, which was $8,728. But in February 1992 she gets a raise to $90,000. Her 10% elected contribution, even with the lower contribution for the month of January, would exceed the $8,728 limit by year end. She must notify her employer to reduce the amount of her contribution so she will be within the limits.

Even though most employers will automatically make adjustments to prevent an employee from overcontributing, Kathy should not rely totally on her employer to prevent excess contribution. The problems which arise if the employer does not stop the overcontribution can be enormous. If the employer does not stop the overcontribution, Kathy may receive an incorrect W-2 at tax time. Because her employer also has until after the end of the plan year (which may not coincide with the tax year) to make corrections and notify you of problems, Kathy may have already paid her taxes, based on an erroneous amount of income. If so, she will have to file an amended federal tax return and perhaps an amended state return as well. If the mistake is not corrected within a year after the overcontribution, the money may be frozen in her 401(k) account. She will have to pay taxes on the contribution and its earnings twice—once in the year the overcontribution is discovered and again when she withdraws it at retirement. The inconvenience of overcontributing is simply too great to rely completely on your employer.

Some 401(k) plans also allow you to contribute after-tax money, which is not subject to the dollar limit but is subject to the 25% of compensation limit. Although you don't get an immediate tax break for these contributions, the earnings on them are not taxed until you withdraw the money.

Withdrawals Before Retirement Age. Congress designed and intended 401(k) plans to be retirement plans, not savings plans, regardless of how your employer may try to "sell" the plan to you as a "savings account." If you leave your employer and take your 401(k) money, you may directly transfer the amount into an IRA or another employer's plan to avoid taxes and penalties. Otherwise, if you withdraw 401(k) money before you retire, reach at least 59½ years old, or become disabled or die, your employer will withhold 20% for federal income tax, you will be liable for ordinary income tax on the money you withdraw, *and you will pay an additional 10% penalty on that withdrawal.* The only exceptions to the 10% penalty tax in such cases are payments from the 401(k) in equal payments over your expected life time or withdrawals to pay for tax-deductible medical expenses in excess of 7.5% of your income. You still pay regular income tax on such withdrawals.

You may not receive your money from the plan before you separate from service for any reason other than "hardship." Even then you will pay the 10% early withdrawal penalty tax, unless you meet one of the penalty exceptions, and income tax on the amount you withdraw. Technically, the IRS will permit the 401(k) plan administrator to determine what constitutes "hardship." But if the plan makes the wrong decision in even one case, the plan can lose its tax-exempt status. As a result, few 401(k) plans permit hardship withdrawals except in cases which the IRS has stated will be "deemed to constitute an immediate and heavy financial need." The general rule is that such a need will be deemed to exist only if:

- ❖ You are about to be evicted or your mortgage is about to be foreclosed.
- ❖ You must have the money to make tuition payments for yourself or a child (this does not include dorm or living expenses).
- ❖ You have or will incur substantial medical expenses.
- ❖ You will use the money for the purchase of a principal residence.

If the withdrawal is for medical expenses, you may be exempt from the 10% penalty for the amount of those expenses exceeding 7.5% of your income.

Even if you satisfy the requirements for severe hardship, you will be further punished for the withdrawal if your plan relies on these *deemed hardship* rules, because the law will not permit you to continue or begin contributing to the plan again for at least 12 months after you made the withdrawal. You will have lost the opportunity to contribute 12 months of retirement savings, earnings on those savings, and any employer match you might have received, in addition to losing the withdrawn amount and paying taxes and penalty on the money.

If the plan sets its own standards for hardship, you may avoid the prohibition against contributing for 12 months. However, you should be prepared to prove to your employer your precise financial position, including the fact you have sought other loans and been refused.

In addition to these limits, you must show that you have no other resources available to you. You may withdraw no more than the amount needed to meet the hardship expenses and to pay the taxes due on the withdrawal.

Loans on 401(k) Plans. Because the hardship withdrawal rules are so strict, many employers permit loans from the 401(k) plan. Under the law, you may borrow against the amount you have contributed to your 401(k) plan. The bad news is these loans must be at market interest rates and cannot extend for more than 5 years except for a mortgage. Loans may not exceed the lesser of (1) $50,000, reduced by any previous loan balance within the last year, or (2) half of the amount in your account. However, for accounts with less than $20,000, the law permits loans of up to $10,000. The plan does not have to permit such loans. The good news is many 401(k) plans will credit your account with the interest you paid on the loan, so you literally borrow the money from yourself and you reap the interest.

Special 401(k) Nondiscrimination Rules. As with all qualified retirement plans, 401(k) plans may not discriminate among employees by limiting the plan only to highly paid employees or by giving other preferences to highly paid employees. In addition to the general non-discrimination rules discussed in Chapters 3 and 6, such as vesting, participation, and contribution and benefit amounts, 401(k)s are subject to very detailed and complex rules regarding how much highly compensated employees may contribute, on average, as compared with other employees' contributions. These rules require the employer to "test" the plan each year to be sure the contributions comply with the rules.

Since compliance with 401(k) nondiscrimination rules is the employer's responsibility, why do you as an employee care? Because, if you are a "highly compensated employee," the amount of money you can contribute to your 401(k) account may be reduced below the $7,000 limit as adjusted that year for inflation if your employer's average lower-paid employees did not put a large enough percentage of their money into the 401(k). Another reason for concern is that the same problems associated with overcontributing in excess of the dollar limit apply to contributions exceeding the nondiscrimination limits.

If you are not highly compensated, you also care, because the employer will be taking steps to encourage you to increase your contributions, such as providing matching contributions. In rare cases, the employer may even give the lower-paid employees additional nonmatching contributions designed to increase the percentage of salary saved by the lower paid.

The rules generally work this way. On average, the percentage of salary contributed by highly compensated employees to the 401(k) cannot be more than one-fourth greater than the average percentage of salary contributed by the other, lower-paid employees. For example, if all the employees who are not highly compensated contribute an average of 2% of their salary, the highly compensated employees cannot contribute more than 2.5% of their salary when averaged together. There are alternative tests which permit some variations to this limit. Employees who contribute nothing to the plan are still included in their appropriate category, but are averaged in as "zeros."

Because highly paid employees are likely to have more discretionary income to save than other employees, more highly paid employees are likely to participate and set aside a higher percentage of salary. On average, the participation rate for those earning between $5.00 to $7.50 per hour is about 42%, as compared to a 79% participation rate for those earning over $20.00 per hour.[8] These limiting rules can dramatically lower the amount you may contribute to the 401(k) plan, if you fall into the definition of "highly compensated," which is generally those earning more than about $64,000 in 1993 (the amount is adjusted for inflation each year). For example, according to *Forbes* magazine, the 401(k) contribution averages for lower-paid employees at a major hotel chain were so low one year that the highly compensated employees could contribute less than $2,000 that year. If you are relying on a 401(k) plan to be your primary employer-provided retirement plan, this kind of limitation could have a dramatic impact on your retirement security, if it continued year after year.

Obviously, these rules place a high premium on significant contributions by all employees. The rules encourage employers to provide matching contributions. If contributions by lower-paid employees are too low to pass the IRS-required tests, some employers may also contribute directly to the 401(k) accounts of lower-paid employees to raise the averages and enable the plan to satisfy the tests.

Paying Taxes on 401(k) Savings at Retirement. When you withdraw money from a 401(k) at retirement, you pay federal income tax on any money which hasn't been taxed before. In most cases this means you will pay tax on all money as you withdraw it. But, if your 401(k) allowed you to put after-tax dollars in the plan and you did so, you will not pay taxes on that amount of money. It is your responsibility to keep track of the amount of after-tax money you have contributed and to calculate the tax properly.

Advantages of 401(k) Plans

Greater Employee Control Over the Retirement Plan. 401(k) plans enable you to have some control over your employer-provided retirement plan. The more money you contribute, the more you will have for retirement. And in plans where the employer also matches your contributions, you can, in effect, give yourself a raise by contributing to the 401(k). For example, if your employer gives a 50% matching contribution and you contribute $20 per week to the 401(k), at the end of the year, you will have savings of $1,560—$1,040 from you and $520 from your employer. And that is $1,560 you will not have to pay federal income tax on until you retire.

The Ability to Control Contributions to Your Retirement Plan. This can be especially valuable if you plan to be off the payroll in the future to start your own business or to care for your family. You have the ability to save heavily during those years with the employer to make up partially for·those years in which an employer will not be contributing toward your retirement.

Deferred Taxes on Savings. The tax advantages make it easier to save. Because you are using pretax dollars, you can save more. You are paying lower federal income taxes.

Savings Are Deducted Automatically. The 401(k) savings are automatically taken from your paycheck. Savings discipline is enforced, so it is easier to save. If you never see the money, you have no chance to spend it.

Flexibility to Borrow or Withdraw Savings. Most 401(k) plans allow you to borrow against your contributions in the plan or allow you to withdraw your money in cases of severe hardship. While a 401(k) plan should never be thought of as a savings account, this ability to borrow or withdraw money does give you a hedge against significant financial disaster.

More Investment Choices. You will probably have some choices about the investment of your 401(k) plan, unlike a pension plan whose investments are solely in the control of the pension plan trustees. Investment control and decisions can be an advantage or a disadvantage, depending on your investment savvy—and luck. As with profit-sharing plans, 401(k) plans usually have several investment choices, especially for the employee's money. The employer's contributions may also be invested in these choices, or the employer may limit its contributions to investment in its stock or in a particular fund, usually a fairly conservative fund.

Employees who are not near retirement should choose the more aggressive investment options which will have a higher rate of return and earn more money. As you near retirement, the funds can be shifted into more conservative investment choices which will have a lower rate of return in some cases, but will also be less subject to fluctuation with the stock market or the economy.

Disadvantages of 401(k) Plans

Difficult to Save Enough for Retirement. No matter how disciplined you may be, you may not be able to save and earn enough in your 401(k) to last a lifetime. While 401(k) plans do have some enforced discipline in savings, you can change your contribution level from time to time. When financial crises arise, you may reduce your contribution level, robbing yourself of retirement security in the long run. Or you simply may not have enough discretionary income to save as much as you need for a woman's long retirement.

Greater Investment Risk. Your 401(k) account will bear the risk of investment because it will grow only if it is wisely invested. If the investments have a poor rate of return, the employer is not obligated to increase its contributions, if any, to the 401(k) plan. Yet you will be limited to those investment choices the employer's plan provides for you. The fewer investment choices your 401(k) provides, the greater the potential disadvantage of lack of diversification in investments. This lack of diversity can become a severe problem if the only investment option is the employer's stock or if the employer's contribution is invested only in the company stock, because you have too many eggs in one basket.

Employer May Provide No Other Retirement Plan. A circumstantial disadvantage can arise from the adoption of a 401(k) plan if the employer terminates an existing pension plan and replaces it with a 401(k) plan as the company's sole retirement plan. Many pension rights advocates argue 401(k) plans are designed simply to force the employee to fund her own retirement plan. Employers would answer these arguments by saying a 401(k) plan is better than no plan at all, a premise difficult to refute.

Clearly, if you could choose whether your employer would have a pension plan or a 401(k) plan, the pension plan will usually be better from the older employee's point of view because the employer pays for all of it in most cases. But few of us get such choices. Unless you are in a position to influence the employer's decision—that is, if you are considering whether to take the job, if you are part of a collective bargaining team, or if you are the director of human resources and helping to decide what plan to choose for the employees—you don't need to be concerned about these philosophic arguments.

If the 401(k) plan is there, use it. Contribute as much as you can, from the minute you can. In many cases the employer will have both a pension and a 401(k) plan. If the employer doesn't have a pension plan, using the 401(k) doesn't prevent you from urging the employer to adopt one.

Stock Bonus Plans

Stock bonus retirement plans receive the employer's contributions in shares of the employer's stock rather than cash to be invested in other securities. Unlike a defined benefit, which is prohibited from holding more than 10% of its assets in stock of the employer, the stock bonus plan will have all or most of its assets held in the employer's stock. These stock contributions may be part of a profit-sharing plan or combined with a 401(k) plan.

By using stock rather than cash to contribute to the retirement plan, an employer gives his employees ownership of the company and a built-in incentive to make the company profitable and sound. If the employer can use unissued treasury stock, rather than stock purchased on the open market, it also saves a great deal of money. The employer is diluting the ownership of the company by issuing the stock to the retirement plan, but the advantages can far outweigh the disadvantages to the employer.

Frequently, stock bonus plans are referred to as employee stock ownership plans. But true ESOPs, as defined by law, are different from ordinary stock bonus plans and deserve special discussion. With a stock bonus plan or an ESOP, both your job and your retirement security may rise and fall with the price of company stock and the market. Some people fear that combination is putting too many eggs in one basket.

Employee Stock Ownership Plans

ESOPs are unique among employer retirement plans because only ESOPs can borrow money from the plan sponsor or permit the plan sponsor to guarantee a loan to the plan. Although this power to borrow does not seem extraordinary on its face, investment bankers have proved differently.

This power to borrow, coupled with some significant tax breaks provided by Congress, has made ESOPs a big favorite as a financing tool for companies. Almost without regard for the purpose of ESOPs as retirement plans, money from ESOP loans has been used occasionally by shaky companies to generate cash flow, to take companies private, and to make or to fight takeover bids, in addition to being used as a device to accomplish the original purpose of the law, that is, enabling employees to buy their companies.

Of the literally thousands of ESOPs, only a relative handful have been abused. But when ESOPs are introduced as a retirement plan, especially if they replace an existing pension plan, you should be aware of the other factors which might be driving the employer to create an ESOP. *And you should be aware that the ESOP may have been created for business purposes totally unrelated to the employees' retirement security or welfare. The retirement benefit impact of the ESOP may not have been the primary focus.*

To the extent ESOPs give you ownership in the company, you and your fortune can grow with the company. But don't start packing up to move into the management suite immediately. In and of themselves, ESOPs do not give you, the employee, management power and authority. If the company is to be truly employee owned, management must share its rights and duties. Additionally, company fortunes don't always prosper even with good management and the best employee productivity and support. With the thrill of ownership can come the agony of a plunging stock market and stock price in spite of your long hours and hard work.

Leveraged ESOPs. When an ESOP borrows money it is called a *leveraged ESOP*. You probably won't find this term in your employee benefits manuals or in the summary plan descriptions of the ESOP, but it does have significance in the rights you may have. In a leveraged ESOP, the employer sets up an ESOP and contributes stock to the plan or sells stock to the ESOP. That stock is placed in a *suspense account*, which means it has not been distributed to any employee's account, but is being held to be distributed eventually among employees. The ESOP or the employer borrows money from a lender to finance the ESOP's purchase of the stock. The loan is secured by the shares of stock in the ESOP's suspense account. Each year as the employer contributes to the ESOP, those contributions are used to pay the original loan. This payment frees an equal amount of stock in the suspense account for distribution to employees. That stock is then distributed to the accounts of employees.

As with most employee retirement plans, the amount of stock contributed to your account can be based on several different factors. Frequently, the amount contributed to you will be based on salary. Some ESOPs do base contributions on a flat rate to each employee or on a formula which takes into account years with the company.

With a leveraged ESOP, the amount of stock issued to your account is based on the loan payment and the number of the stock shares released as a consequence when the loan is paid, not the value of the shares when the shares are distributed into your account. This means, if the value of the shares go up, you can receive greatly increased contributions, even contributions in excess of the IRS's 415 limits. But if the value of the stock goes down, the loan still has to be paid at full value. This can work against you because you will be treated for 415 limit purposes as receiving a proportionate share of the amount used to pay the loan. You will be receiving contributions of stock worth much less than the contributions being made, and at the same time, you may be limited on amounts you could receive in other employee plans or even amounts you could contribute to the employer's 401(k) plan.

Voting Rights on ESOP Stock. Employees must be permitted to exercise the voting rights of the ESOP stock held in their accounts. If the stock is not publicly traded, these rights can be limited to voting on major issues such as dissolving, selling, or merging the company. Shares of the stock in the suspense account which have not been distributed must be voted by the plan trustees for the best interests of the ESOP participants, not the employer. In a perfect world, on any issue the best interests of both the employees and the employer will be one and the same, but this is not always the case.

Diversifying as You Near Retirement. By law the ESOP must permit you to diversify your ESOP stock acquired after 1986 after you have been in the ESOP for 10 years or reach age 55, whichever date comes later. The law recognizes the risk of overinvestment in the employer's stock is too great as you near retirement. The ESOP must permit you to either make other investments within the ESOP, or receive cash from your ESOP account. You have the right to move up to 25% of your remaining ESOP holdings each year for 5 years and up to 50% in the 5th year after you reach the 10-year and age 55 threshold. This ability to diversify gives you some protection against overinvestment in your employer's stock.

Getting Your Stock—or Your Cash—When You Leave. You can elect to receive your ESOP benefits in stock or cash, except in rare cases where state law prohibits the ownership of the stock outside the corporation. If the stock is not freely traded on an open market, the employer must give you a "put option," which means the employer must buy the stock from you at fair market value over as long as 5 years. If you own more than $500,000 worth of stock, the period for repurchase can be longer.

The stock distributions must begin within one year after the close of the plan year in which you retire, become disabled, or die. If you leave for any other reason—you quit, are fired, or are laid off permanently—the employer can delay your benefit payout for up to 5 years after the end of the plan year in which you left. Once you are entitled to begin receiving your ESOP account, regardless of whether you retired or quit, the employer may distribute it to you over 5 years, but the distributions must be in at least annual installments. If you own more than $500,000 of stock, the 5-year payout period can be extended.

For example, suppose Alice has $50,000 in her ESOP account. The ESOP plan year runs from July 1 through June 30. Alice will retire on August 1, 1993. The ESOP stock distribution does not begin until June 30, 1995. This is almost 2 years after Alice retires, but it is still within the 1-year limit after the close of the plan year when she retired. She is entitled to receive one-fifth of her stock or $10,000 in 1995. The plan must give Alice one-fifth of her account each year after that for the next 4 years. She will not receive her final benefit from the account until 1999.

You should bear these potential delays in mind and consult with your employer about when payments can be expected. Most employers do not use the full time permitted by law, but most do need some time to do the paperwork involved. Don't plan on receiving the full account as soon as you leave.

ESOP Advantages. If the employer's stock does well, the ESOP has several advantages:

- ❖ It enables the employer to start a benefit plan with relatively little money. This seed of stock can grow to be a far more generous retirement benefit plan than the employer could have afforded if she had made a cash contribution.

- ❖ As an employee, you own a piece of the company and may see a direct result of your effort.

- ❖ As a stockholder you also have a voice, small though it may be, in the operation of the company. An ESOP enables a young, growing company to share that growth with its employees.

- ❖ In some cases, particularly in enterprises owned by one person or one family, an ESOP may be the only way to carry on the business and keep the worker employed when the family wants to sell out or the owner wants to retire.

- ❖ In other cases, the capital provided by the ESOP loan may provide the financing necessary for the company to regain or improve its financial health and prevent the collapse of the company and loss of jobs.

ESOP Disadvantages

Greater Investment Risk. If the stock does poorly, the retirement plan can become worthless. Many retirement planning experts urge diversification and argue that a retirement program which consists solely of an ESOP is inherently bad retirement planning. The heavy investment in the employer's stock simply makes the plan too vulnerable to the stock price declines affected by all sorts of factors which may have no real relation to the value of the company. Sound companies may have their stock price dragged down by bad market conditions.

Greater Risk of Tying Employment Security and Retirement Security. When the company does undergo bad financial times, the employees may suffer a double hit. The company may decide on layoffs or forced early retirement just when the stock is so low that the employee hasn't enough to live on. By law the retiring employee can take the stock of most companies and hold it until the price of the stock goes up. But if the ESOP is the only retirement plan, the retirees may not have any choice but to sell the stock to help meet daily living expenses.

Less Control over the Retirement Investment. The value of the stock may be influenced by factors far beyond your control as an employee. If management has used the money from the ESOP loan to go on a takeover buying binge, the interest needed to pay the loan may severely strap even a successful, high-revenue company. Many a sound company has recently damaged itself and its stock by becoming so encumbered with debt that even the highest revenues are not sufficient to pay the interest on the debt, pay dividends, and keep the payroll high. If your company is one of these, your ESOP and your job could become nonexistent.

Simplified Employee Pensions

Simplified employee pensions (SEPs) are a relatively little used form of employer-provided retirement benefit. They are essentially IRAs the employer sets up for you, but the contribution is not limited to the $2,000 IRA limit. Theoretically, SEPs are covered by the same 415 limits contribution levels that apply to other defined contribution plans—that is, the lesser of $30,000 or 25% of compensation per employee. However, a SEP is limited to deducting no more than 15% of the company's compensation for employees in the SEP in any year. Contributions in excess of the deductible amount can be carried forward to other years, but the law imposes a 10% excise on *excess contributions* that are not deductible in the year made. It is the rare employer willing to pay a 10% excise tax to give employees extra retirement benefits!

Like other employer retirement plans, SEP contributions are not taxed until you take the money out of the SEP account. Unlike other retirement plans, SEP contributions must be immediately vested. By law the employer cannot limit the withdrawals from SEPs. So if you decide to take the money out of the SEP the day after the employer puts it in, you can. But you will pay both regular income tax plus a 10% penalty on the amount you withdraw before you are age 59½ or meet the other exceptions to the penalty, and you will lose the tax deferral on the earnings the money would have made.

No plan document is required other than a standardized IRS Form 5305-SEP which you and the employer sign. This form does not have to be filed with the IRS or the Department of Labor, and no annual reporting on Form 5500s is required. The employer need not contribute to a SEP each year, nor is there any requirement the contribution be based on the same formula each year. But when a contribution is made, it must be according to a written formula and must bear a uniform relationship to compensation. Some disparity in contributions is permitted for Social Security.

The employers usually leave the choice of investments to the employee, although by law the employers can choose the investment. Usually the investments are certificates of deposits, insurance annuities, or mutual funds. You tell your employer where you want the money invested, and the employer forwards the money to the SEP fiduciary—usually a bank, insurance company, mutual fund family, or stockbroker.

If the employer has 25 or fewer employees, the SEP can also permit salary reduction contributions from the employees, much like a 401(k) plan. At least 50% of the employees must participate in the salary reduction arrangement, putting some level of their own money into the accounts. But this can be a minimal amount, and it is pretax money, just as in a 401(k) plan. Tax-exempt employers and state and local governments may not have salary reduction SEPs regardless of their number of employees.

SEPs have never become very popular with employers, primarily because of their strict participation rules. The employer must contribute for every employee who:

- ❖ is over 21
- ❖ worked for the employer during 3 of the last 5 years
- ❖ received $300 or more in compensation from the employer for the year the SEP applies

The $300 threshold is adjusted for inflation and as of 1993 was $385. Contributions must be made for employees satisfying these criteria even if they are not working for the employer at the time the contribution is made. Any period of service, even a day, counts as having worked for the employer. Thus, part-time employees, including those working a few hours for a few weeks during a busy season, would have to receive a contribution. Every employee must agree to participate in the SEP. If one employee refuses to participate, no contributions can be made. This sounds draconian, but, fortunately, most people rarely refuse to accept money. Given these strict participation and contribution requirements, it is not surprising SEPs have not been overwhelmingly popular.

Advantages and Disadvantages of SEPs. The biggest advantage of SEP is that you may be able to convince your employer to establish one if you don't have a retirement plan at work now. Because the SEP has virtually no reporting and record-keeping requirements and because the employer has the right each year to decide whether and how much to contribute, the employer may agree to establish a SEP even though it has rejected requests for other benefit plans. After all, it would provide the employer with a retirement plan, too. If there are only 25 or fewer of you, you might at least convince your employer to set up a salary reduction SEP, if you can get 50% of your coworkers to agree to contribute. Another great advantage is the fact the SEP contribution is immediately vested.

Finally, the fact most employers permit the employee to choose the investment option can be a big advantage. You can choose an investment option that matches your other retirement financial planning objectives. If there is a mutual fund you have been tracking, but haven't had the money to invest in it, the SEP contribution will be the perfect opportunity. If you still feel comfortable only with certificates of deposit, you may invest your SEP there.

The disadvantage of SEPs is the employer's discretion not to contribute and the ability to change the levels of contribution each year. You never know whether you will have a retirement plan, and if so how much you can count on. Depending on your discipline, the easy access to SEP money can also become a temptation. You essentially control the money, and you can withdraw it from the SEP account at any time. Of course, the heavy taxes you face on the withdrawal can be an effective deterrent.

HYBRIDS—TARGET BENEFIT PLANS AND CASH BALANCE PLANS

So-called *target plans* and *cash balance plans* combine elements of both defined benefit plans and defined contribution plans. In a target plan the employer determines the percentage of your salary it wants you to receive as a retirement annuity payment when you retire. This calculation is based on actuarial assumptions about your life expectancy and likely earnings of the plan trust. Each year the employer contributes an amount to the target plan trust fund calculated to reach that sum for you. Each employee has a separate account.

If the trust fund's investments earn more money than anticipated, you will retire with an amount which exceeds the "target" set for you when you entered the plan. If the invested funds do not earn as much income as anticipated, you will retire with less than the targeted amount.

The important difference between ordinary pension plans and target plans is that the retirement benefit is not a fixed sum; instead, it will vary depending upon the performance of the investments of the fund. Unlike a defined benefit pension plan, the employer is not required to make additional contributions to the trust to make up for disappointing investment performance, nor does she reap the rewards of superior investment results. The fixed contribution burden gives the employer the advantage of fixed costs for retirement benefits.

Cash balance plans, while relatively new, are becoming increasingly popular. They are actually defined benefit plans masquerading as defined contribution plans. The plan defines future retirement benefits, not the contribution to be made each year. But the annual benefit accrual to each participant is expressed as a dollar amount added to each participant's account. These accounts are a mere bookkeeping device, and no individual accounts actually exist. Contributions for the participant are usually based on a flat dollar amount or on a percentage of compensation.

Each account earns interest at a rate stated in the plan or linked to an index stated in the plan, such as the rate on U.S. Treasury bills or notes. This rate is not dependent on the actual rate of return on plan assets. In cash balance plans, unlike target benefit plans, the plan, not the employee, bears the risk of investment. The participant is guaranteed the rate of return envisaged in the plan.

Cash balance plans are insured by the Pension Benefit Guaranty Corporation. Such plans do not accept employee contributions as a general rule.

Benefits are usually available as a lump sum or an annuity. If the retiring employee chooses the annuity, the payments are based on the actuarial equivalent of the lump-sum value. Some cash balance plans also provide a minimum annuity which will be the greater of the employee's cash balance or a sum calculated on a traditional pension basis of years of service times a percentage of pay.

CONCLUSION: MAKE THE MOST OF YOUR EMPLOYER-PROVIDED RETIREMENT PLAN

You now know the various retirement plans employers can provide. If you have an employer-sponsored plan, you have the tools here, coupled with the plan's SPD, to understand how the plan operates and what pitfalls and problems might arise with it. Unfortunately, the law does not require employers to have retirement plans. And only about half of today's working women work for employers that provide retirement plans. Whether you are in the majority or not, in the next chapter we will move on to see how you can set up your own retirement plan—the most important part of your financial security for retirement. Before we look at individual plans, take these steps to maximize your employer-provided benefits:

❖ Review all the employer SPDs you have collected.

❖ Try to determine your accrued benefit to date from each employer-provided plan.

❖ Contact your former and current employers and ask for their records on your accrued benefits.

❖ Compare your estimates of accrued benefits with those of your employer or former employers. If they are not approximately the same, contact the employer in writing to find out why.

NOTES FOR CHAPTER 7

1. Daniel J. Beller and David D. McCarthy, "Private Pension Benefits," in John A. Turner and Daniel J. Beller, eds., *Trends in Pensions 1992* (Washington, D.C.: U.S. Department of Labor, Pension and Welfare Benefits Administration, U.S. Government Printing Office, 1992), Table 4.1, p. 75, and Employee Benefits Research Institute, "Employee Benefit Notes," March 1992, Table 2, p. 6, based on March 1990 and March 1991 *Current Population Survey* data.

2. Joint Committee on Taxation, "Estimates of Federal Tax Expenditures for Fiscal Years 1993–1997," JCS–8–92, April 24, 1992.

3. Daniel J. Beller and David D. McCarthy, "Private Pension Benefits," in *Trends in Pensions 1992*, Table 9.13, p. 206.

4. Ibid., Table A2, p. 590.

5. Ibid., Table A2, p. 592.

6. Ibid., p. 319.
7. Ibid., Table 8.2, p. 163.
8. Ibid., Table 8.11, p. 169.

YOUR INDIVIDUAL SAVINGS FOR RETIREMENT

Your own individual savings constitute the most important leg of your retirement income security stool. You cannot control government policy on Social Security, you cannot control the retirement plan or the rules of the plan your employer may adopt, and you may not always have an employer. But you can control the amount of money you set aside in savings for retirement. Your retirement savings encompass obvious investment accounts like IRAs, but we will also look at retirement security planning devices such as disability insurance, universal life insurance, and possibly, your home.

MAKE PAYING YOURSELF A HABIT

Saving is a habit. As with any habit, the more often you do it, the more likely you are to continue. If you haven't started saving, start today. Don't be discouraged if you can put aside only small amounts. Most habits start small and then begin to grow.

Pay yourself first. If your employer has a payroll deduction plan, use it. If your bank makes automatic withdrawals from your checking account into a savings account, use that option. An even better option is to have your paycheck deposited directly into a money market fund that is your short-term savings account. Then write a check to your checking account for living expenses. You have reversed the psychology of saving. Under this approach everything you take out of your "savings account" is clearly drawing down on your savings. The point is, if you never see the money, you never seem to miss it. If you absolutely need the money at the end of the month, you can always withdraw it from your savings account.

You may feel that there is simply nothing left to spare after covering current necessities. You may be right. But think about current spending you could eliminate so that you could use the money for savings. Skip lunch one day a week. Even a carry-out lunch these days can cost $5. That's a saving of $260 a year—with interest at 8%, it's $280.80. Granted, that's a small start, but it *is* a start. Chances are, once you start looking for expenses to eliminate in order to save, you will find more. Wash those silk blouses and iron them yourself, take public transportation to work instead of paying for parking, walk to work instead of taking public transportation.

Some financial planners even advise keeping track of literally every penny you spend for a week or two to see where the money goes. This kind of tracking may show you spending $10 a week in the junk food vending machines or $70 a week on eating out or $10 a week on magazines at the drugstore. From those figures you can see how seemingly insignificant purchases add up. While you might not want to eliminate them entirely, if you cut them in half you would give yourself $45 a week to save.

All of this probably sounds like repetitive conventional wisdom you've heard a hundred times before. It is. But there is a reason why it's "conventional wisdom." It works!

PUT YOUR MONEY TO WORK—AND ENJOY THE WONDERS OF COMPOUND INTEREST

Chapter 2 showed us the time value of money. Money you have saved is growing into more money through the interest or investment growth it earns. And the interest earns interest. When Albert Einstein was queried about his opinion on the greatest invention in the world, he replied, "Compound interest." Perhaps he had heard compound interest described by one of the Rothschilds as the "eighth wonder of the world."

Compound interest also explains why you should start saving early. When you begin saving at age 30 for retirement, your early money has 35 years to earn compound interest before you retire at age 65. If you wait until you are 55 to start saving, you have only 10 years of interest-earning time. If you invest $1,000 at 7% for 10 years, you will yield $1,967, but if it is invested for 30 years, *it yields* $7,612. At 7%, investing $1,000 a year for 10 years will give you $13,816, or *$3,816 earned on the $10,000 investment*. But $1,000 a year invested for 30 years gives you $94,461, *which is earnings of $64,461 on your $30,000 investment over the years.*

Any sort of savings program is good, but as we learned from Chapter 5, tax-favored savings plans (where taxes can be deferred or where the amounts can be exempt from tax) yield much higher returns. The rest of this chapter focuses on tax-deferred retirement savings vehicles that you as an individual can use.

INDIVIDUAL RETIREMENT ACCOUNTS

Congress first established IRAs with the enactment of ERISA in 1974 for people *without* employer-sponsored retirement plans. In 1981, Congress extended IRAs to cover all employees and spouses, regardless of whether their employers provided a retirement benefit. Tax-deductible contributions of up to $2,000 per year were permitted.

The Tax Reform Act of 1986 eliminated the tax deductibility of contributions to IRAs for persons covered by an employer-sponsored plan or whose spouses are covered by an employer plan, *if* the employee has an income of over $35,000 if single or over $50,000 if married. If you or your spouse is "an active participant" in an employer plan for any part of the year, and your income is more than $25,000 if you are single or over $40,000 if you are married and filing joint income tax returns, your IRA deduction will be reduced proportionately. You may still contribute the full $2,000 amount to the IRA, but only a portion of it will be deductible. Of course, in such cases you could also choose to contribute only the amount that is deductible.

If neither you nor your spouse is "an active participant" in an employer's retirement plan, you may contribute and deduct from your taxes up to $2,000 per year to an IRA of each of you, regardless of your income, so long as you earn at least as much taxable income as you contribute to the IRA.

Anyone who earns money or who has a spouse who earns money can establish and contribute to an IRA until they are age 70½. The earnings on the money in the IRA will be tax deferred until you begin withdrawing the money from the IRA. *But not everyone can make tax-deductible contributions to an IRA.* The rules on the deductibility of

		TABLE 8.1		
		Current Tax Deductibility of IRA		
Adjusted Gross Income				
Individual	Married, Filing Joint Tax Return	Married, Filing Separate Tax Returns	Covered by Employer Plan	IRA Contribution Deductible
$25,000 or under	$40,000 or under	$0	Yes	Fully
$25,000 or under	$40,000 or under	$0	No	Fully
$25,000– 35,000	$40,000– 50,000	Less than $10,000	Yes	Partially
$25,000– 35,000	$40,000– 50,000	Less than $10,000	No	Fully
$35,000 and over	$50,000 and over	$10,000 and over	Yes	Nonde-ductible
$35,000 and over	$50,000 and over	$10,000 and over	No	Fully

Source: Employee Benefit Research Institute, *Fundamentals of Employee Benefit Programs*, 4th ed. (Washington, D.C.: EBRI-ERF Publications, 1990), Table 15.1, p. 126.

the money used to set up the IRA are complicated, and Congress frequently changes the law. Table 8.1 on the current deductibility of IRAs gives you a rough idea of the rules. Then we will describe the details.

Setting Up a Spousal IRA

If you are married and your spouse doesn't earn an income, you can set up an IRA for him of up to $250 per year. Actually, for married couples where one spouse does not work, IRAs worth up to a total of $2,250 per year can be set up and split between the two spouses any way they wish, so long as neither IRA exceeds $2,000. For example, while you are not working after the birth of a child, you and your husband might decide to set up a $2,000 account for you that year and $250 for him, since he earned some retirement benefit from his employer that year and you didn't. Of course, as with any IRA, the earnings on this account are not taxable until withdrawn.

Determining Whether Your IRA Is Deductible in the Case of an Employer Plan

Your "Modified Adjusted Gross Income" Is the Key. Table 8.1 provides a summary of IRA deductibility, but let's examine the details. If your modified adjusted gross income (before taking any deduction for your IRA) is $25,000 or less if you are single or $40,000 or less if you are married, your IRA is fully deductible regardless of whether you or your spouse are covered by an employer's retirement plan for the year. *Modified adjusted gross income* for this purpose includes any income you earn, not just salary. This could include interest, dividends, and freelance income. It must also include any foreign income or foreign housing allowances you may be entitled to. Once you are above these income thresholds, but below $35,000 for singles or $50,000 for marrieds, you need to examine whether you or the spouse you are filing income taxes with is covered by an employer plan.

Are You or Your Spouse an "Active Participant" in an Employer Plan? Just because you are working for an employer that offers a retirement plan, don't automatically assume you are an active participant in that plan. The IRS defines *active participant* or *coverage* by an employer plan very strictly. If your employer has a program for which you are eligible during any time of the calendar year, you are considered to be "covered" and therefore an active participant in the plan. The rules are complicated and subject to change. In fact, the IRS in its IRA booklet gives only a brief explanation of the coverage rules. The IRS primarily suggests you rely upon your W-2, which will tell you whether you are covered by a retirement plan. But your employer may not be accurate, and, if she isn't, you are the one who will suffer for it.

According to IRS publications, coverage by a plan depends on whether the employer plan is a defined benefit plan or a defined contribution plan. If the plan is a defined contribution plan, you are covered if a contribution is made to your account during the plan year that ends in your tax year. Assume you quit working for Acme on December 1, 1991. Acme has a defined contribution plan profit-sharing plan, and on March 31, 1993, it makes a profit-sharing contribution for the plan year which runs from July 1991 to June 1992. You are considered covered by Acme's employer plan in 1992 because Acme made a contribution for its plan year ending in your 1992 tax year. Depending on your income in 1992, you may not have a deductible IRA in 1992. This could be a big problem if you have already filed your 1992 return before the allocation is announced on March 31, 1993. If your employer's plan is a profit-sharing plan and no profits are shared for your tax year, you are not considered covered by a plan for that year.

You are considered "covered" by a defined benefit plan if you are eligible to participate in a plan year that ends in your tax year. You are *not* considered covered by a plan if you are not eligible to participate in the plan at the end of your tax year. For example, suppose you join Acme on December 1, 1991, at a salary of $40,000. Your previous employer had no retirement plan, but Acme has a pension plan which requires a year of service before you become a participant. You can deduct your IRA contribution for tax year 1991. You are not a member of Acme's plan until December 1, 1992, but you may not have a tax-deductible IRA for tax year 1992. Even if you did not work enough during the plan year for your employer to credit service to you that year, for example, if you worked fewer than 1,000 hours in a year and the plan requires 1,000 hours or more to credit service to you for the year, you are considered an active participant. Or you may be covered even after you leave an employer. For example, Beta Company's defined benefit plan year runs from July 1 to June 30. You leave Beta in December 1992 but you are covered until the end of the plan year, ending June 30, 1993. You may not have a deductible IRA in 1993 (depending on your income) because you are considered an active plan participant in 1993.[1]

The moral of the story here is *contribute to your IRA early in the year,* regardless of whether you know if the contribution is tax deductible. You will have an additional 15 months, at a minimum, to earn tax-deferred interest as opposed to your dilatory colleagues who wait until April 15 to fund the previous year's IRA.

If You Are Married, but Filing Separately. If you are married but did not live with your spouse during the year and are filing a separate return, you will not be considered to be covered by any employer plan he may have and you will be treated as a "single" in determining your income for determining deductibility. In this case, if your employer doesn't have a plan, you are not covered, and your IRA contribution is fully deductible. If your employer does have a plan, your income level for determining deductibility eligibility will be the single limits of $25,000 to $35,000, not the married filing separately limit of only $10,000.

Determining Whether Your IRA Contribution Is Partially Deductible. Once you have determined you or your spouse is an active participant in an employer plan and your modified adjusted gross income exceeds $25,000 if you are single and $40,000 if you are married, you must then go on to the next step to determine whether your IRA contribution is partially deductible. If the income figure is between $25,000 and $35,000 if you're single or between $40,000 and $50,000 if you're married and filing jointly, you may still get a partial deduction. But if you or your spouse is an active participant in an employer plan, and you make more than $35,000 for singles and $50,000 for marrieds filing jointly, you will not be able to deduct any part of your IRAs.

The deductibility of the $2,000 IRA limit is reduced by a fraction in which the top number is the amount in excess of $25,000 for singles and $40,000 for marrieds and the bottom number is $10,000. So, if you are single and earn $31,000, the fraction will be $6,000/$10,000 or 3/5 or 60%. That is, 60% of your contribution to your IRA will be nondeductible. If you contributed $1,000 to your IRA, $400 would be deductible and $600 would be nondeductible.

If you are married and have an income over the $40,000, you both must calculate your IRA contributions separately. Do the calculations before you make your IRA contributions because the deductible limits cannot be transferred from spouse to spouse. For example, if the deductible limit for IRA contributions is $690 for each of you, but you contributed $1,200 and your husband contributed $500, you cannot use the $190 of deductible contributions he did not use to increase your deductible amount. To maximize deductibility, it would make more sense for him to contribute an additional $190 and for you to reduce your contribution by $190. From a retirement security point of view, that does *not* make sense. Urge your husband to increase his contributions and keep yours at the current level anyway. The deductible limit won't be reduced below $200 until your income reaches the $35,000 or $50,000 limit.

Another Use for IRAs—Rolling Over Employer Plan Money

IRAs also serve as the place to continue the tax-deferred sheltering of money from employer retirement plans lump sums that you receive when you leave your job or when your employer terminates a tax-qualified retirement plan. If you have your employer plan transfer the money directly into an IRA, a process called a *trustee-to-trustee transfer* or *direct rollover*, no taxes are due until you begin to withdraw the funds. If you receive the funds from the employer, you may still put the money into an IRA within 60 days, but the employer plan must withhold 20% of the amount for federal income taxes. You can put the full value of your lump sum in the IRA and file for a refund of the 20% that was withheld.

For example, Sarah is leaving Midnight Banking. She has $10,000 in her 401(k) at Midnight. She has several options. She can set up an IRA with a bank, savings and loan, mutual fund, stockbroker, or insurance company before she receives the funds and instruct her former employer plan to transfer the 401(k) funds directly to that IRA. The full $10,000 will go directly to her IRA.

But suppose she does not get organized and the employer issues her a check for her 401(k) account because the employer has not been instructed to send the money to an IRA. Sarah will receive a check from her employer for $8,000, representing her account minus the 20% withholding. She may still set up an IRA within 60 days of receiving the check, and she can put the full $10,000 value of her 401(k) account into that IRA. She will need to get the extra $2,000 from other savings. When she files her income tax, she will file for a refund of the $2,000 withheld or apply that amount to any additional federal income tax she owes.

When you leave an employer, *never, never, never spend the money you may have coming to you from the retirement plan*—unless, of course, you are actually retiring. Even then, you won't want to spend it all. You may well want to transfer it directly into an IRA. Remember, this is the money you need to live on during retirement. If you spend it, the money is gone, the potential earnings are gone and you will pay tax on the money. Further, if you are under 59½, a 10% federal tax penalty will be added to the bill.

A quick example will reinforce this admonition. At 35 you leave dear old Acme and receive the $10,000 in your profit-sharing plan. You spend it on a wonderful vacation—well, actually you spend the remainder after taxes. Assuming you are in the 28% bracket and your state income tax is a mere 2%, you will pay $3,000 in state and local taxes. You will also pay another $1,000 in the 10% early withdrawal penalty. You have $6,000 left for your vacation.

If you had rolled the $10,000 directly into an IRA, no taxes would be due until you begin to withdraw the money from your IRA. If your profit-sharing rollover earns 8% annually, when you retire at 65, *your $10,000 rollover is now $100,630.* If the money had earned 9%, by the way, you would have $132,680.

Any lump sum you receive from an employer's tax-qualified retirement plan can—and should—be placed in an IRA. The only exception to this rule is after-tax contributions you may have made to the plan. Any money you contributed on a pretax basis, such as 401(k) contributions, can be rolled over into an IRA. By law, the employer must give you a brief description of the tax treatment of the money you are receiving from the plan. If you have a benefit worth less than $3,500, the employer can simply cash out your interest in the plan and send you or your IRA a check for your accrued benefit. If your accrued benefit in the plan is in excess of $3,500, you must request payout, and you can refuse to accept payouts, if you wish, until you reach the normal retirement age stated in the plan.

A rollover to an IRA is one area where IRS laws are fairly simple, although the law has recently been changed. Now distributions must go directly from your former employer's plan into an IRA, or the employer plan trustee must withhold 20% for federal income taxes. You notify your employer plan of the IRA sponsor location you are using and tell the employer to transfer the value of your lump sum to that account. You may still receive the money and, after you receive the check, set up your IRA for the full value of your benefit before taxes were withheld. But you will receive a smaller amount given the required withholding, and, if you want to set up the IRA for the full value of your original benefit, you will have to find money to make up for the withheld amount out of other savings. You probably will not receive your income tax refund in time to replace the withheld amount in the IRA.

The only restriction on rollovers of pretax money from employer plans into IRAs is that the funds must be placed in an IRA within 60 days of your receiving the money. This time limit is not within 60 days of your terminating or of the date on the check. It is 60 days from the time of actually receiving the check or other assets. IRS is very strict about the time limit. It has disallowed rollovers made 65 days after receipt. However, where individuals have sent the assets to a bank, broker, or other IRA custodian within 60 days and the bank or custodian neglected to get the account set up within 60 days, the courts have required the IRS to allow the rollover IRA in spite of the agent's delay. Obviously, the smarter approach is to set up the IRA before you take the money from your former employer's plan and have the plan transfer the money directly to the new IRA. Then the 60-day limit is immaterial. The plan is not bound by the 60-day rule because the money is held by the plan trustee up to the minute it is transferred to the new IRA trustee. Although an employer plan should not take more than 60 days to forward the account, if the plan does take more time, it will not jeopardize your right to put the money in an IRA.

Where to Set Up an IRA

IRAs can be set up in a number of places—banks, thrift institutions, stock brokers, mutual funds. Just remember to set up the IRA before you receive any money from your plan, to avoid the 20% withholding. You may set up any number of IRAs. Which institution you choose depends largely on the type of investments you wish to make and how you wish to make them. Banks and savings and loans will usually issue you certificates of deposit with no additional charge for an IRA account. Brokerage houses and mutual funds usually have a small charge for handling IRA accounts. These charges are frequently in the $20–30 range, regardless of the size of the account. Most mutual funds will reduce the minimum amount of investment required for IRAs. Some savings institutions offer higher rates on CDs to IRAs. Chapter 13 provides more advice on how to invest.

Advantages of an IRA

❖ The earnings on the money in the IRA are tax deferred. Your savings grow faster. You may also be able to deduct all or part of the initial contribution.

❖ The savings are locked up. You cannot easily fall prey to impulse spending.

❖ IRAs are controlled only by you. Your employer does not have control over the fate of this retirement plan. You won't fail to get a contribution because the company had a bad year, and your IRA cannot be "terminated" because the employer finds the program too expensive.

❖ IRAs are immediately vested. It's always your money. You won't lose IRAs if you move to a new job or take time out of the job market.

❖ IRAs are easy to set up and to maintain. There's a bank on every corner and brokers or mutual funds will set up accounts by phone or mail.

❖ IRAs can invest in almost any financial instrument. This even includes U.S.-minted gold coins. Investments which might otherwise be unattractive because they lock up money for too long are perfect for IRAs because the IRA is locked up until your retirement anyway. Investments that produce a lot of income annually are good for IRAs because the tax is deferred on that income.

❖ IRAs can be used for short-term loans. Use this advantage with extreme caution, but you may withdraw money from your IRA without tax consequences as long as it is replaced within 60 days. You may only do this once a year with the same money or the same IRA. *And you should never do it unless you are absolutely positive you can repay the money within 60 days*. For example, if you go to closing on your new house in June, but don't go to closing on your old house until July 10, it may make sense to use IRA money in the first closing. If you don't repay the loan within 60 days, you will pay tax and penalty on the amount borrowed, and you cannot put the amount back into the IRA.

Disadvantages of an IRA

❖ The law on IRAs has changed frequently. Congress seems to want to use the IRA as both a carrot and stick. Usually, Congress does not make the changes retroactive, but still it is confusing when one year the money is deductible and the next year it isn't unless you satisfy various criteria.

❖ The savings are locked up. If you withdraw the money from the IRA (other than to roll it into another IRA) before you are 59½ the earnings on money and any contributions you deducted from income tax will be taxed at ordinary income tax rates plus a 10% penalty. If you have become disabled or died, you or your estate or survivors may also withdraw the money without the 10% penalty. Otherwise, the only way to avoid the 10% penalty is to take the money out in equal payments over the course of your expected lifetime. However, from a retirement security point of view, this "lockup" is not a disadvantage; it's an advantage. Retirement savings should be used at retirement, not before. If the very worst happens—you become disabled or you die leaving a family dependent on you—the money is there for support without the penalty tax. So these seeming disadvantages really become advantages.

Depending on the amounts you save and the age of your children, IRAs might even be a potential source of college tuition. You can begin to take the money out without the 10% penalty over the course of your lifetime. But this should be a desperation measure only. The best gift you can give your child is a financially independent parent in your old age. It's the best gift you can give yourself, too.

❖ IRAs cannot be borrowed against or otherwise used to secure loans. Unlike an ordinary savings account or brokerage account which may serve as collateral for a short-term loan or other borrowings, IRAs may never be used as security. If you do, the amount will be treated as though it was distributed, and you will owe income and penalty taxes.

ANNUITIES—YOUR HOME-GROWN PENSION

Individual annuities are investments designed to pay out over your lifetime, much like creating your own pension plan. Basically, you and an insurance company enter into a contract in which you invest an after-tax amount of money, generally at least $5,000, to earn a stated rate of interest over the contract period. When the contract expires, usually timed to coincide with your retirement, you begin to receive a payback from the annuity.

The earnings on the amount you originally invested, frequently referred to as *inside buildup*, are not subject to taxes until you begin to receive payments from the annuity. The portion of the money you originally invested, referred to as your *basis in the contract*, is not subject to tax at all, if you have already paid taxes on it.

Usually, there are no direct commissions charged for annuities, because commissions are built into the plan's cost. The annuity issuer may impose substantial early withdrawal penalties should you wish to get your money out of the investment before the end of the contract. You will also face the 10% early withdrawal penalty tax if you receive the money before you are age 59½ in a form other than a periodic stream over the course of your expected lifetime. The penalty will not apply if you become disabled and begin to withdraw the money.

Variations in Annuities

This is the basic outline of annuities, but there are many variations. Each insurance company selling annuities has several different plans and several variations in each plan, for example,

- ❖ You may be able to add to the investment each year.
- ❖ The interest rate may be changed each year.
- ❖ The interest rate may be tied to a stock or bond index.

Variable annuities, sold by insurance companies, mutual funds, and others, permit you to invest money in mutual funds and usually permit you to choose and move in and out of various mutual funds in the "family" of funds covered by your annuity. In the early 1990s, Equitable, Prudential, and Merrill Lynch were among the biggest variable annuity sellers. The basic advantage of a variable annuity is that your investment in mutual funds is allowed to grow without current taxes on the earnings in the mutual funds. As with any other annuity investment earnings, tax is not paid until you begin to withdraw the money.

Receiving the Payout from Annuities

Once the contract has reached the payback date, you may be able to choose a number of ways to begin receiving the money. The traditional form of payment under an annuity is—no surprise—*annuitizing*, which guarantees equal periodic payments over the course of your life. Under such a payment plan, you receive a fixed amount as long as you live, just as you do with an employer-provided pension. If you die a short time after payments begin, the insurance company pockets the money. But if you exceed your life expectancy, the insurance company must keep paying you as long as you live, even if the original investment and earnings have been exhausted.

But there are many other ways to receive payment, including variations on the annuitizing method. For example, you may elect a *joint and survivor annuity* which will reduce your monthly payments, but will pay out as long as you or your named beneficiary is alive. After the death of both you and the beneficiary, no further payments will be made, and any remaining amount is kept by the insurance company.

Another form of annuity payment is the *life-with-years-certain annuity*. This form of payment guarantees you a lifetime income, but also permits you to elect payments for a certain period, even if you die prior to the expiration of that period. For example, you could elect a *life-with-10-years-certain payout*. As long as you are alive, you will receive the established payment, but if you die before 10 years have passed, your estate or a beneficiary would collect payments for the remaining portion of the 10-year period.

Some annuities promise a higher interest rate on your investment but limit you to receiving the money only in the traditional annuity form. Some companies will allow you to take payout under a schedule you set up. This plan of withdrawal is usually referred to as the *systematic withdrawal plan*. With this approach, you can raise, lower, or stop the payments whenever you wish. You could also switch the remaining sum of money into an annuitized form of payment. But under this form of payment, you lose the guarantee of lifetime payments. In most cases, you will also pay tax on all the payments each month until the earnings on your investment are considered to have been exhausted.

You may also take your payment in a lump sum and invest it in some other investment vehicle. Some investment advisers suggest shopping again for an annuity at retirement with the lump sum from your original annuity. You may be able to receive a higher rate of return with a new company, thus increasing the monthly payment you begin to receive.

Safety of Annuities in the 1990s

For years, annuities were considered to be among the safest of investments. Experts viewed them as highly appropriate for conservative investors, especially those age 50 and over who did not mind having their investment locked up until retirement. The collapse of the Baldwin Company, a big seller of individual annuities in the early 1980s, began to change that view. The piano manufacturing company had become infected with takeover mania and diversified into many areas, including insurance companies selling annuities to individuals. Baldwin's fall should have reminded investors and investment counselors that annuities are only as good as the company offering them. But as late as December 1990, the Pension Benefit Guaranty Corporation, charged by the government to insure the safety of employer benefit plans, was stating there was no known case of an annuity purchased by an employer failing to fulfill its payment promises. (This was technically true—Baldwin apparently had no employer-purchased annuities.) Less than six months after PBGC's assertion, Executive Life Insurance in California and Mutual Benefit Insurance in New Jersey all but collapsed, leaving annuityholders, among other debtors, in doubt as to whether they would ever see all their money.

Even if you choose a company that is sound, problems can arise because in most states, an insurance company may sell your annuity contract to another company which is less sound. Theoretically, this should not happen without your knowledge and consent. Annuities are, after all, contracts between you and the company and one party to a contract cannot assign the contract's performance to a new entity without consent of the parties to the original contract. This practice of selling annuities to other companies is sometimes referred to as *assumption reinsurance* and is increasing, according to state insurance officials.[2] At this point there appears to be little defense against such resales other than to watch your statements and your mail closely. If you receive notice of an impending sale, contact the original annuity insurer immediately and withhold your consent until you can review the status of the purchasing company. It may not be all bad news. There is a chance that the purchasing company is more sound than the original company.

The moral of the story: *You should carefully and slowly investigate any annuity and its offering insurance company.* Use an independent insurance broker, not an insurance company agent, to evaluate both the companies and various annuities. If you use an agent who represents only one company, she can only offer you the annuities her company sells, which may not have the highest rates or all the features that are available.

Insurance companies are regulated by the states. Investigate what the state regulatory agency says about the company. But don't rely on state agencies. A few months before the collapse of Executive Life, the state of California was still rating the company positively. Go to a library and look at insurance company rating services such as A. M. Best, Standard & Poor's, or Moody's. You might also consult *Annuity & Life Insurance Shopper* (800-872-6684), a bimonthly newsletter that publishes rates of annuities.

Be particularly wary of any annuity which offers greatly higher interest rates. This can be a sign of a company desperately needing your money to keep the wolf from its door. If the annuity is one which guarantees the interest rate for only one year, ask what rate the same type of annuity purchased in the previous year paid then and is paying this year. Ask what rates for the company's similar annuities have been over the last 5 years. This will give you at least an idea of whether the company lures customers in with high rates and then drops the rates drastically in the future years.

Advantages of Annuities

❖ In spite of the bad publicity of the early 1990s, most annuities are safe and can provide a steady income at retirement.

❖ Annuities don't need to be "managed"; the investment return can be totally controlled by the insurance company.

❖ If you choose an annuity that permits periodic payments, you will be encouraged to add to your savings because the "payment" seems like a bill which must be paid.

❖ Annuities can provide a guaranteed income for life, if you choose that option of payment at retirement.

Disadvantages of Annuities

❖ Your money is tied up in a specific investment. If the interest rate falls, your only recourse is to withdraw from the annuity and that involves substantial penalties in most cases. You will also have to pay tax on any money the annuity investment earned when you withdraw from the annuity.

❖ Your annuity is only as safe as the insurance company sponsoring it. If the company becomes insolvent, you may receive some minimum payments from state reinsurance funds, or you may receive nothing.

KEOGHS—RETIREMENT PLANS FOR THE SELF-EMPLOYED AND MOONLIGHTERS

If you are self-employed, work as a freelancer, or have your own business in addition to being employed by another, you may set up *a tax-deductible Keogh,* or H.R. 10, plan. The earnings from this plan's investments are tax deferred until you begin to withdraw them at retirement. Keoghs (named for Congressman Eugene Keogh who introduced H.R. 10, the legislation creating them) are designed to provide self-employed individuals, sole proprietorships, and partnerships with the same types of retirement plans corporate employers can establish, including the same tax advantages.

Who Can Contribute to a Keogh?

You are eligible to set up a Keogh if you are self-employed. This option is available even if you have a conventional job but derive additional income from self-employment. The IRS gives as an example an attorney who is employed by a corporation during the day but has her own law practice in the evening. However, full-time insurance salespeople, members of religious orders, or ministers are examples of "employees" who cannot set up Keoghs even though their earnings are deemed self-employment income for Social Security purposes. But such people may also be self-employed, in addition to being insurance salespeople or ministers.

For example, a minister may receive a regular salary from her congregation, which is treated as self-employed income for Social Security tax purposes. She may also be "self-employed" for fees reported on Schedule C for performing marriages, baptisms, and other personal services, and the fees for these services may be self-employment income for Keogh plan purposes.[3]

If you have other employees in your business, you will probably need to include them under the Keogh plan. Keoghs are subject to the same rules applied to other employer plans discussed in Chapter 7, so if your employees meet the age and service rules, you will need to include them in your plan.

How Your Employment Status Can Affect Your Keogh

Keoghs can be especially useful for women. During times when we are "out of work" officially, we may be working at home on various consulting projects. Keoghs offer a way to save for retirement even when you are off the payroll. For example, if you take a leave of absence, you may be able to convince your employer to engage you as a "consultant" with independent contractor status to finish up a project in progress or to help out with work overflows. From this self-employment income you can set up your Keogh. If you are shifting to part-time work for an employer in which you would not receive benefits or accrue retirement benefits or service credits, consider whether you could control your work enough to be classified as an *independent contractor* rather than as a part-time employee. You are then self-employed, and you can save in your own retirement plan rather than have no retirement savings growing. As we have seen, growing retirement savings amounts, even if small, can become significant sums over the years.

There are drawbacks to becoming an independent contractor, however. You will have to pay higher Social Security taxes as a self-employed person and be responsible for paying estimated income taxes. The employer cannot withhold for you. You may lose other benefits, such as health and life insurance if your employer provides these benefits to part-timers. Additionally, you really must be "independent" and control your own work performance, factors the IRS has not specifically defined. In determining independent contractor status, the IRS weighs a number of factors, such as setting your own hours, using your own equipment, working in your own premises, working for other clients, and being free to turn down assignments.

For example, suppose you are a graphic arts designer. Your employer's business slowdown makes it necessary to cut work hours. You and she agree you will go off the payroll but be available to do projects for her on an as-needed basis. You work at home, at hours you determine, using your own desktop publishing software. You pay your own expenses and hire any assistants you need without consulting your former employer. The IRS would probably agree you are a "self-employed" independent contractor. But if the same facts applied, except you are expected to be available to your employer every workday between 9 and 12 and you may not work for other clients, the IRS would almost certainly consider you to be an employee.

Setting Up the Keogh

You may set up a Keogh at any time during the tax year. As long as the plan is in place by the end of the tax year, you may contribute to it for that tax year until your tax return filing date, including extensions. In fact, if you choose a defined contribution plan (discussed in the next section), you probably will not be able to fund the Keogh fully until after your tax year closes, because your contribution must be based on net earnings. You generally won't know that figure until you calculate your year-end income and expenses. To maximize the growth of your money, you should be placing some money in the Keogh during the course of the year.

Should Your Keogh Be a Defined Benefit or Defined Contribution Plan? Keogh plans can be defined benefit or defined contribution plans, like corporate employer plans, discussed in Chapter 7. For example, if your Keogh is a defined contribution plan, your contributions are limited to the Section 415 limits, discussed in earlier chapters, of $30,000 or 25% of compensation, whichever is less. The $30,000 figure will be indexed for inflation in coming years.

Also, if you set up your defined contribution plan as a profit-sharing plan, your tax deduction is limited to 15% of compensation for employees, or 13.0435% of compensation for the self-employed. You may make a higher contribution of up to 25% if you set up a *money purchase pension* defined contribution plan, but that plan requires you to contribute a fixed percentage of compensation, regardless of profits. Of course, if you are the only person in the plan, the net income of the business is your compensation, so there is no problem. But if you have employees, the money purchase pension plan may pinch in lean business years.

If you set up a defined benefit plan, you will need an actuary to calculate the amount necessary to contribute to the plan. You must make payments to fund the benefit at least quarterly. The benefit you ultimately receive cannot be in excess of $90,000 adjusted for inflation ($115,641 in 1993) or 100% of compensation, whichever is less. When you retire, if the plan has been in existence for fewer than 10 years or if you retire before your Social Security retirement age, these limits will be "actuarially" reduced.

If you are lucky enough to be concerned about exceeding these contribution and benefit limits, you should recognize that while you are young, the defined contribution limit will permit you to make a greater contribution to your Keogh plan, all things being equal. After you reach middle age, you can probably contribute more money under a defined benefit plan, if you haven't had a defined contribution plan Keogh. If you have, the IRS will look at potential retirement benefits from the defined contribution plan and adjust the amounts you can contribute to the new defined benefit plan accordingly.

Whether a defined contribution plan or a defined benefit Keogh allows you to contribute more money depends on your age when you start contributing. Remember these are simply rules of the growth pattern of money. If you want $1 million at age 65, you can contribute less money each year if you start when you are 30 than you can if you start when you are 40.

The compensation for you as a "self-employed" plan participant is your "net earned income" from the business, minus the deduction allowed for self-employment taxes *and* the deduction you take for your contribution to the Keogh. Compensation in excess of $200,000 (this figure is indexed each year; in 1993 it is $235,840) cannot be taken into account.

Complying with Keogh Requirements. Keoghs must be a trusteed account with a formal, written plan document which incorporates much of the language required in other employer-provided retirement plans. There are many *master plans* or *prototype plans* approved by the IRS and offered without additional charge by banks, mutual funds, insurance companies, and brokerages when you set up a Keogh account. You may also buy annuities with your Keogh assets. If you buy annuities or certificates of deposit from an insurance company, the Keogh does not need a trustee.

You could also have a lawyer draw up your own Keogh plan document, but there is no significant advantage to such an individualized document. And there would be significant expense involved. You would be wiser to use that money for retirement savings and use an "off-the-shelf plan" from the institution where you invest your Keogh.

Which organization you use to hold your Keogh assets depends on the investments you want. If you simply want certificates of deposit, use a bank or thrift. If you want only mutual funds, deal directly with the mutual fund. If you have enough money in your Keogh to diversify investments, a brokerage house makes sense. The broker can purchase stocks and bonds for you, as well as CDs and mutual funds.

Keogh plan assets may not be invested, loaned, or otherwise used for the benefit of any corporation, partnership, or business which is more than 50% owned by you, members of your family, or any fiduciary of the Keogh. If you do, you have engaged in a "prohibited transaction" and must pay a tax of 5% of the value involved in the prohibited transaction. This amount increases to 100% if the "prohibited transaction" is not corrected after the IRS notifies you of the problem.

Keoghs have not been extremely popular among the self-employed, in part because of their complex rules. Also, like other employer-provided plans, Keoghs must file annual reports with the IRS on Form 5500. For single-employee plans, the IRS made available the Form 5500EZ, which requires minimal information and is easy to complete. In the past few years, the IRS has announced that Keoghs with less than $100,000 in assets can omit filing even the Form 5500EZ except upon termination of the plan. The absence of a filing requirement should encourage more eligible parties to set up the accounts.

Advantages of Keoghs

❖ Keoghs are the primary way for self-employed individuals to save substantial retirement benefits in a tax-sheltered plan. The $2,000 permitted to an IRA contribution is simply not adequate to build a substantial retirement savings account.

❖ Keoghs are easy to set up and require little reporting until your account contains substantial assets.

❖ Keoghs can offer a way to keep investing for retirement even when you are officially off the payroll, if you earn money freelancing in your profession.

Disadvantages of Keoghs

❖ The Keogh contribution can be difficult to calculate. IRS Publication 560, "Retirement Plans for the Self-Employed," will give you instructions.

❖ Unless the Keogh is a profit-sharing plan (i.e., if it is a money purchase plan or a defined benefit plan), you must fund it each year or terminate the plan. Because the plan must be intended to be permanent, the IRS will look with disfavor on plans that are terminated after a few years. Of course, since the funding is usually based on your income, the contribution will coincide with the income, except in a defined benefit plan.

❖ If you have other employees, you will need to include most of them in the Keogh.

SIMPLIFIED EMPLOYEE PENSION PLANS

SEPs can also be used as an individual retirement account, a so-called SEP IRA. The same rules apply for these individual SEPs as for employer-provided SEPs discussed in Chapter 7. Recognize that if you set up a SEP for yourself and you later acquire employees, these employees will most likely have to be covered by the SEP as well—and the benefits will be vested immediately.

For all practical purposes, SEPs are subject to the deduction limitation of 13.0435% of your self-employed net earnings and 15% of employees' compensation. In theory you can contribute up to the defined contribution limit to the SEP and carry over used deductions into the next year. In reality, if you do, you may face a 10% excess tax for excess contributions. So it is unlikely you will want to contribute more than the deduction limit.

UNIVERSAL LIFE INSURANCE

Universal life insurance is *not* an ideal retirement savings vehicle, but if you are a single mother on a limited budget, for example, it may be the best vehicle you can afford. Universal life insurance can provide life insurance to protect your dependents and build future value for retirement. The policy uses your premium payment to cover both life insurance, which would provide money to your children if you die, and to cover an investment, giving you a cash value in the policy. The premiums can be divided to purchase different amounts of life insurance and investments, and the premiums can be varied. In the first years of the policy while the children are small and so is your salary, you might want most of the premium to go to insurance. As the children grow up, the premium can move more to the investment side of the policy.

The changes in divisions of the premium might be more up and down. For example, suppose you get a job providing you with twice your salary in life insurance, at no cost to you, and permits you to buy even more life insurance cheaply, if you wish. You can shift most of the premium in your universal life policy to the investment side. Six years later you move to a job without that benefit and the children have just started college. It's time to move more of the premium back to the life insurance side of the policy.

Policies will vary from company to company, so be sure you understand the exact operation of any policy you buy. As always, working with an independent agent should give you the best range of options.

Advantages of Universal Life Insurance

- ❖ If you have dependents, it enables you to buy life insurance to provide for those dependents and produce some savings as well.

- ❖ The premiums are a "bill" which is likely to be paid even in financially tight months when savings deposits would not be made.

❖ The earnings on the invested portion of your premium are not taxed until you withdraw the money.

Disadvantages of Universal Life Insurance

❖ The return on your investment is quite low compared with other returns you could be receiving on the money.

❖ Your "investment" is locked up.

❖ If you don't have dependents, you don't need the life insurance.

DISABILITY INSURANCE

Disability insurance is not usually thought of as part of "retirement" planning. But if you become permanently disabled, you are retired—and without the ability to have planned for retirement. Most likely in this situation, you also lack the years of private savings and accruals of employer retirement benefits you had counted on.

Disability insurance should be one of the most important parts of your financial planning, indeed, the number one priority after a roof over your head and a job. Most individuals need more disability insurance than that provided either through an employer plan or Social Security.

Disability benefits are usually divided into short-term disability, in which there is the expectation you will recover and work again, and long-term disability, under which you are presumed to be incapable of ever rejoining the work force. Disability claims and benefits are also divided into work related and nonwork related.

If your disability is directly work related, you may be covered by worker's compensation. Every state has laws requiring worker's compensation benefits. These laws vary widely from state to state. If you have questions about worker's compensation, you should talk with a local expert. Begin with the state office in charge of worker's compensation enforcement. If the disability is nonwork related, you will not be covered unless you have some form of disability insurance. This discussion focuses on nonwork related, long-term disability.

Qualifying for Social Security Disability Benefits

Social Security may provide some disability benefits. But the qualifications for receiving the payments are rigorous. Social Security disability payments are subject to several requirements:

❖ You must prove you cannot work at any job.

❖ You must prove you are unable to perform any gainful employment, not just being unable to conduct your usual employment. And your impairment must be expected to last at least 12 months.

Social Security has also tightened disability standards, more to help with the federal deficit and the growing Social Security debt than because of any showing of disability fraud.

There is a 5-month wait. You will not receive benefits for the 5-month waiting period. You can expect the Social Security review to take a number of months, but you will be paid retroactively for Social Security's delay in processing your case.

You must have the minimum work history. You must have been covered by Social Security for 40 quarters—10 years—to be eligible for disability benefits. If you were born before 1929, you need fewer quarters. Obviously, if you are just starting out in the job market, you will receive nothing under Social Security if you become disabled. Also, some of those quarters must have been earned recently. That number depends on your age. If you were born between 1948 and 1959, you must have earned 20 quarters in the last 10 years. If you were born after 1960, you must have earned 6 quarters in the last 3 years.

For example, Janet's first job was with a state agency where she worked from 1967 to 1971. She then went to work for the Congress and worked there until 1980. Neither of those jobs was covered by Social Security in those years. She left to have a baby, and in 1982 she went to work for a law firm. In 1985 she took a leave of absence to work as a campaign volunteer and returned in 1986. In 1992 she still does not qualify for Social Security disability or survivors coverage for her dependents because she has only 36 quarters of Social Security coverage from her 9 years at the law firm. After a career spanning 25 years, she still does not qualify for disability coverage under Social Security.

Most jobs, including state and local government positions, are now covered by Social Security, so Janet's situation is extreme. But for those who are not yet qualified, disability insurance becomes even more important.

Social Security disability benefits will be reduced if you are receiving worker's compensation or other disability benefits. Total disability benefits may not exceed 80% of your predisability compensation.

How to Obtain Employer-Provided Disability Insurance

Your employer may provide some disability insurance or may give you the opportunity to purchase such insurance. Only 45% of employees employed by companies with more than 100 workers had disability insurance in 1988.[4] Small employers are even less likely to provide such benefits. If the employer does provide disability insurance, purchase as much as you can. Ideally, you would buy enough to cover your current salary if you become disabled. Usually, if you are disabled, you will need more money to live, not less. Services you once performed for yourself will now need to be done by others who must be paid. However, many policies limit the amount they will pay to a percentage of your compensation before disability. Policies may also offset their payments by disability benefits from other sources such as Social Security, worker's compensation, or your own privately purchased insurance. Check these features carefully. Also check whether benefits cease if you earn a limited income under a new profession. You don't want to be punished for becoming rehabilitated and working at a lower-paid job.

Purchasing Disability Insurance Privately

If you are self-employed or your employer does not provide disability insurance, purchase it on your own. If you belong to a trade association, such as the American Bar Association or a local chamber of commerce, you may be able to purchase a policy through their group at a lower rate. It may be worthwhile to join an organization just to get the group rates for the disability insurance.

Investigate several policies. Ask about the same features we discussed with employer-provided insurance, but be even more alert:

- ❖ What type of disability is covered?
- ❖ Must you be totally disabled from all gainful employment or only from your usual occupation?
- ❖ Who decides—one doctor, a team of doctors?
- ❖ Is there an appeals procedure?

❖ Do they use the Social Security standard? Beware of policies which do because of Social Security's tight standards.

❖ How long must you be disabled before payments begin? One way to reduce the cost of disability insurance is to buy a policy which delays payment for six months or a year after disability. If you have savings that could support you for a time, think of buying this type of policy.

❖ How long will benefits last?

❖ Do you have to submit to periodic examinations?

Weigh the answers to each of these questions carefully. Don't just decide based on price.

LONG-TERM CARE INSURANCE

Long-term care insurance—coverage for nursing home or in-home "custodial" care—is another item you might not ordinarily include in retirement planning. Certainly long-term care insurance is nowhere nearly as important as disability insurance, and, unlike other forms of disability and health insurance, it is relatively new.

Long-term care insurance policies should not be one of the elements of your retirement planning if you are under 40 or if you have limited savings. Unless you have extraordinary medical conditions or histories, such insurance should be a part of your retirement assets only after you have invested close to your maximum savings in other retirement programs. But you might also consider the purchase of long-term care insurance for an elderly parent for whom you have responsibility. Even if you are not paying for the policy, your parent may wish to consult with you on the purchase of the policy.

Long-term health insurance pays for custodial care if you are incapacitated by an illness or accident, or if age simply makes it impossible for you to care for yourself. Medicare and most other health insurance programs do not pay for "custodial" care which merely helps with your ordinary living activities and does not purport to "treat" an illness.

Some employers are beginning to offer long-term care policies covering the employee and her spouse and, in some cases, even the parents and parents-in-law of the employee. Such policies require contributions by the employees. The older the age of the policy beneficiary, the higher the premium.

Individual long-term care policies are also available. Insurance companies have been wary of offering such policies because of the many uncertainties involved, including the period of years in which the need could arise and over which it could last and the rapid changes in medical technology. Many reputable companies are now offering long-term care policies and revising them frequently based on the company's experience. Nevertheless, caution must be your watch word as you look at such policies.

The National Association of Insurance Commissioners has produced a *Shopper's Guide to Long-Term Care Insurance,* which includes a policy comparison checklist as well as a number of recommendations.[5] NAIC notes that most states have a "free look" period after you purchase the policy during which you may cancel the policy.

Questions you should specifically ask include:

❖ What is the nature of the benefit—a fixed dollar sum or a percentage of costs? Is there any inflation protection?

❖ How long will care last?

❖ Is there a day per year maximum?

❖ Can premiums be raised once care begins?

❖ Can the policy be canceled? Why, when, for what reasons?

❖ Can the care be delivered at home or only in an institution?

❖ Is Alzheimer's disease covered?

❖ Are other types of mental impairments covered?

❖ Is there a requirement that you first be hospitalized before you can begin receiving long-term care? Frequently, patients don't require hospitalization before requiring custodial care. You don't want to be forced to be hospitalized as prerequisite to beginning long-term care.

❖ What is the "trigger" for the policy? Inability to complete basic tasks such as dressing, eating? How many such tasks?

❖ Who decides whether these criteria have been met?

❖ What is the level of care? It should be skilled, intermediate, and custodial. Custodial care covers basic needs such as feeding, dressing, and so on. Skilled care involves the services of a licensed medical professional. Intermediate care is the "day care" approach requiring some care everyday, but not round-the-clock service.

In addition to these questions, be certain you are dealing with a reputable and financially stable company. The chances are you will not begin to collect on your long-term insurance for decades. You want to be certain the insurer will still be there when you do need your benefits. As with investigating insurance companies for annuities, look to the independent insurance rating services such as Best or Standard & Poor's. Consult with the state insurance regulatory agency in your state as well.

HOME OWNERSHIP AS A RETIREMENT INVESTMENT

At one time any self-respecting book on financial planning—especially one on retirement financial planning—would have started with the advice to buy the most expensive house you can afford and let it be the primary source of your "savings" in your early work years. Such books would have told you that the first priority after feeding yourself should be a home purchase. Today no less an authority than the National Association of Realtors recommends you purchase a house for shelter, not for investment, according to Linda Goold, the Realtor's director of federal tax programs.

Depending on where you live, buying a home may be risky business. Starting in Texas in the early 1980s, we saw the old "buy a big house" advice go very wrong. People bought houses and a year or two later their value had declined 50% to 75%—if they could sell the house at all. Jobs were lost, mortgage payments were missed, and people with previously sound financial records simply walked away from their mortgage and their home, not to mention the savings they had invested in their home. In the early 1990s the same scenario was played out on the East and West coasts. Women in Los Angeles, Boston, New York, and Washington, D.C., saw their life savings eroded as the overheated value of their homes melted down. If these women also had the misfortune to lose their jobs, their financial security melted, too.

If the same woman had invested in an IRA or 401(k) plan, instead of a house, even if she had lost her job, there would have been no big mortgage payments. As a last resort, she could have used her retirement savings to live on until she found another job. Granted one still has living expenses even without mortgage payments, but it is much easier to break the lease on a three-bedroom apartment and move into an efficiency than it is to sell a three-bedroom house.

Moreover, at retirement you may find yourself house poor. A large portion of your net worth is tied up in your home, and the market may or may not be good. You may find the steady investment in upkeep eating away at your retirement savings. You may want to move to a different locale, or you may be tired of gardening and want a smaller yard and less house to heat, cool, and paint.

Buying a home still can be a wise financial move. You have to live somewhere, and you might as well be paying yourself rent. You also get a tax deduction for the interest you are paying on your mortgage. But ignore any advice to invest all your savings in the down payment and "stretch" to buy a house a bit more expensive than you can afford on the theory that inflation will increase your income, and in two or three years you can easily afford the mortgage payments that first seemed gargantuan.

In considering buying a house—especially in a high real estate market—do your financial calculations on a "worst case scenario" considering the cost of the house, the closing costs, the interest rate, and the monthly payments. After the down payment, closing costs, and incidentals, will you still have enough money to pay the mortgage payments for six months if you lose your job? Will you still be able to save at least enough to fund your employer-provided 401(k) or contribute the maximum to your IRA next year?

If the answers aren't "yes," think long and hard—and very realistically—about whether your job or business is likely to be secure two years from now. Look at the housing market in your area. Has it been stable for the last decade? Has it increased dramatically? How does it compare with the rest of the country? Some of this will be guessing. If you have evidence to suggest your job is safe and the housing market in your area has been stable or is just beginning to climb, you may want to make the investment in a home even if it will deplete your savings.

Remember that homes priced at the lower end of the scale have better resale potential in any kind of market. Although a three-bedroom, two-bath house near a good school may be more modest than the five-bedroom spread with master bath and jacuzzi that you really want, the smaller house may be the better investment. As a bonus, you may find when you retire it is the home you really want to live in instead of a five-bedroom white elephant eating all your retirement income in lawn service fees and new roofs.

CONCLUSION: RECOGNIZE THE IMPORTANCE OF PERSONAL SAVINGS—AND START SAVING *NOW*

You are the single most important source of your retirement savings. It is the source you can control and plan for. Recognizing the importance of your own retirement savings now and taking steps to begin building those savings—no matter how small at the start—is the single most important thing you can do for your retirement planning. Here's a recap of recommendations for your individual retirement plan:

❖ Begin a regular savings program with an eye toward retirement; don't worry if it seems small.

❖ Open an IRA and put as much money as you can afford into it up to the $2,000 limit. Start with a certificate of deposit, if you feel uncomfortable with mutual funds or stocks, but an equity or balanced mutual fund is probably the best investment for growth.

❖ Find out whether you have disability insurance through your employer; if your employer offers disability insurance but doesn't pay for it, buy it; if you don't have access to it at work, buy it on your own.

❖ If you are self-employed, set up a Keogh or SEP even if the initial contribution must be small.

Let's move on to see what you can expect from Social Security and Medicare for retirement security.

NOTES FOR CHAPTER 8

1. All these examples are based on IRS Publication 590, "Individual Retirement Arrangements," and are correct as of 1992, but Congress could change the law or IRS could change its interpretations at any time. This booklet is available from IRS for free by calling 1-800-Tax-Form.

2. Albert B. Crenshaw, "Policyholders, Beware: Insurers May Sell Contracts to Other, Less Sound Firms," *Washington Post*, May 10, 1992, p. H3.

3. IRS Publication 560, "Retirement Plans for the Self-Employed."

4. U.S. Bureau of the Census, *Statistical Abstract of the United States: 1991*, 111th edition (Washington, D.C.: U.S. Government Printing Office, 1991), Table 686.

5. A free copy can be obtained from the National Association of Insurance Commissioners by writing them at: 120 W. 12th Street, Suite 1100, Kansas City, Missouri 64105.

CHAPTER NINE

GOVERNMENT-SUPPLIED RETIREMENT BENEFITS– SOCIAL SECURITY AND MEDICARE

Alice will have Social Security to bolster her retirement income when she retires in 5 years. As a 60-year-old worker earning almost $37,000 annually, Alice has enjoyed slightly above-average earnings over her career. She can expect her Social Security benefits to equal about 35% of her earnings. Coupled with her expected employer-provided retirement benefit of 12% of final earnings, she will have less than half of her previous income for retirement. *Unfortunately, an annual income of less than half of Alice's final earnings today is not likely to be sufficient for her to live on for the next 25 years or so without her own personal savings or assets.* Nevertheless, Social Security and Medicare will provide significant—if not sufficient—benefits in retirement. Let's look at what you can expect from these government-provided benefits and how these benefits will be calculated. We will also see the inequities in the Social Security system for two-earner families.

Since 1935 when Social Security was first enacted, its administrators have warned that its payments to an individual are not sufficient for retirement security and should only be looked upon as a *supplement* to private sources of income. But a majority of Americans continue to ignore Franklin Delano Roosevelt's newsreel advice offered at the bill signing that Social Security is only a cushion against poverty. *Indeed 60% or more of Social Security recipients rely on those Social Security benefits for 50% or more of their retirement income.* In the 1990s Social Security payments will provide about 59% of preretirement earnings to those earning 50% of average U.S. wages, 44% of preretirement earnings for those earning an average income, and 24% for those who had earnings at or over the maximum Social Security taxable wage base.

The Social Security Administration's chart (Table 9.1) shows the approximate amount you can expect from your Social Security in today's dollars and under today's law. Because these figures are given in today's dollars, they give you a better idea of what your ultimate Social Security benefit will be like. If you earn $40,000 now, you take home about $2,500 per month, if you are single. Think about what you could buy in today's dollars with a monthly benefit of $1,263. That amount does not cover much today, and it probably won't cover much 26 years from now when you reach your normal Social Security retirement age, even though it will have been adjusted for inflation. These figures also assume there will be no changes in Social Security to reduce the proportion of earned income replaced by Social Security benefits, an assumption that is questionable at best.

By design Social Security replaces a greater percentage of income for lower-paid employees than higher paid, in part because lower-paid workers pay a higher percentage of their income in Social Security taxes than do those workers whose pay exceeds the maximum taxable Social Security wage base and in part because of the social goal of supporting those whose lower income during working years made it more difficult for them to save individually. Table 9.2 gives a history of the wage replacement ratios for Social Security. For example, 1980 was the peak year for workers with low or average earnings. Social Security paid 63% of final pay to workers who earned less than 50% of the national average (i.e., "low earnings") and 47% of final pay to workers earning average wages. Since then, Social Security benefits have tapered somewhat.

		Your Earnings in 1990				
Age	**Benefits Recipient**	**$20,000**	**$30,000**	**$40,000**	**$50,000**	**$51,300 or More**
45	You	$ 863	$1,124	$1,263	$1,392	$1,422
	You and spouse	1,294	1,686	1,894	2,088	2,133
55	You	783	1,014	1,106	1,181	1,195
	You and spouse	1,174	1,521	1,659	1,771	1,792
65	You	725	926	982	1,021	1,022
	You and spouse	1,087	1,389	1,473	1,531	1,533

**TABLE 9.1
Approximate Monthly Benefits at Normal Retirement Age with Steady Lifetime Earnings Based on 1990 Earnings***

*These figures assume that your spouse is the same age as you. Actual figures will depend on your actual pattern of past and future earnings.

Source: Social Security Administration, "Retirement," SSA Publication No. 05-10035, January 1991, p. 5.

A BRIEF HISTORY OF SOCIAL SECURITY

When first adopted, Social Security covered only employees in industry and commerce, about 60% of workers. Over the years it has expanded coverage to include the self-employed, many state and local government workers, federal workers hired after 1983, and employees of nonprofit organizations. Today approximately 95% of all employees are covered by Social Security.

Social Security was designed to be a self-supporting federal program, financed with payroll taxes and providing not just retirement income, but a host of other insurance programs for workers. In addition

	TABLE 9.2 Ratios of Social Security Benefits to Final Pay, 1955–1992		
Year	Low Earnings*	Average Earnings†	Maximum Earnings‡
1955	52%	35%	33%
1960	49	33	30
1965	46	31	33
1970	48	34	29
1975	60	40	29
1980	63	47	30
1985	61	41	23
1990	58	43	24
1992	59	44	24

*Low earnings are defined as 50% of the national average wage.
†Average earnings are defined as the national average wage.
‡Maximum earnings are those at the top of the Social Security wage base.

to retirement payments to workers and spouses, Social Security benefits include:

❖ Disability benefits for workers and families

❖ Survivor benefits to families of workers

❖ Medicare hospital insurance for retirees, their spouses, and disabled persons receiving Social Security (Medicare Part A)

❖ Supplemental Medical Insurance covering doctors, outpatient treatments, and other treatments for retirees, their spouses, and disabled persons receiving Social Security (Medicare Part B)

These benefits are financed by a payroll tax called the Federal Insurance Contribution Act (FICA), tax paid by you and your employer, or the Self-Employed Contribution Act (SECA) tax, paid only by you if you are self-employed. The "Social Security taxable wage base" subject to these taxes has grown steadily over the years from the original $3,000 wage base to a 1993 wage base of $57,600 for the Old Age, Survivors and Disability Insurance (OASDI) portion and a wage base of $135,000 for the Medicare hospitalization insurance (HI) portion. These wage bases are adjusted annually based on the increases in average wages in the country.

The original maximum employee tax of $30 per year has also increased dramatically. The employer/employee tax rate is 6.2% for the OASDI portion and 1.45% for the HI portion. That amount is paid by both the employee and the employer, resulting in an overall FICA tax of 15.3%. The self-employed tax is also 15.3%: 12.4% for OASDI and 3.9% for HI. *In 1993, the maximum Social Security tax was $5,528.70 for an employee and $11,057.40 for a self-employed person.* Not surprisingly, given this amount of money coming out of the worker's and the employer's pockets, Social Security has come under increasingly dissatisfied attention over the years.

Although Social Security was designed to be a self-supporting program and has largely succeeded in that goal, it has never developed the "trust fund" to draw on for future years which was once anticipated. In the early 1980s policy makers feared the Social Security system would become bankrupt. In 1983, the system was changed significantly to help create a trust fund for the age wave of baby boomers expected to retire after 2020. Currently, the Social Security system's soundness depends on the actuarial and demographic assumptions used. According to the Social Security Board of Trustees' Report in 1990, under one scenario the system continues to be secure beyond 2065; however, under other of the trustees' scenarios, the system will be exhausted in 2028, 2046, or 2060.[1] But their 1991 report was less optimistic, chiefly because of the recession. Under their most realistic scenario, the fund will be running a deficit by 2017.[2]

Because of the changes made to create the "trust fund" for the age wave, Social Security has generated significant surpluses of income over paid-out benefits in the 1980s and 1990s. But this surplus has not been placed in a trust fund. It has been spent by the federal government. The funds from Social Security have played an important role in obscuring how truly large the federal deficit has become because Social Security receipts have been counted into the budget figures. Without the Social Security excess, the deficit would be even larger and require even more federal borrowing. For example, in 1991, if the income from Social Security taxes in excess of the Social Security benefits paid had been properly trusteed and not counted as part of federal revenues, the federal deficit would have been over $320 billion. By counting the Social Security excess as ordinary federal income, the budget deficit was reported as about $270 billion.

The Medicare system is projected to have severe financial problems beginning before the year 2000, according to the Social Security Trustees.[3] Table 9.3 shows the most realistic scenario of the Social Security Trustees. According to the Trustees, figures in Table 9.3, by the time Bonnie, our 40-year-old retires, Social Security will be broke!

TABLE 9.3 Projected Social Security and Medicare Budget Deficits and Surpluses (Social Security Tax Income Less Outgo), 1991–2060			
(in billions)			
Year	OASDI*	HI†	Total
1991	$ 34.7	$ 7.5	$ 42.2
1995	48.3	-2.9	45.4
2000	73.6	-27.7	45.9
2005	101.0	-63.6	37.4
2010	109.0	-128.4	-19.4
2020	-127.4	-429.5	-556.8
2030	-667.8	-1,064.3	-1,732.1
2040	-1,201.2	-2,037.0	-3,238.3
2050	-2,065.1	-3,481.5	-5,546.7
2060	-4,090.8	-6,096.8	-10,187.6

*Old Age, Survivors, and Disability Insurance portion of Social Security.
†Hospital insurance portion of Medicare.

Source: Annual Report of the Social Security Trustees.

The Social Security program has already changed in major ways which are only now being felt. Part of the changes involved adopting the expanded and indexed wage base and higher rates we have now. Another important change was in the increase in retirement age at which full Social Security benefits would be paid. While the increase is gradual and relatively small, it represented a major change in Social Security philosophy. The age 65 retirement limit for full benefits had not been changed since adoption of the Social Security Act in 1935, even though life expectancy for a 65-year-old then was only another 2 years while today the life expectancy of a 65-year-old is another 19 years for females and 15 years for males. In 1935 when Social Security was enacted, most males never reached age 65!

WHEN YOU CAN RECEIVE FULL SOCIAL SECURITY BENEFITS

Today full benefits still begin at age 65 and reduced benefits are available at 62 for those born before 1938. Alice can still retire with full benefits. But Susan, Bonnie, and Jennifer will be under a new schedule to receive full benefits at their "normal retirement age." Table 9.4 illustrates those born between 1938 and 1943 will have to add 2 months to age 65 for every year born after 1937 before they can retire with full benefits. Susan will have to be age 65 and 10 months for full benefits to begin.

TABLE 9.4 Age to Receive Full Social Security Retirement Benefits	
Year of Birth	Normal Age to Retire
1937 and prior	65
1938	65 and 2 months
1939	65 and 4 months
1940	65 and 6 months
1941	65 and 8 months
1942	65 and 10 months
1943–1954	66
1955	66 and 2 months
1956	66 and 4 months
1957	66 and 6 months
1958	66 and 8 months
1959	66 and 10 months
1960 and later	67

If you were born between 1943 and 1954, you must reach age 66 to receive full benefits. Bonnie will fit in this group. Those born between 1955 and 1960 again begin the 2-month addition for each year born after 1954. Those born after 1960 will not receive full benefits until age 67. Jennifer will fit this age group.

Employers have not adjusted their retirement plans to conform with these new Social Security normal retirement ages, in part because ERISA prohibits retirement plans from withholding benefits after the participant reaches age 65. There has been no apparent movement among employers to amend ERISA to achieve a consistency between the two retirement ages. This is probably because many large employers remain eager to ease older workers out of their work force.

If You Retire Before Social Security Retirement Age

You can begin receiving Social Security benefits at age 62, regardless of your birth year; however, you will receive a permanently reduced benefit for the rest of your life. There is an actual reduction in your benefit made by the Social Security Administration ranging from 20% at age 62 for those born before 1939 to 30% at age 62 for those born after 1959. The reduction is correlated in part on the lengthened normal retirement age under the law and in part on your age when you retire. The benefit you would receive at your normal retirement age (under the new retirement schedule) will be reduced by five-ninths of 1% for each month between the time you actually retire and your normal retirement age. The closer to your "normal retirement age," the less the reduction.

Your Social Security benefit will also be reduced by early retirement because you will probably be earning less at age 62 than you would have if you had continued to work until normal retirement age. Your Social Security benefit will not reflect those higher years of pay you could have earned. For example, suppose Alice decides to retire at 63½. Her normal retirement age is 65, and she will be retiring 18 months before that age, so her benefit will be reduced by 18 times 5/9, or 10%. This reduction applies to workers. If you are considering receiving benefits as a spouse, a different reduction factor applies.

If You Retire After Normal Retirement Age

You may also permanently increase your benefit if you delay retirement past your normal retirement age. The Social Security Administration will increase the amount of the normal retirement benefit from 3.5% to as much as 8% per year, depending upon when you were born. The increase is to compensate for the years you did not receive Social Security. And you may also receive a higher benefit because your wages at retirement are higher, increasing the overall wage base for your benefit calculation.

Let's look at Alice. Suppose she decides to delay retirement to age 68. Alice was born in 1932, so her normal retirement age is 65 and her increase in benefits is 5% per year of delayed retirement. She is delaying retirement for 3 years, so her ultimate Social Security benefit will be increased by 15%.

From an actuarial viewpoint, delaying the payment of Social Security benefits past age 65 is usually thought to be an unwise financial move. *But for women, delaying retirement may be worth it.* This depends on a number of factors:

❖ If you haven't worked the maximum number of years for full Social Security credit when you reach normal retirement age, working a few more years will considerably raise your earnings base.

❖ If your salary during your last working years is high, this will also raise your earnings base.

❖ Also, remember women live longer than men and thus you are likely to be receiving benefits longer than the average man, even if you do delay receipt of Social Security benefits past age 65.

❖ Finally, Congress recognized that the small increase in Social Security benefits for delaying retirement was not a sufficient incentive, and as Table 9.5 shows, the incentive is being increased slowly over the years.

In the future retirees like Susan, Bonnie, and Jennifer will have more incentive to delay retirement.

HOW SOCIAL SECURITY BENEFITS ARE CALCULATED

Your benefits are calculated on your income and the number of quarter years during which you paid Social Security taxes. Let's walk through how the benefits are derived.

182 ❖ CHAPTER NINE

TABLE 9.5 Late Retirement Social Security Benefit Increase Factors	
Birth Year	Percentage Increase in Benefit per Year of Delay
Before 1924	3 %
1925–1926	3.5
1927–1928	4
1929–1930	4.5
1931–1932	5
1933–1934	5.5
1935–1936	6
1937–1938	6.5
1939–1940	7
1941–1942	7.5
After 1942	8

Source: Social Security Administration, "Retirement," SSA Publication No. 05–10035, January 1991, p. 9.

You may qualify for Social Security benefits as a wage earner or as a spouse of a wage earner, even if you are divorced, so long as you were married 10 years or more. If you have been married, you need to look at your Social Security qualification as both a wage earner and a spouse because, even though you have worked for many years and qualify on your own earnings, if your spouse's earnings are much higher than yours, you may be entitled to higher monthly Social Security benefits as a spouse. We will discuss how. Let's look at qualification and benefits as a wage earner first. Qualification as spouse will be discussed later in this chapter.

Qualifying for Social Security as a Wage Earner

To qualify for Social Security as a wage earner, you must have 40 quarters of coverage. (If you were born before 1929, you need fewer quarters, but by now you are probably receiving Social Security and you know that.) You must earn a minimum amount of wages in each year. In 1992 a quarter of coverage was granted for each $570 earned, so $2,280 earned in a year entitled you to 4 quarters of coverage. Prior to 1978 you had to earn a minimum amount each quarter, but now the law requires only an annual amount. This change is especially helpful to women who may have taken the summers off to be with the children and earned enough to meet the annual minimum for coverage, but did not meet the minimum earnings test for a particular quarter.

Calculating Your Average Indexed Monthly Earnings. Your benefit as a wage earner will be based on your average indexed monthly earnings (AIME). This is your lifetime earnings history. AIME will be based on the Social Security Administration's records of your earnings. You can get a copy of this record at any time. And you should do so. This record is called your "Earnings and Benefit Estimate Statement," and it can be requested by sending your name, address, and Social Security number and signing the request with a statement that you are requesting your own Social Security record. Send the request to:

> Social Security Administration
> Wilkes-Barre Data Operations Center
> P.O. Box 20
> Wilkes-Barre, PA 18711

There is also a Form SSA-7004 you can obtain to fill in this information and make a request. The form is shown in Exhibit 9.1 or you can call the Social Security Administration at 800-772-1213 between 7 A.M. and 7 P.M. EST and request the form as well as other information on Social Security. The information required is the same whether you use the form or send a letter. If you include your Social Security wages for last year, your estimate for this year and future estimates, and the age at which you expect to retire, the Social Security Administration will also calculate your estimated benefit. This information is free. A popular scam has been charging for the form to submit to the Social Security Administration or charging to complete the form and submit it. Don't pay for the form or for anyone submitting it for you.

Keep Track of Your AIME Throughout Your Career. You should send for your Earnings and Benefit Estimate Statement every 3 years to be certain the Social Security Administration has accurate information. You will receive the Personal Earnings and Benefit Estimate Statement, which lists a history of your Social Security earnings each year through your previous year's wages and gives you the current value

EXHIBIT 9.1

Social Security Form SSA-704
Request for Earnings and Benefits Estimate Statement

First Class Postage Required

SOCIAL SECURITY ADMINISTRATION
WILKES-BARRE DATA OPERATIONS CENTER
P.O. BOX 20
WILKES-BARRE, PA 18711-2030

SOCIAL SECURITY . . . It never stops working!

EXHIBIT 9.1
(cont'd)

SOCIAL SECURITY ADMINISTRATION

Request for Earnings and Benefit Estimate Statement

The Social Security program belongs to you and you can count on it to be there for you. Social Security can protect you in many ways. It can help support your family in the event of your death and provide monthly payments and health insurance when you retire or if you become disabled.

To help you learn how Social Security is a part of your life, we are pleased to offer you a free Personal Earnings and Benefit Estimate Statement.

The Personal Earnings and Benefit Estimate Statement shows your Social Security earnings history and estimates how much you have paid in Social Security taxes. It also estimates your future benefits and tells you how you can qualify for benefits. When you receive your earnings statement, we hope you will use it to start planning for a strong financial future.

To receive your statement, please fill out the form on the reverse and mail it to us. You should receive your statement in 6 weeks or less. We look forward to sending it to you.

GWENDOLYN S. KING
Commissioner of Social Security

EXHIBIT 9.1
(cont'd)

Operations Bldg., Baltimore, MD 21235, and to the Office of Management and Budget, Paperwork Reduction Project (0960-0466), Washington, D.C. 20503. **Do not send completed forms or information concerning your claim to these offices.**

We estimate that it will take you about 5 minutes to complete this form. This includes the time it will take to read the instructions, gather the necessary facts and fill out the form. If you have comments or suggestions on this estimate, or on any other aspect of this form, write to the Social Security Administration, ATTN: Reports Clearance Officer, 1-A-21

Moisten, fold, and seal before mailing.

SOCIAL SECURITY ADMINISTRATION
Request for Earnings and Benefit Estimate

To receive a free statement of your earnings covered by Social Security and your estimated future benefits, all you need to do is fill out this form. Please print or type your answers. When you have completed the form, fold it and mail it to us.

1. Name shown on your Social Security card:

   _____
   First   Middle Initial   Last

2. Your Social Security number as shown on your card:

   ☐ ☐ ☐ - ☐ ☐ - ☐ ☐ ☐ ☐

3. Your date of birth: _____ _____ _____
   Month   Day   Year

4. Other Social Security numbers you have used:

   ☐ ☐ ☐ - ☐ ☐ - ☐ ☐ ☐ ☐

   ☐ ☐ ☐ - ☐ ☐ - ☐ ☐ ☐ ☐

5. Your Sex: ☐ Male   ☐ Female

6. Other names you have used (including a maiden name):

   _____

   _____

7. Show your actual earnings for last year and your estimated earnings for this year. Include only wages and/or net self-employment income covered by Social Security.

   A. Last year's actual earnings:

   $ ☐ ☐ ☐ ☐ , ☐ ☐ ☐ . ☐ 0 ☐ 0
     Dollars only

   B. This year's estimated earnings:

   $ ☐ ☐ ☐ ☐ , ☐ ☐ ☐ . ☐ 0 ☐ 0
     Dollars only

8. Show the age at which you plan to retire: ☐ ☐
                                          (Show only one age)

Form **SSA-7004-PC-OP1** (9-89) Destroy Prior Edition

EXHIBIT 9.1
(cont'd)

| | Form Approved OMB No. 0960-0466 | | SP |

Statement

9. Below, show the average yearly amount that you think you will earn between now and when you plan to retire. Your estimate of future earnings will be added to those earnings already on our records to give you the best possible estimate.

   Enter a yearly average, not your total future lifetime earnings. Only show earnings covered by Social Security. Do not add cost-of-living, performance or scheduled pay increases or bonuses. The reason for this is that we estimate retirement benefits in today's dollars, but adjust them to account for average wage growth in the national economy.

   However, if you expect to earn significantly more or less in the future due to promotions, job changes, part-time work, or an absence from the work force, enter the amount in today's dollars that most closely reflects your future average yearly earnings.

   Most people should enter the same amount that they are earning now (the amount shown in 7B).

   Your future average yearly earnings:

   $ ☐☐☐,☐☐☐.00
   Dollars only

10. Address where you want us to send the statement:

    _____
    Name

    _____
    Street Address (Include Apt. No., P.O. Box, or Rural Route)

    _____
    City   State   Zip Code

I am asking for information about my own Social Security record or the record of a person I am authorized to represent. I understand that if I deliberately request information under false pretenses I may be guilty of a federal crime and could be fined and/or imprisoned. I authorize you to send the statement of earnings and benefit estimates to the person named in item 10 through a contractor.

▶

Please sign your name (Do not print)

_____   _____
Date   (Area Code) Daytime Telephone No.

ABOUT THE PRIVACY ACT
Social Security is allowed to collect the facts on this form under Section 205 of the Social Security Act. We need them to quickly identify your record and prepare the earnings statement you asked us for. Giving us these facts is voluntary. However, without them we may not be able to give you an earnings and benefit estimate statement. Neither the Social Security Administration nor its contractor will use the information for any other purpose.

of your Social Security benefit at the retirement age you designated on the Form SSA-7004, as well as the benefit at your normal retirement age and at age 70. The statement will also tell you what your survivors would receive if you died and what you and family would receive if you became disabled. The information on survivors and disability benefits is helpful right now to determine how much additional insurance you need to buy for adequate disability benefits and for your dependent survivors should you die.

In most cases, the Social Security Administration by law can correct errors only up to 3 years, 3 months, and 15 days after they occur. If you don't get a copy of your earnings history every 3 years and review it, you won't catch errors in time for correction under the law.

Years Needed for Maximum Benefits. If you were born after 1928, you will use your highest paid 35 years of work to determine your earnings records, that is, your AIME. Those born in 1928 may use 34 years, and those born earlier may use even fewer years. If you did not work the minimum number of years, you will be adding zeros into the average, thus greatly reducing your AIME and the subsequent benefit amount, called the primary insurance amount (PIA).

Basically, the Social Security system assumes a 40-year career and allows you to use the 35 years with the highest earnings. This works well for a career like Bonnie's where she works in a job with earnings exceeding the Social Security wage base and she takes fewer than 5 years off. But if a woman today takes 10 years off the payroll to raise her children and perhaps a year or 2 to deal with elderly parents, she may have only 28 years of the needed 35 years. She has to count 7 years as zero. According to former Social Security Commissioner Gwendolyn S. King, each year counted as a zero reduces the monthly Social Security benefit by about $12. Considering the Social Security benefit in 1992 for a wage earner who earned an average wage all her life and worked the required 35 years was only about $960, a loss of $12 each month for each year less than 35 is significant; for example, the woman who has worked only 28 years will receive about $875 per month, for a loss of over $1,000 per year in benefits.

Alice will estimate her benefit based on her expected 43-year career. Alice uses 35 years to calculate her AIME. Because Alice will have worked all but 3 years during her career, the zeros for those 3 years will not hurt her. She can drop those 3 years and the first 5 years of her career that were the lowest paid and still have 35 years of earnings to calculate her AIME. She looks at her earnings in each of the remaining years and multiplies them by an indexing factor used to make the earliest years comparable to today's dollars. She then totals the figures and divides the sum by 35 years times 12 months to get her earnings AIME of $3,062, which entitles her to a PIA benefit of approximately $1,070 per month in 1992 when she retires at age 65.

What if Alice had taken 18 years off to raise her children? Based on the same figures, Alice would have had only 25 years of earnings to count. She would have had to add in 10 years of zeros and to have included all years of earnings including those early low-paid years. Using Commissioner King's estimate of a $12-per-month loss in benefits for each year counted as a zero, Alice would lose $120 per month, leaving her with a monthly benefit of only $950. Those years off the payroll would reduce her benefit by about 11%.

Social Security Benefit Calculations Don't Always Fit Women's Career Patterns. Both the Older Women's League and the Congressional Caucus for Women's Issues have criticized the Social Security system for its treatment of working women. Social Security was designed for different demographics in which a family had one wage earner and one caregiver. Benefits are earned under Social Security for both the wage earner and the "dependents," which include a spouse and minor children. But today's demographics show that, for the vast majority of families, two wage earners are supporting the family or, if only one wage earner supports the family, there is no spouse.

Legislation has been introduced to allow up to 10 years to be subtracted from the number of years used to calculate the AIME if those years were used for child rearing or care of a disabled relative. Chances of this legislation being enacted are very slight. As a practical matter any changes to Social Security that will increase benefits will have to be financed by increased taxes, and no one is eager to increase taxes. There may also be the unstated fear that focusing on the new demographics of a two-wage-earner family will cause "reforms" that pay for the increased benefits for women who have worked outside the home and paid Social Security taxes at the expense of the dependent spouse benefits for women who have not worked outside the home and have not paid Social Security taxes.

There are grave inequities in the system for two-wage-earner families. Table 9.6 eloquently states how working couples compare with the one-wage-earner family. The two-earner family earning the same amount as a one-earner family receives a significantly smaller Social Security benefit. Worse yet, the surviving spouse receives far less in the situations where wives work. Wife A in Table 9.6's scenario who has never worked outside the home or paid Social Security taxes receives a benefit equal to 67% of the total benefit the couple received. Wives B and C, both of whom worked outside the home and paid

TABLE 9.6 Penalty for Working Couples and Survivors			
	Average Monthly Earnings	Couple's Benefit	Survivor's Benefit	Percentage of Couple's Benefit
Couple A				
Husband	$1,000	$526	$526	67%
Wife	0	263	526	
Total	$1,000	$789		
Couple B				
Husband	$ 667	$419	$419	58%
Wife	333	299	419	
Total	$1,000	$718		
Couple C				
Husband	$ 500	$366	$366	50%
Wife	500	366	·366	
Total	$1,000	$732		

*Source: "Women, Caregiving, and Poverty: Options to Improve Social Security," Hearing before the Subcommittee on Retirement Income and Employment of the Select Committee on Aging, U.S. House of Representatives, Committee Pub. 101–779, October 3, 1990, pp. 116–117.

Social Security taxes, receive survivor benefits of only 58% and 50% of the couples' benefits as a reward for their contribution to the Social Security system!

Two-wage-earner families where both spouses earn an average wage are especially hard hit, when you compare the amount those families pay over the years in Social Security taxes. Table 9.7 illustrates disproportionate burden of Social Security taxes in relation to both the original amount earned by such a family, the Bonos, and the benefits they ultimately receive. The Bonos, with both husband and wife making the same amount of salary, earn far less than the Abbotts or the Costellos, *but they pay the same amount of tax as the Abbotts.* Mrs. Abbott never pays Social Security tax, yet she will receive a greater percentage of Social Security benefit as a survivor than Mrs. Bono, who always paid tax, will receive as a survivor drawing on her workers' benefits!

Former congresswoman Mary Rose Oakar (D., Ohio), in a hearing on Social Security benefits to women, said, "It is unbelievable to me that there hasn't been public outrage over this issue." But women have expressed little, if any, outrage. The lack of complaint probably stems from the fact women are unaware of the unjust operation of Social Security until it is too late for them to do anything about it.

Receiving Social Security Benefits as a Spouse

If Alice had worked only before her children were born and after the youngest child left home at 18, she would have been in the workplace only 20 years. In calculating her AIME, she would have to include 15 years of zeros. Depending on her husband's earnings, *Alice might be entitled to receive a higher Social Security benefit as his spouse than she could on her own earnings.*

Any wage earner—male or female—who is married, is widowed, or was married for 10 years and is divorced is entitled to receive benefits based on her own earnings or the spouse's earnings. A spouse who has never worked outside the home is entitled to draw benefits based on the wage earner's work record. Once the wage earner begins receiving benefits and the spouse reaches normal retirement age, she is entitled to a dependent's benefit equal to 50% of the wage earner's Social Security benefit. A spouse may choose to receive a reduced benefit beginning after age 62, but before her normal retirement date. Currently, at age 62 the spouse is entitled to 37.5% of the wage earner's benefit. As the normal retirement age increases above 65 over the

TABLE 9.7 1992 Earnings and Contributions and Monthly Social Security Benefits (1992 Dollars) for Workers Retiring in 2010*			
Earnings	**Abbotts**	**Bonos**	**Costellos**
Husband	$70,000	$27,750	$50,000
Wife	0	27,750	20,000
Family total	$70,000	$55,500	$70,000
OASDI Tax†			
Husband			
Employer	$ 3,441	$ 1,721	$ 3,100
Worker	3,441	1,721	3,100
Wife			
Employer	0	1,721	1,240
Worker	0	1,721	1,240
Family total	$ 6,882	$ 6,884	$ 8,680
Benefits			
Husband	$ 1,420WB‡	$ 1,011WB	$ 1,420WB
Wife	710SB‡	1,011SB	710SB
Family total	$ 2,130	$ 2,022	$ 2,130
Survivor Benefits			
Amount	$ 1,420	$ 1,011§	$ 1,420
As a % of couples, benefits	67%	50%	67%

*Benefits are for workers retiring at age 66 (full benefit retirement age) in 2010. Workers are assumed to have the same relative level of earnings throughout their careers.

†OASDI contributions are based on SSA 1992 tax rate of 6.2% and maximum earnings of $55,500. Earnings above $55,500 are not considered for Social Security purposes.

‡WB, worker's benefit; SB, spouse benefit.

§Spouse continues to collect on own worker's benefit. Survivor benefit does not apply.

Source: Staff-prepared background material for "How Will Today's Women Fare in Yesterday's Traditional Retirement System?" Hearing before the Subcommittee on Retirement Income and Employment of the Select Committee on Aging, U.S. House of Representatives, March 26, 1992.

years, the spouse may still begin receiving a benefit at 62, but she will receive less than 37.5%. As with wage earner benefits at early retirement, this reduction is permanent.

A spouse at any age with a child under 16 or a disabled child can also receive a 50% benefit when the wage earner begins to receive Social Security benefits. The child may also receive a benefit of 50% of the wage earner's benefit, if she (1) is under 18, (2) is under 19 and still in high school, or (3) regardless of age, became disabled before age 22. The total amount of benefits any family can receive based on *one* wage earner's work record is limited. But if both you and your spouse worked and you still have dependent children at home when you retire, you may be able to receive higher benefits if you use both your work records. You can receive benefits for the children under the higher work record of the two of you. The second worker's benefit is not subject to the higher-paid worker's "maximum family benefit" as the limit is called.

A spouse may also retire early based on her own wage earnings. She would receive a reduction in her benefits for early retirement. Then, when her spouse retires at normal retirement age, and she reaches normal retirement age, she could shift to receiving benefits as a spouse, if those benefits are larger. If she has not worked continuously in the work force or has worked for very low wages, as we saw from the Costellos in Table 9.7, it is possible to receive a higher spouse benefit than a wage earner benefit. Under this scenario, her spouse benefit would not be reduced for early retirement, because she did not begin receiving the spouse benefit until she reached normal retirement age.

Divorced Spouses May Receive Spouse Benefits. If you are divorced, the rules for receiving Social Security benefits based on your former husband's work record are a little different. So long as your former spouse is eligible to receive Social Security benefits, regardless of whether the former spouse is actually receiving benefits or not, you can receive benefits once you and your former spouse have reached age 62. But if your spouse is only 62, you must have been divorced for at least 2 years before benefits can begin. The benefits percentages will be the same as a married spouse, and you will be subject to the same reductions in benefits as married spouses. Your benefit will stop if you remarry, unless you remarry someone who is receiving benefits as a dependent of a wage earner.

Special Social Security Rules

Minimum benefits are available for individuals who have worked for many years at low wages. These minimum benefits are paid only if they are higher than the benefits which would be received under ordinary calculations.

If you worked for a local or state government or the federal government and when you retire from that job you are not covered by Social Security taxes, in most cases any Social Security benefit you receive as a spouse or as a widow will be reduced by two-thirds of the amount of your other pension. Because government employee pensions are usually relatively generous, this two-thirds offset rule generally eliminates any benefit from Social Security. Any Social Security benefit you receive based on your own wage record is not affected by this rule.

If you were in the military or you are relying on benefits received as a military spouse, your benefits may be increased by credits counted toward the earnings record.

RECEIVING THE SOCIAL SECURITY BENEFITS

Social Security checks don't just magically appear. You must apply for your Social Security benefits. Depending on the area of the country in which you live, this can take from a month to three or four, so you are wise to begin the application process a few months before you hope to retire. The application process is detailed in Chapter 16.

How Earnings Can Reduce Benefits

You may continue to work after you begin receiving Social Security benefits, but until you reach age 70, you will be subject to an "earnings test." Your benefits (and your family's benefits, if any) will be reduced if you earn more than the limit. If a family member receiving benefits earns more than the limit, only that family member's benefits will be reduced. For example, you and your husband are 68. He is receiving benefits as a wage earner and you are receiving Social Security benefits as a spouse. If your husband exceeds the earnings limit, both of you will have benefits reduced. But, under the same circumstances, if you both are receiving benefits based on your *own* wage earning records, your benefits will not be reduced if his earnings exceed the limit. Likewise, if you were working, but he was not, any of your earnings exceeding the limit would not limit his benefits.

The limit changes annually based on the average earnings in the country. In 1993, recipients between the ages of 65 and 69 could earn $10,560 and those under 65 were limited to $7,680. If you hit the limit and you are under 65, your Social Security benefits will be reduced by $1 for every $2 over the limit you earn; if you are over 65 your benefits will only be reduced $1 for every $3 you earn over the limit. Once you reach age 70, your Social Security payment is not affected by your earnings.

"Earnings" for purposes of the earnings limitation are generally compensation received for services. Usually, the type of income a retired person could expect to receive, such as pensions, interest, dividends, and so on, are not "earnings" subject to this limitation, so you are not penalized for saving and investment before retirement. Noncash payments for domestic service are also not included in earnings. So if you can receive a rent-free apartment in exchange for janitorial services, it is not "earnings."

If you are considering working after beginning your Social Security benefits, you need to *consider carefully the amount of income earned and whether the additional income is worth the trade-off.* Also remember that the amounts you are earning are subject to income taxes and Social Security taxes. The Social Security earnings limits are applied on a pretax basis. But, generally, Social Security benefits are not taxable. Once the taxes are calculated, you may be ahead very little on those earnings exceeding the limitation, especially if you are working between ages 62 and 65 when the reduction is $1 for every $2 earned over the limit.

Social Security Benefits May Be Taxable for the "Wealthy"

Social Security benefits are nontaxable unless you are single with an income of $25,000 per year or are married with an income of over $35,000. Note, the income limit here is not "earnings" like that used in the earnings limitation test. Income, for determining the taxability of Social Security, counts one-half of your Social Security benefit and all non-Social Security income, including all the pension benefits, interest, and dividends from your preretirement savings and tax-free bond interest. If this income exceeds these thresholds, *you pay income tax on half of the income in excess of the threshold or half of your Social Security benefit, whichever is less.*

For example, in Alice's case at 65 she will have a pension of approximately $4,600 a year. She hopes her own savings can generate another $8,000 a year, and for a time she hopes to have a part-time job paying $4,000. Her Social Security benefit will be approximately $12,800. Her taxing threshold is calculated as follows:

Pension	$ 4,600
Savings income	8,000
Part-time job	4,000
½ Social Security	6,400
Total	$23,000

She has includable income of $23,000 per year, well below the $25,000 threshold for taxing Social Security benefits for single individuals, so she will pay no income tax on her Social Security benefits.

Her neighbors, George and Harriet, are not so lucky. Their includable income is:

Pension	$25,000
Savings income	12,000
½ Social Security	9,350
Total	$46,350
Less married threshold limit	32,000
Excess	$14,350

George and Harriet will have to pay income tax on the lesser of half of $14,350, the excess (i.e., $7,175) or half of their $18,700 Social Security benefit (i.e., $9,350). The half excess amount of $7,175 is less than the half of Social Security $9,350 amount, so they will pay taxes on $7,175.

Until the Social Security changes adopted in 1983 to bolster the financial viability of the system, Social Security benefits were not taxable. But with the changes in 1983, it was thought that wealthy individuals who received Social Security should at least pay tax on that half of the benefit representing the portion of tax originally paid by their employer.

OBTAINING SUPPLEMENTAL
SECURITY INCOME

The Social Security system, along with some states, makes available a supplemental benefit to those over 65 and disabled persons, if they have assets less than $2,000 for an individual or $3,000 per couple. Your home, burial plots, burial funds of up to $1,500, and usually, your car and home furnishings do not count toward the asset limits. Income from other sources reduces Supplemental Security Income (SSI) benefits, but the first $65 per month of wages is ignored, as is half the amount over $65. The basic payment to those over 65 is about $400 per month for an individual and about $610 for a couple.[4] Payments may be higher, depending on how much the state adds to the SSI benefit. Or payments may be lower, depending on your earnings. In fact, the average payment is much lower—$209 for singles and $461 for couples in 1990.[5] Obviously, SSI is available to you only if you are in truly desperate circumstances. Of those over 65 receiving SSI payments, 75% are women.[6]

USING MEDICARE BENEFITS AS A SOURCE
OF RETIREMENT "INCOME"

Medicare is the federal health care reimbursement system which pays for a portion of medical care for those age 65 and over. Medicare becomes an important source of retirement "income" because health care costs represent an unusually high percentage of retired persons' income. While this is less true for the "young old" defined as those 65–70, those described as the "old old" over age 80 find this especially true. The average Medicare reimbursement for retirees is about $2,700 per year, with about $1,700 of that amount going for hospital bills and the remainder for other medical services.[7] Of course, this is a somewhat misleading figure because a significant amount of Medicare expenditures are spent on people in the last six months of their lives.

Nevertheless, Medicare reimbursements or payments constitute a substantial portion of the elderly's "income."

Medicare is administered by the Health Care Financing Administration, which like the Social Security Administration, is part of the U.S. Department of Health and Human Services. Both administrations have budgets that exceed the gross national products of most countries in the world. Together the two agencies' benefits payments represent approximately 60% of the federal budget.

Medicare has two parts. Medicare Part A is hospital insurance, paying some of the costs of hospital stays, some related care while you are there, and certain home health care. Medicare Part A is financed by the "hospital insurance" portion of the Social Security tax. If you or your spouse is eligible for Social Security, you pay nothing additional for Medicare Part A. It is automatically provided when you apply for Social Security. Even if you don't qualify for Social Security, you may buy Medicare Part A insurance for a fee after you reach age 65. Medicare Part B covers other medical services such as doctors' fees and outpatient services. Part B is financed in part by monthly premiums deducted from your Social Security check. See Table 9.8. You may opt out of Part B coverage. The monthly premiums, which cover only about one-fourth of the cost of Part B, are adjusted each January. The premiums are calculated for those who enrolled when they were first eligible. If you enroll after you are first eligible or drop in and out of the Part B, your premiums will be higher when you do enroll in Part B.

TABLE 9.8 Medicare Part B Premiums, 1992–1995	
Year	Monthly Payment
1992	$31.80
1993	36.60
1994	41.10
1995	46.10

You may begin to receive Medicare at age 65, regardless of whether you are enrolling for Social Security. However, even if you begin receiving Social Security benefits at age 62, you will not become eligible for Medicare until you are 65. Medicare is also available for the disabled and for those with chronic kidney disease. Even if you plan to continue working past age 65, you should enroll for Medicare coverage. Depending on your age, health, and the benefits your employer is providing, you may opt out of Part B, but if you do, remember you will pay a higher premium later. Chances are highly unlikely you will find a health insurance policy covering the same services for less money—if you can find an individual policy at all.

What Expenses Medicare Pays for—and Which Expenses It Doesn't Cover

Medicare does not pay all medical expenses. Like most other health insurance plans, you pay a "deductible" and a "copayment" for most services. These deductibles and copays are linked to the increases in medical costs and go up each year. For example, in 1992, hospital benefits required a $652 initial deductible and $163 per day after the first 60 days. After 90 days you pay the full amount for hospitalization, or you may choose to pay $326 per day for up to 60 "lifetime reserve" days. This means over the course of your entire lifetime you will have only 60 days of hospitalization at this rate for those periods when you are in the hospital more than 90 days at a time. These benefits also may be paid for skilled nursing care facilities in which you are receiving treatment.

Ordinary nursing home care (in which the services provided are custodial care rather than rehabilitation or treatment) is *not* covered by Medicare. Custodial care becomes a source of serious income depletion for some elderly people when they are unable to care for themselves at home, but have no treatable illness. This is when the long-term care policies discussed in Chapter 8 become crucial. Unfortunately, many younger people still do not realize Medicare does not cover custodial care.

Medicare Part B, also called supplementary medical insurance benefits, pays for doctors' services, X rays, diagnostic tests, physical therapy, necessary ambulance services, drugs that cannot be self-administered, and so on. It will also pay for periodic mammography, the only preventative treatment specifically covered. You must pay the first $100 of Medicare-recognized charges, annually. After that, Medicare will pay for 80% of covered expenses, but only at the "customary" or "prevailing" charge level established by Medicare. If the Medicare prevailing charge for a specific service is $100, but your doctor charges $130, Medicare will pay only $80 for the service, that is, 80%

of the permissible charge of $100. You must pay the remaining amount up to a government-imposed limit.

Doctors deal with Medicare in one of two ways. A doctor may take "assignment" from Medicare and become a "Medicare-participating" physician, meaning that she agrees to charge only the "prevailing" fee set by Medicare for procedures and submit bills directly to Medicare. Medicare pays 80% of the "prevailing charge" after deductibles, and you pay the remaining 20% of the charge. A doctor accepting "assignment" from Medicare may not charge more than the Medicare prevailing charge.

Other doctors may choose not to accept assignment from Medicare and not to be a "Medicare-participating" doctor. In the past, such doctors could charge a Medicare patient whatever the doctor wished. As in the example we just discussed, Medicare would pay 80% of its prevailing fee for the procedure and the Medicare patient had to pay the rest of the bill, regardless of the amount.

Beginning in 1991, Medicare limited the fees *any* doctor, including "nonparticipating" doctors, may charge a Medicare participant. A nonparticipating doctor may still charge more than a participating doctor, but under no circumstances may a doctor charge a Medicare patient more than an established percentage of the Medicare prevailing charge for a procedure. Beginning in 1991 nonparticipating doctors could charge no more than established percentages above the Medicare prevailing charge for an office or hospital visit and other services such as surgery. Doctors charging more are subject to legal action by the U.S. Department of Health and Human Services, Medicare's parent agency. Unfortunately, the Health Care Financing Administration (HCFA) has not been vigorous in enforcing this new ban on overcharges and, as late as spring of 1992, was still supplying forms telling Medicare patients they were responsible for nonparticipating doctors fees, regardless of the amount the doctor charged.[8] The head of HCFA was dealt with severely by the Bush administration for this dereliction of duty in failing to correct the forms. They promoted her to the White House staff!

Purchasing a "Medigap" Health Insurance Policy to Cover Additional Medical Expenses

As you can see, you can still incur significant medical expenses in retirement, even with Medicare. As a result many retirees also purchase a so-called "Medigap" health insurance policy from a private health insurance to cover those expenses such as copays and deductibles. "Medigap" policies do not cover custodial nursing home care. Only a long-term care policy specifically designed for custodial care will cover nursing homes, as a rule. "Medigap" policies became a scandal in the 1980s, and some progress was made in regulating them. The area still remains subject to abuse, although criminal penalties apply for those selling such policies in violation of the regulations.

If you consider a "Medigap" policy, either for yourself at retirement or for your parents, *shop slowly and ask lots of questions.* The Social Security Administration provides the following tips:

❖ Don't believe statements that the insurance is government sponsored; policies to supplement Medicare are not sold by the federal or state governments.

❖ Compare several different policies and companies.

❖ Don't buy more insurance than you need and don't buy several different policies.

❖ Check for "preexisting condition" exclusions that will not pay for treatment of a medical condition you already have or had perhaps years ago.

❖ Be suspicious of any suggestion you give up a current policy and buy a replacement; the new policy may have waiting periods or preexisting condition exclusions.

❖ Check your right to renew; buy only policies that have an automatic right to renew (most states now require this by law).[9]

Financial Future of Medicare

Under its present funding, Medicare is projected to face serious deficits in the mid-1990s. Medicare, like all other health care programs, has suffered from dramatic costs increases. Changes have been made to attempt to control costs by limiting the amount Medicare pays to health care providers such as hospitals through fixed reimbursements based on diagnosis-related groups (DRGs). Physician service payments are now being limited through a pricing control system based on *resource-based relative value scales* (the RBRVS system).

What the Medicare program may look like 20 years from now when the age wave begins to retire is pure speculation. The nation as a whole is concerned about health care availability and affordability. Over the next two decades, changes can be expected in the entire health care delivery system even more dramatic than those seen in the last 20 years. The changes are accelerating. We have gone from a nation spending about $800 per person annually for health care in 1978 to one spending $2,700 per person in 1990. Increasingly, health care, even that provided by private systems through employer insurance or individually purchased health care, is "managed" through health maintenance organizations or medical providers who agree to discounts through "preferred provider organizations" or networks.[10] Given these changes toward more regulation in private systems, it is unrealistic to expect Medicare not to become more "managed."

Yet Medicare is extremely popular among its recipients. It is perceived by an electorate increasingly jaded and disapproving of government as one part of government that works. Medicare recipients tend to be politically powerful. After all, every elected official realizes that retirees have little to do but to work in a political challenger's campaign if the incumbent takes a stand in favor of limiting Social Security or Medicare. Or as the shorthand goes, Social Security and Medicare are the electrified third rail of politics—touch it and you die!

In some form Medicare will be available to future retirees, and it will likely continue to be generous, even if usage is more regulated. But there is the chance it could become more "means tested," with higher-income retirees paying more or that certain medical procedures could be rationed as they are now in other countries providing national health care deliveries.

CONCLUSION: PLANNING FOR SOCIAL SECURITY IN YOUR RETIREMENT SAVINGS PROGRAM

Social Security will probably be a part of your potential retirement income when you retire, but as you have seen, it is not likely to be sufficient to provide a secure retirement—nor was it ever intended to be. While you are still young enough to save for retirement, seeing your projected Social Security benefit will be important "reality therapy" for calculating the additional retirement income you will need to maintain your life-style.

Here are some guidelines for determining your Social Security and Medicare benefits:

❖ Order your Social Security Earnings and Benefit Estimate Statement now, no matter how old you are. Use the form shown in Exhibit 9.1.

❖ When you receive the statement (it usually takes about four weeks), check it carefully for any errors. It is important to check regularly for errors because the Social Security Administration cannot correct old errors in most cases.

❖ Use the estimated Social Security benefits in your current planning and budgeting for retirement saving. Look carefully at the estimated benefit at retirement. It will be given to you in current dollars. Obviously, unless you are very close to retirement, the current dollar figure is not likely to be the same as your actual retirement benefit. But the current dollar figure will give you an idea of the buying power of your Social Security benefit at retirement. As inflation goes up so does your Social Security benefit, at least under the current law version of Social Security. Theoretically, the benefit you actually receive at retirement will have the same buying power as the benefit amount shown to you in your various estimates. Of course, the estimates assume you will continue to work and to earn approximately the same salary. If you stop working, your ultimate benefit will be lower than the estimates. If you begin to receive a higher salary, your final retirement benefit will likely be higher than the estimates you receive.

❖ Order the Earnings and Benefit Estimate Statement about every 3 years. Having these statements will enable you to check for errors and get them corrected within the legal period for corrections, as well as see how much your expected Social Security benefit at retirement is changing.

NOTES FOR CHAPTER 9

1. Report of the Board of Trustees, Federal Old-Age and Survivors Insurance Trust Fund (Washington, D.C.: U.S. Government Printing Office, 1990).

2. Report of the Board of Trustees, Federal Old-Age and Survivors Insurance Trust Fund (Washington, D.C.: U.S. Government Printing Office, 1991), pp. 1–2, 149.

3. Ibid., p. 149.

4. Social Security Administration, "SSI: Supplemental Security Income," SSA Publication No. 05–11000, January 1991.

5. According to statistical publications by the Social Security Administration, the actual average monthly SSI payment for those over 65, including federally administered state supplements, was only $209 to an individual and $461 to couples in 1990. See *Fast Facts and Figures About Social Security 1991*, produced by the Office of Research and Statistics, SSA, table labeled "Average SSI Payment Amounts."

6. Ibid., table labeled "SSI Recipients by Sex."

7. Ibid., table labeled "Benefit Payments."

8. *The New York Times*, March 1, 1992, page A1.

9. Social Security Administration, "What You Need to Know About Medicare and Supplemental Health Insurance," SSA Publication No. 05–10014.

10. KPMG Peat Marwick, "Health Benefits in 1992," a survey of over 1,000 randomly chosen employers that showed that over one-half of all employees are part of an Health Maintenance Organization (HMO) or Preferred Provider Organization, (PPO) arrangement, an increase from only 29% in 1988.

PART

THREE

HOW MUCH TO SAVE AND INVEST

THE ROLE OF BENEFITS
IN TAKING-OR LEAVING-A JOB

Jennifer has just received a call from her boss's colleague who needs an experienced secretary. The colleague has seen Jennifer's work and wants to offer her a job at $2,000 more a year than her current salary of $21,000. Jennifer knows the colleague and the business, and she needs the extra money. She accepted the job. *Jennifer just lost over $1,000 in annual compensation.* She confused "salary" with compensation, and she didn't ask about health, disability or retirement benefits. What happened?

In this chapter we will see how to estimate the value of benefits in calculating your total compensation package. We will also discuss how to protect your benefits when you leave a job for any reason.

If Jennifer had asked, she would have learned the new job does not provide health, disability, or retirement benefits. At her current job she has health benefits worth $2,000; she pays for 25% of cost of health care benefits with pretax dollars. Automatically she has lost

$1,500 in health benefits. She currently pays only a small amount to buy group disability insurance; buying it as an individual will cost much more.

Jennifer has a defined benefit retirement plan under her current job that will pay her $8,000 per year at retirement. There is no retirement plan at the new job, and she will have to save over $700 per year for 30 years to make up for the loss of the retirement benefit. Worse, she is only a few months away from vesting in the benefits she has accrued under her current employer's plan. Because she is leaving before she vests, she has lost the current lump-sum value of the benefits she has earned to date. That amount, $543, seems small, but $543, which could be invested in a tax-deferred individual retirement account (IRA) at 6% for the next 35 years until she retires, would grow to $4,175, and invested at 9% it would grow to $11,080.

Table 10.1 shows the balance sheet for Jennifer's jobs.

TABLE 10.1 Comparison of Benefits at Different Jobs		
	Current Job	New Job
Salary	$21,000	$23,000
Health benefits	1,500	—
Retirement benefit Current value equivalent	700	—
Subtotal	$23,200	$23,000
Loss of accrued retirement benefit	—	(543)
Total	$23,200	$22,457

So Jennifer has lost approximately $2,750 in benefits this year in return for a $2,000 per year in salary for a net loss of at least $750 this year.

But her net loss is really greater when you account for the tax consequences. The $2,000 of salary at the new job is subject to at least 22% in taxes, leaving her with a net salary increase of only $1,560. The $1,500 of health benefits she received at her former job was not subject to tax, and her contribution of $500 toward the health care plan was made with pretax dollars. The equivalent value of the retirement benefit she was accruing is about $700 and that value was tax deferred. She will need over $3,462 in pretax earnings each year to replace the tax-favored employer-provided benefits she was receiving at her former job.* So Jennifer has actually lost $3,462 minus her after-tax salary increase of $1,560 for a total loss of $1,902.

REMEMBER: COMPENSATION EQUALS BOTH SALARY AND BENEFITS

Jennifer's situation is dramatic, but not unusual. Too many employees realize too late that they are working for more than salary; other important benefits need to be counted. Employers are partly to blame for employees' lack of benefits awareness. Each year employers spend literally billions of dollars on retirement, health, disability, and other benefits. ERISA requires employers to disclose information about these benefits and employers comply. But most employers do little to emphasize the value of those benefits in either the ERISA-mandated communications or other employer communications. It's not surprising, but it is regrettable that most employees receiving employer-pro-

---

*The formula to use to compare the values of pretax and after-tax dollars is:

$$\text{After-tax amount needed} \quad \times \quad \frac{1}{1 - \text{Effective tax rate}} \quad = \quad \text{Pretax amount you must earn}$$

So in Jennifer's case the calculation to see how much she would need to earn before taxes to replace her previous tax-favored $2,700 worth of benefits is as follows:

$$\$2,700 \quad \times \quad \frac{1}{1 - 0.22} \quad = \quad \$3,462$$

vided benefits have little, if any, concept of the after-tax value of those benefits.

When questioned about this lack of publicity, employers give two common responses. First, say employers, if we talk about the cost of benefits, employees fear we are preparing to reduce benefits. Second, employers say, "We spend enough on benefits as it is. We don't want to spend more money publicizing them." Both answers seem self-defeating for employers. As a result, when the costs become so high the employer is forced to ask the employees to share in the costs, as has happened frequently with health care benefits, the employees are stunned and resentful at the costs they have to pay. The employees give little thought to the good deal they received from the employer benefits in previous years. Yet even when employers ask for cost sharing, they are reluctant to admit how much the company is still paying for the employer share of the benefits.

The nature of employer funding in defined benefit plans makes it virtually impossible for an employee to know the dollar value of the contribution made on her behalf each year unless the benefits statement contains a rough estimate of the present value of the benefit accrued to date in the plan. Because the contributions are not made to individual accounts and because the amount contributed to the plan depends on a number of variables, as we saw in Chapter 7, the employer could only really state an approximate amount the employee would have to save to match the expected benefit from the employer at retirement. With defined contribution plans, determining the value of the annual employer-provided benefit is easier. The employee usually knows what the profit-sharing plan or 401(k) matching contribution was for last year. And the employer usually includes the value of employer contributions in the annual benefit statement. But still the employer rarely stresses the total amount of benefits and the tax advantages of those benefits.

It is not surprising that Jennifer didn't think about the value of the retirement plan. No one had ever given her a clue about the estimated costs. But you needn't follow her errors.

WHAT TO ASK DURING THE JOB INTERVIEW

The time to learn about benefits—retirement, disability, health, and dependent care—is during the interview process. The health, disability, and dependent care benefits are important to retirement benefits, because the less money you have to spend for those items, the more money you have to save for retirement.

Job candidates are often reluctant to ask many questions about benefits, perhaps for fear of seeming too greedy. But you can pose your questions and still avoid seeming greedy. At an appropriate point in the interview, usually when the interviewer casually and rapidly lists the benefits, say something like, "I recognize that labor costs, including the benefit costs, are an important part of any business's expenses. I really appreciate that and I recognize that compensation is more than just salary; it includes those benefits. I always consider the value of benefits when weighing just what my compensation is."

You have conveyed both your awareness of the employer's expenses and your appreciation of benefits. You don't look greedy; you look cost-conscious for both you and your employer. Then go on to ask specifics about the benefits plan. Asking about the retirement plan should suggest you are a serious, long-term-oriented person, not just someone who is passing through. As the interview concludes ask for the "new employee" packet to look over. Tell the interviewer it will save important work time if you review it now rather than take the time to do so on your first day. Get a copy of the summary plan descriptions (SPDs) and be sure they tell you when you are eligible for the plans and when you vest. If it isn't clear from the materials you receive, call and ask the personnel or human resources office.

What if the answer is, "There are no benefits"? Clearly, you are not going to turn down a wonderful job you want, or even a not so great job you need, because benefits are not included. But bear that in mind in your budgeting and, most important, in your salary negotiations. When the discussion begins to focus on salary, remind your potential employer the job comes without benefits. Give an estimate of how much that is going to cost you out of your paycheck. Have fairly specific figures, that is, individual health insurance will cost so much, additional savings for retirement will need to be so much, and so on. By now you know how much you are going to need for retirement and how much you will have to save to get that sum. Share the information with your employer. Again, you will appear to be a serious person who is inclined to think ahead and prepare for the future, important qualities every employer wants.

Also point out that if the employer had provided retirement or health benefits, the benefits would not be taxable or would be tax deferred. Because you will be paying for them yourself, you will be buying benefits with after-tax dollars, further reducing your income. Your potential employer may not have realized that the full value of your benefits is $2,000–$3,000 before taxes. (You may not have thought about it either before now.) This lesson on the value of employer-provided benefits may give you some leverage to get a higher starting salary.

Clearly, acquiring retirement and other benefits cannot drive your career, but when weighing and considering jobs, benefits may be the factor that tips the balance in staying with your current employer or shifting to a new job. Benefits' value works both ways. A new job at the same salary, but with retirement and health benefits, may give you much more compensation than your current job even though there appears to be no more in your pay envelope at the end of the month.

BENEFITS ISSUES WHEN YOU LEAVE A JOB

Having a firm grasp of the benefits in the job you are leaving is as important as knowing about the new job's benefits. First, you cannot compare existing compensation to the benefits and compensation at the new job unless you are knowledgeable about your current benefits. Second, like Jennifer, you may walk out just before benefits are due to be vested. Leaving a job 4 years and 11 months after you arrived could cost you thousands of dollars' worth of tax-deferred retirement benefits. Those benefits could be transferred directly into an IRA to continue growing on a tax-deferred basis until your retirement. Check vesting schedules for benefits and double-check your years of service and any breaks in service you might have had that would reduce that service. Do these things well before you give any hint of resigning. In fact, right now would be a good time to check with the benefits department on the status of your retirement benefits, regardless of whether you are thinking of moving your career.

If the new employer has pursued you and if your job move would mean a loss of nonvested benefits at your former employer, try to negotiate with your new employer to "buy out" those nonvested benefits you are losing by giving you a "hiring on" bonus or increasing your salary. Even if the new employer offers you the value of the nonvested benefits you are forfeiting at the old job, remember you will not be able to shelter that money in a tax-deferred retirement account. To receive the exact equivalent of the benefits you are forfeiting, the "bonus" would have to be adjusted for this lack of tax deferral.

Understand the Payout Options on Your Old Job's Benefits

Before you leave your current job, be sure you understand all the payment options for your vested retirement benefits. The plan may not release benefits before you reach retirement age under the plan at all. In that case, the burden will be on you to keep the retirement plan administrator informed of your current address until you retire. But most plans today are eager to "cash out" terminating employees because it lowers the plan's administrative costs. In fact, if you have less than $3,500 in accrued benefits, you can be "cashed out" of the plan without your permission. This simply means the plan will transfer the value of your accrued benefit to an IRA you have designated. If you do not designate an IRA for direct transfer, the plan sponsor will issue you a check equal to the value of your accrued benefit with 20% withheld for federal income taxes. You may then roll that amount, plus the value of the 20% withheld if you wish, into an IRA to permit continued growth of your retirement benefit.

If the plan permits preretirement distributions or you are "cashed out," think carefully about where and how you want to invest the money. If the investment managers of your former employer's defined contribution fund have been good managers or there are several investment options you like in the plan, you may want to consider leaving the money in the plan. Check to see whether former employees are charged a management fee or other fees different from those charged current employees. Leaving the money in the plan will avoid your having to pay fees to manage the money in an IRA.

If the money is in a defined benefit plan, your task is more complicated. If you withdraw your benefit as lump sum before retirement, the amount will be reduced by a "mortality factor" as we discussed in Chapter 7. But the growth assumptions used to calculate the present value of the lump sum are usually modest, meaning that you may be able to make the sum grow more than the plan and, hence, provide a larger benefit at retirement under your own management than you would receive under the defined benefit fund. For example, the pension fund may assume a 6% rate of growth in calculating the lump-sum amount needed today to equal the value of your accrued benefit when you reach retirement age. You may be able to make the money grow at the rate of 9%. So if the value of your lump-sum at separation of service is $20,000 and you have 20 years until you reach retirement age, the benefit would have a lump sum value at retirement of $64,140, if left in the plan, but be worth $112,000 if you transferred it into an IRA and achieved your expected 9% rate of return.

Before you make your decision, get both the lump-sum value and the retirement benefit monthly annuity figure at the age you intend to retire. Use the time value of money tables in Appendix A to see how the money would grow at different interest rates. Ask the employer about date of death assumed in calculating the value of the benefits. Take the number of years from the date of retirement to the date of death the employer used, and using the tables again, see how much you could pay yourself each month from the lump sum you have from your investment of the money at different rates of return as compared to the monthly benefit you would receive from the re-tirement plan. Then assume you will live to 95 and, using the tables again, see how much you could pay yourself over those years from your desired date of retirement to age 95. This amount will result in a lower figure because you will be paying yourself over a greater number of years.

If the payout is from a defined contribution plan, learn whether you can take your benefit in cash or in the assets you have in the plan. If the 401(k) portion of your plan matched by your employer is only in company stock and the stock is at a record low, you probably don't want to sell the stock and take cash now. You want to take it as stock and wait for the price to increase. Frequently, when companies announce massive layoffs, the stock is in the doldrums. The announce-ment may have an artificial effect on the price, either up or down. If the price goes up, the higher price is likely to last only a few days and not continue through the long period it may take to sell the stock under the plan.

If the plan does require you to sell the assets or you want to sell the assets and take the distribution as cash, be certain you know the date on which the price of the stock will be fixed for determining the value of your sale. This is the "valuation date" under the plan. Some plans have valuation dates based on a past date such as the last day of the previous quarter, in which case you will know the exact value of the assets when they are sold. But other plans use the transaction date, which might be weeks after you have elected to cash out the assets. The value of those assets, especially if they are employer stock, may fluctuate dramatically between the time you decide to sell and the time the plan actually executes the sale. In most cases you, not the plan, bear the risk of loss or gain. This is another reason why you may want to take your benefit as assets rather than cash, if you can. You can have your employer transfer the assets into an IRA with a brokerage firm, and you will control the date on which the assets are sold.

Transferring the Benefits from the Previous Employer

Of course you won't even *think* of doing anything with the money you receive other than having your employer transfer it into an IRA or your new employer's plan. If the former employer's plan does not transfer the assets directly to an IRA or other employer plan, your former employer's plan must withhold 20% of the value of the benefit for federal income taxes. That's why you must set up an IRA or other employer plan to receive the money.

If you do slip up and receive the distribution directly, you may still put the full amount of your benefit including an amount equal to the withheld sum into an IRA. But you may have difficulty getting the equivalent of the 20% that was withheld from other savings. It will not be refunded by the federal government until you file your regular income tax return the following year.

For example, when you leave Acme in 1993, you are due $20,000 from the profit-sharing plan. You neglect to set up an IRA, so the Acme profit-sharing plan issues you a check for $16,000, representing your benefit minus $4,000 for withholding. You may put the $16,000 into an IRA, and, if you wish, you can add back $4,000, representing the amount withheld for taxes. Because you put the money in an IRA, no taxes are due on the benefit distribution at this time. When you file your income tax return for 1993, you include the $4,000 of tax withheld as tax already paid and seek a refund of that amount.

And get that distribution in that IRA within 60 days of the time you receive it. If you don't you will pay tax on the money and a 10% penalty (unless you are over 59½ or totally disabled). The only exception to this rule is money that represents after-tax dollars you may have contributed to an employer's thrift plan. That money may not be placed in an IRA, but you do not pay taxes on it and there is no 10% early withdrawal penalty on it.

Even if you are out of work and know you will have to spend the money from your former employer's retirement plan, have your employer plan transfer the money into an IRA first. As long as the money is in the IRA, its earnings are tax deferred. As soon as the money is placed in a taxable account, the ability to earn tax-deferred money is lost forever. Withdraw amounts from the IRA as slowly as possible so that you pay taxes and penalties only on the amount you absolutely have to have.

In fact, if you can draw it out in a steady stream based on equal amounts paid over your life expectancy, you will even be able to avoid the 10% penalty, but not the income tax, of course. However, unless the amount in your IRA is quite large, this life stream payment option probably won't give you sufficient amounts to live on if it is your sole source of living expenses. Additionally, once you begin this form of payment, you must continue it until you reach age 59½ and at least 5 years have elapsed since you began receiving the life stream payments from the IRA. For example, you started the life stream of payment when you were laid off from a job at age 53. You could stop that form of payment when you reached age 59½ because 5 years of payments have been received and you are 59½. But if you were 55 when you began receiving the payments, you could not stop them until age 60.

Continue Your Health Insurance Coverage— a Friendly COBRA

If you have current health insurance with your employer when you leave your job, you are entitled by law to continue that coverage at your expense, unless you will receive the same coverage from your new employer immediately. This health care continuation requirement is sometimes referred to as COBRA, an acronym for the Consolidated Omnibus Budget Reconciliation Act which contained the law. You are entitled to the coverage whether you quit or are fired for any reason other than "gross misconduct." The employer may charge only the cost of the coverage plus as much as 2% for administrative costs. Unfortunately, health care coverage is so expensive without any employer contribution that many terminated employees find they cannot afford COBRA coverage.

Because the penalties for not complying with COBRA are so strict, most employers try diligently to comply. But the COBRA law is as difficult and wily as the snake. The law has been amended several times in the few years since its enactment and the rules are not familiar to all employers. If you think you will need coverage under COBRA, inform your former employer and ask for the COBRA election form before you leave that employer. Elect the coverage and pay the premium even if your former employer thinks you are not eligible. Because many employers now have "preexisting condition exclusions" in their coverage, even if you are covered at the new employer, you may not be covered for old health problems or not covered for them for a period of months. COBRA coverage will maintain the coverage for the "preexisting condition" not covered by your new employer. If you find out you are covered at the new employer for all your needs or you really are not eligible for COBRA, your former employer may have to return the premiums you paid. So pay first and ask questions later if you have any doubt about your coverage with your new employer.

IF YOU ARE LAID OFF

The decade of the 1990s has already proved to be the decade of "down sizing," "right sizing," and plain old massive job eliminations. No matter what it is called, it hurts just as much and the financial bind is the same. But if you find yourself "right-sized" out of a job, keep your wits about you as you "negotiate" your severance or examine your "package." You never needed rational planning more than now. Take all the steps outlined to determine your benefits.

If the layoffs are massive enough, the retirement plan may have undergone a "partial termination," which would entitle all plan participants who were affected by the layoffs to immediate vesting in their accrued benefit. If so, you will be eligible for retirement benefits even though you were not vested. Ask your employer about this. Also, even if you are told no such partial termination occurred, insist the benefits department keep your address and tell you the amount of benefit you had accrued to date. The Pension Benefit Guaranty Corporation (PBGC) or the courts have been known to declare a partial termination even when the plan sponsor disagreed. If this happens, you want to be easily reached so that you can receive your benefits.

And you will want to have evidence of what the employer told you those benefits were before the legal actions declaring a partial termination occurred. There may be some differences because interest rate assumptions change over time, but major differences should be brought to PBGC's attention.

Even when not required by law, some companies vest retirement benefits as part of the severance package. Early retirement packages are often available, and if you qualify, investigate the packages closely, even if you have no intention of retiring. These packages frequently are very generous. It may make sense to consult an accountant or an actuary to help you understand the proposals and options and to calculate your benefits under certain options.

COBRA health care continuation applies unless the company shuts down all health care plans. Such total shutdowns are rare, so chances are good you can buy continuation coverage.

IF YOU ARE FIRED

Unlike COBRA even if you are fired for cause, including "gross misconduct," your retirement benefits are unaffected. If you are vested in your retirement benefits, the reason for your dismissal is immaterial. The fact that you were embezzling from the company and got caught red handed in no way reduces your retirement benefits. "Bad girl" clauses are ineffective. Violations of noncompete clauses also cannot affect the payment of your retirement benefits under an ERISA plan. Of course, any "bad girl" clauses contained in a non-ERISA plan such as an executives-only plan or contract may be valid to deny you benefits under those plans.

CONCLUSION: EVALUATE RETIREMENT BENEFITS WHEN CHANGING JOBS

❖ In examining any new job offer, be sure to think in terms of compensation, not just salary, including retirement benefits, as well as health insurance, disability benefits, and dependent care. Include the after-tax value of these benefits from both your current and expected job before you make any decisions.

❖ Contact the benefits office and get an up-to-date statement of your accrued benefits and your vesting status.

❖ Find out what the payout options are from the job you are leaving.

❖ Compare the options carefully. If the sums are very large, consider hiring an expert such as an accountant or actuary to calculate the differences in plan payments.

❖ Decide whether you need health care continuation insurance from your former employer. Be sure your new employer's coverage meets all your needs, if you decide against the continued coverage from the former employer.

❖ If you are terminated and are not vested in your accrued retirement benefits, check to see whether a partial termination of the plan has occurred which would vest you in the benefits.

❖ If early retirement options are offered, examine them carefully. Again, hire an expert if necessary to help you calculate your numbers.

❖ Remember, you cannot lose vested retirement benefits under ERISA regardless of your conduct or the reason for your dismissal. If anyone representing your employer attempts to tell you differently, report them to the Department of Labor.

HOW MUCH DO YOU NEED FOR RETIREMENT?

In order to have a retirement savings goal, you have to know how much you need. Conventional wisdom says you need 60–90% of your preretirement income. But that analysis does not fit women's retirement planning very well because it assumes a man's life expectancy and a man's higher income. Women live longer and will be more subject to the ravages of inflation. Also, the lower paid you are during your working life, the more likely you are to have most of your income taken up by the basic necessities such as food and shelter that don't change after you retire. We will discuss the factors affecting your estimates such as tax rates, inflation and rates of return, as well as how to estimate your needed savings rate. We will also walk through a retirement savings calculation sheet.

How much you will want to save for as goal will depend on several things. Some we can know now; some we can't. Basic questions include:

- ❖ When do you want to retire?
- ❖ What will inflation be like?
- ❖ Will you own your own home by retirement?
- ❖ Is your health likely to be good?
- ❖ Do you want to work part time when you retire?
- ❖ Do you want to travel extensively?
- ❖ Do you want to go back to school?
- ❖ Do you want to indulge expensive hobbies?
- ❖ What sort of life-style do you want—will you be content to say goodbye to expense account restaurants, or will you still want to frequent them; can you switch to having a new car every seven years when you have always had a new car every two years?

IGNORE THE CONVENTIONAL WISDOM ON NEEDING LESS MONEY AFTER YOU RETIRE

The advice that you need less income in retirement is based on the traditionally male career and life span, which doesn't work for women for the reasons already explained. But the advice may be wrong for both sexes. The idea that you need less in retirement is usually supported by reasoning that you will spend less on clothes, lunches, and commuting to work; you will be in a lower paid tax bracket; and your Social Security benefits will not be taxed. Alas, each of these factors is at best subject to review or probably just plain wrong. Experts are reexamining their views on the amount needed for retirement in light of changed tax rates.[1] One study found an increase in the ratios required to match preretirement income based on changes in tax law, but the study assumed a one-male-wage-earner-and-dependent-spouse scenario, so its relevance for women is limited. The study did not purport to look at amounts needed to maintain life style or the effects of inflation over time. The study looked at replacement ratios needed in retirement solely as affected by changes in the tax treatment of income (i.e., no FICA taxes, no income taxes on Social Security in most cases, possibly lower brackets, etc.) and reductions in gift giving and saving.

The following sections debunk these retirement savings myths.

Myth #1: You Will Spend Less Because Work Expenses Will Be Reduced

Will this really be significant enough to make a big difference in your cash flow? Granted, if you are commuting 30 miles by car each way to work, your savings in commuting costs after retirement will be considerable. If you eat lunch out every day and spend even $5 or $6 for each lunch, you may reduce your costs when you retire. Lunch at home can be less than that, but it still costs something. And from time to time you may *want* to lunch out. Certainly, you may need fewer clothes suitable for work. But let's face it, if you were a clothes horse while working, you are unlikely to be content with buying one new outfit a year after you are retired. If you weren't concerned about clothes while you were working, you probably didn't spend that much anyway, so any savings from buying fewer clothes after retirement is likely to be small.

Myth #2: You Will Be in a Lower Tax Bracket

Hopefully, not if you're lucky. Falling into a lower tax bracket after retirement may have been common in the 1970s and early 1980s when there were 15 tax brackets that ranged up to 70%. Unless you are very near retirement now, it is impossible to know what the tax rates may be when you retire. But realistically, it is unwise to count on lower taxes given the huge federal deficit which will haunt the United States for decades to come.

Under current 1990s law there are only three tax brackets, as shown in Table 11.1. The 15% rate applies only to the lowest earnings, and once you reach the 28% rate, there isn't much difference between that and the highest 31% rate.

To fall into a lower bracket you would need to retire with much less income than you were accustomed to. True, Alice, Susan, Bonnie, and Jennifer would each be in a lower tax bracket if they retired with only their employer-provided benefit and Social Security, but they each would also be living on less than half of their former income if that happened. With the top 31% bracket beginning at around $53,000 for singles and around $89,000, for marrieds, there isn't much room for lower brackets. One reduction in your taxes after retirement will be the elimination of FICA taxes. FICA taxes apply only to wages, so these taxes will not be applied to your pension, Social Security, or personal savings income. That saves at least 7.65% of your earnings or 15.3%, if you are self-employed.

TABLE 11.1 Current Federal Income Tax Rates, 1993		
Tax Rate	Annual Income, Filing Single	Annual Combined Incomes, Married and Filing Jointly
15%	Up to $22,100	Up to $36,900
28%	$22,100 to $53,500	$36,900 to $89,150
31%	Over $53,500	Over $89,150

Myth #3: Your Social Security Won't Be Taxed

That is only partially correct, as we saw in Chapter 9. If you have income (including half of your Social Security benefits) of more than $25,000, if single, or more than $32,000, if married, you may be taxed on as much as half your Social Security benefits. For example, if you are single and have a total income of $28,000, including half of your $10,000 Social Security benefit, you will pay tax the lesser of (1) half of the amount over the $25,000 income threshold or (2) half of your Social Security benefit. In this case half of the $3,000 excess income is $1,500, which is less than the $5,000 representing half of the Social Security benefit. Hence an additional $1,500 will be added into "adjusted gross income" and taxed.

Myth #4: You Won't Be Saving for Retirement After You Retire

Once you retire, it is true you need not save for retirement, so not all of that portion of your preretirement income going to savings will be needed. But, if you started saving early, the portion of income going into retirement saving shouldn't be that large a portion of your income just prior to retirement. Also, certainly at the start of your retirement you should still be "saving," even if that saving takes the form of paying yourself less than you could from your own retirement savings. Your life expectancy after retirement may be another two decades or more, and in order to make your retirement savings last that long, you will have to be cautious in the early years of retirement.

Also, in retirement, as in the rest of your life, emergencies occur or special opportunities like an exotic trip arise. Having a fund for those occasions requires some savings.

ASSUME YOU NEED AT LEAST 100% OF PRERETIREMENT INCOME

Certainly in the early stages of your planning, assume you will need 100% of the income you were earning immediately before you retired. Use your current income and the tables in Appendix A to project it forward at a realistic rate. For the cases of Alice, Bonnie, Susan, and Jennifer, salary was projected at 6% per year. The only sure reduction in expenses after retirement will be the elimination of FICA taxes, assuming you are not working then. Using at least 100% of preretirement income is a good rule for planning in your 20s, 30s, 40s, and early 50s, because your actual desired life-style in retirement is impossible to predict so far in advance.

REFINE ESTIMATES OF FINANCIAL NEED AS YOU NEAR RETIREMENT

As you get nearer to retirement, you can begin to refine your estimates for financial needs at retirement, based on better knowledge of what you may be doing and the assets you already own. By the time you reach 55, the house that seemed cramped when you were in your 40s, may seem impossibly large and troublesome or it may be the only place you could ever be happy living. But you will know those things more certainly as you get closer to actual retirement age. Also remember to think carefully about your possible circumstances in retirement. Will you still have children in college? How is your health likely to be?

Assuming you will need 100% of preretirement income is prudent, but if you know that absolutely certain expenses will change, then adjustments can be made. For example, if you know you will own your home, you can reduce your income needs by the amount of mortgage or rent you now pay. But don't make the mistake of assuming your housing costs will be $0. Remember, taxes, insurance, and utilities go on *and* they will increase over the years with inflation. For an easy dose of reality therapy on the issue. of housing costs, if you are in your 30s or 40s now, ask your parents what their mortgage payments used to be and compare that with the amount they now pay in real estate taxes and utility bills.

Condo fees and homeowners' association dues will continue and increase. Repairs will still be needed, and painting and other routine maintenance will be necessary, especially as property ages. In your early years of retirement you may find you have the time and energy to do maintenance you used to hire out and pay for, such as yard work and painting. But as you age, things you used to do routinely yourself will be less appealing or impossible for you to do safely. The cost of these services needs to be considered. And if you are one of those ambitious people who always did all the painting, repairs, and gardening yourself, you will be unpleasantly surprised how much your labor was worth and how much those things cost when others do them.

Statistics tell us that health care costs will be taking a larger portion of your income in retirement. The Social Security Administration estimates retired Medicare participants receive over $2,700 per year, on average, in reimbursements. Certainly, health care costs constitute a large portion of older retirees' expenses and Medicare payments constitute a large portion of their income. At a minimum there will be Medicare Part B premiums. *Don't even think of passing up this insurance.* Of every 1,000 retired Americans eligible for the Part B program, 793 receive benefits under Part B. You can't get it cheaper, because you pay only one-fourth of the cost, and even if you have excellent health, uncovered medical costs aren't worth the risk. In 1992 those premiums were $31.80 per month, and in 1995 they will be $46.10 per month. Assume they will increase at the rate of inflation. You may also wish to purchase additional Medigap insurance, another costly item.

Be realistic about how your health might be in retirement and the costs of health care beyond what Medicare covers. You won't fall apart as soon as you hit 65, but by 75 health problems are likely to arise. The health and longevity of your parents and older siblings are your best guide. If your mother developed late-life diabetes, there is a good chance you will, too. But if she was severely overweight in her later years and you have maintained a normal weight and exercise frequently, those chances go down considerably.

Also factor in the money necessary to do the things you really want to do. If you have always dreamed of completing your master's degree in Shakespeare's works, factor in the cost of tuition, books, and so on. If creating the prize garden is a goal, that costs money, too, so include those fertilizers, exotic seedlings, and the cost of traveling to flower shows.

While you will be better able to estimate your retirement expenses as you near retirement, it is too late then to adjust your retirement savings significantly at that time if you have not saved enough in your 30s to early 50s. That's another good reason to assume you will need at least 100% of your preretirement income in making your savings needs projections.

PLANNING FOR INFLATION

The tables in Appendix A show the way money grows at varying interest rates. They also can be used in the same fashion to show how the purchasing power of money erodes at various inflation rates. The principle (no pun intended only because it would be misspelled) is the same. This is one of the reasons you must assume you need at least 100% of your preretirement income to survive in retirement. For example, let's assume you are earning $50,000 annually when you retire. Your pension, Social Security benefits, and personal savings also provide you with $50,000 annually in retirement. If the inflation rate after you retire is 7%, the average inflation rate in the 1970s, in 5 years you would need $70,000 to have the same purchasing power. If the average inflation rate is 5% as it was in the 1980s, you would need $63,800 to purchase the same goods in 5 years.

A woman of 65 today can expect to live another 18 years. If she was earning $50,000 when she retired and inflation stayed at a low 4% per year each year during the next 18 years, she would need approximately $101,500 to maintain the same purchasing power in her last year of life as she had when she retired. *At a 6% rate, the average inflation rate for the 1970s and 1980s, she would need about $142,500 to maintain purchasing power after 18 years.*

Inflation is the greatest enemy of the retiree. You must understand its effect and plan for it as you save and invest for retirement. As you can see, inflation means that even having a retirement income of 100% of your preretirement income may not keep you financially secure. Very few employer-provided retirement benefits are adjusted automatically for inflation. The exceptions are state and local government retirement plans which are sometimes subject to inflation adjustments, either directly through increases tied to a cost-of-living index or indirectly through payments based on a percentage of the current salary being paid to the position you held while you worked for the government. Private pensions do occasionally provide inflation adjustments to pensions on an ad hoc basis. Such cost-of-living adjustments (COLAs) seem to be dwindling even among employers who have provided them in the past. About 16% of those receiving private pensions received an increase in their pension after they retired according to the Department of Labor.[2] Among retirees who started receiving benefits prior to the 1980s, 24% had received such increases. During the 1980s only 13% received pension increases.[3] If you receive a COLA under your pension plan, celebrate! But in your preretirement planning, *don't assume there will be increases in your pension benefits for inflation,* even if your employer has made such increases in the past. Clearly the trend is away from inflation adjustments.

You can take steps to insulate your retirement savings and later income from inflation, at least partially. Indexed benefits and investments benefiting from inflation help. The next sections describe these steps.

Social Security Provides Some Protection from Inflation

First, Social Security benefits are adjusted for inflation, at least for the present time, so a part of your retirement income is protected from the scourge of inflation. Ironically, the less income you had during your working years, the higher proportion of your retirement income will come from Social Security benefits, and consequently, the more of your retirement income will be protected from inflation.

Some economists argue that because entitlements, including Social Security benefits, are such a large part of the U.S. economy, linking these payments to inflation, in fact, exacerbates inflation. While a majority of Congress has yet to embrace this concept, as more and more retirees are supported by fewer and fewer workers in the twenty-first century, the least obvious way (and hence the most politically salable way) to reduce the Social Security burden would be to limit inflation adjustments. One could also argue such limits would fight inflation and increase or at least stabilize income for both retirees and workers. On balance, the strong protection against inflation which

Social Security provides for today's retirees may not be guaranteed to future retirees.

Choose Investments to Ride with Inflation

Second, your investments for retirement savings and income, especially in your 20s through age 50 or so, should contain primarily assets which will benefit from inflation such as stocks and other investments that give you equity in the asset. The single biggest mistake people make with employer-provided plans such as 401(k) plans or thrift plans that give employees investment options is choosing too "safe" an option. Chapter 13 will discuss in greater detail the relationship between risk and rate of return. For now, recognize in most cases the safer the investment, the lower the rate of return. But if the rate of return is so low that your savings are being dissolved by inflation, the investment isn't safe—it's a waste of money.

Suppose Jennifer's employer institutes a 401(k) plan with three investment options: a stock mutual fund, a government securities fund, and a fixed interest investment option, commonly called a *guaranteed income contract*. As the mutual fund prospectuses always say, "Past performance is no guarantee of future investment return," but over the years the mutual fund has had an average return of 10%, some years losing as much as 10% in value and other years earning as much as 30%. The government securities fund averages about 7% annually, some years going as low as 3% and as high as 12%. The guaranteed income contract (GIC) is guaranteed only by the assets of the insurance company offering it, and its only real "guarantee" is to pay 4% for one year on the money invested. At the end of the year, the GIC will set a new interest rate based roughly on similar interest rates for certificates of deposit.

Faced with those investment options, too many people go with the GIC because they think they understand it (they probably don't) and because they think it is safer than the mutual funds (it probably isn't). GICs' safety is based solely on the financial security of the insurance company underwriting it. At age 30 Jennifer has a lot of time to let her money grow, so even small amounts can become significant. Because she will not need her money for several years, ups and downs in the market have plenty of time to even out. Jennifer decides to put $1,000, about 5% of her current salary, in the 401(k) plan each year until she retires at age 60. How much she will have at retirement varies dramatically depending on the investment mix she chooses. Assume over the next 30 years the funds achieve their historic rates of return.

TABLE 11.2 Comparison of Retirement Savings Earned from Different Investment Options		
	Lump Sum at Retirement	Annual Income for 25 Years*
100% Stock mutual fund, 10% return	$164,494	$15,400
100% Government fund, 7% return	94,461	8,850
100% GIC, 4% return	56,085	5,250
50% Stock mutual fund/ 50% GIC	110,289	10,300
50% Government securities fund/50% GIC	75,272	7,050
*Assumes an 8% rate of return on lump sum after retirement.		

Clearly, Table 11.2 shows how rates of return make a critical difference in the growth of your investments for retirement. Investing the same amount of money, but depending on the investments she chooses now, Jennifer may have an annual income from her 401(k) of $5,250 a year or about three times that much, $15,400. If Jennifer follows the lead of many unsophisticated employees and "safely" invests her money in assets that have a lower rate of return, but presumably lower risk (i.e., assets such as the government securities fund and the GIC), she is likely to have a very risky retirement. She simply won't have enough money, even with Social Security and her employer-provided pension, to maintain her life-style.

As a 30-year-old, Jennifer has decades before she will retire. She can wisely invest in the "riskier" stock mutual fund because, even when the fund has a bad year in which it loses money, she can wait for the value to build up again. In contrast, at 60, Alice cannot wait for the fund to regain value over decades. Therefore, Alice should invest a larger part of her assets in less volatile assets such as a large portion in the government securities fund and perhaps 40% or so of her 401(k) in the stock mutual fund. She should be invested in the GIC which is providing a 4% rate of return, only if she believes her retirement is imminent and she knows she will need money immediately.

One basic rule for retirement savings is to *invest heavily in the assets with higher rates of return and risk early in your career and shift to the lower-risk-and-return assets only as you near retirement.* Even during the early retirement years, some of your funds should be in higher-return assets to protect against inflation during your long years of retirement. The less risk tolerance you have, the more money you must save to reach the same dollar retirement savings goals. The next chapter discusses investment strategies in more detail.

Look at the Real Rate of Return—Subtract Inflation

As you plan for inflation, look at investments in terms of their "real rate of return." A bond returning 8% per year is really only growing at the rate of 8% minus the inflation rate. The "real rate of return" is the interest rate minus the inflation rate. Of course, as inflation increases, so do rates of returns in many investments. That's why buying a 30-year bond toward the end of an inflationary cycle is a very good investment. Chances are it will be paying 10% for the next 30 years, which will provide a very good real rate of return when inflation is 4%. But in the years in which inflation spirals to 11%, you are losing 1% per year on your money. The other problem is knowing when we are at the end of the inflationary cycle. If the financial experts, the White House, and the Federal Reserve Board can't figure it out, you may have a problem discerning the end of an inflationary trend, too.

Beware of the Optimistic Financial Adviser

Many retirement adviser projections do not adequately account for inflation. Several of the mutual fund families and stock brokerage houses produce very worthwhile retirement financial planning guides, but these forms often assume unrealistically low estimates of inflation. Some of these guides even provide you with charts showing inflation averaging 5.5% for the 1980s and then merrily tell you on the next page that their examples and projections will assume a 4% inflation rate. They may be right. After all, inflation in the 1960s averaged only 2.3%. But that was before we had a national debt of $3 trillion and annual deficits running in excess of $200 billion plus "for as far as the eye can see." The 1990s so far suggest it will be a low-inflation decade. But remember you will be planning for and living in the next two to four decades, too. It stretches credulity to think those decades will continue with low inflation.

Table 11.3 shows you inflation rates for the last three decades based on three common indices. The consumer price index (CPI) is the most popularly used guide to inflation; however, the *implicit price deflators* used by the U.S. Department of Commerce are more comprehensive because they cover more items and services. Table 11.3 gives you a history of inflation. Decide for yourself on its future. Unlike most other areas of life, in retirement financial planning pessimism is a better trait than optimism. Think about inflation in all your calculations.

CALCULATING SAVINGS NEEDED TO REACH YOUR RETIREMENT INCOME GOALS

If you are under 55 now, start by assuming you will need at least 100% of your current income. Then subtract from present income Social Security taxes (7.65% up to $57,600 and 1.45% on the remainder up to $135,000 in 1993). There are vast differences in the projected amounts needed, depending on the retirement financial planning method you use and the inflation factors you assume. We will use one approach and suggest ways you can construct your own approach using the time value of money and your own assumptions. Susan's retirement planning will serve as an example, and there are blanks for your own calculations.

The worksheet in Table 11.4 is derived from *Money* magazine and is widely reprinted, especially by mutual funds and brokerage houses in their retirement savings planning brochures. Attached to the worksheet are various time-value-of-money factors, like those contained in the time-value-of-money tables in Appendix A. But

	TABLE 11.3 Common Indices for Rates of Inflation, 1960–1990			
Year	Consumer Price Index	Gross National Product	Gross Domestic Product	CPI Decade Average
1960	1.7%	1.6%	1.6%	
1961	1.0	1.0	1.0	
1962	1.0	2.2	2.2	
1963	1.3	1.6	1.6	
1964	1.3	1.5	1.5	2.3%
1965	1.6	2.7	2.7	
1966	2.9	3.6	3.6	
1967	3.1	2.6	2.6	
1968	4.2	5.0	5.0	
1969	5.5	5.6	5.6	
1970	5.7	5.5	5.5	
1971	4.4	5.7	5.7	
1972	3.2	4.7	4.7	
1973	6.2	6.5	6.5	
1974	11.0	9.1	9.1	7.1%
1975	9.1	9.8	9.8	
1976	5.8	6.4	6.4	
1977	6.5	6.7	6.7	
1978	7.6	7.3	7.3	
1979	11.3	8.9	8.9	
1980	13.5	9.0	9.0	
1981	10.3	9.7	9.7	
1982	6.2	6.4	6.4	
1983	3.2	3.9	3.9	
1984	4.3	3.7	3.7	5.5%
1985	3.6	3.0	3.1	
1986	1.9	2.6	2.5	
1987	3.6	3.2	3.3	
1988	4.1	3.3	3.3	
1989	4.8	4.1	4.0	
1990	5.4	NA	NA	

NA – Not available.

Source: Bureau of the Census, *Statistical Abstract of the United States: 1991*, 111th edition (Washington, D.C.: U.S. Government Printing Office, 1991), Tables 765 and 767.

these factors are limited to an assumption of an 8% rate of return on investments and a 5% inflation rate. These factors will be applied to help in our calculations needed to project the growth of savings and the required savings rate on our worksheet. This worksheet originally called for using 80% of preretirement income as the starting figure, but we will follow our 100% rule.

At 50 Susan is too far from retirement to have an exact idea of her retirement income needs to outline a budget and use that budget figure. We have begun with Susan's current income of $25,200 and current dollar figures for salary, Social Security, and her pension benefits. The real figures will be higher, but this method gives you an idea of where she stands today. We then subtracted Social Security taxes (worksheet line 2) she pays on her current salary from that amount. Remember you don't pay Social Security taxes on nonwage income such as the Social Security benefits themselves or pensions and interest income, so you won't need that amount of money in retirement. We got Susan's estimated Social Security retirement benefits from current law estimates of primary insurance amounts for a person of Susan's age, income, and work history.

Moving down the worksheet for Susan, we added Susan's projected annual employer benefits payments (worksheet line 5) taken from Appendix B and her projected Social Security benefit (worksheet line 4) and then subtracted that sum from her current salary after we had deducted Social Security taxes (worksheet line 3). The result (worksheet line 6) is the amount she will need at retirement from sources other than her employer retirement benefit and Social Security. Unless she wins the lottery, this line 6 amount will have to come from her own savings.

On worksheet line 7 we calculated the amount she will need to have saved by retirement to give her a nest egg large enough to supply this amount of money each year of her retirement. We multiplied her annual needs by the factor A for retirement at age 65. To see how much of that needed nest egg amount on line 7 she still needs to save, on worksheet line 8 we entered the amount she has already saved, which is only $8,000 under our assumption for this exercise. Worksheet line 9 projects the value of that $8,000 by the time she retires by multiplying it by the 15-year growth factor B for a sum of $12,240. Worksheet line 10 subtracts this projected value of current savings from the amount she will need at retirement and reaches a result of $146,294 of personal savings needed by retirement at age 65. To learn how much she must save each year to accumulate that amount by the time she reaches retirement age, we apply the factor C for 15 years to reach the final figure of $7,900 on worksheet line 11, which is the amount Susan must save annually from now until retirement to have 100% of her current income when she retires.

Based on these projections, Susan has an all but impossible task before her. She will have to save over $7,900 annually or about 31% of her pretax income to meet these goals. Of course in Susan's case, if the law remains unchanged, it is not likely she will have to pay taxes on the Social Security benefits she receives. She can live without the income she would have needed to pay taxes on $10,320 of Social Security income. Also, because Social Security is indexed to meet inflation and because Social Security will make up a large part of her income after retirement, she will have some built-in inflation protection. Her employer-provided benefit is stated in today's dollars and will in fact be higher at retirement (but so will her actual income needed at retirement).

The projections also assume Susan has a very low current amount of savings to date of only $8,000. Chances are very good she is likely to have saved more than that by now. Previous savings could dramatically reduce the amount she would need to save in the future. For example, if Susan had saved $20,000 by now, not an unrealistic sum for a woman with her years in the work force, she would need to save approximately $6,900 or about 27% of her current income, per year until retirement to meet her goal. Of course, this is still an ambitious savings goal.

The other difficulty is that these projections do not fully factor in inflation erosion. There is no guarantee that even with 100% of today's salary, she will still be able to maintain her life-style. Of course, both Social Security and her employer-provided pension values used here are stated in terms of today's dollar. Social Security's buying power will increase with inflation, at least under current law. The pension value will increase with inflation until Susan retires, but there will be no increase in its value after the pension amount is fixed at Susan's retirement.

Note that if we had used Susan's accrued benefits as of today, her benefit at retirement would have increased both for inflation and for increased service and salary. But we used her projected benefit at retirement, which includes the value of those years of service and salary increases.

	Susan	You
TABLE 11.4 **Retirement Savings Projection Worksheet** **Based on _Money_ Magazine's Approach,** **Today's Dollars**		
1. Salary at retirement	$25,200	_____
2. Social Security taxes at retirement	1,928	_____
3. Income needed at retirement (line 1 minus line 2)	23,272	_____
4. Annual Social Security retirement benefits (estimated)	10,320	_____
5. Annual pension benefits from defined benefit plans	4,695	_____
6. Annual income needed from personal savings (line 3 minus lines 4 and 5)	8,257	_____
7. Amount to be saved before retirement (line 6 times factor A)	158,534	_____
8. Amount saved for retirement to date, including IRAs, etc.	8,000	_____
9. Projected value of current savings at time of retirement (line 8 times factor B)	12,240	_____
10. Amount of retirement capital still needed (line 7 minus line 9)	146,294	_____
11. Annual savings needed to reach retirement goal (line 10 times factor C)	7,900	_____

TABLE 11.4 *(cont'd)*	
Age at Retirement	Factor A*
55	23.3
56	22.9
57	22.6
58	22.2
59	21.8
60	21.4
61	21.0
62	20.5
63	20.1
64	19.6
65	19.2
66	18.7
67	18.2

Years to Retirement	Factor B*	Factor C*
5	1.15	0.188
7	1.22	0.131
9	1.29	0.099
11	1.36	0.079
13	1.44	0.065
15	1.53	0.054
20	1.76	0.038
25	2.02	0.028
30	2.33	0.022

*These factors assume an 8% rate of return on money invested and 5% rate of inflation.

Source: This worksheet and the factor tables are based on similar table and factors appearing in *Money* magazine and used by permission of the publisher, Time-Warner, Inc.

Susan needs so much individual savings for two primary reasons. First, her employer-provided pension will supply only about 16% of her preretirement income. Second, she started her own personal savings so late in her career.

But when Susan started her career if she had begun saving 5% of her earnings and placed them in a tax-sheltered investment, such as an individual retirement account (IRA) or an employer's saving plan, she would have enough saved to receive an annual income from those savings of $10,600 (in today's dollars) when she retired.

This income from her personal savings, combined with Social Security and her employer-provided pension, would give her an income in retirement of $25,615 a year, in today's dollars. This income does not exceed the $25,000 threshold for taxing some portion of Social Security benefits because only half of Social Security income is counted in that threshold. Thus none of Susan's $10,320 Social Security benefit is subject to income tax, and, of course, her pension and personal savings income are not subject to FICA taxes. As a result Susan would have a slightly higher after-tax income during retirement than she had while working. *The income from her small, but early and consistent, personal savings would give her a greater annual income than either the employer-provided benefit or Social Security and, more important, would reach her retirement income goals.*

From Susan's case, you can see now why retirement planning financial advisers are tempted to assume unrealistically low inflation rates and unrealistically high earnings rates on your savings and investments. Otherwise, they fear you will be so discouraged by the amount you need to save, you will abandon the idea of retirement savings completely. But don't fall into either the trap of unrealistic assumptions or the slough of despondency over the large sums projected for retirement needs. It is better to know the bad news while you are working and young enough to save something than to bury your head in the sand and learn how much you should have saved after it is too late to do anything about it!

Use the Income Projection Worksheet for Your Retirement Planning

Now go through the chart yourself and see what you need to be saving to maintain your current life-style. Start with your current salary. Calculate line 2, Social Security taxes, by using your paycheck stub or by multiplying your salary by 7.65% up to the first $57,600 and by 1.45% for salary above that up to $135,000. Your Earnings and

Benefit Estimate Statement that you ordered from Social Security will supply the estimated annual Social Security retirement benefit figure for line 4. Use your employer's summary plan description (SPD) to calculate your pension benefits from defined benefit plans needed in line 5. For line 8, include all the amounts you have in employer-provided defined contribution plans, such as 401(k) plans and profit-sharing plans, as well as amounts in your IRA, Keoghs, and any other savings you have set aside strictly for retirement. Don't cheat by including in line 8 money you have saved for your children's education or money you are saving for a vacation house. Unless you are age 50, like Susan, you will have to use the appropriate values from Appendix A, rather than the factors in Table 11.4.

You can also construct your own projection sheet, using your own assumptions on inflation rates and rates of return by using the time-value-of-money tables in Appendix A and choosing the appropriate factors. For example, if you have 20 years until retirement and feel you can earn 10% on your line 8 savings, but inflation will be 4%, you will have a 6% real rate of return on your savings. Use Table A.1, the Future Value of a Dollar, and apply a factor of 3.207 (the multiplier for 6% over 20 years) to determine the worth of your current savings at your retirement. If the savings in line 8 are primarily in a tax-deferred IRA or profit-sharing plan invested in sound mutual funds, this might be a fairly accurate assumption. Likewise, once you reach the figure on line 10 for the amount you still need to save, you could use Table A.3, Future Value of an Annuity, to determine how much you must save if you think you can earn a 6% real rate of return (i.e., return minus inflation) on your money after taxes. Since you will be earning 6% over 20 years, find the factor for that amount, 36.786, and divide that amount into the amount on line 10 to determine the amount of money you must save annually to reach your goal for line 11.

As we saw with Jennifer's choices earlier in the chapter, you can see for yourself what a difference a few points on rate of return or inflation make in the amount you need to save and the amount you will ultimately have for retirement. Don't be discouraged if your projected sums seem astronomical. Maybe you won't be able to save that much, but at least you know what your goal should be. Remember, some savings are better than no savings. Also, as you get nearer to retirement, you can calculate your actual needs more accurately. If you begin to see you can live on less than 100% of your current salary, but you have saved based on needing 100% of your current income, you will find you have all the savings you need before you retire, as well as a cushion for retirement.

Seeing the amounts you need to save for retirement well in advance of your retirement will help your planning in other ways. If the amount you need to save seems impossible when you have assumed retirement at age 60, recalculate planning retirement at age 62 or 65. You will be surprised at the difference. Delaying retirement helps in two ways. You have more years to save, and there are fewer years when you are drawing down capital. Or add in an assumption you will work part time after retirement so you will have some earned income during your first years of retirement. If you begin planning for part-time work before retirement is actually upon you, you have time to plan for a different type of work or a second career.

Also, project your retirement needs and savings requirements every few years. These numbers change dramatically at different inflation rates or rates of return on savings. Hopefully, your employer-provided retirement benefits should be growing, too. As the employer-provided benefit grows, you will need less personal savings. But, remember, for planning purposes, use the worst case scenario and set your savings goals based on that scenario, even if you cannot meet the goals. At a minimum you will be safe in most scenarios. If you assumed inflation at 7% and a real rate of return on your retirement investments of 3% in your early saving years, but in fact inflation was only 4% and you received a real rate of return of 4%, when you redo your calculations after a few years you can adjust your future savings. Even if you don't change your future assumptions, your projected needed savings rate will be much lower because you will have already "oversaved" in the early years and will be earning money on a larger pool of assets than you had originally projected.

CONCLUSION: CONSIDER THE EFFECT OF INFLATION AND YOUR INVESTMENT CHOICES WHEN ESTIMATING YOUR RETIREMENT INCOME NEEDS

❖ Project your salary forward to retirement using the tables in Appendix A.

❖ Applying the projected salary, use the *Money* magazine projection worksheet in Table 11.4 and values in Appendix A for your own retirement savings.

❖ If you find the savings requirements impossible to meet, recalculate using a slightly older retirement age.

❖ Regardless of the outcome, *keep saving.*

❖ Assume you need at least 100% of your income just prior to retirement to live comfortably in retirement.

❖ Remember the effects of inflation in calculating your needed retirement income and the savings to produce that income.

❖ In your early years of retirement saving, invest heavily in assets that will give you a higher rate of return, and track inflation such as stocks or stock mutual funds. The difference in the amounts you must save when you are getting a 9% rate of return are vastly lower than the amount you need to save when you are only receiving a 5% rate of return.

❖ Let your projections inspire you to save more than you thought you could. And, remember, future raises will make saving easier, as long as you don't count on them and don't spend the raise before it occurs. Resolve to save every "windfall" such as a bonus or an income tax refund you weren't expecting.

❖ Finally, you may have to adjust your expectations to better fit reality. You can't retire at 55 if you didn't start saving until you were 50.

NOTES FOR CHAPTER 11

1. *See* Bruce A. Palmer, "1991 GSU/AACG Retire Project Report," Georgia State University. Center for Risk Management and Insurance Research.

2. Daniel J. Beller and David D. McCarthy, "Private Pension Benefits," from John A. Turner and Daniel J. Beller, eds., *Trends in Pensions 1992* (Washington, D.C.: U.S. Department of Labor, Pension and Welfare Benefits Administration, U.S. Government Printing Office, 1992), Table 10.11 and p. 223.

3. Ibid.

How to Start
Saving and Investing:
Becoming Familiar with
Investment Vehicles

Nike's advice for an exercise program applies equally well to a savings and investment program—Just do it! Start putting away some amount, no matter how small, immediately. Yes, we said it before, but have you started yet? Waiting to begin saving until you have more money or until you know everything about investments is like waiting to start jogging until you can run 5 miles. It isn't going to just happen. You have to begin, and usually you have to begin in a small way.

As with learning about employer and individual retirement plans, reviewing some basic investment terms helps. Then we'll move on to how to become more knowledgeable about investments, how to begin investing, and how to get good investment advice on a continuing basis. Our focus is on retirement savings, but many of the ideas apply to other financial goals you might have.

Saving money is not enough; you must put those savings to work earning money, too. That requires investment. In any savings or investment instrument, you want to consider three basic elements:

1. Safety of your invested money (your principal)—that is, are you going to get your money back?

2. Rate of return—that is, how much will you earn on your money after the expenses of investment (if any) and after taxes and inflation?

3. Liquidity—that is, when can you get your hands on the money and the earnings?

As a rule, the safer and more liquid your money, the lower the rate of return, and vice versa. Investments like stocks will give you the opportunity to get a relatively high return on your money over the years, but the risk that your investment may be reduced or even lost completely is higher too. By contrast, a savings account or a certificate of deposit will be very safe—guaranteed by the U. S. government up to $100,000 per account—but the interest you earn will be very low. In fact, after paying taxes and accounting for inflation, you may actually lose money. But within any class of investment there are specific vehicles that provide more return with less risk. Learning how to find those specific investments marks you as a true investor.

Generally, your investments should be balanced with a few investments that are very safe, such as certificates of deposit, and most that are more risky with a greater return, such as mutual funds and income stocks. But the specific mix best for you depends partly on your age. At a younger age you can afford to put more money into slightly riskier ventures because you will have more time to correct your mistakes. This is particularly true when investing in stocks and mutual funds because the vagaries of the market often correct themselves over time. As you near retirement, you should shift a greater percentage of investment to the bottom of the pyramid. But even in retirement you cannot have all your capital invested in low-risk/low-return investments because inflation will erode it.

DEBT OR EQUITY INVESTMENTS

All sorts of investments can be referred to as "securities," which in a legal sense means any sort of investment or arrangement from which you expect to receive income without working for it. There are basically two kinds of securities investments—debt and equity. If you invest in debt issues, you are a creditor for which you receive a return in the form of interest. If you invest in "equity," you are an owner and you receive your earnings in the form of dividends. As a creditor you are betting that the underlying entity—a corporation, the U.S. government, a municipality, or whatever—will pay its bills. Debt investments are usually called bonds or notes. In an equity investment you are literally buying a piece of the entity issuing the security. Equities are most frequently sold in the form of stock or limited partnerships. Remember that debtors get paid before owners, so in general bonds will be safer than stocks. But as with all rules of thumb, there are lots of exceptions.

The following sections outline some basic investment vehicles and the pros and cons of each.

Cash Equivalents

Money Market Accounts. Money market accounts are basically checking accounts that pay you interest. Your checking account should definitely be a "money market account" paying you interest and not charging you for checking. If you have your account with a federally insured institution such as a bank, savings and loan, or savings bank, your account will be insured up to $100,000 per institution.

The obvious advantage of these accounts is their safety and liquidity, but the disadvantage is they usually pay a very low rate of return. Money market accounts are not the investment for your retirement funds, because you don't need to access those funds easily and you do need to have as high a rate of return as possible. But money market funds are very good places for your "emergency savings" and for holding funds while you are investigating longer-term investments. Once you have established significant retirement savings, you should have a money market account simply to hold money between buying and selling investments.

Money Market Funds. Money market funds function like money market accounts, but they are not federally insured. They are a type of "mutual fund" holding several different debt instruments. (Mutual funds are discussed in detail later in this chapter.) Because money market funds usually diversify their holdings in short-term debt that have varying maturities, they are considered a very safe investment. The funds are liquid. Again, their rate of return is very low, so these are not good investments for retirement funds, but may be useful as short-term "holding accounts" until you decide on long-term investments.

Certificates of Deposit

These are simply deposits of cash with a bank or thrift institution. The money earns interest for the life of the CD—usually a stated period of months. The longer the period of the CD, the higher the interest rate in most cases. If you redeem the CD before its term runs, there is usually a steep penalty. If the CD is deposited in a state or federally guaranteed institution, your money is guaranteed by the government. In federal institutions the guarantee is up to $100,000. In state institutions, the amount guaranteed will vary from state to state.

CDs are very safe—at least up to the guaranteed amount, as the savings and loan scandal proved—but their rate of return is usually relatively small. Indeed, after taxes and inflation are factored in, you may only be breaking even. If your CDs are for a very long term and inflation rises during the term, you might even lose money when you compare the amount of CD interest with the rate of inflation. Nevertheless, CDs are easily understood and easily purchased. They are relatively liquid, depending on their term. You can make them even more liquid by purchasing at one time a 3-month, 6-month, 9-month and 1-year CD. Thereafter, each time one of the CDs matures, buy a 1-year CD. With this system you always have a CD maturing within 3 months and you will have access to a major part of your savings every 3 months. You will also have the advantage of receiving the higher rate of return that comes with the longer-term CD.

Unless you buy CDs through a broker, who can sometimes get you higher rates than are ordinarily available, you pay no fees or commissions to buy CDs.

Given CDs' low interest rates, which in part is a trade-off for the liquidity of CDs that is unneeded for retirement accounts, CDs are not an ideal investment for your retirement savings. However, until you feel confident in investing, CDs can be a good compromise investment while you are learning about other investment opportunities. Just don't wait too long to branch out into higher-paying investments.

Bonds

Bonds are promises to repay your loan of money at a certain time—the maturity date of the bond. Over the course of the loan, the debtor will pay you interest, often when you submit a "coupon," although for the most part the quaint exercise of actually "clipping coupons" to redeem this interest has gone the way of Model-Ts and one-wage-earner families. Today the interest is usually paid without coupon submission. The U.S. government, most state and local governments, and corporations issue bonds.

When you invest in bonds, always remember that the value of your investment is invariably linked to overall interest rate market, not just to the quality of the bond itself. The value of your underlying principal value will vary—sometimes dramatically—depending on fluctuations of the general interest rates for other debt instruments. As interest rates go up, the value of your principal investment in the bond goes down. As interest rates go down, the value of your bond goes up. The longer the term of your bond, the more the underlying value will be affected by interest rate changes. For example, if you bought a $10,000, 30-year bond paying a rate of 7% and interest rates for other types of debt moves up to 8%, the underlying value of your bond on the secondary market, that is, what another buyer would pay you for your bond, is going to be considerably reduced. Why? Because other investors can now buy newer bonds paying a higher interest rate than your bond. But if interest rates fall to 6%, the value of your bond in the secondary market will considerably exceed $10,000 because there are few other investments that will pay as great an interest rate as your bond. Your bond now looks quite attractive to potential buyers.

Of course, if you keep the bond until maturity, you will receive your $10,000 back and you will have received interest on a periodic basis over the life of the bond. This is one reason why bonds can be good investments for retirement planning. If you buy a 20-year bond, planning to hold it until retirement, the fluctuations in the bond's price in the secondary market over its terms are immaterial to you. You have received a higher interest rate because you are willing to have your money tied up in the bond for a long time and the risk of changes in the underlying value bond before the maturity date aren't a concern for you. But be careful of buying long-term bonds in times of low inflation and low interest rates. If you buy a 30-year bond paying 8% and inflation goes to 10% or more for a decade, you will have lost a considerable amount of money because you could not use the money tied up in the bond to seek an investment with the higher rates of return high inflation brings.

Bonds are rated for safety by several rating agencies such as Standard & Poor's and Moody's Investors Services. The ratings range from AAA to D for Standard & Poor's and Aaa to D for Moody's. As you might expect, the closer to AAA or Aaa, the safer the bond and the lower the rate of return. This guide is helpful for the beginning investor. Ratings can change during the term of the bond, which will change the bond's secondary market value, but not its ultimate redemption price. Most bonds can be purchased through a broker for a fee.

There is a tendency to think of bonds as extremely safe and nonvolatile in their prices. But as illustrated in our examples, the value of bonds can fluctuate greatly, sometimes more than stocks. Investing in bonds should be a long-term proposition. Don't put money in bonds if you are going to need it before the bond's maturity date.

Treasury Bills, Notes, and Bonds. U.S. Treasury debt instruments are backed by the full faith and credit of the U.S. government— and more important, the U.S. taxpayer. "Bills" are debt instruments with maturities ranging from 60 days to 1 year. "Notes" have maturity dates from 1 year to 10 years. Treasury debt instruments for more than 10 years are "bonds." Again, the longer the maturity level, the higher the interest rate usually is, but in recent years during uncertain economic times, shorter-term maturities have occasionally had higher rates of return than the longer-term debts. "Treasuries" can be purchased through brokers or a bank for a fee or from the Federal Reserve Banks. Call the Federal Reserve Bank in your region. For more information write to The Bureau of Public Debt, Department F, Department of the Treasury, Washington, D.C. 20239-1200.

Treasury debt instruments have a "secondary" market, meaning that they can be bought and sold through brokers after they have been issued and before they mature, so they tend to be very liquid. Treasury debt instruments are also exempt from state and local taxes, which can be quite a bonus if you live in a high-tax state such as New York, Maryland, Pennsylvania, New Jersey, or Massachusetts.

For retirement savings, you don't need the liquidity of Treasury bills, especially given their low return. For younger savers Treasury notes and bonds are a good retirement investment only if the rates are competitive with corporate bonds. For older, or very conservative, investors, Treasuries may be an appropriate investment. Also once your portfolio has an adequate level of other investments, Treasury bonds or notes may be an appropriate way to diversify.

Municipal Bonds. These are bonds issued by state and local governments. Their interest is exempt from federal taxes and usually from tax of the jurisdiction issuing the bonds. Because of this tax advantage, the rate of return is usually lower than that of corporate bonds. If you want to compare the tax-exempt bond rate of return to taxable rates, divide the bond's interest rate by the number that equals one minus your tax bracket. Include state tax in that bracket figure if the bonds are exempt from state tax. For example, suppose a municipal bond is offering a rate of 5%. Your federal tax rate is 28% and the state rate is 3%. Your overall rate is 31%. One minus 0.31 is 0.69; 0.69 divided into 5 is 7.25, so you would need to be receiving at least a 7.25% rate of return on a taxable investment to be comparable to the tax-free investment. This formula can be used to compare any type of tax-free amount to a taxable or after-tax sum.

You should never put tax-exempt investments in your IRA or Keogh because when you begin to withdraw money from those plans, all income of the plan will be taxable. Only your original investment will escape taxation. Putting tax-exempt investments in an IRA or Keogh will turn the otherwise tax-exempt income into taxable income, even though the tax will be delayed until you retire. But tax-exempt bonds may be good investments for retirement savings in addition to your IRA or Keogh account. Municipal bonds are best purchased from a broker who specializes in municipals because such brokers are more knowledgeable and have easy access to a wider variety of bonds.

Corporate Bonds. Corporate bonds are simply debt of the corporation. Corporate bonds pay interest at a fixed rate over the term of the bond, usually 10, 20, or 30 years. With corporate bonds, the underlying value of your principal will be affected by interest rates in general, as was true with U.S. Treasury bonds. But with corporate bonds, the value of your principal will also be affected by the overall health of the company to some degree. Highly rated corporate bonds are appropriate retirement savings investments for a small part of your retirement portfolio. As you age, their steady income becomes more important to cash flow, and the portion of your portfolio dedicated to bonds should increase.

Corporate bonds that are guaranteed by the general assets of the company are referred to as debentures. Corporate bonds guaranteed by specific assets of the company are referred to as mortgage bonds.

Zero Coupon Bonds. Zero coupon bonds are offered by the U.S. Treasury, municipalities, and corporations. Zero coupon bonds are sold at a deep discount from the face value; for example, a $1,000 bond may be offered at $300. Over the life of the bond, no interest is paid. Then, at maturity, you receive the face value. The IRS treats these bonds as though interest were paid every year, so you pay taxes even though you have received no interest. Since IRAs and Keoghs do not pay tax on earnings as those earnings occur, some investment advisers urge buying zero coupon bonds for IRAs and Keoghs. They can be a good investment for those accounts, as long as you are receiving a competitive rate of return on the bond.

Junk Bonds a/k/a "High-Yield Bonds" and "Fallen Angels." Junk bonds may begin their lives as junk, or they may descend into junkdom. Some junk bonds are "natural born," issued by companies already heavily in debt or on shaky financial ground. These junk bonds offer a very high rate of return from the date they are issued to make up for the lack of safety. Highly popular in the takeover-crazed 1980s, these "natural-born" junk bonds are less commonly issued today.

Other high-yielding junk bonds are "self-made." At the date of their original issue, these bonds may have had an ordinary yield; however, because of financial reverses of the issuing company, the face value of the bond has fallen so low that, in comparison to the interest being paid on more secure bonds, the yield now is quite high. For example, Modern Buggy Company issues bonds at $1,000 face value, paying 5%. Investors come to view Modern Buggy as out of step with the current world, and the face value of the bond in the secondary market now falls to $500. The 5% interest payments now represent a yield of 10% on the current value of your investment.

Unless you are very young and have a long time to wait for the investment to even out ups and downs in value or you have the extra money to take some higher-than-average risks, junk bonds are not an appropriate vehicle for retirement savings.

Equities

Investments in "equities" representing ownership are usually in shares of stock of the company. They may also be units of a partnership in which you are a "limited partner." As an owner, you will receive income only after all debts are paid. These earnings will be in the form of dividends, usually paid quarterly, for stocks, and "distributions" for limited partnerships. However, you also have the opportunity to share in the growth of the intrinsic value of the company. That growth should represent itself in the increase of the price of the stock or partnership units you bought. Some companies pay no dividends or distributions, and your only return will be from the growth of the stock price, if any.

Publicly Held Stocks. "Common" stock does not refer to ubiquitous stock. Rather, the term means you will receive dividends, if any, from a common pool of earnings. "Preferred stock" means that you will receive dividends, frequently at a stated percentage of your original investment in the stock, before any dividends are paid to the "common" stockholders. Preferred stock may also carry with it different voting rights than common stock. "Convertible preferred stock" is preferred stock that enables you to convert shares of your preferred stock into common stock when the common stock reaches a certain price. You make money because you paid a lower price for the preferred stock. Of course, the common stock may never reach a higher price than the preferred.

Publicly held stocks, meaning those stocks anyone can purchase, are traded on one of a number of stock exchanges. The New York Stock Exchange is the largest and trades most *Fortune* 500 companies. The American Stock Exchange tends to specialize in the shares of slightly smaller, though still significant companies. Many start-up or regional companies are sold in the over-the-counter market. The over-the-counter market is a network of brokers around the country dealing in the particular stocks. This market buys and sells using the National Association of Securities Dealers' Automated Quotation system, called NASDAQ.

Stocks can be purchased through a stockbroker who will charge you a commission, a fee based on a percentage price of the stock you purchase. When you sell the stock through a broker, there will also be a commission. Some companies permit you to buy their stock directly and will reinvest the dividends the stock earns in more stock. For a fee you can get an updated list of these stocks by writing:

National Association of Investors Corporation

1515 E. Eleven Mile Road

Royal Oak, Michigan 48067

The return on stocks can be quite high because you have the chance to receive both earnings and the growth in the value of the basic share price. But the risk is high for many stocks. Values change daily. Often the price of the stock is influenced more by rumors and the general economy than the underlying value or management of the specific company. The bulk of the market is held by so-called institutional investors such as college endowments, pension trust funds and other trusts, and mutual funds. These investors' funds are managed by professional asset managers, some of whom trade based on computer programs designed to respond to interest rates and other economic indicators. From an investor's perspective, it is meaningless to talk about "stocks" in general. Some company's shares are an extremely good value; others may be essentially worthless in a few months. Most lie somewhere in between.

Picking individual stocks for investment is a chancy business, as millions of people on Wall Street—or formerly on Wall Street—can attest. Some investment counselors even caution that the "dart board" method of choosing stocks works about as well as the "experts." For more than 10 years *The Wall Street Journal* has compared the results of the experts against the overall market and against stocks chosen by the staff literally throwing darts at a listing of stocks. The experts lead the dart throwers by a mere 14 to 9.[1]

Does all of this risk mean you should never put your retirement savings into stocks? Absolutely not! It may be a tough game, but it's the only practical game in town to protect your savings from inflation. (Some might argue gold, diamonds, and real estate will also protect from inflation, but these are too speculative for wise investors.) Besides, there is a wonderful way the individual investor who does not want to spend every spare hour analyzing stocks can still play the game—mutual funds.

Mutual Funds

Mutual funds are groups of stocks or bonds or a mixture of other investment assets held by an asset manager. You invest in mutual funds by buying shares of the funds. Using this technique, your small investment in the mutual fund enables you indirectly to hold at least a piece of many stocks.

There are literally thousands of mutual funds with a large assortment of investment goals, strategies, and pricing schemes. Some funds hold only "income stocks," that is, shares of well-established companies such as AT&T, Coca-Cola, and Merck, which consistently pay dividends, but whose prices ordinarily do not fluctuate greatly. Other funds hold only "growth stocks" of young companies which may not even pay a dividend, but whose share price is expected to grow significantly over the years. Some funds hold combinations of these kinds of stocks. So-called "sector funds" hold only stocks of a particular industry such as health companies, high-tech companies, mining companies, and so on. Mutual funds may hold only bonds or only certain types of bonds. Some funds may hold stocks, bonds, and large sums of cash investments for so-called "total" investment. Others, called index funds, simply buy shares of every stock traded on a given exchange. The return and performance of these index funds have the same results as the overall stock market.

The fund's "prospectus" is somewhat like a summary plan description, but the prospectus outlines the goals, expenses, income record, investments, and managers of the fund. The prospectus will also tell you how to buy and sell shares of the fund. The prospectus will be sent to you by the fund or given to you by a broker handling the fund.

Mutual funds are either *closed-end* or *open-end* operations. Open-end funds will accept new investors and new money at any time. The price of the open-end fund shares is determined by the value of the investments held by the fund, divided by the number of shares of the fund.

Closed-end mutual funds operate differently and are valued differently. These funds have only a limited number of shares in the fund to offer to the public. Once that number of shares is sold, the fund is "closed" to new investors—and usually to additional invest-ment by current shareholders as well. Shares of these funds are traded more like stocks, and the shares of the funds may have a greater value than the assets in the fund or a lesser value, depending on the market's view of the overall prospects for the fund to make money in the future.

Stock mutual funds are a perfect investment for your retirement savings, because they are equities that have the promise of keeping up with inflation. They can provide you with a diversity of ownership in assets and give you a way to own stock without tying up significant portions of your investment in one company's stock. They also provide you with an expert "asset manager" who is responsible for analyzing the thousands of investments on the market and trading those invest-ments at the best times.

Mutual Fund Expenses. Of course, this doesn't come for free. Part of the money you invest in a mutual fund goes to pay the funds' expenses, including the funds' asset managers. These expenses are disclosed in the prospectus, and, of course, you should never invest in a fund until you have read the prospectus and done other reading on performance. Operating expenses should be less than 1% of total portfolio value. Mutual funds may charge an initial fee to purchase the fund. These so-called "load funds" charge fees ranging from 1 to 2% to as high as 8% of the investment. Other funds charge a fee when you sell the fund. Usually this "exit" fee is reduced the longer you hold the stock. Other mutual funds have no purchase or exit fees. The funds without such fees are called *no-load funds*. Any list of the "best" mutual funds contains both load and no-load funds. There is no ev-idence to suggest that load funds as a whole perform better than no-load funds, nor do load funds on average have lower expenses than no-load funds.

Mutual funds can be purchased through a broker or directly from the fund itself. Simply call or write the fund and ask for the materials. They will send you a prospectus and an investment form. If you decide to invest in the fund, simply fill out the form and send it back with a check. Some mutual funds also have programs permitting monthly or other periodic investing by making a withdrawal directly from your checking account. Invested amounts can be as low as $50 per month. Mutual funds usually have dividend reinvestment pro-grams which automatically reinvest your earnings by buying more shares of the mutual fund. Always choose this option. It will be forced automatic savings; it avoids receiving small checks that get spent without thinking; and it provides a way for you to average your investment in the funds over the years, sometimes buying when the price is high and sometimes when it is lower.

CONCLUSION: THERE ARE NO PERFECT INVESTMENTS, ONLY GOOD ONES

There is no one investment that is "best" for every person at every time in her life. Most of the investment vehicles discussed in this chapter were probably somewhat familiar to you, and now you should have a better understanding of their differences and advantages and disadvantages for retirement savings.

On balance, a growth and income equities mutual fund is probably the best retirement investment for those just beginning to save for retirement for several reasons:

❖ Such funds do not require a big investment. Many will open IRA accounts for as little as $250.

❖ These funds provide you with equities which will keep up with inflation over the long years between now and retirement.

❖ Because it is a fund of several stocks, you will automatically have some diversity in investment.

❖ Many funds can be purchased with no investment charges so you don't lose any money to "overhead" with your initial purchase.

❖ Such funds will simply give you the best return on your money for the lowest risk. As your savings grow, it will then become wise to add other types of investments, perhaps at first through other mutual funds such as a bond fund.

Highly liquid investments, such as short-term CDs, money market funds, and savings accounts, while safe, are not appropriate for retirement savings. You receive a lower rate of earnings in return for high liquidity. You don't need liquidity for retirement savings that should be locked up for years.

NOTE FOR CHAPTER 12

1. "Darts Beat Pros in Dismal Performances," *The Wall Street Journal*, May 12, 1992, p. C1.

CHAPTER THIRTEEN

HOW TO INVEST WISELY
FOR RETIREMENT

A fiduciary shall discharge his duties with respect to the plan solely in the interest of the participants . . . by diversifying the investments of the plan so as to minimize the risk of large losses.

*—ERISA, Section 404,
defining the legal duties
of pension plan managers.*

Don't put all your eggs in one basket.

—Your grandmother

Whether the advice is from your grandmother or the Congress—two parties expert in laying down the law—the directive is the same: *diversify your investments.* All investment portfolios, even those of a few thousand dollars, should be diversified to avoid big losses. You also need to become more educated on which of the specific investments in each category of investments are most likely to be sound. Professionals can help with this. This chapter discusses how to choose effective professional help and how to become self-educated as well.

Your savings should be diversified both in types of investment vehicles and among different companies and bond issuers within each type of investment. Your accounts should contain several types of assets such as bonds and stocks, and among those bonds and stocks several different types of companies should be represented. For most of us, at least in the early years of retirement planning, we simply don't have enough money to achieve this diversity without mutual funds.

Diversity among types of investment vehicles is important because markets frequently move in opposite directions. When interest rates go up and your money funds or CDs can pay more, the stock market and existing bond values frequently go down. When interest rates go down, the stock market usually goes up. When inflation is high, stocks frequently keep pace with inflation, but bonds may be hard hit by inflation. There are always exceptions, but in general if you are diversified, one asset type such as bonds may lose value, but those losses may be offset by gains from other types of assets. Diversity within assets types is needed so that your investments are not tied to the fate of one company.

ASSET ALLOCATION

This diversity is also referred to as "asset allocation" among financial planners. Generally, advisers divide the available investment options into four segments:

❖ Cash and cash equivalents

❖ Fixed income (bonds, certificates of deposit)

❖ Equities

❖ Tangible assets such as gold, silver, and real estate

How those assets are divided depends on your levels of savings, your goals, your age, and your comfort level. The division also depends on the market for various assets at the current time, but that level of analysis is generally not necessary at the beginning of your savings program.

Everyone needs a minimal amount of savings that is readily available for emergencies, and this must be in cash or cash equivalents. You don't want to sell mutual funds to meet an emergency if their price is down. The rule of thumb for an emergency pool of savings is six months' expenses. This cash can be in money market accounts or funds or short-term CDs. Frankly, it is difficult to have six months of expenses set aside only for emergencies. Ordinarily money set aside for retirement savings should never even be considered available for any other purpose, let alone used for any other purpose. But for beginning savers on a low budget, we have to make an exception.

Don't wait until you have saved your six-month expense reserve before you begin saving for retirement. In the early stages of your retirement savings program, hedge a little bit. For example, if your 401(k) plan permits loans, don't delay funding your 401(k) even if you don't have six months of expenses saved. The 401(k) may have an employer match that you will miss if you don't contribute to the 401(k), and if the plan permits loans, you can always use that as a small part of your emergency fund for most things.

In your early days of saving, consider your IRA as at least some of the "emergency fund." For example, if the worst befalls you and you become disabled, the IRA can be drawn on without penalty. Build toward the six months' expenses emergency reserve at the same time you build toward retirement savings. Until you get the emergency reserve, some of your retirement savings may have to be in a cash-equivalent type of investment such as a money market account. Once that cash emergency reserve is established, you don't need cash assets at all for your retirement savings, at least at the beginning of your savings project.

Case Study #1: Appropriate Asset Allocation for Jennifer

Let's look at Jennifer. At 30 she is just beginning to save for retirement. She has put aside $4,000 as her emergency savings in certificates of deposit with 1-year maturity dates to get higher interest rates, but she has four 1-year CDs, each timed to mature 3 months apart. Each time one matures, she rolls it over for a year. She has saved $2,000 to fund an IRA account this year. She knows CDs are safe, but interest rates are fairly low, and she knows her investments should be diversified, so more CDs aren't a good idea. Given Jennifer's age and the fact she will not be using the money for as long as another 35 years, she should begin looking for mutual funds. Additionally, mutual funds enable her to have her investment supervised by the fund's professional investment manager, a good substitute for hiring a professional financial adviser of her own. She probably cannot afford a personal financial adviser at her present modest income and saving level.

She could place $1,000 in a corporate bond fund, a conservative investment which would probably earn about 6% per year, and $1,000 in an aggressive growth stock mutual fund. The aggressive growth mutual fund is among the riskier investments in mutual funds, but she has a long time to allow the money to grow. Even if the fund has a bad year now and again, she can wait for the price of the fund to go up again because she won't need the money for another 35 years. But Jennifer has never owned stocks before, and she feels she doesn't want the risk and volatility of aggressive growth stocks. She can compromise with a growth and income stock fund that invests in mature companies historically paying dividends and in companies that are still growing and have a potential for stock price increase. With all these investments, she should opt to have all dividends reinvested.

So she has her $6,000 of assets allocated as follows:

$4,000 in cash/cash equivalents	67.0%
$1,000 bonds (mutual fund)	16.5%
$1,000 stocks (mutual fund)	16.5%

As Jennifer saves more, she will proportionately reduce her allocation in cash and cash equivalents. She is too heavily invested in cash now, because she needs the cash emergency reserve. Because Jennifer is just getting started in her savings program and has relatively little saved, in analyzing her "asset allocation," she should not look at just her retirement savings assets, but should recognize her overall financial picture. Investments that may be very good for retirement savings in the future when she has more money, such as zero coupon bonds, are not appropriate for her to hold now, when it is possible a crisis might require that she dip into retirement savings for other short-term needs.

As a younger person, Jennifer could be more aggressive in her asset allocation, if she feels comfortable. As she saves more money and her portfolio grows, she should have as much as 80% of investments in stocks, probably through various mutual funds.

Case Study #2: Bonnie's Asset Allocation

Bonnie, now 40, faces a very different situation. First, Bonnie earns much more money ($85,000 annually), and she has been in the job market longer, so she has saved her emergency reserve. She also saved $13,700 and invested it in tax-deferred IRA plans. She has 22 years before she wants to retire. Because she has more time than Susan or Alice to even out the ups and downs of her investment, she can invest more heavily in aggressive growth stock funds. With less than $14,000 for her portfolio, she probably should not be investing in individual stocks now, but as her portfolio grows, individual stock investments will become appropriate. For now she might want a portfolio invested in mutual funds and stocks like this:

Aggressive growth stock fund	$5,500 (40%)
Growth stock fund	$4,100 (30%)
Growth and income stock fund	$2,050 (15%)
Midterm bond fund	$2,050 (15%)

Bonnie has most of her assets in equities at different levels of risk and only 15% in debt represented by the bonds. This is a riskier portfolio than someone nearer retirement should have, but given her salary level and the years to retirement, it is appropriate for her.

Case Study #3: Susan's Asset Allocation

At 50, Susan has at least 15 years to retirement, and based on her $25,200 salary she has saved her cash emergency reserve long ago. Like Bonnie, she can be much more aggressive with her investments, depending on her own "sleep-at-night" factor for risk tolerance. Some investment advisers recommend that the minimum asset allocation to stock should be a percentage equal to 100 minus your age, or in Susan's case at least 50% of savings in stock. Susan wants to be more aggressive, so in addition to her emergency cash reserve of $10,000 (roughly six months of her after-tax salary), she has her retirement savings allocated among mutual funds with 50% in an aggressive growth fund, 25% in a growth and income fund, 15% in an income fund, and 10% in a long-term corporate bond fund. She is using the dividend reinvestment program in each fund, and she has the income fund automatically deduct enough from her bank account each month to have her IRA fully funded by the end of the year. With this arrangement, the higher income this fund delivers is protected from taxes.

Case Study #4: Alice's Asset Allocation

With only 5 years to retirement, Alice cannot afford to be as aggressive as our other retirement planners. Yet some financial experts would tell Alice even she should have two-thirds of her retirement savings in stocks and the remainder in bonds and then reverse that proportion when she retires. Because Alice will have relatively little from her employer-provided plan, she has decided to take the more aggressive advice and she has one-third of her retirement investments in an aggressive growth mutual fund, one-third in a growth and income fund, and one-third in a fund with investment-grade corporate bonds.

Each of the retirement savers could have chosen other ways to divide their investments that might provide as good a mix of investments. The important thing is that each has allocated her assets in different investments, so that no matter where the economy goes, she will have some protection from market forces.

ACCEPTING HIGHER RISK FOR A HIGHER RATE OF RETURN

Women seem to have a difficult time with accepting the fact of risk in their investments. Pam Harmon, a Washington, D. C., financial planner who counts many women among her clients, finds this risk aversion to be the single biggest mistake women investors make, especially in planning for retirement. To help overcome this risk aversion, Ms. Harmon resorts to charts showing the risk/reward benefits, for example,

❖ If you invest $2,000 per year in your IRA for 20 years in certificates of deposit paying 6% interest, you will have an account of $73,572.

❖ If you invest $2,000 in a mutual fund returning 8%, you will have $91,524.

❖ If you invest $2,000 per year in a mutual fund returning 10%, you will have $114,550.

But, of course, you know the CDs will always pay their guaranteed 6%. With mutual funds or other investments, some years the return will be 3% and some years it will be 20%, and the only guarantee of your principal is the quality of the fund, unlike the CDs which are guaranteed by the federal government.

We already know that the higher the risk, the higher the rate of return—usually. In choosing among individual investments, there are some ways to mitigate risk and maintain a high rate of return. As we have seen, mutual funds are one way to do this, as is asset allocation. Investigating investments before you consider putting in your money is another way. Investigate the ups and downs in the price of the investment you are considering. This "volatility" is charted by investment periodicals such as *Value Line* publications. There are investments that provide a higher rate of return with less volatility. Search them out to help overcome your fear of risk. Choose investments with at least a 10-year record of solid performance. Investigate before you invest; once your money is invested, be patient. Prices of stocks and mutual funds go up and down, so be prepared for that.

Remember millionaire financier Bernard Baruch's guide to the stock market, "Buy low, sell high." This seems rather obvious—and useless advice. But considering how many people ignore this advice, it is apparently a pearl of wisdom rather than ordinary common sense. Consider the behavior of investors in two fairly recent periods. First, recall the stock market crash of October 19, 1987. When the market plunged, many individuals rushed to shift their 401(k) plans, IRAs, and other retirement savings out of the funds that held stocks and into fixed income funds. They sold low, when they should have been buying or at least holding on to their stock investments. During the record-high stock market of early 1992, the same levels in shifting retirement assets were seen, but this time investors are buying into stocks when the price is high. There are bargains to be found in individual stocks, even in high markets, but they are hard to find. Unless you consider yourself a real expert, you really should not try. Don't try to "time" the market by shifting your 401(k) plan funds or IRAs as the market moves up and down. Don't follow the pack. Follow Bernard Baruch's advice. After all, it seemed to work for him.

REGULAR TIMED INVESTING— DOLLAR COST AVERAGING

Another way to mitigate risk is to make small investment purchases in the same fund or stock on a periodic basis, for instance, monthly. This approach to investing, sometimes referred to as "dollar cost averaging," means you will be buying some of the fund when it is relatively high priced and some when it is relatively low priced. For example, you have $3,000 you want to invest in a mutual fund that has been ranging in value from $18 to $21 a share. You could watch the fund's price every day, waiting to buy when the fund is close to $18. This will take some time and become irritating. Or you could begin investing $500 per month, recognizing you will probably buy some shares near the $21 price and some near the $18 price and most at a price in between.

With dollar cost averaging investing, you avoid second guessing yourself about whether you bought too high or should have waited another day or two. Most important, you establish a regular pattern for investing that you are more likely to maintain. When you are buying at low prices, you can congratulate yourself on getting more shares for your money, and when you are buying at higher prices, you can congratulate yourself on how well your investments are doing.

DECIDING WHICH INVESTMENTS TO CHOOSE—READ, READ, READ

Telling Alice and her colleagues to buy a bond mutual fund and an aggressive stock fund hasn't really given them much help. There are hundreds of each of these funds. Which one should they choose and whom should they consult to make their choices? Remember, *The Wall Street Journal's* dart throwers give the expert financial advisers a run for their money, so there don't seem to be any guarantees in investing, even when you consult an expert. Now we get to the difficult part.

Books. Several excellent books provide general investment guidance. Start with Andrew Tobias's *Still the Only Investment Guide You'll Ever Need* (Bantam Books, 1987, $4.95). Tobias takes an appropriately irreverent attitude toward experts, ignores sophisticated tax-driven schemes, and concentrates on sound advice for those of us who don't trade in 1,000-share blocks of stock four times a day. Jane Bryant Quinn's book, *Making the Most of Your Money* (Simon & Schuster, 1991, $27.50), is updated almost annually and provides a full range of investment and money advice. Grace Weinstein's *The Lifetime Book of Money Management* (New American Library, 1987, $13.95 in paperback) is recommended by many, including the American Association of Retired Persons. Weinstein's book covers all basic areas of money management and takes a "life-cycle" approach useful for the lifelong retirement saving that you will be doing. Once you decide to concentrate on studying investments, Matthew Lesko's *The Investor's Information Sourcebook* (Harper & Row, 1988, $9.95) provides a useful directory of sources of information on all aspects of investing.

Magazines and Newspapers. Dozens of periodicals are devoted to investment information on specific stocks, bonds, and mutual funds. *Money, Business Week,* and *Forbes* rank mutual funds at least annually. These magazines, along with *The Wall Street Journal* and *Barron's* newspapers, provide information on stocks and other securities. *Barron's* runs a particularly interesting summary of the various stock brokerages' recommendations on which stocks to buy, sell, or hold. *Kiplinger's Personal Finance Manual* provides helpful advice and is recommended by some financial planners. While you won't want to subscribe to all of these, they are easily available on the newsstand and at the library. Look at each and find one or two you want to subscribe to.

Newsletters. Stock investment newsletters number literally in the hundreds, and a subscription usually costs well over $100 a year. These newsletters provide in-depth analysis of individual stocks and probably have more information than you need on a regular basis. But some of the better-known investment newsletters, such as *Value Line Investment Survey* and *Standard & Poor's Outlook,* are available at larger public libraries. These can be useful when you are considering a specific investment or want to look up a particular stock or industry.

Courses and Seminars. Community colleges and some women's organizations have classes at all levels of financial planning. Jennifer, who is just starting her savings and investment program, may be well served to attend some community college classes on personal financial planning, beginning at the basic budgeting level and then moving on to investments. Alice could find the American

Association of Retired Persons–sponsored local seminars conducted through its "Women's Financial Planning Program" particularly helpful. These focus on the woman nearing retirement, but much of their advice applies to younger women as well.

Stockbrokers, financial planners, and accounting firms frequently hold free seminars on investment or personal financial planning. Obviously, the seminar sponsor hopes to gain you as a customer and may even be pushing a specific product at the seminar. But you will find helpful information as well, such as how to analyze a stock's potential for growth and value based on current price, asset value, and dividend history. Brokers also provide a number of useful publications such as explanations of basic investment terms and how to read a balance sheet, retirement planning kits, and so on. Most of these publications you can get by simply writing. Charles Schwab and Co. (a brokerage firm) provides a quarterly guide to mutual fund performance including the funds it sells.

Other Information Sources. The American Association of Individual Investors (AAII) is dedicated to providing consumer education on investments. AAII produces a magazine, home study courses, and seminars. The association can be reached by writing AAII at 625 North Michigan Avenue, Chicago, Illinois 60611-3110. Its materials are designed for the investor who wants to spend a significant amount of time on investments. You may find AAII publications too technical and time intensive if you are just starting your portfolio, but if you really want to concentrate on planning, the materials will be most educational.

WHO CAN HELP—FINANCIAL ADVISERS, ACCOUNTANTS, STOCKBROKERS

There are always the professionals to fall back on. There is no magic formula for finding good advice, but there are some rules for avoiding bad advice. First, do not expect unbiased advice and do not depend on financial advisers who make money by selling you a specific product such as an annuity or insurance policy. These sellers may provide you with excellent information about *their* products, but it will be only about their products. They are not looking out for the best investment for your portfolio of savings and investment. They are looking out for the best investment for you *that they happen to sell.*

Or worse, they may be looking for the best investment for you that gives them the biggest commission.

Second, remember that as long as any adviser is being paid by commissions, rather than directly by you, she really cannot give totally unbiased advice. Her first loyalty must be to feeding her family, not your financial well-being. This does not mean you should never deal with sellers of investments who are dependent on commissions. Stockbrokers and insurance company agents are very useful people and can provide important guidance. *But don't rely on them for independent advice, and don't rely solely on them for financial advice.*

Pick a financial adviser whose only product is her knowledge and experience and be prepared to pay for that product. After all, she has to make a living, too. All advisers are willing to talk with you initially for free for a short time, but you should not expect to call every six months for free advice. Even women with as little as $2,000 to invest are welcomed by some financial advisers and should consider seeking professional assistance, according to Ms. Harmon.

But you should also do your own homework before seeking a financial adviser. First decide exactly what services you want from a financial adviser. Do you want budgeting advice, credit management help, help with taxes, investment advice, or all of the above? A stockbroker can give you advice on specific investments and perhaps on asset allocation, but she won't be able to help on taxes. An accountant will take care of your taxes, but may or may not be helpful with advice on specific investments. Depending on the individual and her training and background, a "financial planner" may be able to provide advice at every level.

Paying for Advice

You need to consider the cost of financial advice in relation to your "portfolio" at any given time. Investment advisers themselves disagree about how much investment money one needs to have before you should use an investment adviser. Some financial planners will not work with you unless you have a substantial portfolio already— $200,000 or more. Others are willing to start with very small accounts of a few thousand dollars. If you have only $2,000 or $3,000, frankly an adviser will not be very helpful simply for investment advice. Your best avenue may be educating yourself about mutual funds and buying a few different no-load funds you have researched until you reach a portfolio of $20,000 or more. Obviously, if you are paying the adviser by the hour or as information is rendered, she may be glad to advise you, regardless of the amount of your nest egg. But why spend $500 to learn how to invest $2,000? You would have to receive advice that gives you 25% rate of return, just to break even. Be very candid about what you have, what you can save, and how much you want to pay for advice.

Stockbrokers charge on a commission basis. Most accountants charge an hourly fee. Financial planners generally charge in two different ways, either on an hourly fee or per planning session fee or based on a percentage of your portfolio. Some advisers will allow you to choose the fee structure you want. Others will tell you how they charge and say, "take it or leave it." The billing method most advantageous to you depends on your approach to investing. If you want the adviser to take over managing your money with only general direction from you on goals, a percentage-of-portfolio billing approach makes sense. If you intend to take a more active role, sometimes accepting the advice and sometimes rejecting it, an hourly fee may be fairer to both of you.

Be wary of financial planners who charge you a fee directly and also derive a commission from securities you purchase. When you pay a fee to the planner, you ordinarily would assume the planner is not also receiving a commission from investment product sales, too, but this is incorrect. Many financial planners do accept commissions. Be sure you know which investments will yield the planner a commission and which do not and weigh her advice accordingly.

Financial Planners. Financial advisers come in all fashions. Accountants, brokers, lawyers, and insurance agents are all financial advisers. For that matter, so is your mother. But this section limits the discussion to individuals who offer wide ranging financial advice on budgeting, savings, and specific investment recommendations and advertise themselves as *financial planners* or *financial advisers*. We will use the term "financial planner" here to distinguish that individual from brokers, accountants, and lawyers who may also be financial advisers. Some financial planners also have credentials as accountants or lawyers, but simply concentrate on financial advice. Anyone can call herself a *financial planner*. Unlike an accountant, lawyer, or broker, there are no licensing or training requirements in most states. There is virtually no effective regulation of financial planners or other financial advisers who are not regulated by virtue of their status as an accountant, broker or lawyer.

To increase your chances of dealing with a qualified planner, look for the following designations:

- ❖ CFP—certified financial planner, awarded by the International Board of Standards and Practices for Certified Financial Planners, Denver, Colorado
- ❖ Ch.F.C.—chartered financial consultant, awarded by the American College, Bryn Mawr, Pennsylvania
- ❖ APFS—accredited personal financial specialist, awarded by the American Institute of Certified Public Accountants, New York, New York

These designations mean the planner has at least gone through a training program on financial matters given by an accrediting institution. It does not necessarily mean the individual is licensed by the state or has passed any state examinations. Talk to people you know about their financial advisers. Ask a friend or business colleague who appears to be financially sophisticated. Seek someone with experience and a track record.

Financial planners should be registered with the Securities and Exchange Commission (SEC), but do not be impressed with that. The Securities and Exchange Commission is the federal regulatory agency which deals with stock exchanges and the registration and disclosure of *securities*, usually stocks, bonds, and limited partnerships. The role of the SEC in all its regulatory duties is to require *disclosures*, not to approve or disapprove of quality. The agency does not in any way rule on either the quality or the wisdom of either an investment adviser or an investment, so remember this when you are buying securities "registered with the SEC," too.

The Investment Advisers Act of 1940 requires any person who is paid to advise others on the value of securities and the advisability of investing in them to register with the SEC. There are a host of exceptions for newsletter publishers and those whose advice is only incidental to their other duties, such as giving accounting or legal advice. The Investment Advisers Act has absolutely no requirements for training, credentials, or experience for registered investment advisers. As a consequence, among the registered advisers are dress designers, booking agents, floor wax salespersons, and astrologers.[1]

The SEC has been successful in convincing a prison inmate to withdraw his registration, although the inmate had argued that the parole board would be impressed with his efforts to establish a business he could go to as soon as he was released. Presumably, the SEC was not favorably impressed. (Apparently, no dart throwers have registered, perhaps because they rely on the exemption for publishers.)

Some questionable advisers deliberately register with the SEC, knowing the registration will mistakenly convince some customers that the adviser has been "approved" by the SEC. But registration with the SEC as an investment adviser in no way suggests "approval" or screening by the SEC. In fact, SEC Chairman Richard Breeden believes that, if Congress is not willing to appropriate more funds to improve regulation, then registration of investment advisers should be eliminated. The SEC argues the agency does not have the personnel to enforce regulation of investment advisers, and the very fact the adviser says he is "registered with the SEC" creates the impression among investors that the SEC has investigated and "approved" the adviser.

The type of financial adviser you need depends on your own level of sophistication and how involved you wish to be in the management of your money. You can begin by getting a free listing of financial planners from two industry trade associations:

> International Association of Financial Planning
> 2 Concourse Parkway, Suite 800
> Atlanta, Georgia 30328
> 404-395-1605
> (Free "Directory of Registry of Financial Planning Practitioners")

> and

> Institute of Certified Financial Planners
> 10065 East Harvard Avenue, Suite 320
> Denver, Colorado 80231
> 303-751-7600
> (Free listing of five CFPs in your ZIP Code)

The National Association of Personal Financial Advisors (NAPFA) will also provide you with a list of its members. Members of NAPFA work only for fees and are prohibited from receiving any sales commission or other type of product-related compensation. You can write or call:

> National Association of Personal Financial Advisors
> 1130 Lake Cook Road
> Suite 105
> Buffalo Grove, Illinois 60089
> 800-366-2732

Accountants. Many accountants also provide financial and investment advice beyond just completing tax returns and setting up budgets. The *certified public accountant* (CPA) is tested and licensed by the state in which she practices in accounting matters. An accountant may also have the AFPS designation. Accountants generally are particularly well versed in the tax and estate planning areas of retirement planning and financial management. This may be more important as you near retirement than it is in your early retirement planning years. Accountants also are frequently savvy in the operation of employer-provided benefit plans because they or their colleagues in their firm advise employers on retirement plans. The Big Six accounting firms—Arthur Andersen, Coopers & Lybrand, Ernst and Young, Deloitte-Touche, KPMG Peat Marwick, and Price-Waterhouse—usually have *personal financial planning* practices in their local or regional offices. Some small accounting firms also specialize exclusively in personal financial planning.

The Big Six and many other firms work only on a fee-for-service basis, either on a hourly rate or on a flat fee for a project. They do not accept commissions or charge based on a percentage of your portfolio's value. Individual accountants and smaller firms may have relationships with brokers or may deal in certain investments themselves. If you rely upon an accountant as your financial adviser, you will probably also need a broker to execute trades in various stocks and bonds. Accountants will give you independent advice, but it is likely to be expensive since you will be billed on an hourly basis in most financial advising relationships.

Stockbrokers. *Full-service* stockbrokers who offer investment advice work for a commission. If you don't buy or sell a stock, bond, mutual fund, or other securities, they don't get paid. For some products, however, such as new issues of stock, the issuer of the investment may pay the broker, in which case there is no commission charged to you. Because brokers are paid on a commission basis, they are under pressure to move investment products. This pressure is tempered by the fact they want to keep you as a customer. To do that, they realize they must help you make money. They endeavor to balance these goals by giving you the best possible investment advice consistent with shifting your investments from time to time. But because most stockbrokers make money only when you are buying and selling securities, you must be on guard against "churning" your account with frequent sales and purchases that earn you little money—or worse, lose money—but make money for the broker.

Full-service brokers, such as Dean Witter, E. F. Hutton, Merrill Lynch, Paine Webber, Prudential Bache, and Shearson Lehman Brothers, give you some level of investment advice, including recommendations on specific stocks, bonds, and other products as well as overall financial planning. While there may be exceptions, generally the level of advice and assistance you can expect from a full-service broker is directly proportional to the amount you have to invest and how frequently you want to change investments. Unless you have tens of thousands to invest and intend to trade on a regular basis (at least once a month), chances are an experienced broker will be happy to execute the trades for you, but she will not be willing to provide you with in-depth, periodic advice on retirement or other financial planning. Frankly, most of us, especially when we are in our 30s and early 40s—the appropriate time to begin planning for retirement, don't have enough money to invest in individual stocks to be a desirable customer for full-service brokers. Until you have saved a large portion of the amount you need for retirement, you should not be trading in individual stocks often enough to interest the average broker. Even for clients with substantial assets, brokers are also likely to refer clients to affiliated financial planners.

The discount brokers such as Charles Schwab, Inc. and Olde Company simply take orders. Their personnel are paid by salary, not by the commissions from your purchases or sales. Discount brokers do not as a rule give advice on which stocks and investments to buy. The discount brokers do provide some free information and booklets, for instance, on retirement planning and mutual funds. If you are using another type of financial adviser, it makes sense to use a discount broker to execute trades based on the advice the other financial adviser has provided.

Interviewing Financial Advisers

Interview several financial advisers, at least a minimum of three to five is better. If you are interviewing an accountant or broker, some of the questions listed in Exhibit 13.1 for the interview process are not applicable. But most of the questions should be posed to anyone who may be entrusted with your money. Take some steps to prepare for these interviews.

❖ Outline your needs and goals. The level of advice you need will determine in part the type of adviser you want.

❖ Have available a brief summary of your assets, obligations, salary and other income, and employee benefits.

❖ Be very candid about your own finances and goals.

❖ Demand candor from the adviser. If at any point she refuses to answer your questions or appears at all evasive, stop the interview and move on to the next potential adviser. Remember, this person will know the most intimate details about you—your earnings, financial worth, and life's goals. You are entitled to know a great deal about her in return.

❖ Begin with a quick telephone call/interview to be sure the adviser can provide all the services you need and that she is in your price range.

❖ Develop a list of the same questions to ask each adviser. Photocopy the list and fill in the answers. Better yet, have the adviser fill it in as you talk.

❖ Keep the lists from the ones you don't reject immediately. Then after you have two or three possible candidates, sit down with the list, review the answers, and make your choice.

❖ Do not decide in their office. Take time to reflect and make the decision only after you have reviewed your "questionnaire" notes.

SAMPLE QUESTIONNAIRE— QUESTIONS YOU SHOULD ASK

The following questions should serve as the basis of your questionnaire.

Experience and Background of Individual and Firm

What is the background and experience of the firm?

(Find out who the other partners or associates are. Are there experts in various areas who can share knowledge and expertise with your advisers?)

How long have you personally been offering financial planning services?

(You do not want the most junior member of the team, unless that is all you can afford.)

What is your client base like?

(If all the other clients are seeking aggressive growth for fast returns, the adviser probably concentrates on these types of investments and may be less informed about the long-term growth opportunities you need. If all the other clients were millionaires when they joined the firm, you may not receive much attention. If many of the clients are women planning for retirement and putting the children through college, the adviser is likely to be very knowledgeable and current about investments that are perfectly suited to your needs.)

What is the size of an average portfolio you manage?

(Again, if all the other clients are interested in investing millions, your $20,000 portfolio may get short shrift.)

What is your basic investment strategy?

(There is no right answer, other than it should match a philosophy you are comfortable with.)

Exhibit 13.1

What are your results over the last 10 years in terms of average return on investments managed each year?

(This will give you an idea of how the adviser performs in up and down markets. But be sure to get a yearly figure, too. A 10-year average return of 15% based on 5 years of losses in the 10% range balanced off by 5 years of 25% gains is very different for you as an investor than the same average based on returns varying between a low of 5% losses in some years and a high of 20% gains in others. The adviser's performance should have done at least a few points better than the Standard & Poor's 500 Stock Composite Index, and some experts recommend choosing only those who have done considerably better than the Standard & Poor's.[2]

What is your educational background?

College and degree:

Graduate school and degree:

(This is more important for advisers with less experience.)

Which of the following do you hold?

Certified Financial Planner _____

Chartered Financial Consultant _____

Registry or Financial Planning Practitioners _____

Other _____

How much continuing education in financial planning do you pursue each year?

1–14 hours professional education _____

15–30 hours professional education _____

30 or more hours professional education _____

Are you a member of any professional financial planning associations?

Institute of Certified Financial Planners _____

(Exhibit 13.1 *cont'd.*)

National Association of Personal Financial
Advisors   ____

International Association for Financial
Planning   ____

Registry of Financial Planning Practitioners   ____

Services Provided

Does your financial planning service include the following?

A review of my financial and retirement goals

Retirement planning

Cash management and planning

Tax planning

Investment review and planning

Adviser on specific investments for my plan

Insurance needs

Estate planning

Other:_____

Do you provide a written analysis of my specific financial situation and your recommendations for my goals?

(You don't want to pay for an analysis for a typical 40-year-old earning $40,000 per year; you want analysis for your specific financial condition.)

Do you offer assistance with implementation of your recommendations, such as researching appropriate investments and buying and selling individual stocks and bonds, etc.?

Do you offer continuous, ongoing advice regarding my financial affairs, including advice on noninvestment financial issues?

How often will I receive reports on my financial condition and in what format? If I request an additional report, will I be charged for it?

(Exhibit 13.1 *cont'd.*)

(For long-term investments you probably don't need a report more than quarterly. The report should, at a minimum, contain a list of all your investments, and return on each, and the overall return of your portfolio along with a break out of any charges. An occasional request for an additional report each year should not be charged an extra fee, but if you regularly request additional reports or development of specialized reports, you should expect to be charged a small additional fee.)

Do you take possession of, or have access to, my assets?

(Having the adviser actually hold investments is convenient, but probably not a good idea. Unless you are using a well-known brokerage firm, you should always have control over your assets, even if it requires physically moving stock certificates or bonds back and forth when you want to trade these investments.)

What are your provisions for your bonding and insurance?

(If the adviser is handling any of your money directly, even for a brief time, get evidence that the adviser and the company are bonded. While there is no way to guarantee the security of your investments once your money is invested, a company's bond can at least insure partially against the threat of outright thievery.)

Fees and Billing Arrangements

Will we have a written contract?

(Always get a written agreement and insist it be in plain English. Don't sign it until you understand it, and don't rely on oral changes to it.)

How is your firm compensated for the financial services you provide?

_____Fees only (flat or hourly rate)

_____Commissions only from investments purchased
      through the firm

(Exhibit 13.1 *cont'd.***)**

____Fees and commissions

____Fee offset by commissions

(Fee only is the best billing method to ensure the advice you receive is totally unbiased and based only on what is best for you. You do not want advice that is influenced by whether the adviser makes more money if you buy a particular investment.)

How is your compensation calculated?

Fee only based on:

____An hourly rate of $____

____A percentage based on____

____A flat fee based on____

____Commission only from clients that deal with the firm you are associated with

____Fee and commission

____Fee offset; you charge a flat fee against which commissions are offset; if the commissions exceed the fee, is the balance credited to me?

(Broker affiliation can be an advantage. It is easier for your adviser to buy and sell investments for you and the adviser may get a discount rate which she may pass on to you.)

If your fees are based on "fee and commission" or "commission only" (or affiliated with a broker/dealer), what percentage of your firm's income comes from:

Fees____%

Commissions on:

Insurance products____%

Annuities____%

Mutual funds____%

Limited partnerships____%

(Exhibit 13.1 *cont'd.*)

Stocks and bonds_____%

Other (explain)_____%

Will you furnish me with no-load (no sales charge) product alternatives, if available?

Will you consult with other professionals such as accountants, lawyers, actuaries, and stockbrokers about my account? If so, will I be billed for that consultation?

(You may want the answers to complicated tax or retirement planning issues that require the use of outside experts. But you should be clear on who pays for their consultation and who is choosing these experts. Additionally, if brokers' fees are included in the adviser's management fee, your overall costs will be lower than if the brokerage fees are added on to the management fees.)

Do you or any member of your firm act as a general partner or receive compensation from the general partner or from investments which may be recommended to me?

What is the average income in fees from a typical client?

$_____(annual fee income divided by number of clients served)

What is the average income in commissions from a typical client?

$_____(annual commissions income divided by number of clients served)

Compliance with Federal, State, and Professional Boards' Regulation

Is your firm registered as an investment adviser with the Securities and Exchange Commission?

(The adviser should be registered, but remember the fact the firm is registered with the SEC does not mean the SEC has reviewed or approved the quality of the firm or the individual.)

(Exhibit 13.1 *cont'd.*)

If not, which SEC exception for registration applies?

_____Fewer than 15 clients

_____Do not provide generic or specific advice on securities

_____Do not provide financial planning advice for a fee, but only as a registered broker/dealer

Is your firm registered with the state securities office? If not, why not?

(There can be any number of legitimate reasons why the adviser is not registered with the state, including the fact the state may not require registration. But you should know why the individual is not registered.)

Have you ever been cited by a professional or regulatory governing body for disciplinary reasons?

References

Give me three or four references, including one who is no longer a client.

(Obviously, the references given will be only those who were satisfied unless you ask for the one who is no longer a client. Even that reference may be one who was very satisfied but moved out of the area and wanted someone close by. When you talk with the references, ask for additional references. This may get you a better picture of the adviser. Of course, don't rely just on references given. Ask around in the community as well.)

(Exhibit 13.1 *cont'd.*)

Questions the Potential Adviser Should Be Asking You

Questions from the adviser are equally important in showing her approach to helping you. Listen carefully to the questions the advisers are asking you. At a minimum, a financial adviser should be asking you the following questions:

- ❖ What are your goals? What are you saving for?
- ❖ What is your philosophy about money?
- ❖ How involved do you want to be with your investments?
- ❖ If you lost 10% of your investments in 1 year, would you be traumatized by that?
- ❖ If you made 20% on your investment in 1 year, would you stop saving for the next year?
- ❖ How secure is your job and what are your prospects for promotions and raises?
- ❖ Do you expect to inherit any money?
- ❖ Do you expect to support your spouse or your parents or in-laws in their later years?
- ❖ Do you intend to provide your children with financial help in their adult years?

Each of these questions goes to broad issues that won't be reflected in your statement of assets and liabilities and income. They are questions about your needs and your comfort level on money and investments. In investing, your financial adviser must honor your "sleep-at-night" factor. If you are losing sleep over an investment, you should not be in it. Your financial adviser must know your "sleep-at-night" factor and respect it.

Finally, consider how you feel about this person as a person. Although working with a financial adviser is the ultimate business situation, it is, paradoxically, also very personal. She is not a substitute for a psychoanalyst or a best friend, but you must feel comfortable with this person and trust her. It shouldn't be a struggle to get her on the phone, and once you do, it shouldn't be a struggle to talk with her and explain your needs clearly and succinctly. When the two of you are discussing a matter unfamiliar to you, her tone should be one of a colleague instructing you on a new matter, not a teacher dealing with a dull student. If your adviser talks down to you, fails to explain issues, or evades questions, get rid of her. You are better off on your own than dealing with someone you don't trust or cannot communicate with.

ADVICE FROM THE PROS

Don't Get Discouraged, and Don't Be Too Conservative. Pam Harmon, a financial planner introduced earlier in the chapter, finds the second biggest mistake women make in retirement planning is getting discouraged because they feel they cannot save enough to meet their goals. The first mistake is being too conservative. Of course, the more conservative you want to be in your investments, the more you will need to save, so these two attitudes reinforce each other. She stresses the link between level of risk and rate of return, urging clients to avoid discouragement by taking a little more risk to help their investments grow more quickly.

But she poses the key test for investment decisions as, "If your $2,000 investment is only worth $1,500 after one year and that will upset you so much that you cannot plan your finances any more, then don't make the investment." But if you can make yourself realize that you have decades to make back the money, then you can move toward higher-return investments with higher risk.

Start Planning and Saving for Retirement Now. Ms. Harmon also stresses you are never too young to start planning for retirement. Starting young also reduces the discouragement factor. You have already seen how much less you need to save when you start in your 20s as opposed to in your 40s. Another way to avoid getting discouraged is to save in a systematic fashion even if it is a small amount. Also start a "found money" account, preferable a mutual fund. Any windfall that you didn't expect, such as a tax refund, or birthday gift of cash, or money from a dress you returned goes into the *found money fund.* "I give an example of a woman who did this over 10 years, never putting in any amount that was more than $100, yet she now has $10,000 in that mutual fund. I know its true, because I'm the woman," she explained.

Save Realistically—According to Your Present Financial Status. The distinguishing elements between the way women and men invest are disintegrating, according to what Ms. Harmon sees in her practice. "Women are so much more knowledgeable and are taking care of themselves." But she still sees some women with the implicit feeling that "people will be there to take care of me." If a woman is single, Ms. Harmon always plans for her as though she will always be single. Of course, this may not always be true, but it is much easier and more pleasant to adjust savings requirements downward or living standards upward if the client becomes part of a two-earner household than vice versa.

Save for Long-Term Goals as Well as Short-Term Needs. William J. Goldberg, national director of KPMG Peat Marwick's personal financial planning practice, sees a problem in the tendency to focus on saving for one thing at a time, such as the house down payment, then children's education, then retirement. "It takes discipline to get past the idea of just saving for one thing. For retirement, in the early years, it may be enough just to save through your employer's plan, but know when you are going to switch over and begin serious retirement savings."

Don't Rely on the Retirement Plans from Your Parents' Generation. Goldberg also thinks retirement saving and planning is the one area where today's workers still have the *Father Knows Best* view of family life, with father working at one company for a long time, mother staying home, and the children leaving home when mom and dad are still young enough to do a lot of retirement saving. As Mr. Goldberg sees it, "Today's adults see their parents' scenarios of living very well in retirement and they assume they will, too. But they're in a totally different situation. Mom and Dad always saved; Dad stayed with the same company most of his life and has a good pension, and Social Security replaces a big portion of their income before retirement. Today's adults were single until they were in their 30s and they're almost 65 when they get the kids out of college. They didn't save much, and they have been in a number of different jobs, so any employer pension is likely to be modest. And who knows what Social Security benefits will be like when they retire."

You know your life today isn't like your parents' lives when they were your age. What makes you think it will be when you retire? Your retirement benefits from work will be different and Social Security benefits are likely to be different. And your savings pattern needs to be different, too. It should be larger—not smaller—than your parents', if you want to match their level of retirement security.

CONCLUSION: STRATEGY PLAN FOR GETTING STARTED ON WISE SAVINGS AND INVESTMENTS

❖ If you have not started already, begin a payroll deduction plan at work or establish a savings account that automatically withdraws money from your checking account and deposits it in your IRA or other retirement savings or investment account. Better yet, consider depositing your paycheck directly into your savings account and writing yourself a check for living expenses.

❖ Check for local classes on investing and savings; enroll in one.

❖ Look for free seminars on investing and financial or retirement planning sponsored by stockbrokers, accountants, and financial planners. Attend and ask questions—but don't invest anything at that meeting.

❖ Calculate the real return on current investments after taxes and inflation: How much money are you really making?

❖ Look at your existing savings and investment for asset allocation: Do you have all your eggs in one basket or are you diversified?

❖ Review your investments in light of the number of years until you retire and the amount of money you are saving to decide whether your investments are too conservative. If you are on target with your retirement goals with conservative investments paying 5%, you probably shouldn't change, but if you are missing your goals and you have at least 10 years before you retire, you may want to move into more aggressive investments.

❖ Decide whether you need professional advice in helping you plan for investing. If the answer is yes, begin your research process. Interview several advisers and ask around among your business colleagues and friends. Take several weeks to investigate.

❖ Buy—or read at the library—a copy of *Business Week, Money,* or one of the other business magazines or newspapers every other week for a few weeks. Try them all; then subscribe to one for a time.

NOTES FOR CHAPTER 13

1. *See* Louis Loss, *Fundamentals of Securities Regulation* (Boston: Little, Brown, 1983), pp. 745–746.
2. Dorcas R. Hardy and C. Colburn Hardy, *Social Insecurity* (New York: Villard Books, 1991), p. 157.

CHAPTER FOURTEEN

HOW MARRIAGE AFFECTS YOUR RETIREMENT BENEFITS

The old marriage vows of "til death do us part" seem anachronistic today. In every area these vows seem more ignored than honored—except in the area of employer-provided retirement benefits. Here's the good news: your husband's pension and most other retirement benefits will be paid out as a joint and survivor annuity, providing you with an income even after he dies, unless you agree in writing otherwise. Here's the bad news: so will *your* benefits.

That only seems fair you say. And at first glance, you're right. But think a little further. Most women are younger than their spouses, and women have a longer life expectancy even when they are the same age as their husbands. If you are in ordinary health and the same age as or younger than your husband, the chances of your husband surviving you are virtually none. As a practical matter, his chances of receiving a benefit from your pension are practically nonexistent. But if you and he don't agree to opt out of the joint and survivor annuity payment option, you will receive a significantly lower benefit from your employer-provided retirement throughout your life because of the fact he has had the theoretical chance of receiving a benefit after you have died.

Additionally, your retirement benefits are likely to be considerably lower than his in the first place, as described in Chapter 1. You may have sacrificed retirement benefits buildups for family responsibilities. As child-rearing duties and caring for elderly parents came along, it was probably you, not he, who took up the challenge and left your paycheck to work for no money—and no retirement benefits buildup—at home. When career opportunities arose, you usually moved to follow his transfers. As we have seen from nurse Alice's experience, your benefits can be a mere fraction of what they would have been had you not taken those years off or changed jobs to follow your transferred spouse. Finally, you probably earned less money during your career, so your benefits will be based on a lower earnings record.

LAWS AFFECTING SPOUSAL RIGHTS TO BENEFITS

In the past, laws protecting a spouse's right to a worker's retirement benefits have assumed it is always women who are being protected by various restrictions on the distribution of employer-provided benefits. But, remember, the laws are drafted in a nominally sex-neutral manner. So all those protections apply to your husband as well. You may have worked as a single woman for 30 years, but a year after you marry, your husband becomes entitled to a survivor right in your pension. And as soon as you marry, you will need his permission to choose a payout other than the joint and survivor annuity payout method for your retirement benefits or to name a beneficiary other than him to your 401(k) plan. And he will need your permission to do the same.

ERISA always assumed the first choice for payment of retirement benefits would be a *qualified joint and survivor annuity* (QJSA). Under a QJSA, the normal form of retirement plan payment for a married retirement plan participant will be a monthly retirement benefit paid over his lifetime and the lifetime of his wife, if she survives him (which she almost always does). The monthly amount received from a QJSA payment form is smaller than the monthly amount from a single annuity form of payment, reflecting the fact the payments are being paid over two lifetimes rather than one. But originally under ERISA, a retiring worker was not *required* to elect the QJSA option. He did not even have to tell his spouse what method of benefit payment he elected. And because the QJSA payment appeared smaller, the plan participant was likely not to choose the joint and survivor option, even though choosing the single annuity payment meant his wife would be left with no benefit if he predeceased her.

The Retirement Equity Act

The enactment of the Retirement Equity Act (REA as it is frequently called by benefits administrators) in 1984 required an employee who elected any form of payment other than the joint and survivor annuity must obtain the spouse's written, notarized consent or that the spousal consent be witnessed by the plan administrator. As one plan administrator put it, "The enactment of REA has freed me from the most difficult conversations I have ever had to hold. I no longer have the widows calling me the first month after 'John's' death, asking 'Where's my pension check?' I won't have to explain to a sobbing widow that 'John' didn't leave her any pension. He chose to take all the money himself, and now that John is gone, so is the pension. With the enactment of REA, the widow will have a survivor's pension, or she will at least have helped make the decision that there would be no pension for her after John's death."

Only employer-provided plans are covered by REA's provisions requiring employer plans to provide coverage for QJSA and qualified preretirement survivor annuities (QPSAs). Among employer-provided plans, all defined benefit plans are required to provide spousal annuities or receive the spouse's consent not to pay out in such annuities. Most defined contribution plans, including profit sharing plans, 401(k) plans, and Keoghs, are not required to provide QJSAs or QPSAs nor are these plans required to give notice about the joint and survivor or preretirement annuity payment forms, if the plans provide that on the employee's death, her entire vested benefit is payable to the surviving spouse immediately. But if the employee takes the money as a lump sum and transfers that lump sum into an IRA, there will be no requirement that the spouse receive that IRA.

Note: IRAs are not required to pay out QJSAs or QPSAs or to get the spouse's consent for any sort of payout. IRA simplified employee pensions, even though provided by an employer, are not covered by REA. State and local government and church retirement plans are not covered by REA, although some plans provide for spousal consent to waive survivor or preretirement annuities.

THE QUALIFIED JOINT AND SURVIVOR ANNUITY—HOW BENEFITS ARE PAID

Under a QJSA by law the *total* amount of benefits that will be projected to be paid is calculated to be at least as great an amount as would have been paid out in a "single life annuity." For example, if the present value of your accrued pension benefit is $300,000, regardless of the form of benefit payment you choose, the payments must be calculated to pay you that value over the expected lifetimes that the payments will be made. But with a QJSA payment form, the size of the monthly benefits will be smaller than monthly benefits paid over one lifetime because the same amount of retirement benefit is estimated to be paid over two lifetimes, as opposed only to the worker's lifetime. The payments are frequently lowered again at the death of the worker.

The reduction in the monthly payment for two lifetimes is based on actuarial calculations which take into account the possibilities of the spouse surviving and the period over which the spouse would likely continue to receive benefits. But these calculations are based on general mortality tables. They do not recognize individual situations. The calculations frequently assume a male retiree and a female spouse or they use unisex mortality calculations. The reduction calculations do take into account the age of the survivor beneficiary, but cannot legally take into account the gender of the participant or the beneficiary. Because women are likely to live longer than men, the reduction in a woman retiree's monthly pension payments, if she accepts the QJSA survival rights for her husband, is likely to be too high in comparison with the chances the husband will ever receive any payments.

For this reason, when a married woman of retirement age in good health is faced with the choice, she and her husband should usually elect the option which pays her pension *over her lifetime only, with no payments to the husband should she die before him.* This will give her higher pension payments. Conversely, because a woman is likely to survive her husband, the husband should almost always take his pension as a joint and survivor annuity. Recognize both spouses will have to agree on each other's form of payment. But they should not fall into the trap of thinking both parties should elect the QJSA form of benefit.

Within a reasonable time before retirement benefits begin (usually 30 to 90 days before the scheduled retirement date), the retiring employee and the spouse must receive a complete and understandable explanation of the payment election procedures, including a waiver for the spouse to sign and have notarized if the employee wants to receive retirement benefits in any form other than the QJSA. As with the summary plan descriptions, the attempt to explain fully the law and options surrounding the benefit payments usually results in a document that is neither understandable or in plain English. Unless the future retiree's spouse agrees to another form of benefit payment, such as a lump sum or payment over only the retiree's life, and properly executes the form before deadline, the payments will be in the QJSA form. This spousal consent cannot be given more than 90 days prior to the beginning of the retirement plan payments. The consent can be changed prior to the actual beginning of the annuity payments' commencement. But once payment begins in the joint and survivor form, most plans will not let you change the form of payment. You are stuck with that form of payment forever.

If the employer plan does not reduce your retirement benefit in return for the survivor's annuity and does not permit you to waive the survivor's annuity or choose another beneficiary other than your spouse, then no notice to you or your spouse is required.

On balance, unless your employer does not reduce your benefit if you receive the joint and survivor annuity (which is a highly unlikely probability since the post-retirement survivor annuity is expensive to provide), you should not take the joint and survivor annuity under ordinary circumstances. Unless your husband is significantly younger or in better health than you, he most certainly will not survive you to receive any benefit. Under the single annuity payment method, you will have more money being paid out each month which you can both live on.

Of course, your and your husband's plans may have several payout options other than simply a QJSA or a single life annuity. The plans may provide for lump-sum distributions or annuity payments that are guaranteed for the longer of the plan participant's life or a guaranteed number of years, such as 10 years. These payment options present other considerations we will discuss in Chapter 16.

THE QUALIFIED PRE-RETIREMENT SURVIVOR'S ANNUITY—HOW BENEFITS ARE PAID IF THE SPOUSE DIES BEFORE RETIREMENT

REA also requires the retirement benefits to provide for a qualified pre-retirement survivor annuity. Under the QPSA, if a vested worker dies before retirement, her spouse will receive a pension benefit based on the benefit she had accrued at her death. The catch is the law does not require payments to begin until the date the employee would have reached retirement age. Some plans begin payments earlier. Other plans delay payment as long as the law allows. Another drawback is the fact the payment is likely to be small if you die young or after you have only been with the company for a few years. Most plans subject to REA are based on numbers of years worked, resulting in a small benefit for young workers.

Plans may ultimately "charge" your pension for the "insurance" provided by the possibility of survivors receiving a QPSA if you died before you retired. This charge is accomplished by reducing the amount of the retirement benefit you ultimately receive at retirement or your survivors receive, if in fact the QPSA is used by them. For example, your ultimate retirement benefit may be reduced by a few dollars or less per month when you receive it at retirement because you elected during your working years to have the QPSA coverage for your spouse and children. If the plan does make such a reduction, the plan must notify you about the survivor benefit and the reduction as soon as you are affected by it. When you are notified, you and your spouse, if any, can choose not to receive the preretirement survivor coverage, and there will be no reduction in your benefits. But to do so, you must have the written notarized permission of your spouse. And, of course, he must have your consent to waive any right to a QPSA in his employer-provided plan.

Given the low probability of your actually dying and triggering the QPSA, the reduction in the benefit is quite small. Many employer plans, in fact, "subsidize" such benefits and don't make any reduction in your ultimate benefit to account for the fact you had preretirement survivor coverage. If the employer does subsidize the QPSA by not reducing your ultimate retirement benefit, the employer does not need to notify you about the coverage and does not need to permit you to waive the preretirement survivor coverage. Absent the employer's subsidization, the plan must notify you about the details of the QPSA by the time you are 35, become a plan participant, or leave the employer if you aren't yet 35, which ever happens last.

Special Rules for QJSA and QPSA Payments

❖ If a retirement plan subject to REA permits loans or permits a plan participant to use her assets in the plan as security for a loan, the plan must obtain the spouse's consent in writing, notarized or witnessed by the plan administrator, before such loan is made.

❖ Joint and survivor annuities need not be paid if the plan participant and the spouse were not married at least a year before the annuity began or the plan participant died.

❖ If the total value of the QPSA or QJSA is $3,500 or less, the plan sponsor may pay the benefit as a lump sum without the consent of either the participant or the spouse.

PRENUPTIAL AGREEMENTS DON'T AFFECT RETIREMENT BENEFITS

Prenuptial or antenuptial agreements are recognized and enforced in nearly all states, unless there is evidence one of the parties was unduly pressured into the agreement or one of the parties deceived the other by hiding assets. These agreements are entered into prior to marriage and agree that property owned by the parties prior to the marriage and obtained after marriage will not be subject to the usual state laws governing marital property. Generally, the purpose of the agreement is to continue to permit each spouse to own property he or she has acquired individually rather than jointly as is usually presumed for married couples. Prenuptial agreements are useful even if you aren't Donald and Ivana Trump. With serial marriages becoming more common, and women as well as men coming to the marriage with substantial assets, it is sensible for both parties to use a prenuptial agreement to protect their children by previous marriages or elderly parents or to protect themselves if the marriage breaks up.

If your spouse-to-be suggests a prenuptial agreement, it can be advantageous for you both. But think ahead. If you are likely to have children together, the agreement should clearly state how the children will be supported. If the two of you are older, consider the expenses of health. Traditionally, wives nurse husbands through their final illnesses, often with great work and strain on their own health. But traditionally such wives weren't party to prenuptial agreements. When their husbands died, the wives inherited the estate. But with a prenuptial agreement, a faithful wife may find she has used her money and health to nurse her husband through his final illness, but is left with nothing from her husband's estate. The agreement should stipulate how health care costs and caregiving services will be paid for. While this may sound crass or even cruel, not to mention totally unromantic, you won't feel very romantic providing 24-hour-a-day nursing service and spending your money for your husband's serious illness so he can leave adult children a large estate.

If the course of true love runs incredibly smoothly and after years you and your spouse feel there is no reason to have the prenuptial agreement, the two of you together may tear up the agreement and denounce such coldblooded instruments. Send a jointly signed, notarized letter to the lawyer who drew it up, stating you both agree to repeal the agreement. Tell the children and your parents and brag to all your friends about it.

Prenuptial Agreements Do Not Affect ERISA Plans

Prenuptial agreements are creatures of state law. Because ERISA and REA preempt state law, prenuptial agreements cannot override the effects of ERISA and REA. Even if you have a prenuptial agreement in which your spouse waives all rights to your employer-provided pension, unless he has signed a waiver to your specific retirement plans, meeting the REA requirements, the prenuptial agreement will have no effect on those ERISA benefits. Of course, the same is true for your agreements about his ERISA benefits. If you want to ensure your children get your 401(k) money or the lump-sum value of your pension, get your husband to sign an ERISA waiver for the plan, acknowledging he is waiving his rights to such benefits.

For non-ERISA retirement benefits such as IRAs, prenuptial agreements will be controlling. They will also protect your individual savings. As we have seen, your individual savings are critical to your retirement financial security, so it is important that they be protected from you husband's creditors and any divorce proceedings.

Conclusion: Coordinate With Your Spouse on Benefits From Both Your Retirement Plans

❖ Review your current employer-provided retirement plans and IRAs for beneficiary designations. Be certain the beneficiaries you want are named on all plans.

❖ If you want a beneficiary other than your spouse for your employer-provided retirement plan have your spouse execute the appropriate spousal waiver form which your employer (or former employer, if applicable) can provide. Your spouse's signature must be witnessed by the plan administrator or notarized. If it is not, it will not be effective.

❖ Go through the foregoing process even for benefits earned before you were married.

❖ If your benefits are encumbered by a previous divorce agreement, be sure your spouse recognizes that fact and the exact details of the "qualified domestic relations order" from the divorce establishing your prior spouse's rights to the benefits.

❖ Ask your spouse for a listing of his employer-provided benefits and the beneficiaries.

❖ If he has designated or wants to designate beneficiaries other than you and if you agree, be sure to execute the necessary spousal waivers.

❖ If your spouse has been married before, find out the exact nature of any encumbrances on his retirement benefits by a prior divorce decree.

❖ Unless you are extremely wealthy, do not agree to allow your spouse to waive the qualified preretirement survivor annuity.

❖ As part of the retirement savings planning, discuss with your spouse the payment form each of you will choose for your employer-provided retirement benefits. Begin explaining the value of taking his retirement benefits as a joint and survivor annuity and taking your benefits as a single annuity.

HOW DIVORCE CAN AFFECT YOUR RETIREMENT PLANNING

As we saw in the previous chapter, once you have married, you and your spouse have certain joint interests in each other's Employee Retirement Income Security Act (ERISA) retirement benefits. Federal and many state and local government retirement plans also create joint rights for spouses. For many couples retirement benefits can be their largest asset or their second largest asset after their home. In the grief and turmoil surrounding any marriage breakup, rationally visualizing the future is hard. Retirement benefit issues are difficult and complex to deal with in the best of circumstances, demanding a clear head and calm study—two commodities frequently not available during a divorce. You may be tempted just to skip the issue of retirement benefits. Don't yield to this temptation. *In a divorce, you need to be aware of your rights to your husband's retirement benefits and his rights to yours.* For all the reasons we already know, your husband's retirement benefits are likely to be larger than yours, so it is in your best interest to include these benefits in the property discussions from the beginning.

This chapter tracks the protections provided by ERISA for employer plans and the importance of an appropriate court order, the *qualified domestic relations order* (QDRO). A description of Social Security for divorced spouses concludes the chapter.

HOW THE RETIREMENT EQUITY ACT PROTECTS RETIREMENT BENEFITS DURING A DIVORCE

In general, ERISA forbids "alienation" of retirement benefits— that is, permitting someone other than the employee to have an interest in the employee's retirement benefits—even if the employee agrees to grant such rights. After the enactment of ERISA, state courts struggled with the issue of whether retirement benefits could be treated as marital property under state divorce law and, therefore, "alienated" from the employee. In 1984, provisions in the Retirement Equity Act (REA) made it clear that retirement benefits could be subject to state law divisions in *domestic relations situations*, such as divorce and separation. This is one of the rare areas in which ERISA permits a future retirement benefit to become subject to the claims of someone other than the employee who is earning the benefit.

REA strictly limits this domestic relations right to state court orders meeting the statutory requirements for qualified domestic relation orders (QDROs). If your divorce lawyer doesn't know what a QDRO is, get another lawyer—immediately. You already know ERISA law is extremely complex in its operation. When you combine ERISA with state divorce law, the mix becomes fiendishly complex. You want a divorce lawyer who has worked through the hell before. Even then your lawyer is not likely to be as familiar with your husband's plan or your plan as you are. Don't be shy about spelling out what you believe are the important features of the retirement plans. If your lawyer isn't grateful for this, she should be.

HOW THE COURT DISTRIBUTES RETIREMENT BENEFITS

From the outset of property settlement discussions, *you should recognize your retirement benefits (or other property, for that matter) are just as subject to the divorce court's division as your husband's.* Divorce law and property settlement procedures differ from state to state, so the following discussion can only be general in nature. But certain principles apply in almost every state.

Divorce court judges have enormous discretion to divide property based on their concept of fairness. Most state divorce laws simply instruct the court to divide property in an "equitable" fashion. Note, the law does not require the division be "equal," so don't expect a 50/50 split of property. In today's courts, women are not guaranteed continued support from their husbands—this applies even to women who have spent their lives working in the home. Understand that you will need to prove your contribution to the marriage and your level of future earnings ability in very concrete dollars-and-cents terms. Depending on the facts and circumstances surrounding the divorce, judges (still predominantly males) are very sympathetic to the former husband's pleas of poverty and inability to support two households on his one salary. Yet after divorce, the standard of living for most women and children drops significantly, and most men's standards of living increase.

The state courts usually do not have definite rules on the division of retirement benefits. Because the provisions of REA have been effective only since 1985, the law is still developing. Courts run the gamut from awarding everything to the worker to awarding everything to the nonworking spouse, depending on other assets and the facts of the case. In the area of pensions, as with all other divisions of marital property and agreements on child support or alimony, you and your husband will be better off—and probably happier with the outcome—if you can agree to the property settlement yourselves and simply present it to the court for the court's approval. While the court is not required to approve the privately negotiated property settlement, it almost invariably does unless the settlement is egregiously unfair to one of the parties.

Try to Work Out the Property Settlement

No matter how bitterly you feel toward your soon-to-be former spouse, you won't benefit financially by making lawyers wealthy with a protracted battle over finances. Depending on the emotional circumstances, if you can deal peacefully with your spouse, it will make the most sense for the two of you to work out a rough understanding of the property settlement. Then have one of your lawyers draft it for your review and the review of the other counsel. This will be the least costly method of proceeding. Of course, this level of agreement between the two parties is rarely achievable, or they wouldn't be getting divorced in the first place. But try to avoid the trap of spending $5,000 of lawyers' billable time arguing about who gets a $2,000 IRA.

If you can't talk it over face to face, think about exchanging written proposals. Just be sure you label them as "drafts" or "proposals" so your spouse doesn't end up with them in court swearing it's what you agreed to. You can leave all this to the lawyers, and certainly you should not agree to a property settlement until your lawyer carefully reviews it. But if the lawyers have to start from scratch with a property settlement, it will probably cost you more in billable time. Just remember, in divorce, as in much of life, civility saves money.

DETERMINING WHAT RETIREMENT BENEFITS ARE AVAILABLE TO YOUR SPOUSE

The first step is finding out exactly what retirement benefits your spouse is entitled to from previous and current employers.[1] Again, to save money, you may want to pursue this information yourself and then turn it over to your lawyer. You may need your husband's cooperation because retirement plans are not required to give information to anyone other than the plan participants and the government. It may increase your husband's cooperation if you remind him that property settlements are subject to change by the court even years after originally settled, if one of the parties can show fraud because assets were hidden. As a last resort you may have to get the plan from the Department of Labor through the Freedom of Information Act, but before you go to the Department of Labor, try having the judge order your husband to produce information on his retirement plans.

These plans will include defined benefit pension plan, 401(k)s, profit-sharing plans, and some employer "savings" or thrift plans. Try to get the summary plan descriptions (SPDs), the original plan document, and your husband's latest employee benefit statement. The employee benefit statement must be given to him at least annually.

CALCULATING WHAT THE COURT MIGHT AWARD YOU FROM YOUR SPOUSE'S RETIREMENT BENEFITS

There is no way of knowing precisely what the court may award you from these benefits. If your husband earned most of these benefits before you and he were married, the court is unlikely to award you much, if anything, from the retirement plan. This is particularly true if you have worked outside the home and have your own retirement benefits. On the other hand, if you were married for most of the time the retirement benefits were being earned, there is a presumption that you have a valid interest in a portion of those benefits.

The uncertainty of how the benefits might be divided and awarded by the court can be a negotiating tool on your behalf. You may be able to convince your husband at the outset that the best approach might be a cash or other property settlement to you in return for your waiving all rights to his retirement benefits.

ASSESSING THE VALUE OF YOUR SPOUSE'S BENEFITS

Even if you take the cash-settlement approach, you will need to know what benefits he has. Once you have found all the possible various sources of retirement benefits, determine your husband's vested benefits. Then look at the value of those benefits or benefits likely to be vested within a short time. You may consider nonvested benefits as well, but the court will probably not consider them. Nevertheless, they can be part of your negotiations with your spouse.

Determining the present value of the defined contribution plans, such as 401(k) plans, will be relatively easy. That will be the value of his "individual account" in the plan. If the account is invested in nonpublicly traded stocks or guaranteed income contracts, there may be an issue of valuing those assets. But that valuation problem will be no more difficult than valuing the assets if they were outside the plan.

Defined benefit plans will be more difficult to value. Remember these plans are based on a number of variables, including your husband's length of service with the plan sponsor, his age, and usually his salary. Actuarial calculations will be required, too, if you want to know the present value of the benefits accrued to the time of the divorce or to his possible retirement date. Depending on the potential dollar value of the benefits involved, you may need to hire your own actuary to calculate the defined benefit values. While the calculations should be based on the interest and mortality factors contained in the plan, there may be choice of variables for calculating the value to you. Your lawyer should have a pension actuary she has worked with before. Be certain the actuary has the latest plan document and all relevant information regarding your husband's accrued benefits such as his earnings history, length of service, and so on.

NEGOTIATING YOUR FAIR SHARE OF YOUR SPOUSE'S BENEFITS

Once you have calculated the value of all the retirement benefits, you can then begin negotiating your share. There are a number of approaches you—or the court, if you and your spouse cannot agree—can take in calculating your share. Some courts might give you half of a fraction of the retirement benefit under the so-called *time rule.* The fraction is based on the number of years during the marriage when benefits were earned divided by the number of total years the benefits were earned. For example, assume you were married for 15 years and your husband earned benefits all those years and had been earning benefits for 5 years prior to your marriage. His benefit has a present value of $60,000. Under the time rule, you would be awarded one-half of an amount equal to $60,000 times the fraction 15/20, for a value of $22,500.

The time rule usually calculates the award based on current value of the benefit at the time of the divorce, not when your husband could retire. This means you will miss the bigger buildup in the value of a defined benefit plan especially in those last years of work. Remember in defined benefit plans the value really grows in the last years of working. (Refer to Chapter 7 for the discussion on how benefits accrue under defined benefit plans.)

You might ask for a fixed percentage of the pension when your husband retires. Using the example, you could avoid the loss of the last years' buildup by asking for three-eighths of his monthly retirement benefit, assuming payment based on a single life annuity, at normal retirement age.

Don't be surprised if your husband's attorney suggests adding in the value of your retirement benefits during the marriage and dividing the value of the two benefits equally between the parties. Since your benefit is likely to be lower, you will still be a net recipient.

CHOOSING A METHOD OF PAYMENT OF RETIREMENT BENEFITS IN DIVORCE

The dollar figures being equal, far and away the best form of receiving the value of the retirement benefits is cash at the settlement of the divorce. If your husband's retirement plan will release the money pursuant to a QDRO, you may then take the sum represented by the retirement and roll it into your own IRA where it can grow on a tax-deferred basis until you retire. If you do not place the money in an IRA, you will not be subject to the 10% early withdrawal penalty, but you will pay ordinary income tax on the amount, and you will miss the advantage of having the money grow on a tax-deferred basis for several years until you retire or reach age 70½. If your husband gives you a cash-equivalent amount from funds outside the retirement plan, the amount probably will not be eligible for a tax-free rollover into an IRA.

In addition to the rollover advantages, this cash-value approach has other advantages:

❖ You don't have to wait for years to receive the award granted by the QDRO.

❖ You do not have to deal with the plan administrator of your husband's plan for possibly decades until your spouse's retirement eligibility date.

❖ You don't have to worry about the plan's being terminated and possible loss of a portion of your benefits.

❖ There will be no issue about the proper interpretation of the QDRO years after the court issued the order and a different plan administrator now has questions about it.

In short, the money is in your hands and not in a plan with payments scheduled to start years from now.

But the reality is that qualified retirement plans probably will not be willing to issue the benefit in cash and, depending on your husband's age, may not be able to by law. Further, cash is often in short supply when couples divorce, and your spouse simply may not be able to come up with the cash to pay the full value of the retirement benefits to you directly, if the plan cannot or will not pay the amount.

As an alternative, he may suggest purchasing an annuity for you in an amount equal to the retirement benefit you would receive. This may sound like a reasonable compromise, but be careful. It could be difficult to force him to continue making the payments for the annuity, or the company issuing the annuity may permit him to change the annuity beneficiary or cash in the annuity. Finally, if you and he do elect the annuity purchase option, be certain the annuity is held in your name, by you. Choose a highly rated company. (Refer to Chapter 8 for a discussion on purchasing individual annuities.) Also, be alert to changes in the law on the income tax treatment of annuities. Congress has consistently shaved away at the tax-favored status of annuities, and you could find yourself paying taxes on the income from the annuity even though you haven't received the income yet.

If neither of these options is suitable, you will have to rely on the QDRO to spell out your rights to retirement benefits for the plans holding those benefits.

KNOW YOUR RIGHTS UNDER THE QUALIFIED DOMESTIC RELATIONS ORDER

By law a QDRO must contain certain information listed in the statute. But the QDRO should also very clearly define the benefit you (whom the QDRO identifies as the alternate payee) are to receive under all the contingencies you can imagine. The QDRO must be a court order pursuant to state domestic relations law involving marital property rights, child support, or alimony to a spouse, former spouse, or dependent of a plan participant. And the QDRO must create or recognize the right of an alternate payee to receive benefits from a qualified plan that would otherwise not be required to honor such an order because of the protections offered by antialienation provisions of ERISA.

A QDRO will take precedence over any other required payment except an earlier filed QDRO, regardless of the dates of the marriage. If your spouse has been married before and has an existing QDRO applying to his retirement plan, that earlier QDRO must be paid and any benefits you receive from your QDRO are based only on the benefits left after the first QDRO is satisfied.

By law the QDRO must contain the following items, which we will discuss in detail later in the chapter:

- ❖ The name and last known mailing address of the plan participant—the plan participant is your former spouse.

- ❖ The name and address of all alternate payees—the alternate payee is usually you, but if the decree gives the children rights in the retirement plan, be sure they are included as well.

- ❖ The amount or percentage of the participant's benefit to be paid to each alternative payee or the method to be used by the plan administrator to determine the amount to be paid to the alternate payees.

- ❖ The number of payments or the period of time the QDRO covers.

- ❖ The name of each plan covered by the QDRO.[2]

Some plan sponsors will provide a model QDRO which they will accept. Contact your husband's plan to see whether it will supply such a model. If so, get the form, but use it only as a guide. The model was developed by the plan administrator and reflects the procedures and payment forms that are in the best interests of the plan and the most efficient for the administrator. But these procedures are not necessarily in *your* best interests. The model will still be a useful guide for your attorney to follow, but you are not required by law to follow it slavishly.

Before drafting the QDRO, your attorney should talk with the plan administrator about any unusual provisions in the plan or the most common errors the plan administrator finds in QDROs. This discussion may avoid having the QDRO rejected by the plan's administrator, which would then require redrafting, resubmission to the court for its approval and then resubmission to the plan administrator. According to surveys, over 70% of plan administrators find handling QDROs "difficult and time consuming," and over 80% find the language spelling out the amount to be paid to the spouse to be unclear or uncertain.[3] A phone call may save costly and embarrassing delays. Moreover, once the QDRO is issued and approved, you will become a plan participant. Over the years you are likely to have many dealings with the plan administrator. You should begin to impress her now with your diligence and attention to detail.

The QDRO should first of all get the name of the plan correct. This seems obvious enough, but many plan administrators complain the QDRO arrives with an incorrect name. Most plan sponsors have several plans all with similar names, so the plan administrator may not know which plan you have the claim against. If your QDRO seeks payment from the "ACME Retirement Security Plan," but the real name of the plan is the "ACME Retirement Income Security Plan," the plan administrator would be violating ERISA and her fiduciary duties to honor the QDRO.

The QDRO should spell out exactly the benefit you are getting in a dollar sum, a percentage of the benefit, or a combination of both. Give the date on which the benefit value is to be fixed, if the award is percentage of his benefit. For example, is the percentage based on the accrued benefit as of the date of the divorce, the spouse's benefit at his earliest retirement date, or at his normal retirement age? If your benefit is defined in terms of a percentage of your former spouse's benefit, be sure you describe the benefit payment form used in your calculation. For example, a single life annuity form of benefit will give him the largest monthly annuity sum. Even though he might not take his benefit in that fashion, you should specify your percentage is based on a single life annuity payment, if you are taking your benefits in annuity form. That way, if your husband remarries and takes his benefit in the lower paying form of a joint and survivor annuity for his new spouse, your benefit won't be reduced. The QDRO should also specifically state your benefit is based on the gross value of his benefit, exclusive of deductions for taxes, health insurance, union dues, and so on. This stipulation will have no effect on the taxes you must pay. But it will mean the difference between your receiving 50% of the pretax pension of, say, $1,000 per month as opposed to 50% of the after-tax pension amount of $720 per month, for example.

The QDRO cannot require the plan to give you any form of benefit or use any type of payment option which is ordinarily not available to any participant under the plan. For example, if the plan does not provide for lump-sum payments, the QDRO cannot compel a lump-sum payment. However, a QDRO can require that you begin to receive payments before your former spouse leaves the company or reaches normal retirement age. Such payments can begin at the *earliest* of the following dates:

❖ Your husband's potential early retirement date under the plan

❖ His 50th birthday, if he would also be entitled to take the benefit, if he left the employer then

❖ The earliest age over 50 when he could begin receiving the benefit, if he has already left the employer.

For example, assume under your husband's plan, early retirement is age 60, payout could be received any time he left the company regardless of his age; and he is 50 years old. Your QDRO could ask for payments to begin immediately because he is 50, and he would be able to get payouts under the plan if he left. But suppose the same facts, but your husband is only 49. Your QDRO cannot get a payout until he becomes 50.

Or let's assume another plan which sets early retirement at age 62, but does not permit any other payout if you leave until you reach 59½. Your husband is 50. The earliest date your QDRO can demand payment is age 59½, because that is the earliest date on which he could get the money. It doesn't matter that your husband is 50 now. Because he could not receive a payout under the plan if he left now, you can't either.

Be sure the QDRO spells out what happens if your husband dies before he is eligible to receive his retirement benefit and what happens when he dies after retirement. You should be designated in specific terms in the QDRO as the "surviving spouse." Otherwise, you may not receive the benefits of a survivor under the plan. For example, under the Retirement Equity Act, most plans must provide for a benefit for the surviving spouse, but once you divorce, unless the QDRO names you as the surviving spouse, the plan may decide there is no "surviving spouse." Hence, no benefit is payable even though you have a QDRO stating you are entitled to half of your spouse's benefit at retirement. If he dies before retirement, he didn't retire so there is no benefit. If the QDRO names you as the "surviving spouse," you receive the benefits of a surviving spouse under REA.

You need to decide whether you want your benefit paid over your lifetime or in some other form. You are entitled to use any payment form offered under the plan, except the joint and survivor option. For example, if the plan permits a lump-sum payment, you may want to take your QDRO benefit in a lump sum as soon as you could receive it under the plan. Even if you are not retired at that time or don't want the money then, you may transfer the sum into an IRA on a tax-deferred basis.

If you elect a periodic form of benefit payments, be sure the QDRO requires the plan send you a check directly. If your husband receives the full amount of the benefit and then writes you a check, you will have a needless delay in receiving your benefit. And if he is short of money one month, he may be tempted to "borrow" from you. If creditors begin to pursue him or he should declare bankruptcy, they will go after your benefits in his bank account.

SUBMITTING THE QDRO TO YOUR SPOUSE'S BENEFITS PLAN ADMINISTRATOR

Once the divorce judge authorizes the QDRO, you or your lawyer—*not* your former husband—should submit the QDRO to the plan administrator. Be sure you do this promptly and be sure you have evidence, such as a signed return receipt, that the plan administrator in fact received the QDRO. The QDRO is not effective until it is in the plan administrator's hands. The plan administrator then has a "reasonable period" to decide whether the QDRO is, in effect, qualified. The law does not define the "reasonable" period, but you should count on giving the plan administrator about 90 days to review fully and rule on the QDRO. About a month after sending the QDRO, however, your attorney or you should call the plan administrator to ask whether there are any problems.

Common problems with QDROs include:

❖ The order demands payment in a form the plan does not permit.

❖ The exact amount of the benefit the alternate payee is entitled to cannot be determined from the order.

❖ The order is not clear as to when the benefit is to be paid to the alternate payee.

❖ The name of the plan is incorrect on the order (61% of the problem cases involve this mistake).

❖ The form of the payment, lump sum, annuity, and so on, is not clear from the order.[4]

The plan can withhold your benefits up to 18 months while it decides on the validity of the order. This delay is an issue only if you are entitled to benefits immediately. Once a valid order is issued, if you are entitled to receive the benefits immediately, you must receive the withheld benefits immediately.

If the plan administrator refuses to honor the QDRO on the grounds it is not qualified, you have two courses of action. If the mistake is clearly an error due to your or your lawyer's lack of knowledge about the plan, try to get a written explanation of the problem, redraft the QDRO, and take it back to the judge for re-issuance. The difficulty with this approach will depend on the law of the state issuing the QDRO and sometimes on the judge's nature.

If you or your lawyer feel the plan administrator is incorrectly interpreting the plan or is simply being overly persnickety, you may appeal the decision pursuant to the plan's appeal procedures required by ERISA. Unless there is a clear error on your part, you should use the claims appeal procedure first and then return to the court if the appeal under the plan is denied. Once the court reviews the QDRO and determines it is, in fact, correct, the plan administrator must honor it.

If the plan administrator feels the court's QDRO is incorrect, resulting in a violation of ERISA or the Internal Revenue Code, the administrator may intervene in your divorce on behalf of the plan to explain the concerns about the plan and the order directly to the judge. Again, trying to involve the plan administrator from the outset may avoid this kind of misunderstanding and delay.

DIVIDING IRA ASSETS IN A DIVORCE PROPERTY SETTLEMENT

Individual retirement accounts (IRAs) are also subject to division in divorces, although no QDRO is required because IRAs are not qualified retirement plans. A transfer from an IRA under a divorce decree is not a taxable event to the former IRA holder. At the time of the transfer of assets, the assets will be treated as though a new IRA was created for the benefit of the receiving spouse. You should immediately set up an IRA with any money you receive from your former husband's IRAs. That money will continue to grow in the IRA on a tax-deferred basis and, as with any other IRA, if you take the money out before you reach age 59½, you will pay immediate tax on it and a 10% early withdrawal penalty, absent one of the exemptions for IRA withdrawals such as disability.

SOCIAL SECURITY FOR DIVORCED WIVES

As a divorced spouse if you were married for 10 years, you are eligible to receive Social Security benefits based on your husband's earnings when you reach age 62, even if he is not yet receiving such benefits and even if he is remarried. Your spouse also must be at least age 62. If he is not retired then, the divorce must have occurred at least 2 years before you can receive benefits. Benefits based on your former spouse's earnings will cease if you remarry, unless your new spouse is receiving Social Security as a widower, parent, or disabled child. Chapter 9 on Social Security and Medicare gives more detail on the rights of divorced spouses under Social Security.

CONCLUSION: KNOW YOUR RIGHTS TO YOUR SPOUSE'S RETIREMENT BENEFITS IF YOU DIVORCE

❖ Recognize that accrued retirement benefits of both you and your spouse are subject to division by the courts during a divorce.

❖ Be sure your divorce lawyer is fully familiar with ERISA law governing the treatment of qualified retirement plans.

❖ Find and value all your husband's accrued retirement benefits from current and former employers. These include 401(k) plans, profit-sharing plans, thrift plans, and ESOPs, as well as traditional pension plans.

❖ Talk to each plan administrator about their plan's requirements for QDROs and common problems to avoid. Ask if a model QDRO for the plan exists.

❖ If the potential amounts of benefits are very large, consider hiring an actuary to produce precise figures for the court to use in determining the value of the benefit.

❖ Be sure the QDRO specifically spells out the benefit you are to receive and the benefit payment form to be used for calculating the benefit; include the time at which the accrued benefit will be fixed—date of divorce, date of retirement, and so on.

❖ Be sure you are listed as a "surviving spouse" for plan purposes; otherwise, if your former spouse dies before he retires, you may receive no benefit.

NOTES FOR CHAPTER 15

1. For an extensive discussion of divorce rights, including specific discussions of rights under the Federal Civil Service Retirement, the Military Retirement, the Railroad Retirement, and the Foreign Service Retirement systems, see *Your Pension Rights at Divorce: What Women Need to Know*, written by Anne E. Moss for the Pension Rights Center. This book can be ordered through the Pension Rights Center, 918 16th St., N.W., Suite 704, Washington, D.C. 20006, for $16.50.

2. See Internal Revenue Code §414(p).

3. Buck Consultants, Inc., "QDROs: A Survey of Employer Practices," May 1991 (Washington, D.C.).

4. Ibid., p. 6.

CHAPTER SIXTEEN

IF YOU ARE NEAR RETIREMENT

This chapter is for those of you who feel you are 2 to 3 years away from retiring, which does not necessarily mean for those of you who are 62 to 65. Remember, when you retire depends on when you want to. If you think you must retire only because you are near 65, this isn't true: you cannot be forced to retire at 65 or any other age.

Under the Age Discrimination in Employment Act (ADEA), you cannot be forced to retire or be demoted because of your age. And unlike other discrimination in employment laws, such as those protecting you from sex and race discrimination, if you sue under ADEA, you will be able to bring your case before a jury (lots of older people serve on juries) and receive attorney's fees, costs and damages if the employer acted willfully to deny your rights. You probably won't be surprised that employers take ADEA complaints seriously. Once an employer is gently reminded about ADEA and its remedies, the employer's hints to older employees about slowing down, enjoying time away from work, and so on, magically cease in most cases. Of course, ADEA does not and should not protect you against dismissal, if you really are not capable of doing your job and your performance on the job is showing that.

Ask yourself why you feel you are near retirement or ready to retire. The only appropriate answer is because you want to—and because you have enough money to live comfortably for the next 25 years. If you did not give those answers, save this chapter for a few more years.

Once you really do want to leave the work force, begin a set of planned steps for leaving your job. Start at least a year before you intend to leave.

SET UP YOUR RETIREMENT BUDGET

If you are within a year or so of retiring, you can now refine the budget estimating we did in Chapter 11, How Much Do You Need for Retirement? Set up the budget you think you can live with. Hypothetical budgeting is always an annoying task because it involves lots of speculation and pondering on the unpredictable. But start with last year's checkbook and credit card receipts to see how you spent your money for a year. Once you have done that, modify the unusual and nonrecurring expenses, but add in expenses which might come up in the first year of retirement. For example, if you have decided to move, add in those expenses. Or if you plan to take an art course, add tuition into your budget.

Depending on how realistically you have compiled your budget, the next step might be even more annoying, or it may be intensely gratifying. *Try living for six months now on the retirement budget you set up.* Granted, there may be some significant differences between your cost of living while working and after retirement. But trying to live now with your retirement budget will give you some valuable insight, before you approach your boss with your advice about your replacement on the job and what he might do with the job. It may also change your ideas about when you want to retire!

Part of your retirement budget must encompass the income side of your plan. Begin looking at your three-legged stool of retirement income with a precise measuring stick for its legs and a sharp pencil. You should review your personal savings, find out what your Social Security benefits will be, and calculate the total of your employer-provided retirement benefits. The next sections of this chapter describe these calculations in detail.

REVIEW YOUR OWN SAVINGS

Start calculating how much money you will need for retirement by reviewing your own personal savings, which are easiest to calculate. You know all of those. If you want to know what sort of a monthly income you could expect from them, consult Appendix A. Choose the number of years you think you will live and the average rate of return you think your savings and investments can realistically receive over those years, and you will derive a rough idea of the amount of monthly withdrawal you can make until your money runs out.

For example, let's assume the following scenario:

❖ You have saved $100,000.

❖ You are retiring at age 65.

❖ You will live until age 90 (another 25 years).

❖ You believe you can earn 10% per year during your retirement on your savings.

In this case, you know the present value of your "annuity." It is $100,000. So you divide that amount by the factor for 10% interest over 25 years, which from Table A.4 is 9.077. Therefore, you may withdraw $11,000 annually from your savings until you are 90, when your savings will be exhausted. Try several calculations to see how the amount can vary based on the assumed interest rate and number of years of assumed life. For example, under the same situation, if you assume you can earn only 7% annually, you could only withdraw about $8,600 annually. And don't forget the effects of inflation on the buying power of that annual amount in the later years of your retirement. (See Chapter 11 to review the effects of inflation.)

FIND OUT WHAT YOUR SOCIAL SECURITY BENEFITS WILL BE

Social Security will provide an important part of your retirement income once you reach the age of eligibility. There are a number of variables involved in determining exactly how much your benefit will be. It is important to look at all the options before you elect to begin benefits. Once you begin receiving benefits under your earnings history, you are usually locked in. For example, when will you start receiving the benefit? You can start as young as 62. Will you receive the benefit based on your own earnings history or as a spouse based on your husband's or former husband's earnings history? Remember, Social Security benefits are based on your highest earnings for 35 years of your working life, and if you have fewer working years than that, the nonearning years will be averaged in as zeros. You may find you could substantially increase your benefit by working a few more years, especially if your current salary is considerably larger than earlier salaries, as is usually the case, or if you have not yet been in the work force for 35 years.

Submit another SSA-7004 Form, Request for Earnings and Benefit Estimate Statement, to the Social Security Administration to get an updated estimate of your Social Security wage history and potential benefits. (See Exhibit 9-1, which provides a sample form.) It will take a few weeks to receive this form, which will contain your Social Security earnings history. If you have been submitting the form and getting your estimated benefits statement every 3 years or so, you can be fairly certain you have kept the wage history accurate. Regardless, check the estimated benefits statement carefully. If you find mistakes, call the number on the form and then follow up in writing to Social Security. In most cases the Social Security Administration can correct errors occurring only within the last 3 years or so.

The statement will also tell you how many quarters of coverage you have earned. You must have 40 quarters to be eligible to receive benefits based on your own earnings history. That is about 10 years of work.

Call the Social Security Administration at 800-772-1213 and ask for its informational booklets. Also ask your employer's human resources or personnel department if it has information on Social Security. Many employers provide excellent information on Social Security; others supply nothing. For an excellent layperson's brochure, see "Guide to Social Security and Medicare," which is updated each year, and can be ordered from:

William M. Mercer, Inc.
1500 Meidinger Tower
Louisville, KY 40202-3415
502-561-4541

The cost is about $6.

Should You Begin Social Security Benefits Early?

Once you know approximately what your retirement benefit from Social Security will be, you can plan more realistically. From your statement, you will readily see the difference between benefits received at different ages. It will also show you your normal retirement age which will be past 65 if you were born after 1937. (Because of the differences in normal retirement age under Social Security based on when you were born, we will refer to "normal retirement age" as the time you receive your highest ordinary Social Security benefit rather than age 65.) If you elect to retire before your normal retirement age, remember your benefit will be reduced and will always remain reduced, although you will receive the cost-of-living adjustments applied to all Social Security benefits. You will not receive the higher benefit when you reach normal retirement age. You are not required to begin receiving Social Security benefits when you retire, even if you begin to receive employer-provided retirement benefits.

If you are retiring before your normal retirement age and you can live without the Social Security payments for a few years, you will need to consider whether to delay receiving the benefits to receive ultimately higher benefits. For example, if you want to work part time at a job paying more than the Social Security earnings limit during the early years of retirement, it may make sense for you to delay receipt of Social Security. Otherwise, you face a reduction in your Social Security benefits based on the earnings limitation in addition to the reduction for receiving the benefits before your normal retirement age, and, depending on how much you earn, you may even wind up paying taxes on part of your Social Security benefit.

From your Social Security benefits statement, you will also see the significant benefit you receive from delaying benefits past normal retirement age. Of course, you are delaying both the time value of having the money early and you are reducing the number of years you will receive payments. You can roughly calculate the number of years it would take you to "break even" in terms of receiving the same total amount of benefit by making three columns headed "Age 62 or Current Age Benefit," "Normal Retirement Age Benefit," and "Age 70 Benefit". Multiply the monthly benefit listed on your statement from Social Security and for each age column add each year's benefit to the previous year's total to see when you reach the break-even point. Table 16.1 shows a person at the top of the wage scale whose normal retirement age is 66. The benefits are estimated to be $1,005 at age 62, $1,370 at normal retirement age and $1,830 per month at 70, according to her Social Security estimated benefits statement.

	TABLE 16.1 Break-Even Points for Early or Delayed Receipt of Social Security Benefits		
Age	Benefit at Age 62	Benefit at Normal Retirement Age	Benefit at Age 70
62	$ 12,060	$ 0	$ 0
63	24,120	0	0
64	36,180	0	0
65	48,240	16,440	0
66	60,300	32,880	0
67	72,360	49,320	0
68	84,420	65,760	0
69	96,480	82,200	0
70	107,540	98,640	21,960
71	120,600	115,080	43,920
72	132,660	131,520	65,880
73	144,720	147,960	87,840
74	156,780	164,400	109,800
75	168,840	180,840	131,760
76	180,900	197,280	153,720
77	192,960	213,720	175,680
78	205,020	230,160	197,640
79	217,080	246,600	219,600
80		263,040	241,560
81		279,480	263,520
82		295,920	285,480
83		312,360	307,440
84		328,800	329,400

Of course, these figures don't correct for the time value of money. Depending on our example's confidence in her longevity, she may not want to wait until she is 70 to retire, since it takes her until age

84 to break even. But if she waits to normal retirement age to begin her benefit, by the time she is 73, she breaks even. Given a woman in her early 60s can expect to live until over age 83 these days,[1] she may be well advised to delay the receipt of Social Security payments to normal retirement age.

Should You Receive Benefits as a Spouse or on Your Own?

If you are married or were married for 10 years and are now divorced, check to see whether you could receive a higher benefit as a spouse based on your husband's earnings record. Because women earn so much less than men and because women's time out of the workplace is counted as a zero in calculating the average indexed monthly earnings (AIME) on which Social Security benefits are based, even a woman who has worked steadily over the years may receive a lower Social Security benefit based on her own earnings record than she can receive as a spouse under her husband's record.

When you order your own earnings and benefit estimate statement, ask your spouse to order his as well. Each of you must order your own statement because the federal privacy laws prohibit giving Social Security information to anyone other than the individual in ordinary cases. Each statement will show both the benefit estimate for the wage earner and an estimated benefit for the spouse based on the wage earner's earnings. In rare cases, your husband could earn a higher benefit filing under your earnings history, but it is highly unlikely given most women's earnings histories. Unlike most employer-provided retirement benefits, the wage earner's retirement benefit is not reduced if a spouse also claims benefits based on that wage earner's history. Since there is no penalty for using the spouse's earnings history rather than your own, if the spouse's history gives you a bigger benefit, file under his benefit. In most cases when you apply for Social Security, they will tell you which benefit is larger and automatically give you the larger benefit.

If you are married, your husband must be receiving *his* Social Security benefits before you can receive benefits based on his earnings record. However, if you were married 10 years and are now divorced, you do not need to wait for your former spouse to begin receiving benefits. You may receive Social Security benefits if he is at least 62 even though he may still be working. The catch here is you must have been divorced at least 2 years or he must have been entitled to benefits when you divorced. For example, assume you and John were married for 23 years and divorced when he was 61 and you were 62. John is still working. You must wait 2 years until you can file for benefits as a spouse based on his earnings. If he had been 63 when you divorced, you could file immediately.

Applying for Social Security Benefits

Once you have decided you want to begin receiving your Social Security benefits, you must begin the application process. *You must apply for Social Security. The checks don't just start coming when you reach normal retirement age.* Start by calling the Social Security Administration's number for applications, 800-772-1213. Most, if not all, of the work for your application can be done by phone. You will need a certified copy of your birth certificate, not just a photocopy. If you don't have an extra certified copy you can give Social Security, start to work on this today. It may be as easy as writing the records division of the state in which you were born, or it may be a long process. It all depends on the jurisdiction. If you do not have a copy of your birth certificate, other documentation will be accepted, such as the birth certificates of your children showing your age. If you are relying on your spouse's wage history, you will need a certified copy of your marriage certificate and, if you are divorced, a certified copy of the divorce decree.

If you don't have these documents, it can take time to get them together, so start early. Do not delay beginning the application process just because you do not have these documents. Begin the application process and keep working on the documentation search. The Social Security Administration will give you tips on ways to find documents, or, if you don't have documentation, they will tell what sort of alternative documentation is acceptable.

File your application at least three months before you want to begin receiving benefits. It's even better to file your application the January before you want benefits to begin. If you are retiring at normal retirement age, Medicare Part A (hospitalization) and Part B (doctors and other medical services) will be covered automatically, unless you tell the Social Security Administration you do not want Medicare Part B coverage. You will pay for Part B coverage; there is no premium for Part A.

If you intend to work part time after you begin receiving Social Security benefits, remember the earnings limitation. After you have reached that limitation, your Social Security benefits will be reduced by $1 for every $2 over the limit if you are under 65 and by $1 for every $3 over the limit between ages 65 and 69. You may file for Social Security benefits as soon as you become eligible and continue working that year until you reach the earnings limitation and then retire.

Chances are you will have no trouble receiving your appropriate benefit once you have provided the needed data. However, if you do have problems, be sure you document your case in writing. Get names of the people you are dealing with and persevere. If after a few months you continue to have problems, contact the staff of your Congressional U.S. representative's staff, not the representative directly. Your representative will know little or nothing about the details of applying for Social Security. But there will be a person on the staff who does little else but deal with Social Security benefits issues for constituents. Make this contact in writing, but you might start with a phone call to the local office for the name of the staff person.

If all else fails, you may want to consult a lawyer for assistance. But be sure you choose one who specializes or is highly experienced in Social Security issues. Avoid a generalist. She will spend too much time learning about the Social Security system at your expense.

CALCULATE THE VALUE OF YOUR EMPLOYER-PROVIDED RETIREMENT BENEFITS

Hopefully, your employer-provided retirement benefits will supply a significant portion of your retirement income. This is when your knowledge of retirement benefits learned in Chapters 6 and 7 will serve you well. Begin by reading your retirement summary plan description and your most recent employee benefits statement. The summary plan description (SPD) will outline the payment options, if any, you can choose for the receipt of your retirement benefits. Your most recent employee benefits statement should show you the monthly payment you could expect from your pension or the balance in your defined contribution account.

Once you have refreshed your memory about the payment options and your estimated benefits, schedule an appointment with the human resources department. Reconfirm your understandings about payment options and your benefit amount. Ask about any recent changes not reflected in your SPD. Be sure both you and the human resources representative are working from the most recent SPD or plan provisions. *Do not rely on anything you do not get in writing.* Only the actual plan provisions control, and while oral promises might be enforced after a long and expensive court case, you don't want to be the one bearing the expense of trying to get your employer to live up to the oral promise made by the human resources clerk.

As you already know, retirement benefits administration is complex and difficult. The employers who provide their employees with retirement benefits are in good faith, and the person dealing with retirement benefits wants to do it right and give you your full benefit, but sometimes the knowledge does not match the good intentions. This is the time to ask lots of questions. The knowledge of the human resources person giving you information will vary widely. Some personnel have in-depth knowledge of both the plan and ERISA and know more about retirement planning with your employer's plan than expert financial planners and ERISA attorneys. Others may not know as much as you do about the plan. They may be new to the job, or they may have been administering the plan for the last 15 years—and doing it wrong every time. It does happen!

If what you are being told doesn't match your understanding of your options or the amount you think you should be receiving, say so. In a non-confrontational manner, ask the plan administrator to look at the provisions again or re-do the calculations. Point out where you think there are problems. Acknowledge that benefits calculations are complex. If you still feel that your payment options or benefits are not being properly calculated or offered, you have the right under ERISA to appeal the decisions and you must receive a reply to your appeal within a reasonable time. If your plan is not covered by ERISA, chances are it also has an appeals procedure. Inquire about it or ask for the plan document and look it up yourself.

Don't limit your benefits inquiries to just your current employer. Contact all your former employers and any unions you may have joined. For some of the former employers, you may *know* you are entitled to a benefit. It is your responsibility to notify the employer of your whereabouts and to ask to begin receiving your benefits. Ask for the current SPD and an estimate of your benefits. Once you receive these materials, do some digging around in your records to try to match the benefit estimate with what you think you are entitled to.

Contact former employers even if you do not think you are entitled to a benefit from them. Things do change. You may have forgotten a benefit program or you may be unaware of benefits changes or new benefits that were adopted. Send a letter to your former employers including your Social Security number, the approximate dates you worked for them, and the name and location of the division you worked in. Again, it is your responsibility to keep in contact with your former employers who may hold benefits for you. Contacting them all may not turn up any forgotten benefits, but you are only investing a little time.

Choosing a Benefit Payment Option

Payment options basically fall into the periodic annuity payment schedule of payments every month for life or lump-sum payments in which you receive the full value of your benefit immediately when you retire. There are variations on both of these approaches. The *decision tree chart* in Figure 16.1 provides a visual picture of most of the options available and their tax consequences. Which is best for you depends on your family situation and on your ability to manage large sums of money.

Some plans have no options: you simply receive an annuity of monthly payments as long as you live, and if you are married as long as your husband lives, if he survives you. Other plans have a number of options. In most cases the tax treatment of the benefit distribution does not have to be a controlling factor because lump sums can be transferred directly into an IRA on a tax-free basis. You then pay taxes only on the money you withdraw from the IRA. You *must* begin receiving periodic payments from your IRA when you reach age 70½, just as you must begin receiving benefits from an employer plan at that age.

Annuity Form of Payment. If you are married, the ordinary method of payment of your ERISA defined benefit retirement plan (and many non-ERISA plans as well) will be a joint and survivor, that is, payment in monthly installments to you for your lifetime and to your surviving spouse. In most cases this is *not* the form of payment you want. Under the qualified joint and survivor annuity (QJSA) payment option (described in detail in Chapter 14), your benefit payments will be reduced because the benefit is being paid over two lifetimes

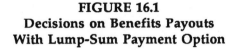

FIGURE 16.1
Decisions on Benefits Payouts
With Lump-Sum Payment Option

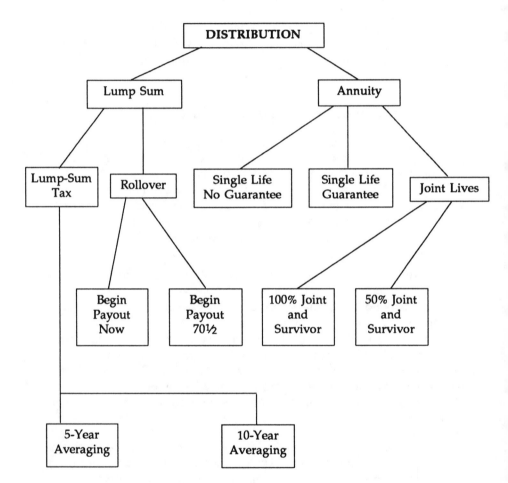

Note: The 10-year averaging option is available only if you were 50 or over in 1986. For 10-year averaging, the tax rates applicable in 1986 must be used, not current tax rates.

rather than one. It may be reduced again for your survivor when you die. But as a woman you are likely to outlive your husband, and there will be no survivor. You will have received a reduced benefit for nothing in return. Of course, if you are in very poor health and your husband is very healthy or your husband is much younger, a QJSA option may make sense. You will need your husband's written, notarized consent to avoid taking the QJSA payout option. Also there are a few plans which "subsidize" the survivor annuity by not reducing the amount paid originally if a survivor annuity option is taken. If yours is one of these rare plans, then there is no penalty for taking the QJSA, and you should take it.

If you are not married, the ordinary way your defined benefit pension would be paid is through a "single life annuity" in monthly installments as long as you live. Your plan may give you the option of choosing a QJSA and naming a survivor. As with a married couple, your initial benefit will be reduced to compensate for the expected payments to the survivor.

Other options for annuity payments include "life and 10 years certain" or some other year figure. Under these payout options, for example, if you retire at age 65 and begin receiving benefits and live to 100, you receive your benefits until you die and nothing is paid to your beneficiary. But if you were killed in a sky diving accident at age 67, your named beneficiary would continue receiving a benefit for the 8 remaining years of the 10-year certain time span.

Lump-Sum Payment. Lump-sum payment options are the normal form of payout for most defined contribution plans such as profit-sharing plans and 401(k) plans. Many defined benefit plans also provide for a lump-sum payment option. Lump-sum distributions require careful thought and treatment. You can transfer the lump sum directly into an IRA, deferring the tax until you withdraw the money, or you can pay taxes immediately, possibly using a 5-year or 10-year income tax averaging technique. Your overriding consideration is to remember that this money must last you a lifetime—and it may be a far longer lifetime than you expect. Other considerations are your comfort level with managing large sums of money, the immediate need for large cash sums if you are considering relocating, and so on, and estate and tax considerations. Unlike the annuity form of payment which in most cases pays for your lifetime no matter how long you live so you cannot outlive your capital, with a lump sum you are managing; once all the money is gone, it's gone.

To get an idea of how long you can live on periodic payments from your lump sum, we can use the same analysis we used for your individual savings. Look at the lump-sum value of your benefit. Suppose you have a 401(k) plan worth $150,000. You are 65 and you think you will live to be age 90. You conservatively estimate you can invest the money at 6%. Referring to the present value of an annuity table in Appendix A.4, we find the value factor for an annuity at 6% for 25 years and divide that into the present value of our "annuity" of $150,000. You can "pay" yourself a little over $11,700 per year under these facts. You have used conservative estimates for a low rate of return and a long life.

If you have a defined benefit with payout options of an annuity or a lump sum, it is easier to compare annuity payments from your management of the money with your employer's management. Let's use Alice as an example. When she retires she will receive annual annuity payments of $4,633, or she can take a lump sum of $39,191. Using the same assumptions, rolling over the lump sum and earning 6% on it while paying herself an annual payment for 25 years, Alice could give herself benefits of only $3,065 annually. Receiving the annual benefit is the better value under these assumptions. But if Alice thought she could make 10% on the money and would only live another 15 years until she is 80, she could pay herself $5,150 annually, clearly a better payout than the employer's annuity. But these high rate of return and early mortality assumptions would be far too optimistic to really rely on. Alice should stick with her employer's annuities. Be very careful with this lump sum versus employer's annuity analysis if you begin to use more optimistic figures on rates of return you could earn on your management of a lump-sum distribution. Using the time value of money tables in Appendix A, you can see what a dramatic difference changing the assumptions makes. For example, if you assume you could earn 10% on your $150,000 lump sum, you could pay yourself over $16,500 annually until you were 90. But that would take more aggressive money management to achieve those returns.

Changing interest rates can also have a dramatic effect on the size of your defined benefit lump-sum, if you choose to take a lump sum rather than the annuity. By law in distributing lump sums, the employer must use a Pension Benefit Guaranty Corporation (PBGC) interest rate assumption. PBGC generates these interest rates based on market rates for annuities. In times of very low interest rates, the lump-sum value of your defined benefit plan accrued benefit will be much larger than in times of higher interest rates. This is because the interest rate is used to estimate how much the lump sum will earn over the course of your remaining life to give you the equivalent of the monthly benefit you would have received under the annuity payout. If interest rates and, hence, earning assumptions are low, you will need a larger lump-sum amount of money to pay the same annual benefit each year than you would need to pay the same benefit annually when interest rates were high and the lump sum was earning more money.

Depending on the sum involved and your age and length of service, the difference in amounts can reach into the tens of thousands of dollars. At a time of very low interest rates, such as we saw in 1992, taking a lump-sum payout from a defined benefit plan may result in a significantly larger benefit than you might have received in annuity form. The disadvantage is that you probably *will earn less* on your money. You will need to be very confident of your money-managing and investment abilities.

Of course, if your defined benefit plan has a cost-of-living adjustment factor, which is very rare for private sector pension plans, but more common in government plans, the lump-sum option is almost always a poor choice. In such cases, if you receive a lump-sum payment, you will not receive any future cost-of-living adjustments under most circumstances.

Lump-Sum Transfers into an IRA. If you elect the lump-sum payment option, except in extraordinary cases, you should have your employer transfer the money directly into an IRA to avoid paying taxes and withholding on the money at that time. IRAs can be invested in almost any traditional securities. Also, you may change your IRA investments at any time, so don't worry about being locked in once you put the money in an IRA. Even if you want to buy a retirement home with your lump sum, you should hold the money in an IRA until the transaction is completed. You can continue to keep the remainder of the money in the IRA until you are 70½ when you must begin minimum withdrawals. You will be earning tax-deferred money, and you will pay taxes only on the amounts you withdraw from the IRA.

There are only two situations in which it would not make sense to transfer a lump-sum distribution directly into an IRA. One such scenario would be if you knew income tax rates were going to increase dramatically within the next few years. Unless you are a clairvoyant with an exceptional record, such knowledge of the future is a relatively unlikely scenario. Income tax rates are likely to increase within the next few years, but most of us won't be able to read Congress's collective minds to know when or how much. And if the increases are only modest, you are still better off having your money in an IRA.

The other non-IRA transfer scenario would be if you anticipated receiving a combined income from all your tax-deferred retirement plans, such as employer plans, IRAs, Keoghs, and so on, in excess of approximately $140,000 annually. Income from tax-favored retirement plans in excess of that amount annually is subject to a 15% "excess distribution" excise tax, as are lump-sum distributions in excess of about $700,000.[2] This is a "problem" most of us will not face and if you have it, congratulations. May all your problems be of this nature. In such problem cases it does make sense to take at least some of the employer plan distributions and pay the tax in the year of distribution. You may be eligible to use another tax break for retirement distributions called "lump-sum averaging." Once you have paid tax on the amount, future distributions from that amount or earnings on the amount will not be counted toward the excess distribution limit for excise tax purposes. But you have lost the ability to shelter the earnings from that amount in a tax-deferred retirement account.

Lump-Sum Averaging. If you do not place the money in an IRA, you may be able to use a *lump-sum averaging technique* to reduce taxes on the money. If you were age 50 or over in 1986, you can use an averaging period of 10 years and the pre-1986 tax rates. Otherwise, the averaging period is 5 years at ordinary income tax rates. You pay tax on all the money in the year in which you receive it, but at a tax rate applied as though you received the money over 5 years (or 10 years, if applicable).

These averaging rules are extremely complicated and you may use averaging only once in your lifetime, so if you later receive another lump sum from a qualified plan such as your profit-sharing plan, you cannot use averaging for it.

On a *grossly* oversimplified basis, here's how lump-sum averaging works. You take your 401(k) distribution of $150,000 in a lump sum and elect not to put it in an IRA. You divide that amount by five to find the amount used to set the tax rate applicable to the distribution. The sum is $30,000, part of which will be subject to a 15% rate and part of which will be subject to a 28% rate. You then multiply the amount of tax due on $30,000 times five and pay that amount of tax on $150,000, for a tax bill on the lump sum of less than $42,000. Without 5-year averaging, you would pay a 31% rate on most, if not all, of the $150,000 distribution, for a tax bill of $46,500. The actual tax amount will depend on the other income on your tax return for the year, but this illustration gives you the basic outline.

Tax treatment for distributions from retirement plans is an area where you really need expert advice. If you elect to receive a lump sum and do not transfer it into an IRA, find an experienced tax accountant or financial adviser before you take any distribution. Work with her to be sure your lump sum will qualify for averaging and that it is done correctly. In seeking for such a person, ask them how many IRS Form 4972s (the form for reporting tax on lump-sum averaging) they complete each year. Unless the answer is several, keep looking for your tax adviser.

Maybe It's Time to Call in a Pro?

Even if you are not using something so complicated as lump-sum averaging, clearly you must consider a great many financial plans and options for your employer plans and savings as you retire. The decisions you make now on the payment options from your employer-provided plans and on the timing of applying for Social Security are literally once-in-a-life time decisions. You will have to live with the consequences for the rest of your life and those decisions will largely govern your life-style. Although you may not have used a financial adviser in the past, this may be the time to consider one who specializes in financial planning at retirement to help you in calculating the dollar value of the options. You should always make the final decisions, but having experts to check plan calculations and the latest tax treatment of retirement plan income can be invaluable. If your employer plans provide you with a number of payment options or if you have a plan that makes only lump-sum distributions, you should seriously consider seeking some professional advice, if you do not already have an adviser. The tax savings alone may more than pay for the advice.

Consult the checklist in Chapter 13 for qualities to look for in a financial adviser. As always, experience and up-to-date knowledge are the key qualities, followed by listening skills and responsiveness. Also be sure the adviser is expert in interpreting retirement plan provisions and either has actuarial skills or has access to an experienced pension actuary who can provide advice at a reasonable fee.

Make clear from the outset your primary goal is a set of reports showing the payout options available to you and the tax consequences of each one. Any investment advice should come only after you have decided on the payout and tax options. With investment advice, the sleep-at-night factor is the primary guide. After all, the whole reason for retirement planning is to create security. You're not secure if you are worrying about investments. But unlike the decisions on benefits payments, your investment decisions can, and definitely should, be revised from time to time. There is no great urgency in *how* you invest your retirement savings, but *there is urgency in making the right decisions on the form of payment and tax consequences.*

WHAT TO DO IF YOUR BENEFITS ARE NOT ENOUGH TO LIVE ON

Like Alice you may find once you have totaled your potential Social Security benefits, employer-provided retirement benefits, and your savings, it simply isn't enough to live. "Keep working" is the first and obvious response. That option has advantages in addition to the income it will provide. By delaying retirement, you will increase the benefits you receive from Social Security, from your employer's plan, and from your own savings. You will likely receive at least a cost-of-living raise during the years you work, and that, along with the additional years of service you will have put in, will increase your other retirement benefits.

Change Partners, but Keep Dancing—Try Part-Time Work or a Different Job

But there are also other options. It may be possible to find another, less demanding full-time job. Or part-time work can provide necessary income as well as ease the transition from full-time, heavily scheduled workdays to seemingly endless unstructured time in retirement. About 25% of full-time workers return to the workplace after "retiring" from their longest held job. Partial retirement is increasing among 62- to 67-year-olds and with the highest increase among the 66- to the over 70-year-olds, suggesting that part-time work for older workers is both available and desired by those workers.[3]

Your employer might be eager to arrange a part-time position to keep your expertise available while reducing her payroll. The bias against older employees is eroding. Many employers are recognizing the value of older employees. Studies show that older employees have better attendance records, lower turnover, and the ability to learn tasks just as rapidly as their younger colleagues. Some employers such as the Days Inn hotel chain and the McDonald's fast-food chain have an aggressive hiring program for older employees. Even the bad economic times of the early 1990s can be turned to your advantage. Employers who cannot afford full-time help can use experienced part-timers, lowering their cost of salaries and benefits.

You have a lifetime of contacts both in the workplace and in the community. Use them in seeking part-time employment. If you have been volunteering, find out if the organization can use some part-time paid help. You have already proved your usefulness, now ask to be paid for it. If there is no money, but a clear task to be performed or service to be given through the nonprofit program, offer to seek a grant for the money with the understanding that if your proposal results in a grant, you will be hired to do the work. Make that clear in the proposal, too.

Unless you feel the work is beneath you, don't be deterred by discussions about your being "overqualified" from either your friends and family or the potential employer. You aren't looking for a career track, you are looking for income and a way to employ your skills. Remind the person interviewing you that one way to meet the constant mandates from her boss to "do more with less" is hiring you, especially if you are "overqualified." It is an opportunity for her to "do more with more" in your case. Be aggressive in your job search and do not be modest about your accomplishments. You have years of talent and skill to offer. You're not bragging about it. You're just stating the facts.

Put Your Home to Work—Consider Reverse Mortgages and Sale and Leaseback

The biggest areas of expense are likely to be taxes and housing expenses, and a move can reduce both of these. Other ways to reduce housing expenses and perhaps take some equity out of your house are through a "sale and leaseback," a "reverse mortgage," or other types of home equity conversion loans. These options are designed to enable you to remain in your own home while "spending" some of the equity you have in it. "Home-Made Money: Consumer's Guide to Home Equity Conversion," published by the American Association of Retired Persons and updated periodically, is an excellent and highly detailed guide to the various home equity conversion programs available along with the names, addresses, and telephone numbers of lenders.

For more information and publications on these arrangements write:

AARP Home Equity Information Center
Consumer Affairs Section
American Association of Retired Persons
601 E Street, N.W.
Washington, D.C. 20049

American Bar Association
Commission on Legal Problems of the Elderly
1800 M Street, N.W.
Washington, D.C. 20036
202-331-2297

National Center for Home Equity Conversion
1210 East College Drive, Suite 300
Marshall, Minnesota 56258

With a reverse mortgage, also called a reverse annuity mortgage (RAM), you receive a stream of monthly payments from the mortgage company. The mortgage is then repaid from the proceeds of the house after your death. You retain title to the house and full responsibility for its upkeep, and so on. Should you wish to sell the house at some point, you can do so and repay the "mortgage" under most arrangements. According to lenders, the typical borrower is a 76-year-old widow who was once solidly in the middle class, but now needs the money to cover medical or other living expenses. She receives about $350 per month from her reverse mortgage.[4]

Reverse mortgages are not permitted in every state, and before you enter into any agreement you should seek expert advice and get all your questions answered in writing. For example, what happens if you live beyond the mortgage payments? Who owns the appreciation in the house etc.? Also reverse mortgages tend to be expensive ways to borrow money. When fees are included, the overall interest rate charged is relatively high. If your house appreciates in value over the years after you have acquired the reverse mortgage, there may still be some value left for your heirs or estate when you die. But if values hold steady, there may be little or nothing left at the end of the mortgage term.

Also some RAMs are gender biased. Because of women's longer life expectancies, these RAMs will give you a lower monthly payment than a man would receive based on the same home value. RAMs guaranteed by the Federal Housing Authority (FHA) cannot use this gender bias. The FHA can provide you with a list of lenders in your area who provide FHA-guaranteed RAMS. Call the local U.S. Housing and Urban Development office for the information.

Under a sale and leaseback you convey title to your home to the buyer. You continue to live there paying a monthly "rental." Appreciation and upkeep of the home belong to the buyer, not you. The advantage of a sale and leaseback arrangement is that it permits you to use the older homeowners, tax break of a one-time exclusion from federal income taxes for up to $125,000 of capital gain. You and all other owners of the house, such as your spouse, must be over 55 and have used the house as your principal residence for at least 3 of the 5 years prior to the sale. You may use this exclusion only once.

You should undertake any of these approaches only with independent expert advice from a lawyer or real estate expert whom you have hired and who you know has experience in these transactions and in your community. If you are retiring at 65 today, neither of these should be your first choice in affording retirement. In most cases, you will be too young to receive a significant monthly income from them, and you may run the risk of outliving your "payments" from the mortgage company. But you should be aware of these options for consideration later in your retirement.

Change Your Life-style

As a last resort, think about changing your life-style to reduce expenses. Maybe you *can* live on less. Early in your retirement selling your home and buying a less expensive, lower-maintenance house might be a much better approach than the home equity conversion plans. It will not only give you extra cash now to invest for income, it will reduce expenses.

But be very realistic in examining the life-style change alternative. Moving to a state with lower taxes and a lower cost of living will save you money, but if you don't know anyone there and you miss your former community, the trade-off isn't worth it. Selling your house might give you a huge nest egg, but if you hate apartments, you will be miserable and feel trapped. You may be happier continuing to work and maintaining your current life-style than making dramatic changes. On the other hand, if you have dreaded yard work for years and longed to move back to the small town where you went to college, you may find you can get along financially and emotionally very well with that change in life-style.

CONCLUSION: STRATEGY PLAN
IF YOU ARE NEAR RETIREMENT

❖ File Form SSA-7004 with the Social Security Administration to receive your most recent estimated earnings and benefits.

❖ Read your most recent Employee Benefits Statement from your employer's plan; check the benefits for accuracy.

❖ Review your employer's plans' Summary Plan Descriptions.

❖ Review your own retirement savings. Using Appendix A, calculate how much you can "pay" yourself each month under various scenarios.

❖ Construct a "retirement" budget and try to live within it for six months.

❖ Consider hiring a financial adviser to calculate various pay-out methods for your employer-provided benefits and other retirement benefits.

❖ Begin the application process with Social Security Administration at least 3 months before you expect to receive benefits. You can do this by phone.

❖ Contact all former employers about retirement benefits; include your Social Security number and approximate dates of employment.

❖ Schedule an appointment with your employer's human resources department to discuss retirement plan options and confirm benefits level.

❖ Think about beginning to reposition some of your investments in light of retirement.

NOTES FOR CHAPTER 16

1. U.S. Bureau of the Census, *Statistical Abstract of the United States: 1991*, 111th edition (Washington, D.C.: U.S. Government Printing Office, 1991), Table 106.

2. This amount is based on five times the annual limit and will cease indexing at $750,000. The 1992 limit is $722,755.

3. Employee Benefit Research Institute, "The Work and Retirement Patterns of Older Americans," EBRI Issue Brief No. 121, December 1991.

4. "Older Homeowners Slip into Reverse," *The Wall Street Journal*, May 5, 1992, p. B1.

EPILOGUE

Retirement planning for women requires the same elements as for men. Social Security will provide a subsistence, retirement benefits earned while working will add no more than a third of necessary retirement income, and the remaining 40% to 70% needed for retirement must come from individual savings. Indeed retirees, especially women, may need as much as 80% of their retirement income coming from their own savings because they may have no employer benefits. And that percentage required from personal savings is likely to get higher, not lower, as the baby boomer age wave ages. Social Security cannot politically or economically justify the high taxes needed to continue today's relatively generous benefits. Employers are moving away from generous pensions and toward simply helping employees save for their own retirement through defined contribution plans like 401(k) plans, which require a contribution from the employee before the employer adds its contribution.

But retirement planning is more challenging for women for all the reasons discussed in this book. It is especially more difficult because we earn less money and, consequently, have less to save, and, because almost all employer retirement benefits are based on salary, we earn lower retirement benefits.

So we end where we started—save and invest. If you don't want to join millions of your sisters in poverty in your retirement years, you can really rely only on your own savings.

Focus on seven basic principles:

1. The sooner you start saving, the less you will have to save, because money doesn't grow on trees, but it does grow in investment accounts.

2. Even small amounts of saving are important; remember the magic of compounding.

3. Know what employer plans are available to you and take full advantage of them. Remember, any money you contribute to a retirement plan is always fully vested and missing a matching contribution from an employer is like turning down a raise.

4. Never, never spend retirement plan distributions when you leave a job; this is your retirement security, and it should be preserved in an IRA or other retirement account.

5. A bad tax-favored investment is still a bad investment; don't let taxes drive investment decisions.

6. Don't get discouraged with the size of your savings and investments; always keep saving something.

7. Learn to accept greater risks for more return, especially when you are younger.

TABLES FOR CALCULATING THE TIME VALUE OF MONEY

TABLE A.1
The Future Value of a Dollar

Period	1%	2%	4%	6%	7%	8%	9%	10%	11%	12%	14%	16%	20%
1	1.010	1.020	1.040	1.060	1.070	1.080	1.090	1.100	1.110	1.120	1.139	1.160	1.200
2	1.020	1.040	1.082	1.124	1.145	1.166	1.188	1.210	1.232	1.254	1.297	1.346	1.440
3	1.030	1.061	1.125	1.191	1.225	1.260	1.295	1.331	1.368	1.405	1.478	1.561	1.728
4	1.041	1.082	1.170	1.262	1.311	1.360	1.412	1.464	1.518	1.574	1.683	1.811	2.074
5	1.051	1.104	1.217	1.338	1.403	1.469	1.539	1.611	1.685	1.762	1.917	2.100	2.488
6	1.062	1.126	1.265	1.419	1.501	1.587	1.677	1.772	1.870	1.974	2.183	2.436	2.986
7	1.072	1.149	1.316	1.504	1.606	1.714	1.828	1.949	2.076	2.211	2.487	2.826	3.583
8	1.083	1.172	1.369	1.594	1.718	1.851	1.993	2.144	2.305	2.476	2.833	3.278	4.300
9	1.094	1.195	1.423	1.689	1.838	1.999	2.172	2.358	2.558	2.773	3.226	3.803	5.160
10	1.105	1.219	1.480	1.791	1.967	2.159	2.367	2.594	2.839	3.106	3.675	4.411	6.192
11	1.116	1.243	1.539	1.898	2.105	2.332	2.580	2.853	3.152	3.479	4.186	5.117	7.430
12	1.127	1.268	1.601	2.012	2.252	2.518	2.813	3.138	3.498	3.896	4.767	5.936	8.916
13	1.138	1.294	1.665	2.133	2.410	2.720	3.066	3.452	3.883	4.363	5.430	6.886	10.699
14	1.149	1.319	1.732	2.261	2.579	2.937	3.342	3.797	4.310	4.887	6.185	7.988	12.839
15	1.161	1.346	1.801	2.397	2.759	3.172	3.642	4.177	4.785	5.474	7.045	9.266	15.407
16	1.173	1.373	1.873	2.540	2.952	3.426	3.970	4.595	5.311	6.130	8.024	10.748	18.488
17	1.184	1.400	1.948	2.693	3.159	3.700	4.328	5.054	5.895	6.866	9.139	12.468	22.186
18	1.196	1.428	2.026	2.854	3.380	3.996	4.717	5.560	6.544	7.690	10.409	14.463	26.623
19	1.208	1.457	2.107	3.026	3.617	4.316	5.142	6.116	7.263	8.613	11.856	16.777	31.948
20	1.220	1.486	2.191	3.207	3.870	4.661	5.604	6.727	8.062	9.646	13.504	19.461	38.338
25	1.282	1.641	2.666	4.292	5.427	6.848	8.623	10.835	13.585	17.000	25.888	40.874	95.396
30	1.348	1.811	3.243	5.743	7.612	10.063	13.268	17.449	22.892	29.960	49.626	85.850	237.376

TABLE A.2
The Present Value of a Dollar

Period	1%	2%	4%	6%	7%	8%	9%	10%	11%	12%	14%	16%	20%
1	.990	.980	.962	.943	.935	.926	.917	.909	.901	.893	.878	.862	.833
2	.980	.961	.925	.890	.873	.857	.842	.826	.812	.797	.771	.743	.694
3	.971	.942	.889	.840	.816	.794	.772	.751	.731	.712	.677	.641	.579
4	.961	.924	.855	.792	.763	.735	.708	.683	.659	.636	.594	.552	.482
5	.951	.906	.822	.747	.713	.681	.650	.621	.593	.567	.522	.476	.402
6	.942	.888	.790	.705	.666	.630	.596	.564	.535	.507	.458	.410	.335
7	.933	.871	.760	.665	.623	.583	.547	.513	.482	.452	.402	.354	.279
8	.923	.853	.731	.627	.582	.540	.502	.467	.434	.404	.353	.305	.233
9	.914	.837	.703	.592	.544	.500	.460	.424	.391	.361	.310	.263	.194
10	.905	.820	.676	.558	.508	.463	.422	.386	.352	.322	.272	.227	.162
11	.896	.804	.650	.527	.475	.429	.388	.350	.317	.287	.239	.195	.135
12	.887	.788	.625	.497	.444	.397	.356	.319	.286	.257	.210	.168	.112
13	.879	.773	.601	.469	.415	.368	.326	.290	.258	.229	.184	.145	.093
14	.870	.758	.577	.442	.388	.340	.299	.263	.232	.205	.162	.125	.078
15	.861	.743	.555	.417	.362	.315	.275	.239	.209	.183	.142	.108	.065
16	.853	.728	.534	.394	.339	.292	.252	.218	.188	.163	.125	.093	.054
17	.844	.714	.513	.371	.317	.270	.231	.198	.170	.146	.109	.080	.045
18	.836	.700	.494	.350	.296	.250	.212	.180	.153	.130	.096	.069	.038
19	.828	.686	.475	.331	.277	.232	.194	.164	.138	.116	.084	.060	.031
20	.820	.673	.456	.312	.258	.215	.178	.149	.124	.104	.074	.051	.026
25	.780	.610	.375	.233	.184	.146	.116	.092	.074	.059	.039	.024	.010
30	.742	.552	.308	.174	.131	.099	.075	.057	.044	.033	.020	.012	.004

TABLE A.3
The Future Value of an Annuity
of One Dollar per Year

Period	1%	2%	4%	6%	7%	8%	9%	10%	11%	12%	14%	16%	20%
1	1.000	1.000	1.000	1.000	1.000	1.000	1.000	1.000	1.000	1.000	1.000	1.000	1.000
2	2.010	2.020	2.040	2.060	2.070	2.080	2.090	2.100	2.110	2.120	2.139	2.160	2.200
3	3.030	3.060	3.122	3.184	3.215	3.246	3.278	3.310	3.342	3.374	3.436	3.506	3.640
4	4.060	4.122	4.246	4.375	4.440	4.506	4.573	4.641	4.710	4.779	4.914	5.066	5.368
5	5.101	5.204	5.416	5.637	5.751	5.867	5.985	6.105	6.228	6.353	6.597	6.877	7.442
6	6.152	6.308	6.633	6.975	7.153	7.336	7.523	7.716	7.913	8.115	8.514	8.977	9.930
7	7.214	7.434	7.898	8.394	8.654	8.923	9.200	9.487	9.783	10.089	10.697	11.414	12.916
8	8.286	8.583	9.214	9.897	10.260	10.637	11.028	11.436	11.859	12.300	13.184	14.240	16.499
9	9.369	9.755	10.583	11.491	11.978	12.488	13.021	13.579	14.164	14.776	16.017	17.519	20.799
10	10.462	10.950	12.006	13.181	13.816	14.487	15.193	15.937	16.722	17.549	19.243	21.321	25.959
11	11.567	12.169	13.486	14.972	15.784	16.645	17.560	18.531	19.561	20.655	22.918	25.733	32.150
12	12.683	13.412	15.026	16.870	17.888	18.977	20.141	21.384	22.713	24.133	27.104	30.850	39.581
13	13.809	14.680	16.627	18.882	20.141	21.495	22.953	24.523	26.212	28.029	31.871	36.786	48.497
14	14.947	15.974	18.292	21.015	22.550	24.215	26.019	27.975	30.095	32.393	37.301	43.672	59.196
15	16.097	17.293	20.024	23.276	25.129	27.152	29.361	31.772	34.405	37.280	43.486	51.660	72.035
16	17.258	18.639	21.825	25.673	27.888	30.324	33.003	35.950	39.190	42.753	50.531	60.925	87.442
17	18.430	20.012	23.698	28.213	30.840	33.750	36.974	40.545	44.501	48.884	58.555	71.673	105.931
18	19.615	21.412	25.645	30.906	33.999	37.450	41.301	45.599	50.396	55.750	67.694	84.141	128.117
19	20.811	22.841	27.671	33.760	37.379	41.446	46.018	51.159	56.939	63.440	78.103	98.603	154.740
20	22.019	24.297	29.778	36.786	40.995	45.762	51.160	57.275	64.203	72.052	89.960	115.380	186.688
25	28.243	32.030	41.646	54.865	63.249	73.106	84.701	98.347	114.413	133.334	179.048	249.214	471.981
30	34.785	40.568	56.085	79.058	94.461	113.283	136.308	164.494	199.021	241.333	349.829	530.312	1181.882

TABLE A.4
The Present Value of an Annuity of One Dollar per Year

Period	1%	2%	4%	6%	7%	8%	9%	10%	11%	12%	14%	16%	20%
1	.990	.980	.962	.943	.935	.926	.917	.909	.901	.893	.878	.862	.833
2	1.970	1.942	1.866	1.833	1.808	1.783	1.759	1.736	1.713	1.690	1.649	1.605	1.528
3	2.941	2.884	2.775	2.673	2.624	2.577	2.531	2.487	2.444	2.402	2.326	2.246	2.106
4	3.902	3.808	3.630	3.465	3.387	3.312	3.240	3.170	3.102	3.037	2.920	2.798	2.589
5	4.853	4.713	4.452	4.212	4.100	3.993	3.890	3.791	3.696	3.605	3.441	3.274	2.991
6	5.795	5.601	5.242	4.917	4.767	4.623	4.486	4.355	4.231	4.111	3.899	3.685	3.326
7	6.728	6.472	6.002	5.582	5.389	5.206	5.033	4.868	4.712	4.564	4.301	4.039	3.605
8	7.652	7.325	6.733	6.210	5.971	5.747	5.535	5.335	5.146	4.968	4.654	4.344	3.837
9	8.566	8.162	7.435	6.802	6.515	6.247	5.995	5.759	5.537	5.328	4.964	4.607	4.031
10	9.471	8.983	8.111	7.360	7.024	6.710	6.418	6.145	5.889	5.650	5.237	4.833	4.192
11	10.368	9.787	8.760	7.887	7.499	7.139	6.805	6.495	6.207	5.938	5.475	5.029	4.327
12	11.255	10.575	9.385	8.384	7.943	7.536	7.161	6.814	6.492	6.194	5.685	5.197	4.439
13	12.134	11.348	9.986	8.853	8.358	7.904	7.487	7.103	6.750	6.424	5.869	5.342	4.533
14	13.004	12.106	10.563	9.295	8.745	8.244	7.786	7.367	6.982	6.628	6.031	5.468	4.611
15	13.865	12.849	11.118	9.712	9.108	8.559	8.061	7.606	7.191	6.811	6.173	5.575	4.675
16	14.718	13.578	11.652	10.106	9.447	8.851	8.313	7.824	7.379	6.974	6.298	5.668	4.730
17	15.562	14.292	12.166	10.477	9.763	9.122	8.544	8.022	7.549	7.120	6.407	5.749	4.775
18	16.398	14.992	12.659	10.828	10.059	9.372	8.756	8.201	7.702	7.250	6.503	5.818	4.812
19	17.226	15.678	13.134	11.158	10.336	9.604	8.950	8.365	7.839	7.366	6.587	5.877	4.843
20	18.046	16.351	13.590	11.470	10.594	9.818	9.129	8.514	7.963	7.469	6.662	5.929	4.870
25	22.023	19.523	15.622	12.783	11.654	10.675	9.823	9.077	8.422	7.843	6.916	6.097	4.948
30	25.808	22.396	17.292	13.765	12.409	11.258	10.274	9.427	8.694	8.055	7.049	6.177	4.979

PENSION PORTABILITY STUDIES AND BENEFITS CALCULATIONS

APPENDICES B.1–B.4

Explanation of Retirement Calculations for Alice, Susan, Bonnie, and Jennifer

The following appendices show actual calculations of retirement benefits for four different women: Alice, a nurse now age 60; Susan, a middle manager now age 50; Bonnie, a lawyer now age 40; and Jennifer, a secretary now age 30. For each woman there are also comparisons with what her benefits would have been had she stayed in one job for her entire working career.

Each appendix segment (B.1–B.4) consists of five pages. The first page of each segment provides data on the individual woman, as well as the economic assumptions and the provisions in the employer plans used to generate the hypothetical retirement benefits paid under the various scenarios.

Part I of the first page gives the woman's career history, showing the number of jobs, the age at which she was hired and the age at which she terminated from each job, whether she worked full-time or part-time, and the type of retirement plan the job provided.

Part II gives a profile of the individual woman, with her age, salary, retirement age under the employer's plan and the age at which she wishes to retire, and the assumed rate of salary increase. The scenarios all assume a 6% rate of salary increase for each woman.

Part III shows the economic assumptions used to calculate the retirement benefits, including the inflation rate of 5%. The same assumptions are used for each woman.

Part IV defines the provisions of each employer-provided retirement plan used in the scenarios. These, too, are the same for each woman.

The four tables of each appendix segment show a different retirement benefit payout option on each page for the woman, depending on whether she takes the value of her retirement benefit as a lump sum all at once when she retires or takes the money in periodic payments over the remainder of her life after retirement and depending on whether amounts are rolled over into tax-deferred retirement savings accounts or left with the employer where they were earned until retirement. Each of those following four pages, under the heading "Benefit Earned over One Job Career," shows the amount of retirement benefit a person who stayed in one job for her entire career would have accrued at each age under three different types of plans:

- ❖ A defined benefit plan which does not take Social Security into account ("unit defined benefit plan")

- ❖ A defined benefit which does take Social Security into account ("integrated defined benefit")

- ❖ A defined contribution plan

The next set of columns on each of the pages carry different headings for Alice, Susan, Bonnie, and Jennifer. The column heading for each woman shows the type of plan the individual woman is assumed to have had with each of her employers and, listed under that plan, the dollar value of the plan benefit (in 1992 dollars) she had earned at each age. The final column, "Total All Jobs," lists the total value for all of the benefits Alice, Susan, Bonnie, or Jennifer earned from each job she has had. Depending on the page used, these dollar values will represent "annual income" or "lump-sum values." The percentage figures listed at the bottom of the page show the percentage of her total final salary represented by all the retirement benefits she has earned over her entire career from all her employers.

The first of the four payout options shows retirement benefits if the benefits are received as an annual benefit over the woman's lifetime, assuming she had left the benefits with the employer when she left each job and received the benefits only at retirement. The next page shows her benefits valued as "lump sum," if taken in one lump sum at retirement, also assuming the benefits remained with the employer until retirement. The page following that shows an annual benefit payout, assuming benefits were taken from each employer at termination and transferred into an IRA or other employer plan, that is, the annual benefit with rollover scenario. The last scenario assumes lump-sum payments with amounts having been taken from earlier employers at termination and transferred into an IRA or other employer plan, that is, the rollover scenario.

Remember, all the dollars are expressed in 1992 constant dollars, meaning inflation is corrected for in each calculation. For example, while each woman is assumed to receive a 6% wage increase each year, if you look at the actual numbers under the column "annual earnings" in the pages following the first page, the increase in annual earnings is only 1%. That is because an inflation rate of 5% is assumed. With a 6% wage increase coupled with a 5% inflation increase, the real increase in wages is only 1%. Because we are using only 1992 dollars, we use only the 1% actual increase to show the annual earnings. Likewise, the other figures such as payments at retirement are also in 1992 dollars. At the women's actual retirement date, the dollar figure they receive may be much larger, but the buying power in terms of today's dollars will be the amount shown in the appendices.

More important for comparisons, the percentage of current salary at retirement represented by the retirement benefit the woman will receive remains the same regardless of whether we use only 1992 dollars or nominal dollars which have not been adjusted for inflation. These percentages are also important in comparing the "one job career" benefits shown in the appendices with the actual career paths of women like Alice, Susan, Bonnie, and Jennifer and, indeed, most women.

Let's walk through a page of Alice's projections to see exactly what the tables show. Alice's Table B.1.1, annual income, shows at age 29, a hypothetical employee with a "unit defined benefit" plan would have accrued an annual pension benefit of $443 (expressed in 1992 dollars) and at age 29 Alice has accrued an annual benefit of $415, as shown under the column "Integ. D.B. Job 1." (Remember under defined benefit plans, you earn very little in your early years on the job.) But Alice leaves that job at age 30. Because she did not vest in her accrued benefit, she loses her $415 benefit and the remainder of that column shows "0" as the benefit value from her first job.

At age 57, the hypothetical one-career employee has earned an annual benefit from the defined contribution plan of $11,584. Alice at age 57 has accrued "0" dollars in benefits from jobs 1 to 4, as those columns show, and has accrued an annual benefit of $1,670 under job 5. At 58, Alice leaves job 5, but she has vested in the $1,670 annual benefit from job 5, so she will receive that at retirement. At age 64 the "Total All Jobs" column shows Alice receiving a grand total of $4,633 annually: $1,670 from job 5 and $2,963 from job 6.

Looking under the heading "Annual Retirement Income at Age 65," the subheadings "Deferred Payments," "Cashout/Spend," and "Cashout/Rollover" show the different amounts Alice would have earned depending on what she did with her money when she left different jobs. For example, in Table B.1.1 Alice did defer payments of benefits earned in order to receive her $4,633 annually. Had she cashed out and spent the value of the $1,670 benefit earned at job 5, she would have an annual benefit of only $2,963 at retirement; in contrast, had she cashed out and rolled over the value of the job benefit, she would have had annual benefits of $4,457. The figures under the heading "Annual Retirement Income as a Percentage of Final Earnings" simply translate those dollar benefits shown under "Annual Retirement Income at Age 65" into percentages, comparing the total annual benefits to Alice's final earnings.

I. CAREER SUMMARY

TOTAL NUMBER OF JOBS   6

JOB NUMBER	AGE AT HIRE	AGE AT TERMINATION	TYPE OF PLAN	STATUS
1	22	29	INTEGRATED DEFINED BENEFIT	FULL-TIME
2	31	34	INTEGRATED DEFINED BENEFIT	FULL-TIME
3	36	42	INTEGRATED DEFINED BENEFIT	FULL-TIME
4	43	50	INTEGRATED DEFINED BENEFIT	FULL-TIME
5	52	57	INTEGRATED DEFINED BENEFIT	FULL-TIME
6	58	64	INTEGRATED DEFINED BENEFIT	FULL-TIME

II. PROFILE OF WORKER

AGE IN 1992	60
ANNUAL SALARY IN 1992	$36,750
SALARY INCREASE RATE	6.0% PER ANNUM
NORMAL RETIREMENT AGE	65
ACTUAL RETIREMENT AGE	65

III. ECONOMIC ASSUMPSIONS

INTEREST RATE IN DEFINED CONTRIBUTION PLAN	7.50% PER ANNUM
INTEREST RATE IN ROLLOVER AMOUNTS	7.50% PER ANNUM
RATE OF INFLATION	5.00% PER ANNUM
RATE OF INCREASE IN AGE 65 COVERED COMPENSATION	5.50% PER ANNUM

IV. PLAN PROVISIONS

UNIT DEFINED BENEFIT FORMULA :   1.25% OF THE FINAL FIVE YEAR AVERAGE EARNINGS TIMES YEARS OF SERVICE TO A MAXIMUM OF 30 YEARS

INTEGRATED DEFINED BENEFIT FORMULA :   1.00% OF FINAL FIVE YEAR AVERAGE EARNINGS BELOW COVERED COMPENSATION PLUS 1.65% OF FINAL FIVE YEAR AVERAGE EARNINGS ABOVE COVERED COMPENSATION TIMES YEARS OF SERVICE TO A MAXIMUM OF 30 YEARS

DEFINED CONTRIBUTION FORMULA :   5.00% OF ANNUAL EARNINGS EACH YEAR

VESTING :   100% VESTED AFTER FIVE YEARS OF SERVICE (TEN YEARS OF SERVICE REQUIRED PRIOR TO 1989)

APPENDIX B.1
Pension Portability Study for Alice, a 60-Year-Old Nurse

AGE	ANNUAL EARNINGS	UNIT DEFINED BENEFIT	INTEGRATED DEFINED BENEFIT	DEFINED CONTRIBUTION	INTEG. D.B. JOB 1	INTEG. D.B. JOB 2	INTEG. D.B. JOB 3	INTEG. D.B. JOB 4	INTEG. D.B. JOB 5	INTEG. D.B. JOB 6	TOTAL ALL JOBS
22	$25,635	$41	$40	$407	$40						$40
23	$25,879	85	81	809	81						81
24	$26,125	131	124	1,204	124						124
25	$26,374	181	169	1,595	169						169
26	$26,625	233	216	1,980	216						216
27	$26,879	296	276	2,359	276						276
28	$27,135	366	342	2,733	342						342
29	$27,393	443	415	3,102	415						415
30	$0	529	495	3,466	0						0
31	$27,918	623	584	3,825	0	68					68
32	$28,183	726	683	4,179	0	140					140
33	$28,452	840	791	4,528	0	214					214
34	$28,723	964	910	4,872	0	291					291
35	$0	1,101	1,041	5,211	0	0					0
36	$29,272	1,250	1,184	5,545	0	0	92				92
37	$29,551	1,414	1,342	5,875	0	0	188				188
38	$29,833	1,592	1,514	6,200	0	0	289				289
39	$30,117	1,787	1,702	6,521	0	0	393				393
40	$30,404	1,999	1,908	6,837	0	0	502				502
41	$30,693	2,231	2,133	7,149	0	0	640				640
42	$30,986	2,483	2,378	7,456	0	0	793				793
43	$31,281	2,757	2,645	7,759	0	0	0	140			140
44	$31,579	3,056	2,937	8,058	0	0	0	286			286
45	$31,879	3,380	3,254	8,353	0	0	0	439			439
46	$32,183	3,732	3,599	8,643	0	0	0	598			598
47	$32,489	4,114	3,975	8,930	0	0	0	764			764
48	$32,799	4,529	4,383	9,212	0	0	0	974			974
49	$33,111	4,978	4,826	9,491	0	0	0	1,207			1,207
50	$33,427	5,465	5,308	9,766	0	0	0	1,464			1,464
51	$0	5,993	5,830	10,037	0	0	0	0			0
52	$34,066	6,353	6,190	10,304	0	0	0	0	240		240
53	$34,391	6,734	6,572	10,567	0	0	0	0	490		490
54	$34,718	7,138	6,978	10,827	0	0	0	0	752		752
55	$35,049	7,566	7,409	11,083	0	0	0	0	1,026		1,026
56	$35,383	8,020	7,867	11,335	0	0	0	0	1,311		1,311
57	$35,720	8,501	8,352	11,584	0	0	0	0	1,670		1,670
58	$36,060	9,011	8,868	11,830	0	0	0	0	1,670	343	2,013
59	$36,403	9,552	9,415	12,072	0	0	0	0	1,670	702	2,372
60	$36,750	10,125	9,996	12,311	0	0	0	0	1,670	1,077	2,747
61	$37,100	10,732	10,613	12,546	0	0	0	0	1,670	1,468	3,138
62	$37,453	11,376	11,267	12,778	0	0	0	0	1,670	1,878	3,548
63	$37,810	12,059	11,962	13,007	0	0	0	0	1,670	2,392	4,062
64	$38,170	12,783	12,699	13,232	0	0	0	0	1,670	2,963	4,633

ANNUAL RETIREMENT INCOME AT AGE SIXTY-FIVE

	UNIT DEFINED BENEFIT	INTEGRATED DEFINED BENEFIT	DEFINED CONTRIBUTION	INTEG. D.B. JOB 1	INTEG. D.B. JOB 2	INTEG. D.B. JOB 3	INTEG. D.B. JOB 4	INTEG. D.B. JOB 5	INTEG. D.B. JOB 6	TOTAL ALL JOBS
DEFERRED PAYMENTS	$12,783	$12,699	$13,232	$0	$0	$0	$0	$1,670	$2,963	$4,633
CASH OUT - SPEND	$12,783	$12,699	$13,232	$0	$0	$0	$0	$0	$2,963	$2,963
CASH OUT - ROLLOVER	$12,783	$12,699	$13,232	$0	$0	$0	$0	$1,494	$2,963	$4,457

ANNUAL RETIREMENT INCOME AS A PERCENTAGE OF FINAL EARNINGS

	UNIT DEFINED BENEFIT	INTEGRATED DEFINED BENEFIT	DEFINED CONTRIBUTION	INTEG. D.B. JOB 1	INTEG. D.B. JOB 2	INTEG. D.B. JOB 3	INTEG. D.B. JOB 4	INTEG. D.B. JOB 5	INTEG. D.B. JOB 6	TOTAL ALL JOBS
DEFERRED PAYMENTS	33.49%	33.27%	34.67%	0.00%	0.00%	0.00%	0.00%	4.38%	7.76%	12.14%
CASH OUT - SPEND	33.49%	33.27%	34.67%	0	0.00%	0.00%	0.00%	0.00%	7.76%	7.76%
CASH OUT - ROLLOVER	33.49%	33.27%	34.67%	0.00%	0.00%	0.00%	0.00%	3.91%	7.76%	11.68%

TABLE B.1.1
Alice's Annual Income Starting at Age 65*

*In 1992 dollars, 5 years' vesting (10 years' vesting prior to 1989).

		BENEFIT EARNED OVER ONE JOB CAREER			SIX JOB CAREER / SINGLE SUM VALUES						
AGE	ANNUAL EARNINGS	UNIT DEFINED BENEFIT	INTEGRATED DEFINED BENEFIT	DEFINED CONTRIBUTION	INTEG. D.B. JOB 1	INTEG. D.B. JOB 2	INTEG. D.B. JOB 3	INTEG. D.B. JOB 4	INTEG. D.B. JOB 5	INTEG. D.B. JOB 6	TOTAL ALL JOBS
22	$25,635	$103	$99	$1,282	$99						$99
23	25,879	218	208	2,606	208						208
24	26,125	345	326	3,975	326						326
25	26,374	485	455	5,388	455						455
26	26,625	641	596	6,847	596						596
27	26,879	836	778	8,354	778						778
28	27,135	1,059	988	9,910	988						988
29	27,393	1,315	1,229	11,516	1,229						1,229
30	0	1,608	1,506	13,173	0						0
31	27,918	1,941	1,821	14,882	0	213					213
32	28,183	2,319	2,181	16,646	0	446					446
33	28,452	2,749	2,590	18,464	0	700					700
34	28,723	3,236	3,054	20,340	0	977					977
35	0	3,788	3,581	22,274	0	0					0
36	29,272	4,411	4,178	24,268	0	0	325				325
37	29,551	5,114	4,854	26,324	0	0	681				681
38	29,833	5,908	5,617	28,442	0	0	1,071				1,071
39	30,117	6,802	6,479	30,625	0	0	1,496				1,496
40	30,404	7,808	7,451	32,874	0	0	1,961				1,961
41	30,693	8,941	8,547	35,192	0	0	2,564				2,564
42	30,986	10,214	9,782	37,579	0	0	3,261				3,261
43	31,281	11,645	11,173	40,038	0	0	0	592			592
44	31,579	13,253	12,738	42,570	0	0	0	1,242			1,242
45	31,879	15,060	14,500	45,178	0	0	0	1,956			1,956
46	32,183	17,089	16,482	47,862	0	0	0	2,739			2,739
47	32,489	19,368	18,713	50,626	0	0	0	3,599			3,599
48	32,799	21,929	21,224	53,472	0	0	0	4,716			4,716
49	33,111	24,806	24,050	56,400	0	0	0	6,012			6,012
50	33,427	28,040	27,231	59,415	0	0	0	7,512			7,512
51	0	31,675	30,813	62,516	0	0	0	0			0
52	34,066	34,612	33,727	65,708	0	0	0	0	1,307		1,307
53	34,391	37,848	36,942	68,992	0	0	0	0	2,756		2,756
54	34,718	41,417	40,493	72,371	0	0	0	0	4,364		4,364
55	35,049	45,357	44,418	75,846	0	0	0	0	6,148		6,148
56	35,383	49,714	48,765	79,421	0	0	0	0	8,127		8,127
57	35,720	54,541	53,587	83,098	0	0	0	0	10,717		10,717
58	36,060	59,901	58,949	86,880	0	0	0	0	11,104	2,281	13,385
59	36,403	65,860	64,917	90,769	0	0	0	0	11,518	4,838	16,356
60	36,750	72,500	71,577	94,767	0	0	0	0	11,962	7,709	19,671
61	37,100	79,920	79,027	98,879	0	0	0	0	12,439	10,934	23,373
62	37,453	88,233	87,385	103,106	0	0	0	0	12,956	14,564	27,520
63	37,810	97,577	96,791	107,451	0	0	0	0	13,517	19,358	32,875
64	38,170	108,112	107,409	111,918	0	0	0	0	14,129	25,062	39,191

SINGLE SUM RETIREMENT INCOME AT AGE SIXTY-FIVE

DEFERRED PAYMENTS		$108,112	$107,409	$111,918		$0	$0	$0	$0	$14,129	$25,062	$39,191
CASH OUT · SPEND		$108,112	$107,409	$111,918		$0	$0	$0	$0	$0	$25,062	$25,062
CASH OUT · ROLLOVER		$108,112	$107,409	$111,918		$0	$0	$0	$0	$12,636	$25,062	$37,698

ANNUAL RETIREMENT INCOME AS A PERCENTAGE OF FINAL EARNINGS

DEFERRED PAYMENTS		33.49%	33.27%	34.67%		0.00%	0.00%	0.00%	0.00%	4.38%	7.76%	12.14%
CASH OUT · SPEND		33.49%	33.27%	34.67%		0.00%	0.00%	0.00%	0.00%	0.00%	7.76%	7.76%
CASH OUT · ROLLOVER		33.49%	33.27%	34.67%		0.00%	0.00%	0.00%	0.00%	3.91%	7.76%	11.68%

TABLE B.1.2
Alice's Lump-Sum Values*

*In 1992 dollars, 5 years' vesting (10 years' vesting prior to 1989).

		ONE JOB CAREER			BENEFIT EARNED OVER SIX JOB CAREERS						
AGE	ANNUAL EARNINGS	UNIT DEFINED BENEFIT	INTEGRATED DEFINED BENEFIT	DEFINED CONTRIBUTION	INTEG. D.B. JOB 1	INTEG. D.B. JOB 2	INTEG. D.B. JOB 3	INTEG. D.B. JOB 4	INTEG. D.B. JOB 5	INTEG. D.B. JOB 6	TOTAL
22	$25,635	$41	$40	$407	$40						$40
23	25,879	85	81	809	81						81
24	26,125	131	124	1,204	124						124
25	26,374	181	169	1,595	169						169
26	26,625	233	216	1,980	216						216
27	26,879	296	276	2,359	276						276
28	27,135	366	342	2,733	342						342
29	27,393	443	415	3,102	415						415
30	0	529	495	3,466	0						0
31	27,918	623	584	3,825	0	68					68
32	28,183	726	683	4,179	0	140					140
33	28,452	840	791	4,528	0	214					214
34	28,723	964	910	4,872	0	291					291
35	0	1,101	1,041	5,211	0	0					0
36	29,272	1,250	1,184	5,545	0	0	92				92
37	29,551	1,414	1,342	5,875	0	0	188				188
38	29,833	1,592	1,514	6,200	0	0	289				289
39	30,117	1,787	1,702	6,521	0	0	393				393
40	30,404	1,999	1,908	6,837	0	0	502				502
41	30,693	2,231	2,133	7,149	0	0	640				640
42	30,986	2,483	2,378	7,456	0	0	793				793
43	31,281	2,757	2,645	7,759	0	0	0	140			140
44	31,579	3,056	2,937	8,058	0	0	0	286			286
45	31,879	3,380	3,254	8,353	0	0	0	439			439
46	32,183	3,732	3,599	8,643	0	0	0	598			598
47	32,489	4,114	3,975	8,930	0	0	0	764			764
48	32,799	4,529	4,383	9,212	0	0	0	974			974
49	33,111	4,978	4,826	9,491	0	0	0	1,207			1,207
50	33,427	5,465	5,308	9,766	0	0	0	1,464			1,464
51	0	5,993	5,830	10,037	0	0	0	0			0
52	34,066	6,353	6,190	10,304	0	0	0	0	240		240
53	34,391	6,734	6,572	10,567	0	0	0	0	490		490
54	34,718	7,138	6,978	10,827	0	0	0	0	752		752
55	35,049	7,566	7,409	11,083	0	0	0	0	1,026		1,026
56	35,383	8,020	7,867	11,335	0	0	0	0	1,311		1,311
57	35,720	8,501	8,352	11,584	0	0	0	0	1,670		1,670
58	36,060	9,011	8,868	11,830	0	0	0	0	1,494	343	1,837
59	36,403	9,552	9,415	12,072	0	0	0	0	1,494	702	2,196
60	36,750	10,125	9,996	12,311	0	0	0	0	1,494	1,077	2,571
61	37,100	10,732	10,613	12,546	0	0	0	0	1,494	1,468	2,962
62	37,453	11,376	11,267	12,778	0	0	0	0	1,494	1,878	3,372
63	37,810	12,059	11,962	13,007	0	0	0	0	1,494	2,392	3,886
64	38,170	12,783	12,699	13,232	0	0	0	0	1,494	2,963	4,457
RELACEMENT RATIOS		33.49%	33.27%	34.67%	0.00%	0.00%	0.00%	0.00%	3.91%	7.76%	11.68%

TABLE B.1.3
Alice's Annual Income Starting at Age 65 with Rollover Election*
*In 1992 dollars, 5 years' vesting (10 years' vesting prior to 1989).

			ONE JOB CAREER			SIX JOB CAREER / SINGLE SUM VALUES						
AGE	ANNUAL EARNINGS		UNIT DEFINED BENEFIT	INTEGRATED DEFINED BENEFIT	DEFINED CONTRIBUTION	INTEG. D.B. JOB 1	INTEG. D.B. JOB 2	INTEG. D.B. JOB 3	INTEG. D.B. JOB 4	INTEG. D.B. JOB 5	INTEG. D.B. JOB 6	TOTAL ALL JOBS
22	$25,635	•	$103	$99	$1,282	$99						$99
23	25,879	•	218	208	2,606	208						$208
24	26,125	•	345	326	3,975	326						$326
25	26,374	•	485	455	5,388	455						$455
26	26,625	•	641	596	6,847	596						$596
27	26,879	•	836	778	8,354	778						$778
28	27,135	•	1,059	988	9,910	988						$988
29	27,393	•	1,315	1,229	11,516	1,229						$1,229
30	0	•	1,608	1,506	13,173	0						$0
31	27,918	•	1,941	1,821	14,882	0	213					$213
32	28,183	•	2,319	2,181	16,646	0	446					$446
33	28,452	•	2,749	2,590	18,464	0	700					$700
34	28,723	•	3,236	3,054	20,340	0	977					$977
35	0	•	3,788	3,581	22,274	0	0					$0
36	29,272	•	4,411	4,178	24,268	0	0	325				$325
37	29,551	•	5,114	4,854	26,324	0	0	681				$681
38	29,833	•	5,908	5,617	28,442	0	0	1,071				$1,071
39	30,117	•	6,802	6,479	30,625	0	0	1,496				$1,496
40	30,404	•	7,808	7,451	32,874	0	0	1,961				$1,961
41	30,693	•	8,941	8,547	35,192	0	0	2,564				$2,564
42	30,986	•	10,214	9,782	37,579	0	0	3,261				$3,261
43	31,281	•	11,645	11,173	40,038	0	0	0	592			$592
44	31,579	•	13,253	12,738	42,570	0	0	0	1,242			$1,242
45	31,879	•	15,060	14,500	45,178	0	0	0	1,956			$1,956
46	32,183	•	17,089	16,482	47,862	0	0	0	2,739			$2,739
47	32,489	•	19,368	18,713	50,626	0	0	0	3,599			$3,599
48	32,799	•	21,929	21,224	53,472	0	0	0	4,716			$4,716
49	33,111	•	24,806	24,050	56,400	0	0	0	6,012			$6,012
50	33,427	•	28,040	27,231	59,415	0	0	0	7,512			$7,512
51	0	•	31,675	30,813	62,516	0	0	0	0			$0 .
52	34,066	•	34,612	33,727	65,708	0	0	0	0	1,307		$1,307
53	34,391	•	37,848	36,942	68,992	0	0	0	0	2,756		$2,756
54	34,718	•	41,417	40,493	72,371	0	0	0	0	4,364		$4,364
55	35,049	•	45,357	44,418	75,846	0	0	0	0	6,148		$6,148
56	35,383	•	49,714	48,765	79,421	0	0	0	0	8,127		$8,127
57	35,720	•	54,541	53,587	83,098	0	0	0	0	10,717		$10,717
58	36,060	•	59,901	58,949	86,880	0	0	0	0	10,972	2,281	$13,253
59	36,403	•	65,860	64,917	90,769	0	0	0	0	11,233	4,838	$16,071
60	36,750	•	72,500	71,577	94,767	0	0	0	0	11,501	7,709	$19,210
61	37,100	•	79,920	79,027	98,879	0	0	0	0	11,775	10,934	$22,709
62	37,453	•	88,233	87,385	103,106	0	0	0	0	12,055	14,564	$26,619
63	37,810	•	97,577	96,791	107,451	0	0	0	0	12,342	19,358	$31,700
64	38,170	•	108,112	107,409	111,918	0	0	0	0	12,636	25,062	$37,698
RELACEMENT RATIOS		•	33.49%	33.27%	34.67%	0.00%	0.00%	0.00%	0.00%	3.91%	7.76%	11.68%

TABLE B.1.4
Alice's Single-Sum Amounts if Benefits from Defined Benefit Plans Are Rolled Over*

*In 1992 dollars, 5 years' vesting (10 years' vesting prior to 1989).

I. CAREER SUMMARY

TOTAL NUMBER OF JOBS   5

JOB NUMBER	AGE AT HIRE	AGE AT TERMINATION	TYPE OF PLAN	STATUS
1	20	23	NO PENSION	FULL-TIME
2	24	28	INTEGRATED DEFINED BENEFIT	FULL-TIME
3	29	38	INTEGRATED DEFINED BENEFIT	FULL-TIME
4	39	43	INTEGRATED DEFINED BENEFIT	FULL-TIME
5	44	64	DEFINED CONTRIBUTION	FULL-TIME

II. PROFILE OF WORKER

AGE IN 1992	50
ANNUAL SALARY IN 1992	$25,200
SALARY INCREASE RATE	6.0% PER ANNUM
NORMAL RETIREMENT AGE	65
ACTUAL RETIREMENT AGE	65

III. ECONOMIC ASSUMPSIONS

INTEREST RATE IN DEFINED CONTRIBUTION PLAN	7.50% PER ANNUM
INTEREST RATE IN ROLLOVER AMOUNTS	7.50% PER ANNUM
RATE OF INFLATION	5.00% PER ANNUM
RATE OF INCREASE IN AGE 65 COVERED COMPENSATION	5.50% PER ANNUM

IV. PLAN PROVISIONS

UNIT DEFINED BENEFIT FORMULA :   1.25% OF THE FINAL FIVE YEAR AVERAGE EARNINGS TIMES YEARS OF SERVICE TO A MAXIMUM OF 30 YEARS

INTEGRATED DEFINED BENEFIT FORMULA :   1.00% OF FINAL FIVE YEAR AVERAGE EARNINGS BELOW COVERED COMPENSATION PLUS 1.65% OF FINAL FIVE YEAR AVERAGE EARNINGS ABOVE COVERED COMPENSATION TIMES YEARS OF SERVICE TO A MAXIMUM OF 30 YEARS

DEFINED CONTRIBUTION FORMULA :   5.00% OF ANNUAL EARNINGS EACH YEAR

VESTING :   100% VESTED AFTER   10 YEARS OF SERVICE

APPENDIX B.2
Pension Portability Study for Susan, a 50-Year-Old Middle Manager

Table header spanning: "BENEFIT EARNED OVER ONE JOB CAREER" and "10 YEARS VESTING — TEN YEARS PRIOR TO 1989 — BENEFIT EARNED OVER FIVE JOB CAREERS"

AGE	ANNUAL EARNINGS	UNIT DEFINED BENEFIT	INTEGRATED DEFINED BENEFIT	DEFINED CONTRIBUTION	NO PENSION JOB 1	INTEG. D.B. JOB 2	INTEG. D.B. JOB 3	INTEG. D.B. JOB 4	DEFINED CONTRB. JOB 5	TOTAL ALL JOBS
20	$18,963	$28	$23	$316	$0					$0
21	19,143	57	46	627	0					0
22	19,326	88	71	934	0					0
23	19,510	121	97	1,237	0					0
24	19,696	156	125	1,535	0	29				29
25	19,883	199	159	1,829	0	59				59
26	20,073	246	197	2,119	0	90				90
27	20,264	298	238	2,406	0	122				122
28	20,457	355	284	2,688	0	158				158
29	20,652	418	334	2,966	0	0	39			39
30	20,848	487	390	3,240	0	0	80			80
31	21,047	563	451	3,511	0	0	122			122
32	21,247	647	518	3,777	0	0	165			165
33	21,450	739	591	4,040	0	0	211			211
34	21,654	839	671	4,300	0	0	268			268
35	21,860	949	759	4,555	0	0	332			332
36	22,068	1,068	856	4,807	0	0	403			403
37	22,278	1,199	964	5,056	0	0	482			482
38	22,491	1,342	1,082	5,301	0	0	569			569
39	22,705	1,497	1,211	5,543	0	0	569	72		641
40	22,921	1,666	1,352	5,781	0	0	569	147		716
41	23,139	1,850	1,505	6,016	0	0	569	224		793
42	23,360	2,050	1,673	6,248	0	0	569	304		873
43	23,582	2,268	1,856	6,477	0	0	569	387		956
44	23,807	2,504	2,055	6,702	0	0	569	0	225	794
45	24,034	2,760	2,272	6,924	0	0	569	0	447	1,016
46	24,262	3,039	2,508	7,143	0	0	569	0	667	1,236
47	24,493	3,340	2,765	7,359	0	0	569	0	883	1,452
48	24,727	3,667	3,044	7,572	0	0	569	0	1,096	1,665
49	24,962	4,021	3,347	7,782	0	0	569	0	1,306	1,875
50	25,200	4,262	3,558	7,989	0	0	569	0	1,513	2,082
51	25,440	4,518	3,782	8,193	0	0	569	0	1,717	2,286
52	25,682	4,789	4,020	8,395	0	0	569	0	1,918	2,487
53	25,927	5,076	4,272	8,593	0	0	569	0	2,117	2,686
54	26,174	5,381	4,541	8,789	0	0	569	0	2,313	2,882
55	26,423	5,704	4,826	8,982	0	0	569	0	2,506	3,075
56	26,675	6,046	5,129	9,173	0	0	569	0	2,696	3,265
57	26,929	6,409	5,451	9,360	0	0	569	0	2,884	3,453
58	27,185	6,793	5,793	9,545	0	0	569	0	3,069	3,638
59	27,444	7,201	6,157	9,728	0	0	569	0	3,251	3,820
60	27,706	7,633	6,543	9,908	0	0	569	0	3,431	4,000
61	27,969	8,091	6,953	10,085	0	0	569	0	3,609	4,178
62	28,236	8,577	7,389	10,260	0	0	569	0	3,784	4,353
63	28,505	9,091	7,852	10,433	0	0	569	0	3,956	4,525
64	28,776	9,637	8,344	10,603	0	0	569	0	4,126	4,695

ANNUAL RETIREMENT INCOME AT AGE SIXTY-FIVE

	UNIT DEFINED BENEFIT	INTEGRATED DEFINED BENEFIT	DEFINED CONTRIBUTION	NO PENSION JOB 1	INTEG. D.B. JOB 2	INTEG. D.B. JOB 3	INTEG. D.B. JOB 4	DEFINED CONTRB. JOB 5	TOTAL ALL JOBS
DEFERRED PAYMENTS	$9,637	$8,344	$10,603	$0	$0	$569	$0	$4,126	4,695
CASH OUT · SPENT	$9,637	$8,344	$10,603	$0	$0	$0	$0	$4,126	4,126
CASH OUT · ROLLOVER	$9,637	$8,344	$10,603	$0	$0	$461	$0	$4,126	4,587

ANNUAL RETIREMENT INCOME AS A PERCENTAGE OF FINAL EARNINGS

	UNIT DEFINED BENEFIT	INTEGRATED DEFINED BENEFIT	DEFINED CONTRIBUTION	NO PENSION JOB 1	INTEG. D.B. JOB 2	INTEG. D.B. JOB 3	INTEG. D.B. JOB 4	DEFINED CONTRB. JOB 5	TOTAL ALL JOBS
DEFERRED PAYMENTS	33.49%	29.00%	36.85%	0.00%	0.00%	1.98%	0.00%	14.34%	16.32%
CASH OUT · SPENT	33.49%	29.00%	36.85%	0.00%	0.00%	0.00%	0.00%	14.34%	14.34%
CASH OUT · ROLLOVER	33.49%	29.00%	36.85%	0.00%	0.00%	1.60%	0.00%	14.34%	15.94%

TABLE B.2.1
Susan's Annual Income Starting at Age 65*
(*In 1992 dollars.)

| | | BENEFIT EARNED OVER ONE JOB CAREER | | | FIVE | JOB | CAREER / | SINGLE | SUM | VALUES |
AGE	ANNUAL EARNINGS	UNIT DEFINED BENEFIT	INTEGRATED DEFINED BENEFIT	DEFINED CONTRIBUTION	NO PENSION JOB 1	INTEG. D.B. JOB 2	INTEG. D.B. JOB 3	INTEG. D.B. JOB 4	DEFINED CONTRB. JOB 5	TOTAL ALL JOBS
20	$18,963	$66	$54	$948	$0					$0
21	19,143	139	112	1,928	0					0
22	19,326	220	176	2,940	0					0
23	19,510	310	248	3,986	0					0
24	19,696	409	328	5,065	0	76				76
25	19,883	534	427	6,180	0	158				158
26	20,073	677	541	7,331	0	247				⁻247
27	20,264	840	672	8,519	0	346				346
28	20,457	1,027	821	9,744	0	456				⁻456
29	20,652	1,239	992	11,009	0	0	117			117
30	20,848	1,481	1,185	12,313	0	0	243			243
31	21,047	1,756	1,405	13,659	0	0	380			380
32	21,247	2,066	1,653	15,046	0	0	527			527
33	21,450	2,418	1,934	16,477	0	0	691			691
34	21,654	2,815	2,252	17,952	0	0	901			901
35	21,860	3,263	2,611	19,473	0	0	1,142			1,142
36	22,068	3,769	3,021	21,040	0	0	1,422			1,422
37	22,278	4,338	3,487	22,654	0	0	1,744			1,744
38	22,491	4,978	4,014	24,318	0	0	2,113			2,113
39	22,705	5,698	4,608	26,033	0	0	2,167	275		2,442
40	22,921	6,506	5,278	27,798	0	0	2,224	575		2,799
41	23,139	7,414	6,033	29,617	0	0	2,282	900		3,182
42	23,360	8,434	6,882	31,490	0	0	2,342	1,252		3,594
43	23,582	9,577	7,838	33,419	0	0	2,405	1,633		4,038
44	23,807	10,860	8,914	35,405	0	0	2,470	0	1,190	3,660
45	24,034	12,299	10,124	37,450	0	0	2,537	0	2,420	4,957
46	24,262	13,914	11,486	39,555	0	0	2,607	0	3,691	6,298
47	24,493	15,725	13,017	41,721	0	0	2,681	0	5,004	7,685
48	24,727	17,757	14,741	43,951	0	0	2,757	0	6,359	9,116
49	24,962	20,037	16,680	46,246	0	0	2,837	0	7,759	10,596
50	25,200	21,868	18,254	48,607	0	0	2,921	0	9,203	12,124
51	25,440	23,880	19,988	51,036	0	0	3,010	0	10,695	13,705
52	25,682	26,094	21,901	53,535	0	0	3,102	0	12,233	15,335
53	25,927	28,533	24,013	56,106	0	0	3,200	0	13,821	17,021
54	26,174	31,224	26,348	58,751	0	0	3,304	0	15,459	18,763
55	26,423	34,194	28,932	61,471	0	0	3,413	0	17,148	20,561
56	26,675	37,479	31,795	64,268	0	0	3,530	0	18,890	22,420
57	26,929	41,118	34,973	67,145	0	0	3,653	0	20,686	24,339
58	27,185	45,159	38,510	70,103	0	0	3,785	0	22,538	26,323
59	27,444	49,651	42,450	73,144	0	0	3,926	0	24,447	28,373
60	27,706	54,657	46,850	76,271	0	0	4,077	0	26,414	30,491
61	27,969	60,251	51,776	79,485	0	0	4,240	0	28,441	32,681
62	28,236	66,518	57,307	82,790	0	0	4,416	0	30,530	34,946
63	28,505	73,562	63,535	86,186	0	0	4,607	0	32,683	37,290
64	28,776	81,505	70,570	89,677	0	0	4,816	0	34,899	39,715

SINGLE SUM RETIREMENT INCOME AT AGE SIXTY-FIVE

		UNIT DEFINED BENEFIT	INTEGRATED DEFINED BENEFIT	DEFINED CONTRIBUTION	NO PENSION JOB 1	INTEG. D.B. JOB 2	INTEG. D.B. JOB 3	INTEG. D.B. JOB 4	DEFINED CONTRB. JOB 5	TOTAL ALL JOBS
DEFERRED PAYMENTS		$81,505	$70,570	$89,677	$0	$0	$4,816	$0	$34,899	$39,715
CASH OUT - SPENT		$81,505	$70,570	$89,677	$0	$0	$0	$0	$34,899	$34,899
CASH OUT - ROLLOVER		$81,505	$70,570	$89,677	$0	$0	$3,898	$0	$34,899	$38,797

ANNUAL RETIREMENT INCOME AS A PERCENTAGE OF FINAL EARNINGS

		UNIT DEFINED BENEFIT	INTEGRATED DEFINED BENEFIT	DEFINED CONTRIBUTION	NO PENSION JOB 1	INTEG. D.B. JOB 2	INTEG. D.B. JOB 3	INTEG. D.B. JOB 4	DEFINED CONTRB. JOB 5	TOTAL ALL JOBS
DEFERRED PAYMENTS		33.49%	29.00%	36.85%	0.00%	0.00%	1.98%	0.00%	14.34%	16.32%
CASH OUT - SPENT		33.49%	29.00%	36.85%	0.00%	0.00%	0.00%	0.00%	14.34%	14.34%
CASH OUT - ROLLOVER		33.49%	29.00%	36.85%	0.00%	0.00%	1.60%	0.00%	14.34%	15.94%

TABLE B.2.2
Susan's Lump-Sum Values*
(*In 1992 dollars.)

| | | ONE JOB CAREER | | | BENEFIT | EARNED | OVER | FIVE | JOB | CAREERS |
| | | | | | | | | | | |
AGE	ANNUAL EARNINGS	UNIT DEFINED BENEFIT	INTEGRATED DEFINED BENEFIT	DEFINED CONTRIBUTION	NO PENSION JOB 1	INTEG. D.B. JOB 2	INTEG. D.B. JOB 3	INTEG. D.B. JOB 4	DEFINED CONTRB. JOB 5	TOTAL ALL JOBS
20	$18,963	$28	$23	$316	$0					$0
21	19,143	57	46	627	0					0
22	19,326	88	71	934	0					0
23	19,510	121	97	1,237	0					0
24	19,696	156	125	1,535	0	29				29
25	19,883	199	159	1,829	0	59				59
26	20,073	246	197	2,119	0	90				90
27	20,264	298	238	2,406	0	122				122
28	20,457	355	284	2,688	0	158				158
29	20,652	418	334	2,966	0	0	$39			39
30	20,848	487	390	3,240	0	0	$80			80
31	21,047	563	451	3,511	0	0	$122			122
32	21,247	647	518	3,777	0	0	$165			165
33	21,450	739	591	4,040	0	0	$211			211
34	21,654	839	671	4,300	0	0	$268			268
35	21,860	949	759	4,555	0	0	$332			332
36	22,068	1,068	856	4,807	0	0	$403			403
37	22,278	1,199	964	5,056	0	0	$482			482
38	22,491	1,342	1,082	5,301	0	0	$569			569
39	22,705	1,497	1,211	5,543	0	0	$461	$72		533
40	22,921	1,666	1,352	5,781	0	0	$461	$147		608
41	23,139	1,850	1,505	6,016	0	0	$461	$224		685
42	23,360	2,050	1,673	6,248	0	0	$461	$304		765
43	23,582	2,268	1,856	6,477	0	0	$461	$387		848
44	23,807	2,504	2,055	6,702	0	0	$461	$0	$225	686
45	24,034	2,760	2,272	6,924	0	0	$461	$0	$447	908
46	24,262	3,039	2,508	7,143	0	0	$461	$0	$667	1,128
47	24,493	3,340	2,765	7,359	0	0	$461	$0	$883	1,344
48	24,727	3,667	3,044	7,572	0	0	$461	$0	$1,096	1,557
49	24,962	4,021	3,347	7,782	0	0	$461	$0	$1,306	1,767
50	25,200	4,262	3,558	7,989	0	0	$461	$0	$1,513	1,974
51	25,440	4,518	3,782	8,193	0	0	$461	$0	$1,717	2,178
52	25,682	4,789	4,020	8,395	0	0	$461	$0	$1,918	2,379
53	25,927	5,076	4,272	8,593	0	0	$461	$0	$2,117	2,578
54	26,174	5,381	4,541	8,789	0	0	$461	$0	$2,313	2,774
55	26,423	5,704	4,826	8,982	0	0	$461	$0	$2,506	2,967
56	26,675	6,046	5,129	9,173	0	0	$461	$0	$2,696	3,157
57	26,929	6,409	5,451	9,360	0	0	$461	$0	$2,884	3,345
58	27,185	6,793	5,793	9,545	0	0	$461	$0	$3,069	3,530
59	27,444	7,201	6,157	9,728	0	0	$461	$0	$3,251	3,712
60	27,706	7,633	6,543	9,908	0	0	$461	$0	$3,431	3,892
61	27,969	8,091	6,953	10,085	0	0	$461	$0	$3,609	4,070
62	28,236	8,577	7,389	10,260	0	0	$461	$0	$3,784	4,245
63	28,505	9,091	7,852	10,433	0	0	$461	$0	$3,956	4,417
64	28,776	9,637	8,344	10,603	0	0	$461	$0	$4,126	4,587
RELACEMENT RATIOS		33.49%	29.00%	36.85%	0.00%	0.00%	1.60%	0.00%	14.34%	15.94%

TABLE B.2.3

Susan's Annual Income Starting at Age 65 with Rollover Election*

*In 1992 dollars.

| | | ONE JOB CAREER | | | 10 YEARS VESTING
TEN YEARS PRIOR TO 1989
FIVE JOB CAREER / SINGLE SUM VALUES | | | | | |
AGE	ANNUAL EARNINGS	UNIT DEFINED BENEFIT	INTEGRATED DEFINED BENEFIT	DEFINED CONTRIBUTION	NO PENSION JOB 1	INTEG. D.B. JOB 2	INTEG. D.B. JOB 3	INTEG. D.B. JOB 4	DEFINED CONTRB. JOB 5	TOTAL ALL JOBS
20	$18,963	$66	$54	$948	$0					$0
21	19,143	139	112	1,928	0					0
22	19,326	220	176	2,940	0					0
23	19,510	310	248	3,986	0					0
24	19,696	409	328	5,065	0	76				76
25	19,883	534	427	6,180	0	158				158
26	20,073	677	541	7,331	0	247				247
27	20,264	860	672	8,519	0	346				346
28	20,457	1,027	821	9,744	0	456				456
29	20,652	1,239	992	11,009	0	0	117			117
30	20,848	1,481	1,185	12,313	0	0	243			243
31	21,047	1,756	1,405	13,659	0	0	380			380
32	21,247	2,066	1,653	15,046	0	0	527			527
33	21,450	2,418	1,934	16,477	0	0	691			691
34	21,654	2,815	2,252	17,952	0	0	901			901
35	21,860	3,263	2,611	19,473	0	0	1,142			1,142
36	22,068	3,769	3,021	21,040	0	0	1,422			1,422
37	22,278	4,338	3,487	22,654	0	0	1,744			1,744
38	22,491	4,978	4,014	24,318	0	0	2,113			2,113
39	22,705	5,698	4,608	26,033	0	0	2,163	275		2,438
40	22,921	6,506	5,278	27,798	0	0	2,215	575		2,790
41	23,139	7,414	6,033	29,617	0	0	2,268	900		3,168
42	23,360	8,434	6,882	31,490	0	0	2,322	1,252		3,574
43	23,582	9,577	7,838	33,419	0	0	2,377	1,633		4,010
44	23,807	10,860	8,914	35,405	0	0	2,434	0	1,190	3,624
45	24,034	12,299	10,124	37,450	0	0	2,492	0	2,420	4,912
46	24,262	13,914	11,486	39,555	0	0	2,551	0	3,691	6,242
47	24,493	15,725	13,017	41,721	0	0	2,612	0	5,004	7,616
48	24,727	17,757	14,741	43,951	0	0	2,674	0	6,359	9,033
49	24,962	20,037	16,680	46,246	0	0	2,738	0	7,759	10,497
50	25,200	21,868	18,254	48,607	0	0	2,803	0	9,203	12,006
51	25,440	23,880	19,988	51,036	0	0	2,870	0	10,695	13,565
52	25,682	26,094	21,901	53,535	0	0	2,938	0	12,233	15,171
53	25,927	28,533	24,013	56,106	0	0	3,008	0	13,821	16,829
54	26,174	31,224	26,348	58,751	0	0	3,080	0	15,459	18,539
55	26,423	34,194	28,932	61,471	0	0	3,153	0	17,148	20,301
56	26,675	37,479	31,795	64,268	0	0	3,228	0	18,890	22,118
57	26,929	41,118	34,973	67,145	0	0	3,305	0	20,686	23,991
58	27,185	45,159	38,510	70,103	0	0	3,386	0	22,538	25,922
59	27,444	49,651	42,450	73,144	0	0	3,465	0	24,447	27,912
60	27,706	54,657	46,850	76,271	0	0	3,548	0	26,414	29,962
61	27,969	60,251	51,776	79,485	0	0	3,632	0	28,441	32,073
62	28,236	66,518	57,307	82,790	0	0	3,718	0	30,530	34,248
63	28,505	73,562	63,535	86,186	0	0	3,807	0	32,683	36,490
64	28,776	81,505	70,570	89,677	0	0	3,898	0	34,899	38,797
RELACEMENT RATIOS		33.49%	29.00%	36.85%	0.00%	0.00%	1.60%	0.00%	14.34%	15.94%

TABLE B.2.4
Susan's Single-Sum Amounts If Benefits from
Defined Benefit Plans Are Rolled Over*

*In 1992 dollars.

I. CAREER SUMMARY

TOTAL NUMBER OF JOBS   5

JOB NUMBER	AGE AT HIRE	AGE AT TERMINATION	TYPE OF PLAN	STATUS
1	25	25	NO PENSION	FULL-TIME
2	26	27	NO PENSION COVERAGE	FULL-TIME
3	28	31	DEFINED CONTRIBUTION	FULL-TIME
4	33	37	INTEGRATED DEFINED BENEFIT	FULL-TIME
5	38	61	INTEGRATED DEFINED BENEFIT	FULL-TIME

II. PROFILE OF WORKER

AGE IN 1992	40
ANNUAL SALARY IN 1992	$85,000
SALARY INCREASE RATE	6.0% PER ANNUM
NORMAL RETIREMENT AGE	62
ACTUAL RETIREMENT AGE	62

III. ECONOMIC ASSUMPSIONS

INTEREST RATE IN DEFINED CONTRIBUTION PLAN	7.50% PER ANNUM
INTEREST RATE IN ROLLOVER AMOUNTS	7.50% PER ANNUM
RATE OF INFLATION	5.00% PER ANNUM
RATE OF INCREASE IN AGE 65 COVERED COMPENSATION	5.50% PER ANNUM

IV. PLAN PROVISIONS

UNIT DEFINED BENEFIT FORMULA :   1.25% OF THE FINAL FIVE YEAR AVERAGE EARNINGS TIMES YEARS OF SERVICE TO A MAXIMUM OF 30 YEARS

INTEGRATED DEFINED BENEFIT FORMULA :   1.00% OF FINAL FIVE YEAR AVERAGE EARNINGS BELOW COVERED COMPENSATION PLUS 1.65% OF FINAL FIVE YEAR AVERAGE EARNINGS ABOVE COVERED COMPENSATION TIMES YEARS OF SERVICE TO A MAXIMUM OF 30 YEARS

DEFINED CONTRIBUTION FORMULA :   5.00% OF ANNUAL EARNINGS EACH YEAR

VESTING :   100% VESTED AFTER FIVE YEARS OF SERVICE

             (TEN YEARS OF SERVICE REQUIRED FOR VESTING PRIOR TO 1989)

APPENDIX B.3
Pension Portability Study for Bonnie, a 40-Year-Old Lawyer

		UNIT DEFINED BENEFIT	INTEGRATED DEFINED BENEFIT	DEFINED CONTRIBUTION		NO PENSION JOB 1	NO PENSION JOB 2	DEFINED CONTRB. JOB 3	INTEG. D.B. JOB 4	INTEG. D.B. JOB 5	TOTAL ALL JOBS
AGE	ANNUAL EARNINGS		BENEFIT EARNED OVER ONE JOB CAREER					BENEFIT EARNED OVER FIVE JOB CAREERS			
25	$73,734	$159	$188	$948		$0					$0
26	74,437	328	386	1,883		0	0				0
27	75,146	507	595	2,805		0	0				0
28	75,861	696	816	3,714		0	0	909			909
29	76,584	897	1,048	4,610		0	0	1,805			1,805
30	77,313	1,141	1,334	5,493		0	0	2,689			2,689
31	78,049	1,411	1,651	6,365		0	0	3,560			3,560
32	0	1,709	2,001	7,224		0	0	0			0
33	79,543	2,039	2,388	8,071		0	0	0	301		301
34	80,301	2,401	2,814	8,907		0	0	0	619		619
35	81,066	2,799	3,283	9,731		0	0	0	953		953
36	81,838	3,237	3,799	10,543		0	0	0	1,306		1,306
37	82,617	3,717	4,365	11,344		0	0	0	1,679		1,679
38	83,404	4,244	4,985	12,133		0	0	0	1,679	404	2,083
39	84,198	4,819	5,665	12,912		0	0	0	1,679	830	2,509
40	85,000	5,449	6,409	13,680		0	0	0	1,679	1,279	2,958
41	85,810	6,137	7,222	14,437		0	0	0	1,679	1,753	3,432
42	86,627	6,888	8,111	15,184		0	0	0	1,679	2,253	3,932
43	87,452	7,707	9,080	15,920		0	0	0	1,679	2,867	4,546
44	88,285	8,599	10,137	16,646		0	0	0	1,679	3,548	5,227
45	89,125	9,571	11,289	17,362		0	0	0	1,679	4,301	5,980
46	89,974	10,629	12,543	18,067		0	0	0	1,679	5,131	6,810
47	90,831	11,778	13,908	18,763		0	0	0	1,679	6,047	7,726
48	91,696	13,028	15,392	19,450		0	0	0	1,679	7,055	8,734
49	92,570	14,385	17,005	20,126		0	0	0	1,679	8,162	9,841
50	93,451	15,858	18,757	20,794		0	0	0	1,679	9,378	11,057
51	94,341	17,456	20,658	21,451		0	0	0	1,679	10,712	12,391
52	95,240	19,189	22,721	22,100		0	0	0	1,679	12,172	13,851
53	96,147	21,066	24,958	22,740		0	0	0	1,679	13,770	15,449
54	97,062	23,100	27,382	23,371		0	0	0	1,679	15,517	17,196
55	97,987	24,486	29,041	23,992		0	0	0	1,679	17,424	19,103
56	98,920	25,956	30,799	24,606		0	0	0	1,679	19,506	21,185
57	99,862	27,513	32,665	25,210		0	0	0	1,679	21,776	23,455
58	100,813	29,164	34,643	25,807		0	0	0	1,679	24,250	25,929
59	101,773	30,913	36,741	26,395		0	0	0	1,679	26,943	28,622
60	102,743	32,768	38,965	26,974		0	0	0	1,679	29,874	31,553
61	103,721	34,734	41,325	27,546		0	0	0	1,679	33,060	34,739

ANNUAL RETIREMENT INCOME AT AGE SIXTY-TWO

DEFERRED PAYMENTS		$34,734	$41,325	$27,546		$0	$0	$0	$1,679	$33,060	34,739
CASH OUT - SPENT		$34,734	$41,325	$27,546		$0	$0	$0	$0	$33,060	33,060
CASH OUT - ROLLOVER		$34,734	$41,325	$27,546		$0	$0	$0	$1,435	$33,060	34,495

ANNUAL RETIREMENT INCOME AS A PERCENTAGE OF FINAL EARNINGS

DEFERRED PAYMENTS		33.49%	39.84%	26.56%		0.00%	0.00%	0.00%	1.62%	31.87%	33.49%
CASH OUT - SPENT		33.49%	39.84%	26.56%		0.00%	0.00%	0.00%	0.00%	31.87%	31.87%
CASH OUT - ROLLOVER		33.49%	39.84%	26.56%		0.00%	0.00%	0.00%	1.38%	31.87%	33.26%

TABLE B.3.1
Bonnie's Annual Income Starting at Age 62 in 1992 Dollars.   361

		BENEFIT EARNED OVER ONE JOB CAREER				FIVE YEARS VESTING TEN YEARS PRIOR TO 1989 FIVE JOB CAREER / SINGLE SUM VALUES					
AGE	ANNUAL EARNINGS	UNIT DEFINED BENEFIT	INTEGRATED DEFINED BENEFIT	DEFINED CONTRIBUTION		NO PENSION JOB 1	NO PENSION JOB 2	DEFINED CONTRB. JOB 3	INTEG. D.B. JOB 4	INTEG. D.B. JOB 5	TOTAL ALL JOBS
25	$73,734	$521	$616	$3,687	*	$0					$0
26	74,437	1,100	1,297	7,496	*	0	0				0
27	75,146	1,743	2,048	11,432	*	0	0				0
28	75,861	2,454	2,876	15,497	*	0	0	3,793			3,793
29	76,584	3,241	3,787	19,696	*	0	0	7,713			7,713
30	77,313	4,226	4,940	24,030	*	0	0	11,762			11,762
31	78,049	5,356	6,266	28,505	*	0	0	15,944			15,944
32	0	6,651	7,786	33,123	*	0	0	0			0
33	79,543	8,130	9,522	37,889	*	0	0	0	1,201		1,201
34	80,301	9,816	11,504	42,806	*	0	0	0	2,529		2,529
35	81,066	11,734	13,761	47,878	*	0	0	0	3,996		3,996
36	81,838	13,913	16,326	53,110	*	0	0	0	5,615		5,615
37	82,617	16,384	19,237	58,506	*	0	0	0	7,399		7,399
38	83,404	19,183	22,536	64,069	*	0	0	0	7,588	1,826	9,414
39	84,198	22,349	26,270	69,804	*	0	0	0	7,784	3,849	11,633
40	85,000	25,926	30,492	75,716	*	0	0	0	7,987	6,087	14,074
41	85,810	29,964	35,262	81,810	*	0	0	0	8,196	8,560	16,756
42	86,627	34,519	40,646	88,089	*	0	0	0	8,412	11,290	19,702
43	87,452	39,654	46,719	94,559	*	0	0	0	8,637	14,753	23,390
44	88,285	45,439	53,566	101,224	*	0	0	0	8,870	18,748	27,618
45	89,125	51,955	61,281	108,091	*	0	0	0	9,112	23,345	32,457
46	89,974	59,292	69,975	115,163	*	0	0	0	9,365	28,626	37,991
47	90,831	67,554	79,769	122,446	*	0	0	0	9,628	34,682	44,310
48	91,696	76,856	90,803	129,947	*	0	0	0	9,903	41,618	51,521
49	92,570	87,327	103,233	137,669	*	0	0	0	10,191	49,552	59,743
50	93,451	99,119	117,236	145,619	*	0	0	0	10,492	58,618	69,110
51	94,341	112,401	133,019	153,804	*	0	0	0	10,809	68,973	79,782
52	95,240	127,372	150,818	162,228	*	0	0	0	11,143	80,796	91,939
53	96,147	144,254	170,900	170,898	*	0	0	0	11,495	94,290	105,785
54	97,062	163,300	193,569	179,820	*	0	0	0	11,867	109,689	121,556
55	97,987	178,835	212,096	189,000	*	0	0	0	12,260	127,258	139,518
56	98,920	196,014	232,595	198,446	*	0	0	0	12,677	147,310	159,987
57	99,862	215,048	255,315	208,164	*	0	0	0	13,121	170,210	183,331
58	100,813	236,180	280,552	218,161	*	0	0	0	13,595	196,387	209,982
59	101,773	259,675	308,623	228,444	*	0	0	0	14,101	226,324	240,425
60	102,743	285,857	339,918	239,021	*	0	0	0	14,644	260,604	275,248
61	103,721	315,110	374,898	249,898	*	0	0	0	15,229	299,919	315,148

SINGLE SUM RETIREMENT INCOME AT AGE SIXTY-TWO

DEFERRED PAYMENTS	*	$315,110	$374,898	$249,898	*	$0	$0	$0	$15,229	$299,919	$315,148
CASH OUT - SPENT	*	$315,110	$374,898	$249,898	*	$0	$0	$0	$0	$299,919	$299,919
CASH OUT - ROLLOVER	*	$315,110	$374,898	$249,898	*	$0	$0	$0	$13,015	$299,919	$312,934

ANNUAL RETIREMENT INCOME AS A PERCENTAGE OF FINAL EARNINGS

DEFERRED PAYMENTS	*	33.49%	39.84%	26.56%	*	0.00%	0.00%	0.00%	1.62%	31.87%	33.49%
CASH OUT - SPENT	*	33.49%	39.84%	26.56%	*	0.00%	0.00%	0.00%	0.00%	31.87%	31.87%
CASH OUT - ROLLOVER	*	33.49%	39.84%	26.56%	*	0.00%	0.00%	0.00%	1.38%	31.87%	33.26%

TABLE B.3.2
Bonnie's Lump-Sum Values*

*In 1992 dollars.

		ONE JOB CAREER				FIVE YEARS VESTING TEN YEARS PRIOR TO 1989					
						BENEFIT	EARNED	OVER FIVE	JOB	CAREERS	
AGE	ANNUAL EARNINGS	UNIT DEFINED BENEFIT	INTEGRATED DEFINED BENEFIT	DEFINED CONTRIBUTION		NO PENSION JOB 1	NO PENSION JOB 2	DEFINED CONTRB. JOB 3	INTEG. D.B. JOB 4	INTEG. D.B. JOB 5	TOTAL ALL JOBS
25	$73,734	$159	$188	$948		$0					$0
26	74,437	328	386	1,883		0	0				0
27	75,146	507	595	2,805		0	0				0
28	75,861	696	816	3,714		0	0	$909			909
29	76,584	897	1,048	4,610		0	0	$1,805			1,805
30	77,313	1,141	1,334	5,493		0	0	$2,689			2,689
31	78,049	1,411	1,651	6,365		0	0	$3,560			3,560
32	0	1,709	2,001	7,224		0	0	$0			0
33	79,543	2,039	2,388	8,071		0	0	$0	$301		301
34	80,301	2,401	2,814	8,907		0	0	$0	$619		619
35	81,066	2,799	3,283	9,731		0	0	$0	$953		953
36	81,838	3,237	3,799	10,543		0	0	$0	$1,306		1,306
37	82,617	3,717	4,365	11,344		0	0	$0	$1,679		1,679
38	83,404	4,244	4,985	12,133		0	0	$0	$1,435	$404	1,839
39	84,198	4,819	5,665	12,912		0	0	$0	$1,435	$830	2,265
40	85,000	5,449	6,409	13,680		0	0	$0	$1,435	$1,279	2,714
41	85,810	6,137	7,222	14,437		0	0	$0	$1,435	$1,753	3,188
42	86,627	6,888	8,111	15,184		0	0	$0	$1,435	$2,253	3,688
43	87,452	7,707	9,080	15,920		0	0	$0	$1,435	$2,867	4,302
44	88,285	8,599	10,137	16,646		0	0	$0	$1,435	$3,548	4,983
45	89,125	9,571	11,289	17,362		0	0	$0	$1,435	$4,301	5,736
46	89,974	10,629	12,543	18,067		0	0	$0	$1,435	$5,131	6,566
47	90,831	11,778	13,908	18,763		0	0	$0	$1,435	$6,047	7,482
48	91,696	13,028	15,392	19,450		0	0	$0	$1,435	$7,055	8,490
49	92,570	14,385	17,005	20,126		0	0	$0	$1,435	$8,162	9,597
50	93,451	15,858	18,757	20,794		0	0	$0	$1,435	$9,378	10,813
51	94,341	17,456	20,658	21,451		0	0	$0	$1,435	$10,712	12,147
52	95,240	19,189	22,721	22,100		0	0	$0	$1,435	$12,172	13,607
53	96,147	21,066	24,958	22,740		0	0	$0	$1,435	$13,770	15,205
54	97,062	23,100	27,382	23,371		0	0	$0	$1,435	$15,517	16,952
55	97,987	24,486	29,041	23,992		0	0	$0	$1,435	$17,424	18,859
56	98,920	25,956	30,799	24,606		0	0	$0	$1,435	$19,506	20,941
57	99,862	27,513	32,665	25,210		0	0	$0	$1,435	$21,776	23,211
58	100,813	29,164	34,643	25,807		0	0	$0	$1,435	$24,250	25,685
59	101,773	30,913	36,741	26,395		0	0	$0	$1,435	$26,943	28,378
60	102,743	32,768	38,965	26,974		0	0	$0	$1,435	$29,874	31,309
61	103,721	34,734	41,325	27,546		0	0	$0	$1,435	$33,060	34,495
RELACEMENT RATIOS		33.49%	39.84%	26.56%		0.00%	0.00%	0.00%	1.38%	31.87%	33.26%

TABLE B.3.3
Bonnie's Annual Income Starting at Age 62 with Rollover Election*

*In 1992 dollars.

		ONE JOB CAREER			FIVE YEARS VESTING TEN YEARS PRIOR TO 1989 FIVE JOB CAREER / SINGLE SUM VALUES					
AGE	ANNUAL EARNINGS	UNIT DEFINED BENEFIT	INTEGRATED DEFINED BENEFIT	DEFINED CONTRIBUTION	NO PENSION JOB 1	NO PENSION JOB 2	DEFINED CONTRB. JOB 3	INTEG. D.B. JOB 4	INTEG. D.B. JOB 5	TOTAL ALL JOBS
25	$73,734	$521	$616	$3,687	$0					$0
26	74,437	1,100	1,297	7,496	0	0				0
27	75,146	1,743	2,048	11,432	0	0				0
28	75,861	2,454	2,876	15,497	0	0	3,793			3,793
29	76,584	3,241	3,787	19,696	0	0	7,713			7,713
30	77,313	4,226	4,940	24,030	0	0	11,762			11,762
31	78,049	5,356	6,266	28,505	0	0	15,944			15,944
32	0	6,651	7,786	33,123	0	0	0			0
33	79,543	8,130	9,522	37,889	0	0	0	1,201		1,201
34	80,301	9,816	11,504	42,806	0	0	0	2,529		2,529
35	81,066	11,734	13,761	47,878	0	0	0	3,996		3,996
36	81,838	13,913	16,326	53,110	0	0	0	5,615		5,615
37	82,617	16,384	19,237	58,506	0	0	0	7,399		7,399
38	83,404	19,183	22,536	64,069	0	0	0	7,575	1,826	9,401
39	84,198	22,349	26,270	69,804	0	0	0	7,756	3,849	11,605
40	85,000	25,926	30,492	75,716	0	0	0	7,940	6,087	14,027
41	85,810	29,964	35,262	81,810	0	0	0	8,129	8,560	16,689
42	86,627	34,519	40,646	88,089	0	0	0	8,323	11,290	19,613
43	87,452	39,654	46,719	94,559	0	0	0	8,521	14,753	23,274
44	88,285	45,439	53,566	101,224	0	0	0	8,724	18,748	27,472
45	89,125	51,955	61,281	108,091	0	0	0	8,932	23,345	32,277
46	89,974	59,292	69,975	115,163	0	0	0	9,144	28,626	37,770
47	90,831	67,554	79,769	122,446	0	0	0	9,362	34,682	44,044
48	91,696	76,856	90,803	129,947	0	0	0	9,585	41,618	51,203
49	92,570	87,327	103,233	137,669	0	0	0	9,813	49,552	59,365
50	93,451	99,119	117,236	145,619	0	0	0	10,047	58,618	68,665
51	94,341	112,401	133,019	153,804	0	0	0	10,286	68,973	79,259
52	95,240	127,372	150,818	162,228	0	0	0	10,531	80,796	91,327
53	96,147	144,254	170,900	170,898	0	0	0	10,782	94,290	105,072
54	97,062	163,300	193,569	179,820	0	0	0	11,038	109,689	120,727
55	97,987	178,835	212,096	189,000	0	0	0	11,301	127,258	138,559
56	98,920	196,014	232,595	198,446	0	0	0	11,570	147,310	158,880
57	99,862	215,048	255,315	208,164	0	0	0	11,846	170,210	182,056
58	100,813	236,180	280,552	218,161	0	0	0	12,128	196,387	208,515
59	101,773	259,675	308,623	228,444	0	0	0	12,416	226,324	238,740
60	102,743	285,857	339,918	239,021	0	0	0	12,712	260,604	273,316
61	103,721	315,110	374,898	249,898	0	0	0	13,015	299,919	312,934
RELACEMENT RATIOS		33.49%	39.84%	26.56%	0.00%	0.00%	0.00%	1.38%	31.87%	33.26%

TABLE B.3.4
Bonnie's Single-Sum Amounts If Benefits from Defined Benefit Plans Are Rolled Over*
*In 1992 dollars.

I. CAREER SUMMARY

TOTAL NUMBER OF JOBS   3

JOB NUMBER	AGE AT HIRE	AGE AT TERMINATION	TYPE OF PLAN	STATUS
1	21	21	INTEGRATED DEFINED BENEFIT	FULL-TIME
2	22	24	DEFINED CONTRIBUTION	FULL-TIME
3	26	64	INTEGRATED DEFINED BENEFIT	FULL-TIME

II. PROFILE OF WORKER

AGE IN 1992	30
ANNUAL SALARY IN 1992	$21,000
SALARY INCREASE RATE	6.0% PER ANNUM
NORMAL RETIREMENT AGE	65
ACTUAL RETIREMENT AGE	65

III. ECONOMIC ASSUMPSIONS

INTEREST RATE IN DEFINED CONTRIBUTION PLAN	7.50% PER ANNUM
INTEREST RATE IN ROLLOVER AMOUNTS	7.50% PER ANNUM
RATE OF INFLATION	5.00% PER ANNUM
RATE OF INCREASE IN AGE 65 COVERED COMPENSATION	5.50% PER ANNUM

IV. PLAN PROVISIONS

UNIT DEFINED BENEFIT FORMULA :   1.25% OF THE FINAL FIVE YEAR AVERAGE EARNINGS TIMES YEARS OF SERVICE TO A MAXIMUM OF 30 YEARS

INTEGRATED DEFINED BENEFIT FORMULA :   1.00% OF FINAL FIVE YEAR AVERAGE EARNINGS BELOW COVERED COMPENSATION PLUS 1.65% OF FINAL FIVE YEAR AVERAGE EARNINGS ABOVE COVERED COMPENSATION TIMES YEARS OF SERVICE TO A MAXIMUM OF 30 YEARS

DEFINED CONTRIBUTION FORMULA :   5.00% OF ANNUAL EARNINGS EACH YEAR

VESTING :   100% VESTED AFTER FIVE YEARS OF SERVICE (TEN YEARS OF SERVICE REQUIRED PRIOR TO 1989)

APPENDIX B.4
Pension Portability Study for Jennifer, a 30-Year-Old Secretary

AGE	ANNUAL EARNINGS	UNIT DEFINED BENEFIT	INTEGRATED DEFINED BENEFIT	DEFINED CONTRIBUTION	INTEG. D.B. JOB 1	DEFINED CONTRB. JOB 2	INTEG. D.B. JOB 3	NO PENSION JOB 4	NO PENSION JOB 5	TOTAL ALL JOBS
21	$19,283	$30	$24	$314	$24					$24
22	19,466	61	49	623	0	309				309
23	19,652	94	75	928	0	614				614
24	19,839	129	104	1,228	0	915				915
25	0	167	133	1,525	0	0				0
26	20,219	212	170	1,817	0	0	32			32
27	20,411	262	210	2,105	0	0	65			65
28	20,606	318	254	2,389	0	0	101			101
29	20,802	379	303	2,669	0	0	139			139
30	21,000	446	357	2,946	0	0	178			178
31	21,200	520	416	3,218	0	0	227			227
32	21,402	602	481	3,487	0	0	281			281
33	21,606	691	553	3,752	0	0	340			340
34	21,812	789	631	4,013	0	0	406			406
35	22,019	896	717	4,271	0	0	478			478
36	22,229	1,013	810	4,524	0	0	557			557
37	22,441	1,141	913	4,775	0	0	644			644
38	22,654	1,280	1,024	5,022	0	0	740			740
39	22,870	1,432	1,146	5,265	0	0	844			844
40	23,088	1,598	1,279	5,505	0	0	959			959
41	23,308	1,779	1,423	5,742	0	0	1,084			1,084
42	23,530	1,975	1,580	5,976	0	0	1,221			1,221
43	23,754	2,189	1,751	6,206	0	0	1,371			1,371
44	23,980	2,421	1,937	6,433	0	0	1,533			1,533
45	24,208	2,674	2,139	6,656	0	0	1,711			1,711
46	24,439	2,947	2,358	6,877	0	0	1,904			1,904
47	24,672	3,244	2,595	7,095	0	0	2,115			2,115
48	24,907	3,566	2,853	7,309	0	0	2,344			2,344
49	25,144	3,915	3,132	7,521	0	0	2,592			2,592
50	25,383	4,293	3,435	7,729	0	0	2,862			2,862
51	25,625	4,551	3,641	7,935	0	0	3,155			3,155
52	25,869	4,824	3,859	8,138	0	0	3,473			3,473
53	26,116	5,113	4,091	8,338	0	0	3,818			3,818
54	26,364	5,420	4,337	8,535	0	0	4,193			4,193
55	26,615	5,745	4,611	8,730	0	0	4,611			4,611
56	26,869	6,090	4,903	8,921	0	0	4,903			4,903
57	27,125	6,456	5,213	9,110	0	0	5,213			5,213
58	27,383	6,843	5,542	9,297	0	0	5,542			5,542
59	27,644	7,253	5,892	9,481	0	0	5,892			5,892
60	27,907	7,689	6,264	9,662	0	0	6,264			6,264
61	28,173	8,150	6,659	9,841	0	0	6,659			6,659
62	28,441	8,639	7,079	10,017	0	0	7,079			7,079
63	28,712	9,157	7,526	10,191	0	0	7,526			7,526
64	28,986	9,707	8,000	10,362	0	0	8,000			8,000

ANNUAL RETIREMENT INCOME AT AGE SIXTY-FIVE

		UNIT DEFINED BENEFIT	INTEGRATED DEFINED BENEFIT	DEFINED CONTRIBUTION	INTEG. D.B. JOB 1	DEFINED CONTRB. JOB 2	INTEG. D.B. JOB 3			TOTAL ALL JOBS
DEFERRED PAYMENTS		$9,707	$8,000	$10,362	$0	$0	$8,000			8,000
CASH OUT - SPENT		$9,707	$8,000	$10,362	$0	$0	$8,000			8,000
CASH OUT - ROLLOVER		$9,707	$8,000	$10,362	$0	$0	$8,000			8,000

ANNUAL RETIREMENT INCOME AS A PERCENTAGE OF FINAL EARNINGS

DEFERRED PAYMENTS		33.49%	27.60%	35.75%	0.00%	0.00%	27.60%			27.60%
CASH OUT - SPENT		33.49%	27.60%	35.75%	0.00%	0.00%	27.60%			27.60%
CASH OUT - ROLLOVER		33.49%	27.60%	35.75%	0.00%	0.00%	27.60%			27.60%

TABLE B.4.1
Jennifer's Annual Income Starting at Age 65 in 1992 Dollars.

		BENEFIT EARNED OVER ONE JOB CAREER				FIVE YEARS VESTING TEN YEARS PRIOR TO 1989 THREE JOB CAREER / SINGLE SUM VALUES					
AGE	ANNUAL EARNINGS	UNIT DEFINED BENEFIT	INTEGRATED DEFINED BENEFIT	DEFINED CONTRIBUTION		INTEG. DEFINED D.B. JOB 1	DEFINED CONTRB. JOB 2	INTEG. D.B. JOB 3	NO PENSION JOB 4	NO PENSION JOB 5	TOTAL ALL JOBS
21	$19,283	$72	$58	$964		$58					$58
22	19,466	152	122	1,960		0	973				973
23	19,652	241	193	2,990		0	1,979				1,979
24	19,839	339	271	4,053		0	3,018				3,018
25	0	448	358	5,151		0	0				0
26	20,219	584	467	6,284		0	0	87			87
27	20,411	740	592	7,454		0	0	184			184
28	20,606	919	735	8,662		0	0	292			292
29	20,802	1,124	899	9,909		0	0	411			411
30	21,000	1,356	1,085	11,194		0	0	543			543
31	21,200	1,621	1,297	12,521		0	0	707			707
32	21,402	1,921	1,537	13,889		0	0	897			897
33	21,606	2,262	1,809	15,300		0	0	1,113			1,113
34	21,812	2,647	2,117	16,755		0	0	1,361			1,361
35	22,019	3,082	2,465	18,255		0	0	1,644			1,644
36	22,229	3,573	2,858	19,801		0	0	1,965			1,965
37	22,441	4,127	3,301	21,395		0	0	2,330			2,330
38	22,654	4,750	3,800	23,037		0	0	2,745			2,745
39	22,870	5,452	4,362	24,729		0	0	3,214			3,214
40	23,088	6,241	4,993	26,472		0	0	3,745			3,745
41	23,308	7,129	5,703	28,268		0	0	4,345			4,345
42	23,530	8,126	6,500	30,117		0	0	5,023			5,023
43	23,754	9,245	7,396	32,022		0	0	5,788			5,788
44	23,980	10,502	8,401	33,983		0	0	6,651			6,651
45	24,208	11,912	9,530	36,003		0	0	7,624			7,624
46	24,439	13,496	10,797	38,082		0	0	8,720			8,720
47	24,672	15,273	12,219	40,222		0	0	9,956			9,956
48	24,907	17,269	13,815	42,425		0	0	11,348			11,348
49	25,144	19,510	15,608	44,693		0	0	12,917			12,917
50	25,383	22,027	17,622	47,026		0	0	14,685			14,685
51	25,625	24,053	19,243	49,427		0	0	16,677			16,677
52	25,869	26,284	21,027	51,897		0	0	18,924			18,924
53	26,116	28,741	22,993	54,439		0	0	21,460			21,460
54	26,364	31,451	25,166	57,053		0	0	24,327			24,327
55	26,615	34,443	27,645	59,742		0	0	27,645			27,645
56	26,869	37,752	30,393	62,508		0	0	30,393			30,393
57	27,125	41,418	33,444	65,352		0	0	33,444			33,444
58	27,383	45,488	36,841	68,278		0	0	36,841			36,841
59	27,644	50,013	40,626	71,285		0	0	40,626			40,626
60	27,907	55,055	44,854	74,378		0	0	44,854			44,854
61	28,173	60,689	49,589	77,558		0	0	49,589			49,589
62	28,441	67,002	54,906	80,826		0	0	54,906			54,906
63	28,712	74,098	60,896	84,186		0	0	60,896			60,896
64	28,986	82,098	67,664	87,640		0	0	67,664			67,664

SINGLE SUM RETIREMENT INCOME AT AGE SIXTY-FIVE

	UNIT DEFINED BENEFIT	INTEGRATED DEFINED BENEFIT	DEFINED CONTRIBUTION		JOB 1	JOB 2	JOB 3			TOTAL ALL JOBS
DEFERRED PAYMENTS	$82,098	$67,664	$87,640		$0	$0	$67,664			$67,664
CASH OUT - SPENT	$82,098	$67,664	$87,640		$0	$0	$67,664			$67,664
CASH OUT - ROLLOVER	$82,098	$67,664	$87,640		$0	$0	$67,664			$67,664

ANNUAL RETIREMENT INCOME AS A PERCENTAGE OF FINAL EARNINGS

DEFERRED PAYMENTS	33.49%	27.60%	35.75%		0.00%	0.00%	27.60%			27.60%
CASH OUT - SPENT	33.49%	27.60%	35.75%		0.00%	0.00%	27.60%			27.60%
CASH OUT - ROLLOVER	33.49%	27.60%	35.75%		0.00%	0.00%	27.60%			27.60%

TABLE B.4.2
Jennifer's Lump-Sum Values in 1992 Dollars.

		ONE JOB CAREER			FIVE YEARS VESTING TEN YEARS PRIOR TO 1989 OVER THREE JOB CAREERS					
					BENEFIT EARNED	DEFINED	INTEG.	NO	NO	TOTAL
	ANNUAL	UNIT DEFINED	INTEGRATED DEFINED	DEFINED	INTEG. D.B.	CONTRB.	D.B.	PENSION	PENSION	ALL
AGE	EARNINGS	BENEFIT	BENEFIT	CONTRIBUTION	JOB 1	JOB 2	JOB 3	JOB 4	JOB 5	JOBS
21	$19,283	$30	$24	$314	$24					$24
22	19,466	61	49	623	0	309				309
23	19,652	94	75	928	0	614				614
24	19,839	129	104	1,228	0	915				915
25	0	167	133	1,525	0	0				0
26	20,219	212	170	1,817	0	0	$32			32
27	20,411	262	210	2,105	0	0	$65			65
28	20,606	318	254	2,389	0	0	$101			101
29	20,802	379	303	2,669	0	0	$139			139
30	21,000	446	357	2,946	0	0	$178			178
31	21,200	520	416	3,218	0	0	$227			227
32	21,402	602	481	3,487	0	0	$281			281
33	21,606	691	553	3,752	0	0	$340			340
34	21,812	789	631	4,013	0	0	$406			406
35	22,019	896	717	4,271	0	0	$478			478
36	22,229	1,013	810	4,524	0	0	$557			557
37	22,441	1,141	913	4,775	0	0	$644			644
38	22,654	1,280	1,024	5,022	0	0	$740			740
39	22,870	1,432	1,146	5,265	0	0	$844			844
40	23,088	1,598	1,279	5,505	0	0	$959			959
41	23,308	1,779	1,423	5,742	0	0	$1,084			1,084
42	23,530	1,975	1,580	5,976	0	0	$1,221			1,221
43	23,754	2,189	1,751	6,206	0	0	$1,371			1,371
44	23,980	2,421	1,937	6,433	0	0	$1,533			1,533
45	24,208	2,674	2,139	6,656	0	0	$1,711			1,711
46	24,439	2,947	2,358	6,877	0	0	$1,904			1,904
47	24,672	3,244	2,595	7,095	0	0	$2,115			2,115
48	24,907	3,566	2,853	7,309	0	0	$2,344			2,344
49	25,144	3,915	3,132	7,521	0	0	$2,592			2,592
50	25,383	4,293	3,435	7,729	0	0	$2,862			2,862
51	25,625	4,551	3,641	7,935	0	0	$3,155			3,155
52	25,869	4,824	3,859	8,138	0	0	$3,473			3,473
53	26,116	5,113	4,091	8,338	0	0	$3,818			3,818
54	26,364	5,420	4,337	8,535	0	0	$4,193			4,193
55	26,615	5,745	4,611	8,730	0	0	$4,611			4,611
56	26,869	6,090	4,903	8,921	0	0	$4,903			4,903
57	27,125	6,456	5,213	9,110	0	0	$5,213			5,213
58	27,383	6,843	5,542	9,297	0	0	$5,542			5,542
59	27,644	7,253	5,892	9,481	0	0	$5,892			5,892
60	27,907	7,689	6,264	9,662	0	0	$6,264			6,264
61	28,173	8,150	6,659	9,841	0	0	$6,659			6,659
62	28,441	8,639	7,079	10,017	0	0	$7,079			7,079
63	28,712	9,157	7,526	10,191	0	0	$7,526			7,526
64	28,986	9,707	8,000	10,362	0	0	$8,000			8,000
RELACEMENT RATIOS		33.49%	27.60%	35.75%	0.00%	0.00%	27.60%			27.60%

TABLE B.4.3
Jennifer's Annual Income Starting at Age 65 with Rollover Election*
*In 1992 dollars.

		ONE JOB CAREER			FIVE YEARS VESTING TEN YEARS PRIOR TO 1989 THREE JOB CAREER / SINGLE SUM VALUES					
AGE	ANNUAL EARNINGS	UNIT DEFINED BENEFIT	INTEGRATED DEFINED BENEFIT	DEFINED CONTRIBUTION	INTEG. D.B. JOB 1	DEFINED CONTRB. JOB 2	INTEG. D.B. JOB 3	NO PENSION JOB 4	NO PENSION JOB 5	TOTAL ALL JOBS
21	$19,283	$72	$58	$964	$58					$58
22	19,466	152	122	1,960	0	973				973
23	19,652	241	193	2,990	0	1,979				1,979
24	19,839	339	271	4,053	0	3,018				3,018
25	0	448	358	5,151	0	0				0
26	20,219	584	467	6,284	0	0	87			87
27	20,411	740	592	7,454	0	0	184			184
28	20,606	919	735	8,662	0	0	292			292
29	20,802	1,124	899	9,909	0	0	411			411
30	21,000	1,356	1,085	11,194	0	0	543			543
31	21,200	1,621	1,297	12,521	0	0	707			707
32	21,402	1,921	1,537	13,889	0	0	897			897
33	21,606	2,262	1,809	15,300	0	0	1,113			1,113
34	21,812	2,647	2,117	16,755	0	0	1,361			1,361
35	22,019	3,082	2,465	18,255	0	0	1,644			1,644
36	22,229	3,573	2,858	19,801	0	0	1,965			1,965
37	22,441	4,127	3,301	21,395	0	0	2,330			2,330
38	22,654	4,750	3,800	23,037	0	0	2,745			2,745
39	22,870	5,452	4,362	24,729	0	0	3,214			3,214
40	23,088	6,241	4,993	26,472	0	0	3,745			3,745
41	23,308	7,129	5,703	28,268	0	0	4,345			4,345
42	23,530	8,126	6,500	30,117	0	0	5,023			5,023
43	23,754	9,245	7,396	32,022	0	0	5,788			5,788
44	23,980	10,502	8,401	33,983	0	0	6,651			6,651
45	24,208	11,912	9,530	36,003	0	0	7,624			7,624
46	24,439	13,496	10,797	38,082	0	0	8,720			8,720
47	24,672	15,273	12,219	40,222	0	0	9,956			9,956
48	24,907	17,269	13,815	42,425	0	0	11,348			11,348
49	25,144	19,510	15,608	44,693	0	0	12,917			12,917
50	25,383	22,027	17,622	47,026	0	0	14,685			14,685
51	25,625	24,053	19,243	49,427	0	0	16,677			16,677
52	25,869	26,284	21,027	51,897	0	0	18,924			18,924
53	26,116	28,741	22,993	54,439	0	0	21,460			21,460
54	26,364	31,451	25,166	57,053	0	0	24,327			24,327
55	26,615	34,443	27,645	59,742	0	0	27,645			27,645
56	26,869	37,752	30,393	62,508	0	0	30,393			30,393
57	27,125	41,418	33,444	65,352	0	0	33,444			33,444
58	27,383	45,488	36,841	68,278	0	0	36,841			36,841
59	27,644	50,013	40,626	71,285	0	0	40,626			40,626
60	27,907	55,055	44,854	74,378	0	0	44,854			44,854
61	28,173	60,689	49,589	77,558	0	0	49,589			49,589
62	28,441	67,002	54,906	80,826	0	0	54,906			54,906
63	28,712	74,098	60,896	84,186	0	0	60,896			60,896
64	28,986	82,098	67,664	87,640	0	0	67,664			67,664
RELACEMENT RATIOS		33.49%	27.60%	35.75%	0.00%	0.00%	27.60%			27.60%

TABLE B.4.4
Jennifer's Single-Sum Amounts If Benefits from Defined Benefit Plans Are Rolled Over*

*In 1992 dollars.

GLOSSARY

Accrued Benefits   Retirement benefits earned to date by an employee. In a defined benefit plan, these benefits will usually be stated in terms of years of service to date times a percentage of current salary. In a defined contribution plan, these benefits will equal the amount in the employee's account. Accrued benefits may or may not be vested (that is, actually owned by the employee) depending on the employee's length of service with the employer.

Actuary   A mathematical technician who calculates employee benefits, required funding levels for benefits plans, and risks based on life expectancies of employees, employee turnover rates, and other statistical data. Actuaries must be used to calculate funding for pensions if those pension plans are to be considered "qualified plans" by the IRS and receive tax breaks.

Age Discrimination in Employment Act (ADEA)   The federal law forbidding job discrimination based on age and prohibiting mandatory retirement at any age except in certain limited circumstances.

AIME   (Average Indexed Monthly Earnings) Your average salary for your 35 highest years of earnings; AIME will be used to determine your Social Security benefit at your normal retirement age.

Annuity   A contract or type of pension payment that guarantees regular payments over a period of time defined in the contract. This time period is usually the life of the retiree and her surviving spouse, but the period may also be a stated number of years such as 20 years. An annuity is also a method of payment on a periodic basis over a stated term of years or a lifetime.

371

Cash or Deferred Arrangement (CODA) An employee retirement plan under which an employee may receive a portion of her salary in cash or may defer that portion into a retirement plan; such plans are also called *salary reduction plans* or *401(k) plans* (named after the section of the Internal Revenue Code that permits these deferrals).

Cliff Vesting A vesting schedule that provides an employee will own 100% of her accrued benefits to date after a specified number of years of service with the employer. Under current ERISA law, this period can be no more than 5 years of service with the employer, but the plan can permit vesting in fewer years. Before 1989, an employer could postpone cliff vesting for as long as 10 years, and multiemployer plans may still use 10-year cliff vesting. *Cliff vesting* is the alternative to *graded* or *graduated vesting,* defined later.

COBRA (Consolidated Omnibus Budget Reconciliation Act) A federal law that requires employers with more than twenty employees who offer health insurance to permit terminated employees to continue that coverage for 18 months at the employee's expense. Dependents of employees are also allowed to continue coverage in circumstances of divorce, death of the employee, and other limited circumstances at the employee's or the dependent's expense.

Defined Benefit Plan The traditional "pension" plan that sets out a formula for calculating benefits to be paid to the employee at retirement on a regular basis for the life of the retiree; the plan document "defines" the benefit which will be paid. This term is a description of one of two basic forms of retirement plans; the other type is a defined contribution plan (see below).

Defined Contribution Plan One of two basic forms of retirement plans. A defined contribution plan sets out the amount the employer will contribute for each employee each year. The contributions remain in an account for the employee, and at retirement the amount of money in the account is the retirement benefit. This sum is usually paid out in a lump sum at retirement.

Employee Retirement Income Security Act (ERISA)

The federal law enacted in 1974 governing all aspects of employee retirement and welfare benefit plans. The law does not require employers to provide employee plans; however, if employers do provide plans, they must follow the rules of ERISA; ERISA requires adequate funding of retirement benefits, the vesting of retirement benefits and certain survivor rights, information to beneficiaries, and disclosures.

Employee Stock Ownership Plan (ESOP)

A defined contribution retirement plan with the contributions in the form of employer stock and fitting the specific requirements of IRS regulations (which include the right to receive certain voting rights and to sell the employer's nonpublicly traded stock to the employer at retirement). ESOPs may also be referred to as *stock bonus plans*.

Exclusive Benefit Rule

One of the requirements of ERISA that dictates that the assets in any employee benefit plan be used only for the *exclusive benefit* of the beneficiaries of that plan; the needs and desires of the employer cannot be considered by the plan fiduciaries in making decisions regarding the investment or use of plan assets; only the best interests of the plan beneficiaries are to be weighed.

FICA

(Federal Insurance Contribution Act) Federal law that taxes both the employee and the employer on wages paid up to the taxable wage base for Social Security benefits under the Old Age, Survivors and Disability Insurance (OASDI) Program and for the hospital insurance portion of Medicare.

Fiduciary	When used in connection with ERISA plans, any person who exercises discretionary authority over assets in an ERISA plan. Such an individual is required to use such assets for the exclusive benefit of the plan beneficiaries and to pay for reasonable administrative costs of the plan and to conduct the business of the plan under the so-called *prudent man rule,* which dictates that all actions are to be those undertaken by a prudent man with the same goals and purposes of the fiduciary.
401(k) Plan	A type of defined contribution retirement plan in which the employee may choose to set aside a portion of her salary into a retirement plan. The employee pays no federal income tax on this portion of the salary set aside or on the earnings until the money is withdrawn. Most employers also contribute some amount to such plans, frequently on a matching basis. These plans are also referred to as *salary reduction plans* or *cash or deferred arrangements*. The 401(k) plan is named after the section of the Internal Revenue Code that permits these set-asides.
Graded or Graduated Vesting	A type of vesting in which the employee earns ownership rights in accrued benefits gradually over a period of years; by law graduated vesting must occur at the rate of 20% of accrued benefits per year after 2 years of service with 100% of the benefits vested at the end of 7 years. The other type of permitted vesting schedule is called *cliff vesting* (see earlier).
Highly Compensated Employee	A specialized IRS term that roughly identifies those employees who:

❖ Earn more than $75,000 per year,

❖ Earn more than $50,000 per year and are in the top 20% of highest-paid employees,

❖ Are officers paid more than $45,000 per year, or

❖ Are owners of more than 5% of the stock.

The dollar figures are adjusted for inflation each year. The term is important because tax-qualified plans may not operate to favor highly compensated employees disproportionately when compared with other employees; highly compensated employees' benefits are compared with other employees' benefits under elaborate *nondiscrimination rules* to ensure there is no favoritism.

Individual Retirement Account (IRA)	An account that any person with earned income can establish and fund up to $2,000 per year; the earnings on this account are tax deferred until retirement; the contribution may be tax deductible if the account owner's employer or her spouse's employer does not provide a retirement plan. Portions of the contribution may be tax deductible if the account owner earns less than $35,000 if single, or $50,000 if married and filing a joint tax return.
Integration	See *Social Security Integration.*
Joint and Survivor Annuity	A type of pension plan payment form that pays the earned retirement benefit over the life of the retiree and over the life of her spouse or other beneficiary after the retiree's death. Under the law, most retirement plans must be paid in this form unless the retiree specifically chooses another payment form and the spouse agrees to the other payment form in writing witnessed by a notary or by the plan administrator.
Keogh Plan	Named for its originator (Eugene Keogh), this retirement plan for self-employed individuals allows them to deduct from taxes and set aside up to $30,000 or 25% of annual net compensation earned from self-employment (whichever is less).

Lump-Sum Averaging   A tax break that permits certain legally defined lump-sum payments from qualified retirement plans to be taxed as though received over 5 or 10 years, thus reducing the tax on the payments.

Lump-Sum Payment   A type of retirement plan payment in which all of the benefit is paid out at once at the plan participant's retirement, death, or disability. This type of payment is the alternative to an annuity payment over the lifetime of the plan participant or her beneficiary.

Medicare   The federally run health insurance plan for those age 65 and over. Once you enroll for Social Security and are age 65, you are automatically covered for the hospitalization portion of Medicare, referred to as Part A; for an additional monthly premium you can also be covered for doctors' and other health care providers' services under Part B of Medicare.

Medigap Policy   A privately offered health insurance policy that will cover a portion of the health care expenses not covered by Medicare.

Money Purchase Pension Plan   A defined contribution retirement plan in which the employer commits to contribute a set sum or percentage (usually based on salary) each year to a plan participant.

Multiemployer Plan   A plan developed as part of a collective bargaining agreement to which more than one employer contributes by virtue of its employees being covered by the collective bargaining agreement. An employee in such a plan has full portability of service when she moves from employer to employer, so long as she continues to work for an employer contributing to the plan.

Nondiscrimination Rules   Several IRS rules that prohibit a plan or a plan sponsor from granting disproportionately larger benefits to highly compensated employees as compared with benefits to other employees. These rules require certain specific tests for various types of retirement plans.

OASDI

(The Old Age, Survivors and Disability Insurance Program) The portion of Social Security that pays retirement and disability benefits, as well as benefits to surviving children and spouses.

Participant

When used in the retirement benefits context, an employee who is actually accruing benefits under the plan even if she is not yet vested in those benefits.

Pension

Usually, a retirement plan that pays a benefit over the life of the retired plan participant, but the term is also sometimes used to refer to any retirement plan, regardless of its payment pattern.

Pension Benefit Guaranty Corporation (PBGC)

Independent federal corporation that insures defined benefit plans, regulates the termination of such plans, and guarantees payment to plan participants should a plan's trust fund prove inadequate.

Plan Document

The document that sets out the provisions of the retirement or other welfare benefit plan. Retirement benefits plans must be operated according to the provisions in the document, and the document must be given to employees covered by the plan, if requested.

Plan Sponsor

In plans established by a single employer, that employer; in plans in which several employers contribute, the plan sponsor is the organization that has established the plan (usually a union or a board of trustees consisting of union representatives and representatives from employers contributing to the plan whose employees are covered by the plan).

Portability

When used in the retirement benefits context, the right to preserve benefits earned with one employer after an employee leaves that employer. Portability takes several forms, including permitting the employee to take the vested benefits with her, to retain the benefits with the employer and claim them at retirement age, or to count years of service with another employer in calculating benefits.

Prenuptial Agreement

A legal agreement recognized in most states entered into before marriage in which the parties agree to the division of asset ownership owned before marriage and acquired during marriage and to the division of property should a divorce occur. ERISA benefits are not affected by prenuptial agreements, regardless of language in the prenuptial agreement to the contrary.

Preretirement Survivor Annuity

The standard payment form for preretirement survivor rights. Once an employee vests in a defined benefit plan, the spouse will be paid in this form should the employee die before retiring.

Preretirement Survivor Rights

The right of a surviving beneficiary to receive retirement benefits if a vested plan participant dies before retirement by law, such rights for spouses must be part of a tax-qualified defined benefit plan.

Primary Insurance Amount (PIA)

The amount of benefit one will receive at normal retirement age from Social Security. The actual Social Security benefit may be higher or lower depending on whether one retires earlier or later than her normal retirement age.

Profit-Sharing Plan

A defined contribution plan in which the employer has the discretion to decide whether and how much to contribute to the plan each year. Under the law, it is not necessary for an employer to have profits to contribute, nor is an employer under a duty to contribute if the company has a profit.

Prudent Man Rule	The principle in ERISA and fiduciary law that requires all fiduciaries of ERISA retirement plans to conduct the business of the plan as "a prudent man" with similar goals and duties would; fiduciaries violating this rule will be liable to the plan and its participants.
Qualified Domestic Relations Order (QDRO)	An order issued by a state domestic relations court requiring the division of an employee's ERISA retirement plan accrued benefits between the employee and a spouse or children. Because of the antialienation rules prohibiting the attachment of ERISA benefits, this is one of the few ways anyone other than a plan participant may receive benefits of an ERISA plan.
Qualified Plan	A retirement plan that meets all the IRS rules for such plans and therefore is entitled to special tax treatment exempting the income of the trust from tax and the participants of the plan from tax on the value of the benefit until they actually receive the benefit and permitting the employer to deduct contributions to the plan trust in the year of the contribution.
Retirement Equity Act (REA)	A federal law enacted in 1984. REA established rules requiring the consent of a spouse to waive rights to benefits in the form of *qualified joint and survivor annuities* and *qualified preretirement survivor annuities*. REA also lowered the required age and minimum service period for plan participation. And REA liberalized the *break-in service rules* to permit an employee's past service to be counted for vesting and benefit accrual if the time away from the employer did not exceed 5 years or the period of time the employee originally worked for the employer (whichever is greater). Maternity and paternity leave of less than 501 hours does not count as a "break in service."

Reverse Mortgage   A financing device in which the lender pays the homeowner a monthly payment for a term of years based on the homeowner's equity in the house; when the homeowner sells the house or dies, the amount of money borrowed through these monthly payments, plus interest, is then repaid to the lender.

Rollover   When used in a retirement benefits context, this is the act of transferring money or assets from one tax-qualified employer plan to another, or from one IRA to another, or from an employer plan to an IRA, or vice versa. Rollovers enable the account to maintain the tax-favored status protecting the account from most taxation until the money is withdrawn from the account. The term *rollover* is frequently used to describe the situation in which the participant receives the assets from the plan and then places those assets into another IRA or employer plan. "Rollover" is sometimes also used to describe a direct transfer from one plan by that plan's trustee to another plan at the request of the participant, although the more accurate description of this type of transfer is a *direct trustee-to-trustee transfer*. There may be taxes withheld on a rollover, whereas no taxes are withheld on most trustee-to-trustee transfers.

Salary Reduction Plan   A benefit plan in which the employee may "buy" or contribute to a benefit by reducing her salary. When such plans are retirement plans, they are also called 401(k) plans or *cash or deferred arrangements*.

Simplified Employee Pension (SEP)   A retirement plan under which the employer contributes to an individual retirement account for each employee. Such contributions may be up to $30,000, and contributions are immediately vested. If the employer has no more than 25 employees, the employee may also contribute to the SEP through salary reductions up to the 401(k) limits.

Single Life Annuity	A form of retirement plan payout in which payments are made over the life of one individual (usually the retiree), with no rights of payment for any survivor.
Social Security Integration	The provisions in a retirement plan that allow the plan's benefits or the contributions by the employer to be reduced to reflect the fact the employer has paid Social Security taxes on certain portions of the wage base. Since 1989, this integration may not reduce the benefit the employee would receive absent this integration by more than 50%.
Stock Bonus Plan	A defined contribution retirement plan in which at least a portion of the employer's contribution is in the form of employer stock.
Summary Annual Report	A report on the financial and funding status of a qualified benefit plan which must be given to plan participants annually.
Summary Plan Description	A layperson's description of a qualified benefit plan, drafted in language calculated to inform the average plan participant of her rights and duties under the plan and to cover fully the provisions of the plan, including certain information specified in ERISA.
Target Benefit Plan	A retirement plan that establishes a "target" retirement benefit for each participant and makes annual contributions designed to reach that target; regardless of the earnings of the plan, the contribution does not vary; if the plan earns more than originally projected, the participant has a larger-than-anticipated benefit; if the earnings are lower, the benefit is lower than anticipated.
Tax Deferred	An employee benefit or other type of income on which you do not pay taxes as the income or benefit is earned, but do pay taxes at a later date; for example, money an employer contributes to

	your retirement plan is not taxed when you accrue the right to it; it is taxed when you actually withdraw the money from the plan.
Tax Exempt	Income or benefits for which you never pay taxes; for example, you never pay tax on the value of the health insurance benefits your employer pays you; interest on most bonds issued by state and local governments is never taxed.
Thrift Plan	A retirement plan funded by the employee's own contributions; any employer contributions are based on the employee's contribution to the plan. Such plans are usually funded with after-tax dollars.
Trust Fund	When used in the context of a retirement plan, the fund that holds all assets of the plan. The trust is owned by the plan, and the plan sponsor has no ownership rights to the trust other than possible reversion rights to assets if the plan is terminated with extra assets and if the plan document reserves this right for the employer.
Trustee-to-Trustee Transfer	Used to describe the process of moving plan assets from one employer's plan to another employer plan or to an IRA, usually at the request of the participant; in a participant-directed trustee-to-trustee transfer, there will be no federal income tax withholding.
Vest	The point at which the employee acquires a nonforfeitable right to receive earned benefits at a certain date, regardless of whether she continues to work for the employer.

INDEX